PERSON
PLACE
THING
/
WAY
SHAPE
FORM
a poememoir, in 9 parts, with a coda, in three parts,
comprised of journal entries, mythic gossip & poor fugitive scrawl

written, edited, purloined, etc. by **darrell larson**
with all apologies

Darrell Larson

Coyote

FOR AVA, that sparkle right from the get go
approbation right out of the gate,
delight and love all of our lives!
12/13/2020

ISBN: 978-0-9998695-7-4

Each of my chapters begin with a quote from Dr. David N. Daniels (1934 to 2017), one of the founding fathers of today's Enneagram. David and his writings have inspired me and inspired my life. David's work and his legacy are carried on at www.drdaviddaniels.com.

front cover photo: Gilbert Gaytan
back cover photo: Margaret Von Biesen
author photo: Rory Lewis
book jacket design: Jeanne Field

f-stop books

for
Susanna
Emma
& Lilah

for
Tavish

for
Ace

for
Rob Sullivan
with eternal gratitude

and especially for
Jeanne Field

1. **PERFECTIONIST:** WE ARE ALL ONE AND WE ARE PERFECT AS WE ARE, *or* people are not accepted for who they are. their good behavior is expected and taken for granted. their bad behavior and impulses are judged negatively and punished.

"coyote: coyote was sent by earthmaker on a mission, which was to bring the waterfall to earth. he bounced around for awhile, doing the best he could. he's not good, and he's not bad, but he's tricky."—murray mednick, 'the coyote cycle'

"the maternal darkness endeavors to give birth and miscarries twice, then bears twin boys, who grow up to quarrel constantly about which of them was born first...prankish, lecherous, accident-prone coyote, and his [brother (trickster)], the unpredictable creators of the world"—rebecca solnit, 'on coyote', new yorker magazine

"the creation of the world did not occur at the beginning of time, it occurs every day."—marcel proust, 'remembrance of things past: the sweet cheat gone'

PREAMBLE
that place where every
person or thing
each moment
brings new awareness

of what has been lost
dylan's voice in 1964
a perfect snarl
of spanish leather and manischevitz
some far found
country we yearn for
the cared for
one

STATING THE OBVIOUS
you feel that you are finally
your own person
but you also feel that this
(or any) moment
is not actually
here.
this is not real steam
or rain
or radio.
you are pretending (to yourself) to listen.
yes this is music
but you are not wrapping the notes in attention
as they enter your ears.
the lights are off
and

this is because of all the bad things you did.

*"the space we **hear** is a space without places."—victor zuckerandl, 'sound and symbol'*

from *Samuel Johnson's Dictionary*:
(whole kit and)
CABOODLE (calaboodle): an entity, group or lot; the entire lot of people or things
COHORT: a company or band united in some common purpose; assistant, colleague or accomplice.

in CAHOOTS: in league with; company, partnership, collusion

"remember that the fool to the eyes of the gods and the fool to the eyes of man are very different…the real fool, such as the gods mock and mar, is he who does not know himself'"— oscar wilde, 'de profundis'

"one lives among gods and monsters, a stranger to peace of mind."—marcel proust, 'remembrance of things past: in the shadow of young girls in flower'

"when he left his father's house, he left god. on to something of his own devising. he built a shrine to james dean, steve mcqueen, and naked marilyn monroe…my beautiful father and his golden idols who died early. they were all poised to explode".—emma larson, 'in the cornucopia of your ear'

it seems that there is often some iconoclastic aspect, something isolating, some element of outsiderness, that establishes the iconic performer—and this is almost always supplied by the inner life of the performer themselves. (mcqueen in *hell is for heroes,* even *great escape,* finds him outside the system of the other prisoners, soldiers, shipmates, poker players, cycle riders), but somehow they remain representative, an avatar, for all of us. being ON OUR OWN, is a basic human reality, (especially re: DEATH), and our most primal fear. the iconic character is abandoned and embraced simultaneously. to be outside is also to be free—but it is a freedom that terrifies us. ('*to live outside the law/ you must be honest'—bob dylan*) we abandon ourselves into highly suspect ecstasy. those who embody this liberation from the ordinary slumber, become heroes to us, subsequently saints and then, of course, angels….

STATEMENT OF PURPOSE
i keep seeing women on the subway who look just like charlotte gainsbourg

i should have done better

i am sure it is my doing

i've come quite undone

4

in that provocative way that drains you of

and then again
one must decide
mustn't one
on the constancy of embarkation
on the brandishing of the lance
on the irrelevancy of exclamations
no one makes proclamations any more
or emblazons themselves for peace

o, yoko

you must revolve your own nest
into absolute alignment
all silent letters cease
to exist
what i can do with an alphabet
resembles as they say

i believe i am nothing
some myth-drenched ripoff
some fortunate scam
impaled on error
some other girl.
—2010

     from Samuel Johnson's Dictionary:
     SCIOMACHY: battle with a shadow
     LUSTRE: the space of five years
     to INLAW: clear of outlawry or attainder
     ORGASM: sudden vehemence
    LYCANTHROPY: a kind of madness, in which men have the qualities of
wild beasts, (specifically **wolves,** or smaller canines, such as **coyotes**)

*"he who makes a beast of himself…gets rid of the pain of being a man."—
samuel johnson*

I DON'T (KNOW HOW TO) PRAY

THE SKY'S ON FIRE
THE SKY'S CHANGING COLOR
THE SKY is FOLDING
THE SKY is mumbling
        FLOODING OVER
the sky is erupting

we can take a picture, but we can't GIVE a picture.
(although MARILYN could).

MARILYN
how many voices in the room
blanked at her pages
rustling of vision
sliced at her wanting
petals drying
matches struck
those who climb between lines
know what she must have felt
must have
diving through mystified
wide-eyed
maybe it was the pain
or the rain
or the waterfall
wriggling deliciously into the mist
who knows
somewhere a piano is making that sound from black crow
dance making

      as she came
      someone hid her face

revealing her forever.

*"the star enjoys life and love on behalf of the whole world. she has the mystical greatness of the sacred prostitute. in the lethe of each dark auditorium her body purifies and immolates itself. her partners are of little consequence: it is **love** who visits her, **love** she is waiting for, **love** who guides her."—edgar morin, 'stars'*

this is a quincunx disaster for the wench

ALL THE DOOMED BLONDES: A String of Pearls/ Part One
*"you must understand that blondes are men's dreams. that's all they are."—amy greene (*wife of milton greene, who took some of the most memorable pictures of marilyn monroe, and became her producing partner with *bus stop* and *the prince and the showgirl)*

so many golden-haired women who bore the love goddess's wreath:
jean harlow, carole lombard, frances farmer, veronica lake, marilyn monroe, barbara loden, jean seberg, kim stanley, carroll baker...many of them died young, some committed suicide, or died by accident, some just seemed to be devoured, fleeing into obscurity, drowning in alcohol, singed by the spotlight.

"the question is: yes or no? and with women like that, the answer is always yes, even if that choice launches a thousand ships, or destroys an empire. no matter what it will cost, the poor guy simply can't help himself. history has bequeathed to us an array of femme fatales so potent that some have captivated our imaginations for millennia, from **eve** *to* **pandora** *to* **persephone** *to* **rapunzel** *to* **quinevere***, to* **helen of troy***…. but since the invention of celluloid, the pictures that once had to be conjured by poets and playwrights have been visible to us all, and the gallery of dangerous sirens has expanded to fill our imaginations with images as timeless as they are unforgettable. their faces haunt our memories."—leslie bennetts in 'vanity fair'*

*"**BUT THIS GODDESS MUST BE CONSUMED**….the star system derives from the old religion of immortality and from the new all-powerful religion in a mortal scale:* **love***…the stars are like the gods: everything and nothing."—edgar morin, 'stars'*

*"..JEAN HARLOW, YOU ARE IN BEAUTY ON DARK EARTH
WITH WHITE FEET!...*
*slaying the dragon is not more wonderful than you. To air
you give magical sleekness..." — michael mcclure, 'le plus blanche'*

jean harlow: was twenty six years old when she died of nephritis, kidneys
lacerated, rotting from the inside, a malady usually associated with much
older people. but the truth was, she had always seemed preternaturally
experienced beyond her years, daring the fates, or whatever restrictions
might come along to try to slow her down. even as a teenager she swung her
nubile body like a seasoned whore. according to david thomson: *"her neglect
of underwear seemed aggressive just because her breasts and the oceanic
roll of her hips were so mature...she winked, she liked her nipples to pout, as
if to say, 'get a load of this.' "* at the age of sixteen she eloped, with a
millionaire from her hometown of kansas city. the newlyweds drifted to los
angeles and after a quick divorce she began to work as an extra. she was
joined by her dominating mother. escaping from her mother was in fact a
major reason for her elopement. now the mother insisted she take *her* name,
jean harlow. jean herself had been born harlean carpenter. the mother was a
more opulent replica of her daughter — platinum hair and all. she brought
along her florid gigolo/husband, marino bello, and the two lived off of harlow
for the rest of her life. bello would periodically write graphic love notes to
harlow, accompanied by fairly constant gropings and midnight visitations,
which jean spurned, sometimes violently.

the real emergence of jean harlow, movie star, owed itself to howard
hughes, millionaire aviator/inventor/movie producer/one of hollywood's most
prolific lotharios, who bought her contract and put her in his hit film *hell's
angels,* in which the aerial pyrotechnics don't stand a chance against her
exuberant raciness. robert sherwood, critic for *life,* said she was
"obstreperously alluring." she was eighteen years old. hughes lent her out,
fairly indiscriminately. he basically owned her, and she did what she was told.
she had real impact in william wellman's *public enemy,* starring james
cagney, who notices her undulating down the sidewalk, and quickly pulls over
in his big white convertible. the flashy tough guy offers her a ride. she climbs
into the back seat, giving him a full view of the delights to come, and cagney
can't resist a sprightly, very sexy, tap shuffle. as they parade down the

boulevard, sprawled in the back seat, while his buddy takes the wheel, the delightfully carnal conversation makes her screechy, untrained voice entirely immaterial. later that year frank capra gave her the actual vehicle to iconic status, her limo to glory, in a genuinely randy comedy called *platinum blonde.* the original title had been *gallagher,* the name of the character played by the intended star of the film, loretta young, at the height of her considerable beauty, (and later had clark gable's illegitimate child) but harlow managed to steal the picture basically with one long tracking shot moving along behind her. (this is a direct precursor to marilyn's justly famous, long, sinuous, stroll away from the camera, two decades later, in *niagara.*) harlow was made, even though she was barely believable as an upper class heiress. hughes then sold her to MGM, cashing in on her elevated value. the studio contrived a picture just for her, called *red-headed woman,* written by anita loos (who was most famous for a serialized set of stories, and a subsequent collection as a book, called *gentlemen prefer blondes*, which sold like 'bathtub gin'; then it was made into a 1928 paramount movie, 1950 broadway musical and the 1953 movie version of the musical, starring another hughes discovery, the buxom jane russell, and another platinum blonde named marilyn monroe.)

according to loos, when harlow met with irving thalberg who ran MGM, to discuss the idea for *red-headed woman* the boy-wonder mogul asked jean if she thought she could make an audience laugh. she said, "*with me, or at me?*" *at* you!" "*sure, people have been laughing at me all my life.*" she breezed out, with "*a quick, bright, little nod*" thrown back as she swung through the door. thalberg remarked, "*i don't think we need to worry about miss harlow's sense of humor.*" for *red-headed woman,* anita loos came up with a scene to open the film in which 'red' is trying on a sheer little number in a store's dressing room. she rhetorically asks, "*so gentlemen prefer blondes, do they*?" then she holds out her skirt, sashays in front to the mirror, and inquires sweetly of the saleslady, "*can you see through this*?" when an offscreen voice responds, "*i'm afraid so*," harlow breaks into a devastating grin and says "*i'll wear it then*", thereby making it clear just '*what kind of woman* 'she was, neatly circumventing the hays office dictates against open expression of immorality.

but jean was always lonely; she longed to find companionship in a lover, one with wit enough to respond to her compulsive wisecracks. underlying her raffish sense of humor was a resignation unusual for one so young. nothing would ever surprise harlow. she knew exactly how people were going to react to her; if men were stupid, they'd fall for her; if they had good sense, they'd laugh her off. when she married paul bern, thalberg's right hand man, she knew he worshipped her, that he was good, kind and gentle. bern may have counted on his marriage to work a miracle, that with an inspiration like jean harlow, the sexiest woman in the world, he could conquer his life-long impotence. what can be gleaned is that instead, out of intimidation or humiliation, or just plain fantasy, he took to staying out all night, alluding to attendance at orgies, and various other kinky liaisons. jean's response to these tales was, *"just do anything you like, sweetheart, but count me out of those sessions."* when he left for one such *'date'* jean kissed him tolerantly and wished him a good night. the next morning she found a note under her bedroom door. it said, *"i hope you understand that last night was a farce. now i'm yours forever, paul."* bern lay sprawled out on his bedroom floor in a pool of blood. there was a bullet hole in his head and he was naked. he had killed himself while looking into a full-length mirror.

coming on the heels of the controversial *red-headed woman*, not to mention her well-known proclivity for occasional public nudity, her refusal to wear underwear, coupled with a general air of dissolution, after bern's death harlow was henceforth considered the worst kind of femme fatale. and her faith in men was down to a new low. her next picture was the torrid *red dust*—in which she played opposite clark gable for the first time, and delivers her most sexually uninhibited performance yet. she and gable hit it off, on and offscreen, and they did four more pictures together, including her final film, *saratoga,* again written by anita loos. in the interim she made the indelible *dinner at eight,* directed by the incomparable george cukor, and in 1935 she made *reckless,* in which she co-starred with william powell. back to anita loos:

"bill had all the qualities that jean despaired of ever finding in a sweetheart. he was a gentleman, urbane, witty and charming. it began to flash on her consciousness that sex need not be snide and degrading. she turned her full battery of charms on bill. but bill happened to have been the victim of another (doomed) blonde. he had been married to carole lombard, whose incredible glamour made him feel inferior: reduced his ego practically to the situation of paul bern. bill needed some 'little miss nobody 'in order to regain polarity. so he walked out on jean...after bill's rejection, jean seemed to lose interest in

everything, (except drinking…) and when stricken with acute nephritis, she refused to put up a fight. it was as if she took advantage of (what could have been) *a relatively minor ailment to escape from life. jean's funeral at forest lawn was an orgy of grief, with mobs of weeping fans, monitored by mounted police. l.b. mayer sent a heart of red roses five feet tall pierced by a golden arrow. but those of us close to the bier were more impressed when bill powell strode up to place a single white rose on her breast."*

"jean harlow created a totally new standard for sex goddesses. jean was a sacred-whore type whose unabashed vulgarity was integral to the spell she cast. quite a few veils of illusion had been brutally torn off: evidently the sex goddess was no lady if, as harlow, she could be a downright slut. nobody sensed it then..but a great symbol was being debunked. there could be no question about harlow's *real fleshliness, all over and through and through, if only because nothing seemed to exist between her filmy dresses but a little perspiration….once, being a sex goddess was to skip all mundane considerations and assume that lust meant* **aphrodite***…in harlow, sex bloomed miraculously, nakedly, gaudily from the gutter."—parker tyler, 'the awful fate of the sex goddess'*

OUT OF THE WOUND
     cavorting like toddlers with splinters in their fingers
mirror upon mirror it accumulates

"i'll be your mirror, reflect what you are/ in case you don't know/ i'll be the **wind***, the* **rain** *and the* **sunset***/ the light on your door/ to show that you're home'—lou reed, 'i'll be your mirror'*

MOVING EAST, FIRST DAY, 10 to 15 to 70, Los Angeles, California, to Beaver, Utah. 1995.
A Day With Two Breakfasts
woke up at norbert and tandy's, having slept (none too well) in the bed nancy and i purchased together in…1972, i think, (oak, old, authentic colonial). drove to the airport twice. but i'll get to that later. at the first breakfast, in the nook at the superba house, susanna says i have conducted myself in an

exemplary fashion during the entire process. (the practice of not expressing negative emotions pays off.) i love it when she praises me.

went to the airport twice because the styrofoam cooler stuffed with stuff: three plastic jars of brown cow yogurt, one plastic jar of hydroxy-tryptophan, cocoa star-goons, and a plastic jar full of silk-worm eggs; this small, white, light but sturdy chest is made even safer with packing tape wrapped around it twice, but alas despite this 'put-me-in-coach 'outfitting, the poor thing was left behind, forlorn, in the middle of tandy and norbert's living room.

when our (my) negligence is fully grasped, i rush back to secure it, driving like steve mcqueen in *bullitt* and then shoot right back to the airport with the precious cargo, all to keep the girls content, and the entire universe in order. susanna sprints up to the car in the dropoff area with great urgency. suddenly we're in some film like *waterloo bridge*, and she leaps into the car to kiss me, saying fervently, *"i love you...i'm going to miss my plane."* then she grabs the cooler and dashes from the car.

the second breakfast is at elinor's house. there to collect my co-pilot for this journey across the entire country. she is cheerful and simple and kind, as always in this phase of her life. the coffee is excellent. the peaches and raspberries on the fresh yogurt are delicious. tavish is slightly truculent (so what else is new) and obviously got very little, if any, sleep. neither did i. not restful, not at all, hot, cramped and sweaty. the wrong pillows. not our bed.

where is our bed?

back at norbert's, the three of us (n,d,t) shuffle the bags from car to car, somewhat hurriedly. norbert and i hug each other warmly, and sincerely, and he says something into my ear which i do not understand, (i literally did not hear him, even though he spoke quite loudly). we do agree however that we might have one more *coyote cycle* in us.

at mark's we determine who will drive which vehicle. mark has waked and baked and is ready to roll.

the three of us head out in the two volvos, the family wagon (me and tav), and my sedan (mark).

we go to the gas station.

we go to paul gold's for the dubs of the recordings of *"rock and roll in literature"* readings.

finally we hit the road. its only ten o'clock, and we make good time. covering a lot of ground. tavish plays me some music he digs. (phish and parts of a trip-hop compilation.) we stop and eat the turkey legs tom vinetz made, at a rest stop near barstow. the sun, the air, is bracingly, blazingly hot. we smoke a joint. and we're on the road, again.

we stop in baker at the mad greek's for an espresso. we see the bloody carcass of a large black dog.

just before vegas mark starts to have trouble with the car overheating, i feel that my car is also laboring. there is a gradual but grueling grade coming into vegas from the west. he puts his light on as a sign of distress. i slow down and get really concerned. this is just the beginning and we're already experiencing serious mechanical difficulties. (i remember a time when i ran out of gas, with tavish in the car. i think he was around 6. i felt like such a fucking loser, and inadequate to the task of caring for this extraordinary little person entrusted to me. i was always running out of gas, or nearly so, or having my brakes fail coming down from laurel canyon, or having the hood fly up in the wind in the 60something oldsmobile, going sixty on the 10, looking through the windshield at nothing but twisted metal. then there was the car i just walked away from, broken down on dead man's curve. i believe it was an impala. could have been that same doomed oldsmobile.) smoke starts to billow out of the engine. we both pull over and we all clamber out of our cars. i start muttering, *"give me the water"* over and over until i get the old-school burlap purse. by the time the bag is in my hand however, i have come to notice that there is plenty of water. the smoke is not steam and it has stopped billowing. mark has restarted the car. it seems fine, if a bit overheated. aren't we all.

we drive gingerly into las vegas, low on gas. we pull into a gas station which offers no mechanical help. we cruise vegas, spy an obvious automotive/industrial section, scope an auto repair shop, looking incredibly disheveled and greasy. dark and rusted. a guy with 'bob 'on his soiled overalls waves at me with both arms, like a guy guiding a 747 into place, except he is clearly indicating *"GO AWAY".* we pull in anyway, he cringes at the word 'volvo', and refuses to even open the hood, but he does let me use the yellow pages, and i call a place and the guy is cool and gives me directions to his garage, while also diagnosing the problem just from my description, which is comforting. oh, i forgot to mention, the windows of the volvo in question are not working. stuck open. no power. and the steering is getting stiff and hard to move.

anyway, we got there, the guy is *literally* cool. his office is air-conditioned and sunny. his workplace is immaculate—not as if no work is done, but that the work is done in an orderly fashion. he knows exactly what is wrong, its the air conditioning belt. also the fuse is blown to the compressor so there's no power steering. he replaces the fuse with good humor, giving me an extra fuse in the bargain. NO CHARGE! (this is a definite motif in my life. some so-called disaster befalls me and then i am rescued by some kind stranger, just like blanche dubois.) there is nothing left to be done and we go on our way, restored and with clear directions to the freeway.

we stop at the virgin river rest area and call the production office in moab for *'riders of the purple sage'*. they call us back in a few minutes, while i watch two young navaho girls play together. their mother has spread jewelry out on blankets & pads in the shade of the rest area. for some reason i think we can get all the way to moab in less than two hours. the map has deceived me or my legendary skewed sense of time has once more bitten me in the ass. either way we do manage to get as far as beaver, utah, where we dine at the timberline cafe and all flirt with the waitress shamelessly. she seems to respond especially well to tavish's forays. we get a very odd-shaped room, room 33 at the sleepy lagoon motel. seems like they just broke through to a toolshed attached to the building and made that a second bedroom. a suite. but it has three beds. we saw no lagoon.

the drive from the virgin river gorge to beaver is remarkably beautiful, and with the sun setting and the endless fields of new mown hay, overpoweringly fragrant and redolent, reminding me of bucking hay with my cousindale, and how damn good we were at it. i realized i was going to be within sixteen miles of my father's birthplace.

CATEGORIES OF SOULS
okay. so there are twelve categories of souls. maybe nine.
you know their names, or should i say, their *various* names, personas, demarcations…
there are twelve **astrological signs**, *in both the sidereal and tropical systems:* aquarius, pisces, scorpio, capricorn, sagittarius, leo, libra, virgo, cancer, gemini, taurus, aries;

twelve *chinese zodiac* **animals** *(zodiakos; circle of little animals):* rat, ox, tiger, rabbit, dragon, snake, horse, goat, monkey, rooster, dog, pig; there are the **laws** *of the twelve tables* (first attempt to codify a system of laws, established by the romans, in 450 BC.
and, of course, twelve **months** *of the year.* twelve **jurists,** twelve **apostles**, or perhaps there are nine divisions:
planets *[in astrology, 12 sections of the heavens, 9 planets + sun, moon and 'vulcan', [hidden planet, although when the astrological charts were originally devised, neptune, uranus and pluto had not yet been discovered, so…? and now they say pluto isn't a planet, so..well, anyway..]:* mercury, venus, earth, mars, jupiter, saturn, uranus, neptune, pluto.
personality **types,** *(according to 'the essential enneagram', which lend their names to the titles of the 9 sections of this...book.)***: perfectionist, giver, performer, romantic, observer, loyal skeptic, epicure, protector, mediator;**
seducers *(from 'the art of seduction'):* siren, rake, ideal lover, dandy, natural, coquette, charmer, charismatic, star, anti-seducer.

this particular **one**'s name is darrell ray larson: *sagittarius, tiger, jupiter, epicure, natural.*
he's twisted like a corkscrew, a twister, a tornado, a spiral, a toilet flushing, a water spout, (*"whirlpool of hilarity and horror"—mallarme*), a merry-go-round…

so…well,…suppose everything is a circle, a wheel in a wheel:
*"…****the generally miraculous character of the circle and of all circular movement. the circle is both convex and concave; it is made by a fixed point and a moving line, which contradict each other; and whatever moves in a circle moves in opposite directions. nevertheless, movement in a circle is the most 'natural 'movement."****—aristotle*

"relations end nowhere…the exquisite problem of the artist is…to draw, by a geometry of his own, the circle within which they shall happily **appear** *to do so."—henry james*

"and i think a lot of people, when they think of CAROUSELS, think, 'please, mama, take me back to your breasts—i'm not sure i like this world."—francis staub, millionaire who financed the restoration of the carousel on federal island, nyc (may the ancient lovingly carved horses, dragons, and griffons, the benched booths so lustrous, gold ring so available, at the martha's vineyard pier, and clear across the continent to the crenellated carousel at the santa monica pier, many stinging nights, coked up, wailing everly brothers (another twofer) songs into the night, may they all circle on forever..) but then there's the devilishly raked, wildly, murderously spinning merry-go-mad of *'strangers on a train'.* two personalities spinning around each other, funhouse mirror images, frantic guy/ grinning bruno, and of course, the thousands of other twins-who-are-not-twins: tweedle-dee/tweedle-dum, prometheus/ epimetheus, romulus/remus, cain/abel, jesus/lucifer; isaac/ishmael, jacob/esau, agni/soma, vladimir/estragon, **coyote/trickster**, john/paul, the glimmer twins: mick and keith…
or: as in shakespeare's *'comedy of errors',* two sets of twins, masters and servants, the dual duos seemingly identical, but all four living separate narratives, (i did a production of this perfect little gizmo of a play—playing both antipholi, the masters, and directing to boot…why?…the fun? the fear? the puzzle? how can two characters be played by one actor? what happens when both characters are onstage at the same time? you might well ask…of course, every performance by an actor is a kind of twinship…)

then there's love—two identities striving for unity, somehow **in** themselves, but matched, or bridged, or tethered, so that one is never

ALL/ONE.

INDIVIDUAL.

a circling of types,
> *reconciling to bonding, momentary or forever.*
> like square dancers, doh-say-dohing
> couples decoupling, spinning around each other,

16

                going on to the next, clasping, circling, all joining for a fleeting
moment, in fourths, spinning eights, sixteens…infinite patterns of
attraction…joining up…

who could she possibly be?

        so, there are twelve (maybe nine) points of view. twelve ways (okay
nine) of seeing, or better yet, reacting to the present, the gift of the moment.
so we, the twelve types (or nine), often (always) misunderstand the present,
misinterpret, we are hung-up in the past, anxious about the future, our feet
are not on this ground, standing still and upright. we are simply not present.
not right **now** anyway
                for the **now** moves
                        incorrigibly fast
a cloud in our palms,
mist wisping through our fingers.
before we could possibly experience the moment clearly, it is gone, never to
return, it never stops *going*, like some creature that is born and dies in the
same instant, and we are reacting to this incessant flow, with very little time
to perceive it, but changing it, transforming it into *our* version, even in our
memory of it, the subject is us. or rather..me.

*"**coyote:** once it's happened, it's gone. it doesn't matter where you look. you
can look up, you can look down…while it's happening it's gone." murray
mednick,' the coyote cycle'*

*"in acting, the personal quality of the actor is a part of the material that the art
works in, precisely as a **voice**, or a **hand**, or a **mind**."—stark young*

BUSTER TUMBLING
as we fall into his eyes
a steaming train approaches us
in geologic time

as we pratfall into his gaze
we gain a new understanding
of the inner core spinning

as he leans out from the rigging
most improbably perched
regarding the horizon with precarious solemnity
curious but accepting
alarmed but prepared
engaged but in love
as he flees from
hundreds of brides
thousands of cops
millions of eyes
the significant word is painless
plain triumph over gravity
true levity
and in his eyes
the patience of a cow being milked for laughs
in this buster is godlike
as he asks:
"where is this immense wind coming from,
which sets my home reeling?"
so the clapboard facades fall
into his eyes
the eloquent stillness
and the perfect stance.

"think slow, act fast."—buster keaton

ENCOMIUM FOR LOIS SMITH
i see a long hallway, with many doors and a girl with a broom,
gazing silently at the boy,
hanging back,
as he stumbles down the hallway
toward his fallen mother's door.
the girl is myself.
(so is the boy).
she lags behind the boy,
they had exchanged words,
as he shuffled in the yard, and she lingered at the backdoor,

18

eyes wide, hiding behind the screen door.
the boy wears sneakers, white jack purcell sneakers, and a light sweater over
a soiled shirt,
all askew.
later he flees,
perched atop a boxcar,
hugging himself tightly around the knees,
on the shuddering train, all the way to salinas,
straight shot home.

saint joe of the automat,
in hushed tribute to her luminous,
eternal
nature,
contrives an impeccable box,
deep in his basement hideaway,
using the same blue he gave bacall,
then stands in wait, in the alley, by the stage door,
scurrying up to her,
pressing the precious gift into her hands,
then scuttling away, head down,
not realizing
she knew perfectly well
who he was, this furtive genius,
honoring her with his art.

as my mother in *dog logic*
she prowls the american place stage,
her skirt slit up to here,
revealing her still shapely legs.
in her voice, her lyrical infatuation with loss.
her eyes see me, to my core,
shared sadness
loves to dance
mutual devastation and delight.

on *route 66*
she has a vision of a burning barn,
while an enormous mastiff peacefully guards her prophecies.
later, she foretells
the boy's panic, back in the *east of eden,*
and the violent blocks of ice,
formed from frozen tears,
big as steamer trunks as they
hurtle down the chute,
like bisons, red with revenge.
nothing can prevent his tragic stumble,
poor smashed spyder
flung all over the wind.

APRIL 27, 2013
i find myself in washington square (golden memories of susanna, new love,
her place on jones st., wonderfully freckled smile just for me) i pay 25 cents
to two young girls holding a sign offering free advice. in my question i allude
to lilah. they say *'wait, she'll come around.* 'then i stroll through the arch, not
my usual path, only to realize i am on the very spot where *'our scene* was
shot in *stepmom* (that's what julia called it). having noticed earlier in the day
that the film was to be aired on showtime that night.
        did i bring myself to this spot on purpose? with intent? and what could
that intention possibly be? *"in obedience to what possible course"*?

*"NEXUS RERUM: the connections of everything with everything else which
alone gives meaning to life...but we can't always see them, indeed we
mustn't, because then we would be paralyzed, trapped."—roberto calasso,
'ka'*

LATE FOR THE TRAIN
despite the selfish scuffs
and anxious nostril leather
of their footwear
revenge is ecstasy
exstasy is revenge

       the subway has fun
       worming into your belligerent hair
       mussing your glossied orifice
oh
there it is
so radiant
so rampant
so accidental, teeth squealing
thems the brakes, amigo,
sullen breakage
of last year's gnashing,
all the interglobular chewing
we all indulged in
incessantly.
madness, my dears,
delirious and doomed.
1/15/10, nyc

i'd much rather regret having done it, than NOT having done it at all. [there's
your problem, pal...]

if they're watching me i must be dangerous.

I DO NOT ALLOW MYSELF THE SOLACE OF PRAYER.
AND YET
I CRY OUT IN ANGUISH
WITH INCREASING CONSTANCY.

'you sensed his soul. you sensed that he was fighting against something.'—
faye dunaway on steve mcqueen

"the first thing an actor needs is soul. the actor with soul feels his part, he is
living his role, and the result is a good picture.'—d.w. griffith

"if you amount to nothing, your art in the end amounts to nothing; that is a
fact almost biological in its brutal certainty. the actor's business is to remain
himself forever; but to cause to grow in himself such flexibility and fluidity and

*eloquent magnetism of body, and such sympathy of the imagination, as may
be translated into compelling presentations of human character and living.
only through this translation of the character into himself can an actor profess
to be an artist at all, and the 'lord of another's soul.'"—stark young*

IN ACTING, what we seek is a perfect balance between **CLARITY OF
INTENT** and **SPONTANEITY**

SIMPLE QUESTIONS
mama crow
cauling the fetus
with marsh sludge
smearing the blue-eyed boy

why do you want to die?

     dynamics provided by the need.
hopelessness is lazy,
    indulgence is evil

why are you so mad at your mommy?

here comes the big moment
    you see it rising like a negative sun, a hole of light
left to be gnawed on by rabid dogs
    wounds over most of your body
forget all about your beauty
    who you were with
    in whose custody or care,

anyone at HOME?

something you lack
blocks the exit.

*"As it was with icarussssss,
imprisoned in the labyrinth of his father's creation,*

punished by the echoes of a monster's satisfaction
let ring
> *let ring*
exclusion of earth
> > *let ring"*
—jack larson, 'the relativity of icarus'

AFTER SEEING SUPERMAN ON THE DAY BEFORE FATHER'S DAY
i am feeling
pleasantly apocalyptic,
like when we glided past 1999,
at peace with kronos and kali.

and **now**,
perhaps,
really is the end.
such a relief really
unleash the planet engine
or was that
unfurl?
let loose?
release the planet engine.
give me back my dream.

a sadder sound has never been made.
elvis has left the planet.
and so has his missing twin.

let us be silent
just
for a moment.

and maybe take hands, or arms?
against this sea?
not in opposition,
only

to get from here
to there.

*"a certain solitude envelops me in the midst of a society that has lost its way. industrial society is monstrous. political competitiveness is contemptuous of human beings. cruelty is organized. modern society is careening toward destruction...but the human heart has not changed since mankind lived in caves. in giving me life, i was given an integrated, magnetic body, with the universe for parents. it tells me what i have to do, which is to connect with this universe...i want us all to participate in reconstructing the temple, heal the planet, which is a masterpiece in danger. the knowledge of ourselves and our bodies seems to me a salvation. i want it taught to children. it radiates, the **respect, dignity, tenderness** and **religiosity** we should have for each other."—jean-louis barrault*

LUGGING MY INFLATED AGENDA
my paltry gift
receipt to your animal appreciation
my promise to heal heartfelt and wriggling
lugging my inflated agenda through polished airports
warsawing throughout the universe
you are my only one
all my nights in the open
that place
where your neck flows into your shoulder
springfed pool laced with popular song
why not live in the play of our sunlight
i make my breath a love poem
on this the personalized place
that time of day when the bamboo shadows play
on the vineyard couch
for a succulent helping of you.

EIGHT DAYS IN RUSSIA, Warsaw Airport, March 19, 2007
i'm surprised how restful it is to be a stranger, to not understand the language, to be alien. i realized as i was getting on the plane at JFK that i had never traveled outside the united states alone. i've always been

cushioned by families or troupes, cocooned by my cohorts, in cahoots, always dependent on other's language skills and experience. that part of me, the Youth, who struck out On His Own, has been dormant, even neutered. i enjoy traveling with this guy—as tentative and over-polite as he is sometimes. putting on the rube (even when i *am* a rube.) the feeling of autonomy and invisibility is pleasantly scary. i'm on my way to kaliningrad, in russia—wherever that is.

THE TRUTH LIES
vestiges of lost pavilions
dream canals
forced to forget the privileges of beauty
or skirmishes in soul canyon
with all the evil predecessors and their muscled shadows
all stained by scandal because the story is better that way
a possible elephant lurks just at the edge of vision
conniving with cannonballs
LOOK
the splintered sky
above the only house the blizzard hit
now obscured by lucidity
coaxed by furtive chirps
into believing
what must not be seen.

"a man's work is nothing more than to rediscover, through the detours of art, those one or two images in the presence of which his heart first opened.'—albert camus

TOTEM: an emblem, a badge, a symbol, a token
my totem, my clan, is **coyote**

COYOTE NOON
sky blue circles under feet of steam.
you've walked so far and wandered reckless with stretched strides
flung yourself and given up flinging
coveting your next moment

adding to the raging river
spanned by quicksilver bridges.
in vengeance for your absence
your total lack of authentic participation
your utter shoelessness
your bare feet balancing on your heels
will you listen to nothing but destruction
even in yourself
to notice movement
something must be standing still.
—1974

COYOTE DUSK
i am up a tree
waiting to fall from the sky
by sliding down the spider's web
tasked by earthmaker with bringing the waterfall to earth.
and i leap
into the imaginal realm
i am animal
human
divine
acting in a grove of trees
in my black leather jacket, silver arrow on my back,
i bounce around, doing the best i can
i'm not good and i'm not bad
but i'm tricky
and then trickster bursts up out of the ground
and the stalking begins

COYOTE NIGHT
who is who exactly?
am i the actual person?
who is that pointing at me?
is it me or my enemy?

as far as i can tell, coyote claimed me sometime around 1974. or rather he recognized me. we became aware of each other. somehow i felt myself to be in the clan. by 1977 i was playing coyote in a project called *the coyote cycle,* written and directed by murray mednick, with norbert weisser playing trickster, coyote's other half, his twin-who-is-not-a-twin, his loyal ally and bitter rival.

from the winnebago trickster cycle:
 1.coyote/trickster cohabits with woman before war party
 5. coyote/trickster makes his right arm fight his left.
 7. children die because coyote/trickster breaks rules.
 11. coyote/trickster mimics man pointing.
 15. penis placed in box.
 16. penis sent across the water.
 24. coyote/trickster falls in his own excrement.
 38. chipmunk causes coyote/trickster to lose part of his penis.
 39. discarded pieces of penis thrown into lake and turn into plants.
 —from *paul radin, 'trickster: a study in american indian mythology'*

all of the above events occur in *'coyote one: the pointing'.* over the years more coyote tales, culled from various native american tribes, inspired us in the making of seven plays. details from our own lives became part of the mythology of the epic journey as well. we worked on each new chapter of the cycle, from 1977 to 1984, at a writer's workshop called *padua hills playwright's workshop/festival.* we performed all of the plays outside, sometimes with elaborate sets that seemed to grow out of the dirt. with all seven completed, we presented the entire cycle, in marathon all-night performances, from dusk to dawn. and the waterfall came to earth.

48. waterfall is forced to fall on land by coyote/trickster
49. coyote/trickster eats his final meal on earth and retires to heaven

COYOTE DAWN
to play a character that is **animal, human** and **divine**, and claim to actually understand that task, let alone achieve it, is a delusional hubris, and plain foolishness. at the time it seemed necessary, somehow inevitable, and in the doing, surprisingly believable—to myself and others. over the years the

project entered into legend. people on the street still hail me as '*coyote*'! even after more than 20 years since the last performance. the project lasted for nine straight years, (with an ill-fated reprise on martha's vineyard in 2000) and obviously had a tremendous impact on my work and my life. coyote is a holy fool, a reckless idiot—he believes he cannot die. he is always on the run, going nowhere in particular. he falls into his own shit, again and again. and yet…he is promethean, with an essential role in the making of this world. he is inspired and inspiring, and able to do anything he sets his sights on. to his great peril, as it happens. to say my life has been influenced and shaped by coyote, is to minimize his impact. in a real sense, i am coyote. and he is me. and as with most things, the very good and the very bad are inextricably bound. just like coyote and trickster. just like **me, myself** and **i.**
—*2020*

"how much do we actually see, and how much do we read into what we think we have seen?"—henry james

"to achieve accurate knowledge of others, if such a thing was possible, we could only ever arrive at it through the slow and unsure recognition of our own initial optical inaccuracies. however, such knowledge is not possible: for, while our vision of others is being adjusted, they, who are not made of mere brute matter, are also changing; we think we have managed to see them more clearly, but they shift; and when we believe we have them fully in focus, it is merely our older images of them that we have clarified, but which are themselves already out of date."—marcel proust, 'remembrance of things passed;'in the shadow of young girls in flower'

"once, there was a blond-haired, green-eyed man in a black leather jacket and i believed every word he said."—emma larson, 'in the cornucopia of your ear'

ALOHA SUITE/ COYOTE GOES TO KAUAI/ Part One, 2015
henceforth
my name shall be BigD.
i live in a house
of mutterers

muttering.
we tell ourselves what we are doing
so as to keep on doing so.
we are in paradise
or somewhere pretty close,
maybe the next valley over,
where it is even quieter than here.
we have a view of a corner of the shimmering sea
a darker shade of blue than the whole bowl of the radiant sky.
over there is an inconstant cascade,
white as a bridal veil, streaming from the jagged mountaintop.
once it was my task, as coyote, freely fallen from the firmament,
to bring the waterfall to mother earth.

now i busy myself with the moment at hand,
rapidly flowing through my fingers,
dreaming of love long past,
absorbing the news of the day,
future holding fast.
perpetual quick change
into
and out of
multicolored costumes.

trees murmur in concert with the chiming wind
and the simple wonder of sunlight.

*"at bottom no **one** in life can help any**one** else in life; thus **one** experiences over and over in every conflict and every perplexity: that **one** is al**one**."— rilke, from 'letters on love'*

"keep, keep, you know, keep a thing happening all thru it."—john coltrane

2. **GIVER**: EVERYONE'S NEEDS ARE EQUALLY AND FREELY MET IN
THE NATURAL FLOW OF GIVING AND RECEIVING.

           or to get, you must give. to be loved you must be needed.

*"coyote can run a thousand miles and never get tired! he is never even out of
breath! coyote can fly over the land in leaps and bounds!...wait a minute!
this is a funny place! someone has been fooling around with the gravity
around here!..."—murray mednick, 'the coyote cycle'*

saw a mother and daughter walking hand in hand on the west 4th street
platform of the A train. [the very spot on which i once embraced susanna,
drawing her to me with the collar of her blue overcoat fur trim quick kiss as
the train barreled in] and i thought "*am i to be deprived of the pure joy of
observing such as this, sweet interactions with sisters daughters mothers. for
the rest of my natural days? as punishment for what crime? and who
determined this sentence? is there no one to whom i can appeal? i'd rather
be dead than live in this solitary confinement, this banishment.*"

*"we can't become our real selves in the absence of others..we even start to
unravel without their presence in our lives."—re: solitary confinement as
torture*

30

earliest memories: walking with dad in the towering damp of the redwoods, the path beginning right outside our trailer, near fort bragg, our tin house trailer dwarfed but also somehow guarded, protected, by the enormous trees.

the tick in jerry's belly, he's around two years old, standing on the toilet seat, screaming, in pain and outrage, in the tiny closet-like bathroom, in the singlewide trailer, where five of us lived.

the tiger on my bunkbed, crouched at the foot, in the middle of the night, loudly purring. (i think it was actually my mom..)

my mom…sobbing, weeping, inconsolable, behind the flimsy accordion partition which separated their bed from our bunks.

the davey crockett hat, with the raccoon tail, and the power it bestowed on me.

the curtain call of 'puss in boots', done by an amateur theatre troupe in fort bragg. daddy was the grinning hero, basking in the applause, mommy was a resplendent puss-in-boots.

"in life there is really no great or small thing. all things are of equal value and of equal size."—oscar wilde, 'de profundis'

ALL THE DOOMED BLONDES: Part Two
carole lombard didn't give a fuck, and she was famous for saying so. although she died when only thirty-four, she had made forty-two talking pictures, and a slew of silents, including a stint as a bathing beauty in a dozen or so comedy shorts produced by mack sennett. most importantly she appeared in four of the finest comedies america has ever produced: *twentieth century, my man godfrey, nothing sacred* and *to be or not to be.* in these and many other films, she is still as enchanting and witty as any hollywood actress, then or now. her brusque, blonde superiority, her offhand hints of sexuality, and especially the exposure of feelings beneath the screwball comedy genre made lombard something of a legend in her own time. her tragically early death, and the way that cut short a very happy marriage to clark gable, ensured her reputation as someone slightly more than human. a

goddess, in short. she made her film debut in 1921, playing a 'tomboy 'part in a silent film called *a perfect crime.* the director spotted her playing baseball in the street. in 1930 she was put under a seven-year contract with paramount, where she established herself as aromantic comedienne, most effectively in *man of the world*, with william powell, whom, as we have seen, she married.

in 1925 she had just graduated from the ranks of starlets, when the brakes failed on the car ahead of the bugatti automobile in which she was riding with some other hard partiers. the car in front slid backward, shattering the windshield and severely slicing carole's face along the left cheekbone. for an actress considered just a *'pretty face',* the result could have ended her career before it had a chance to start. she had to endure having her face stitched back together by a plastic surgeon *without* anesthesia, subsequently lying immobile for a week and a half. fox summarily dropped her, even before they could see how the recovery went. though the wound would eventually heal with very little trace of a scar, it did cause carole to reappraise herself at the critical age of eighteen. she resolved not to be seen as superficial and to develop other elements beside her physical attractions. she would emphasize her positive energy, love of life, and unbridled spirit. given the random nature of the accident, she became fatalistic about the unforeseen, the plot twist that could change your life—or end it.

she had a very healthy regard for making love. she was amorous with the ex-hoofer, gangster/movie star, george raft; publishing magnate horace liveright; and the aviator/film producer **howard hughes**. she had learned about single malt whiskeys from william powell, who was hollywood's idea of a most eligible bachelor. he insisted on being immaculate, endlessly fussing about the smallest detail of haberdashery, both on-and-off camera; but he was enough of a rake to pull it off, enhanced by a dry and resilient wit. on june 26, 1931, after making a second movie together, *ladies 'man,* they wed, announcing powell's entrance into hollywood high society. the marriage lasted twenty-eight months.

with each project, lombard was assembling the elements that would define screwball comedy, the genre she would come to embody. it was carole's manner—the sass, a barely repressed energy that hovered just shy of manic, and a salty disposition. she was one of the boys, and one of the girls; the thin frame and draping of a model, and a mouth that could talk a blue streak. she could be ultrafeminine, born to the long gown and perfectly drawn face, but she could be as tough as any guy, and loved raising eyebrows. when making *we're not dressing* with bing crosby, she came down to breakfast one morning and loudly inquired, so that the whole company could hear her, "*bing, dear, did i leave my nightie in your room last night?*" crosby and lombard became fast friends, although at the time, carole was engaged to bing's crooning rival, russ columbo. columbo died in a bizarre shooting accident at the age of twenty-six. carole called russ *"the great love of my life"*. she sobbed uncontrollably at his funeral, comforted by bing, who served as a pallbearer. five years later she married gable. again, anita loos:

"carole lombard was clark's third wife and the wish fulfillment of every man in and out of hollywood; a natural blonde who, both a lady and a hoyden, had a sense of humor and lack of pretense that seldom go with beauty as glittering as hers. i recall the one day she was strolling down a road and a passing truck offered her a lift. carole accepted and, because the driver had charisma, she drove with him all the way to bakersfield. but before long the young man began to sense that he'd picked up an angel [goddess] *unawares. 'know something baby? 'he ventured. 'you remind me of carole lombard.' 'if you compare me to that floozy, i'll get right off your truck!" carole flared up. so the driver apologized."*

"in the early years of world war II, carole was asked to launch a war bond drive in her native state of indiana. she had been warned to avoid airplanes, still considered unreliable and dangerous. so lombard set off by train, selling bonds at various stops en route to indianapolis. gable had to stay behind to start work with **lana turner** *on 'somewhere i'll find you'. miss lombard left a pneumatic blonde dummy in gable's bed, as a substitute for miss turner, with a note that said, 'so you won't be lonely.' gable chortled and spent three days building a male dummy, expectantly erect, to welcome her home. ('i'm really nuts about him, 'carole once said to garson kanin. 'and it isn't all the great-lover crap because if you want to know the truth, i've had better.') unfortunately, neither of the mannequins proved barrier enough to prevent* **lana turner** *from sharing gable's bed. the element of betrayal was to add enormously to gable's subsequent grief. lombard sold two million dollars worth of bonds, but she wouldn't wait for the train on which she already had a*

ticket. on the night of january 16, she boarded a TWA DC-3 bound for home. a few minutes after take-off from las vegas, the plane somehow strayed off course. beacons that might have warned the pilot had been blacked out because of the fear of japanese bombers. the plane crashed into a cliff near the top of potosi mountain. the first reports to reach hollywood said only that the plane was missing, but somehow everyone knew what had happened. a dazed gable asked to join the search parties but was persuaded to wait in las vegas. it was eddie mannix, the studio's general manager, who accompanied the stretcher-bearing mules up into the snow-covered mountains and retrieved the charred and decapitated corpse of carole lombard. gable was distraught for months. he bought a motorcycle and drove wildly through the canyons north of hollywood. he refused to speak to anyone, or else talked compulsively about his dead wife. of the many diamond necklaces and rings and bracelets he had showered on her, only one mangled fragment was found at the site of the crash, and he wore that around his neck for the rest of his life."—otto penzler, 'city of nets'

LUSTRATION FOR LOS ANGELES
los angeles is truly honeysuckle city
dangerous diners immune to mad cow disease
unforgiven cattle in the imminent river
new grass calmly in the cracks
popcorn in the aisles forlor
threadbare satin and pompom pumps scuffling the boulevard
where tension is protection

just jacarandaopolis
not an entrance exact
a working out place
a bruise
somewhere south of your aspirations
wild and ornamental.
would that the skies *could* be scraped
or licked
skylickers
or sucked
skysuckers.

when the smoke clears,
brothers and sisters, we all will drown.

los angeles is an oleander capital
a motorcycle midnight
where language has been retongued and tongued again
all the erotic vowels of clittoral poets
rubbing on every street corner
and when they speak we all understand.

LA is bougainvilleaville
a rhythm of lips and guitars
gutters of freeways
frenzy on the patios
we are all in this together
and together
and together
and now
the grit caress
hair damp at the back of the neck
a tattoo of a planetary city
a toilet taboo
a paradise

we are agave, lupine and poppy
we are helplessness after dark.
in the flailing of our history
we are all snakebit
headlights livid out on the highway
one heel missing from our boots
blood dripping down our sleeves
hunkered in the shadow of an illegible street sign
an arm dangling from a car window
made a wing by the wind.
to reiterate:
a city of earth

scud of the great sea
home to various witnesses to waste.

this is eucalyptusland
where we grow decay and emulate
where we embrace
where we fast forward through smut
masking our disappointment
but we are all in this together
no one
is immune.
we all clench this same fair air
and run shrieking into the sea
this is our common beach
our stately palms
our share.

HIGH FALLS INTERLUDE
observing the pterodactyls and boys
diving into the river
for sustenance
for pride
for fun,
just to enter the current is cleansing
and to drift with the hovering flitting dragonflies.

why did she abandon dragonflies?

when the wind says rustle stand your ground
going so far as to lean rakishly far
out
over
the flow
hold to the earth firm
in your boldness
steady in your aspirations
what we call rapids

have not moved forward for centuries

in that membrane where gymnast fish
do their tricks
the girl named cat finally breaks through
and plunges, screaming into gravity
pinwheeling her limbs
the suntanned crowd cheers in acclimation.
paddling back to the warm rocks she trills and shrieks,
insisting, breathless,
"oh my god i will never do that again…i'm gonna die"
chattering and clambering back into place
to make her second leap.

"today like every other day
we wake up empty and scared
don't open the door of your study and read
take down a musical instrument
let the beauty we love be what we do
there are hundreds of ways
to kneel and kiss the earth."
—rumi

MONGREL TONGUE/ AMBULANT CARRION
dragonflies draw flame
delighted to be seen being delighted
shadow of frenzied raptors
taking the flaccid shredded remains
of purple balloons
no red no orange no periwinkle
spurted in the streets
thrilled to be authorized
authenticated by other's interest
or better yet
desire
craving
to be able to arouse

obsession
that is:
to be perceived as prey
thrilled to be seen as thrilling

o dysphoria
thou art mighty in thy pleasures
in thy fatal absence
his gloves become sleek ravens
dark paper money
horrid to see
hurtful to recollect
apparition in place of a person
emission vanishing from being seen
nothing (air) remains (toxic)
flung pennies changed
into soaring birds flapping
jangly wings
if you can't read
order the corpse to do it.

carrion buzzes bloated
open like the slaughtered angels
they are.

what have we done?

why did we do it?
someone will pry open the black box
and inhale the fumes of paradise

the best of us has not returned.
--7/20/2014, nyc

*"my father told me of a recurring dream he'd had as a child in which his own
father would sneak up behind him with a long sharp needle and try to pierce
him through the ear. my first nightmare, i must have been three or four: my*

father folding crab-like into his own ear, the evil angels chasing him, a background of murky brown. my mother, slim, columnar in a long white dress, my sister on her hip, and me beside her, all standing before my father, watching him retreat into his own holes."—emma larson, 'in the cornucopia of your ear'

'parents are broken and full of error...being hurt by those you love is awful, but its less awful if you know they meant to help...perhaps the immutable error of parenthood is that we give our children what we wanted, whether they want it or not. we heal our wounds with love we wish we received, but are often blind to the wounds we inflict.'—mark jacobsen 'far from the tree'

"you don't know me; you never knew my heart. no man knows my history. i cannot tell it; i shall never understand it. i don't blame anyone for not believing in my history. if i had not experienced what i have, I could not have believed it myself."—joseph smith, april 7, 1844

PATRIATE BY ORDER OF THE PROPHET/ SONG OF MY GRANDAD
1.
let his name be carl, son of lars. carl found the truth. well, she found the truth, his harsh german bride, anna stoker, she found it and she shared it with him, sparingly, like a loaf of stale bread, one small morsel at a time. he would hold the crumb in his mouth to moisten it, then swallow it slowly.

they have been riding in this horrid, gaseous, heaving, sea-bound prison for weeks, maybe forever, a pilgrim barge, crammed into the hold with so many others, summoned to america by the prophet, joseph smith. they are not in the first triumphant wave, but several detritus-ridden breakers later, and thus they come to new york harbor, a glance at the massive woman in the harbor, herded onto a belching train in barely converted boxcars still stinking of cowshit and dank hay, sleeping on the reeking straw. their meager belongings crammed in battered luggage, their holdings held close, she with her fragile and carefully wrapped cups and saucers, paper thin and hand painted, her delicate plates festooned with filigrees and perfectly rendered fruit, all brought from the black forest, transylvania (her family name 'stoker ' just like bram, a distant cousin, who wrote *dracula*.) carl with his threadbare stockings and thick, gnarled boots.

they crossed the plains, not with pushcarts like the proud first pioneers, in the wake of the martyring of the prophet of the lord. the astounding pilgrimage of the mormons, brigham young the moses of the age, nineteen centuries after the death of christ, all the way to deseret, their name for the territory, anchored by a massive lake of salt, called utah by everybody else. usurping the tribal name of some local savages.

and he, carl, son of lars, would build a sod house in the desolate land near moab, another name borrowed from the heathens, and he would start a farm, and he would give anna twelve children. one, a girl named violet, would die. the other eleven would survive, although the youngest child, harold, contracted polio at seventeen in the epidemic that seared the nation, spending his life with a withered leg and a prominent limp. in pictures, carl held his face like a pioneer, his right ear especially protuberant, with an odd point near the crest, just like my dad's, just like mine.

i know he, carl, son of lars, heard wild music, on the wind, across the fields he had plowed and planted with some animal kind of love. she harried him and threw up her hands in rage at his foolishness, fists forced into her apron, moving her reddened hands like she was strangling a crow, or some other struggling vermin.

and he would walk away often at dusk, stiff-gaited, down to the river.
and listen.

2.

my sons, some of them, went mad. my daughters, all of them, married the wrong man. that's what anna says. me, i kept plowing and planting and sowing and reaping, and drinking when i damn well needed to. and i loved to dance, so i danced, jigs, reels, doe-say-doeing. i could sing to beat the band. so could my boys. some of them. i taught 'em how. beautiful barbershop harmonies, "*under the old apple tree, that's the only place for me..*" the girls would fuss and warble, pound the piano and slap the boys away, even the ones that weren"t their brothers. a couple of those boys i saw myself in STRONG, some of them took after anna, and i threw up my hands, straightened my hat to let some of the sweat out, and spit in the dirt.

she don't own me. god don't own me. if anything the ground, the dirt, the earth owns me. and the water. the sure and precious water. that's what owns me. the rest of it be damned.

in the spring we'd go up the mountain, through the meadows, and we'd drive up there and canoe on the lake, birch canoes like the injuns used, and we'd fish with rods we made ourselves from willow shoots. and we swam in the snowfed lake at midnight with just the moon and the stars to show our way.

she'd stay back at the camp, stewing. sometimes that rascally mary, occasionally even the stern vera, would join me and the boys, come with us skinny-dipping, safe in the dark. it felt like floating in pure moonlight, and i was glad the girls could steal a little magic out from under anna's nose, with her severity and piety and complaining. but mostly, this grace was grasped only for a moment, then snatched away by a shrill shout, *"you girls get back here right now or i'll blister your bottoms. bad enough he's got the boys out there in their all together. shame on all of you…!"*
 and so on.

i know she's trying to squash the very life out of poor harold, especially once he took sick. like he's her last chance to win out. but after the terrible plague almost took him…her rage could fill the whole territory. she prayed so hard it musta singed the pearly gates.

i'll give him credit. he pushed back. turns out he's as stubborn as she is. or me, to be honest. i got a goat in me. so he pushed on, but i kept my distance because, well, she wore me out. but the boy played sports, basketball, even tennis, damn good, too. he went after it—like any boy should.

but no, something did go out of him. my youngest, little limping harold, or something latched on to him and got him in a death grip, sorry to say, a plain terror that i couldn't help him with, her anger magnified unto a thousand times a thousand. i kinda feel sorry for his children, though. all those years of ear-pulling and recrimination and shame from her, his kids will probably take the brunt of his revenge. ain't that the way it always works?

HOW I BECAME RACIST
as a mormon child, an incipient saint, as it were,
i was solemnly informed,
by way of the story of the first murder,

cain, the first man born of woman,
bashed his brothers brains out with a rock,
out of jealousy,
for everybody loved abel more.
he was goldenlocked and good,
cain was dark and glowering,
a bully.
cain hit abel with a rock when they were out on the edge.
working or something, and the brothers quarreled
and cain picked up a rock and smashed his brother's skull.
and the parents found out and cast cain
out of the garden
to the east of eden
and god cursed him with coal black skin so everybody would know he had
sinned
terribly
black skin was the mark of cain
and all his children and all of their descendents were negroes from then on.
just so everybody would know they cursed.
that was what i was taught in sunday school. so black men were not quite
men. they couldn't *'hold the priesthood'* like i would someday at 12 or 13, if i
behaved myself, i would be *'endowed'* with it. the gospel said so. and i
believed the gospel truth. or at least they told me i did.

then i heard rockandroll.
it was as simple as that.
my life was saved by it.
just like the song said.
I heard little richard
good golly miss molly
chuck berry
sweet little sixteen
shake rattle and roll
I heard motown.
please mr. postman
the supremes
james brown

a whole other level of being
and of course elvis and the everly brothers and bill haley and jerry lee and
then the beatles and the stones and…
but those white guys obviously got their mojo from the black priests of the
real power
and right around in there, 1963 or something,
i started seeing marchers,
and hearing martin luther king
and becoming increasingly aware of the civil rights movement
and bob dylan and the beautiful blackhaired songbird joan baez, whom even
some grownups liked
and SIDNEY POITIER,
and what the fuck are these people i am growing up amongst talking about?
superior? they gotta be kidding.

so I say
curse me, baby,
curse me and make it stick!

i started leaving the dinner table when my father used the word ██████.
that did not go over well. pounding the table and flinging of chairs
i started seriously drawing away from the precepts and tales
i had been stuffed with from birth.
of course, the divergence had started earlier on,
but now the split was really complete.
and besides, rockandroll was sexy…

but in 9th grade bussing was instituted and black kids, from the other side of
the levee (i swear to god) were brought to our school every morning. black
guys with impossibly high pompadours, processed and covered with scarves
sometimes. were doing a rhythmic strutstride they called a pimp stroll. like
they were going forward and back in the same movement. the girls were
softer and more open, at least for me. and i made friends. but i was the
'president 'of the student body. i was prominent. and therefore a target. one
day in gym i was assigned to be the captain of a soccer team. i was shit at
physical education, especially combat sports. but, this was just for the day,
but i had to assign positions. i asked one of the black kids to be the goalie.

he refused. i insisted, mostly because i didn't give a flying fuck about it. he got pissed. i got annoyed. he said he was going to wait for me after school and kick my ass. i was terrified. when i got to the next class i wrote a note to a friend, who i hoped could arbitrate a peace agreement. i said, *"the ███ ███s are after me."* i was furious for several reasons—for one thing--i was on *their side.* didn't they know that? and i was scared shitless. i knew he would not be there alone. i pictured myself being beaten. to a pulp. after school i slunk home, which fortunately was quite close to the school, avoiding capture. but the next morning, as i sat at my usual spot in the cafeteria before home room started, i was surrounded by what seemed like the entire black population of the school. some taking swipes at my head, and poking at me. i sat facing forward, as if i was still doing some last minute homework. the only white children left in the room were two kids who tried to protect me. one was a boy named dave messier, who was not a close friend, but just felt like i needed some help. he stood with his back to me, fending off whomever he could. and a girl named delores martin, who was a pretty good friend of mine, got a handful of forks, and climbed up on the table, waving her arms around above my head. after some very tense moments, the english teacher, mrs. robertson, a feisty, short, redheaded woman came plowing through the crowd and ordered everybody to stop harassing me and get to class! for some reason they all did. i was consigned to the principal's office. my father was called. he brought a black city councilman, whom i had no idea he knew, to arbitrate. but it was decided that really this was just a personal problem i was having. the bussing thing was going fine. the next morning i was required to resign as student body president, reading a statement i had written over the public address system. an audible shout went up all over the school, and kids came running up to the office, including many african-american students, demanding that i be reinstated. the rest of the year was tense but peaceful.

a few years later—in high school, i helped to organize an inter-racial group who met after school to discuss the issues facing us as young people on the front lines of forming a new, less racist society. at one of the early meetings i developed a crush on a graceful, beautiful black girl named jackie wardlow. i could tell she liked me, too. her friends were resistant and advised her to reject my advances. and then, a member of the group asked me why i had put up a big sign in front of the junior high school saying i hated ███████s,

44

how could i claim to be an ally of black people? i tried to explain—but it sounded lame even to me. that pretty much did it for me and jackie.

as for my own children—by the time my son was born, in 1977, while racism continued, obviously, the society had changed, and had become more integrated. i had marched many many times for civil rights, and to end the war, and the draft, and nukes, etc. i had many black friends, as was the cliche white people used to claim our support for justice and equality. but, i did. and so did my son, who in fact, went to a school with about half the population black or brown, all the people he admired in the culture, every poster on his wall, were black entertainers—hiphop was his music—in fact he took it on as a life's work, as a producer and an international dj. his sisters, born in 1988 and 1990, are activists like their parents and less racist, by a matter of degrees. two of their godmothers are black women, and so on.

and now the nation is going up in flames. white violence and oppression of black people in this country, from the 1619 to the present, has reached a tipping point, as have all of the inequities and fault lines in our society. is there a bridge to get us across this vast chasm, the last river to cross to the promised land? is the curse we were born with going to prove deadly and irrevocable for the entire human race? stay tuned…

ON OUR OWN/ MY FATHER'S FUNERAL
my dad is lying in his open coffin, at the far end of an anonymous chapel in a funeral home in a town he never lived in. funeral and home are words that don't quite go together. not exactly oxymoronic just ill-fitting, like the suit they've got him in. and the way they've combed his hair.
    each of the children born while he was married to my mother are in the room. and some of the children of those children, and even some of their spouses. we all keep our distance at first, lingering in the back pews, as if approaching a still dangerous but ancient, weakened beast. not out of piety, or even respect--a bit of awe at the finality and universality of death. we all just hang back quietly.
    four of my six siblings: jerry, who looks just like him, but shorter, thicker, nicer, and to whom he never sent so much as a birthday card, and to whom he once said, *"well, if you want to think of me as your father, that's all right with me,"* or some such don't-do-me-any-favors kind of insensitive crap.

at least he wasn't openly, deliberately, actively cruel to jerry, as he was to my sister, lou ree, who devoted herself to him for most of his hostile life.
[and then last month it hit me, like waking up in sweat-soaked pajamas, my dad had polio when he was 17. he almost died. he endured unimaginable pain, just as he was coming into full manhood. in his final years, that pain came back to tighten the screws again. so my father and i both carried a dormant virus in our bodies for much of our lives. I acquired HIV sometime in the mid-80s.]

my brother, kevin, the youngest of the four, and the one elected least bitter, although our father refused to accept kevin as his child, either, who has striven honorably and with good cheer to make a good life for himself (went into the show business like me, as a hardworking stuntman) and his autistic son, shane, in partnership with a truly beautiful, diligent wife, fatima.

and then me. our father did claim me. as his own. and then some. so i became the escapee, lamster, outlier, the one who got away. (still married at the time of my dad's funeral, i was soon to engineer another escape from the home i sought for my entire life, but could never allow, could not let myself have.) my father had been forced to tell me, more than once, that my immortal soul was damned. unless i changed my ways. and now here he lies. gone gone gone.

his erstwhile progeny shuffle and contemplate, nobly, like wild animals approaching a possibly poisoned waterhole. not raising our voices, but nevertheless slightly triumphant. we're still here, after all.

then kevin approaches the corpse.

"his hair is wrong. he would never wear it that way."

and of course it's true. they, the morticians, (that word is always comical to me somehow), have brushed it straight back, revealing the loss of substance and amplitude. dad combed it over. to make it seem fuller.

"anybody got a comb?"

slight pause to consider that nobody carries a comb anymore.

my sister scurries to her purse, stashed in the front pew, and comes up with a brush.

my dear brother steps right up to the coffin and adjusts the soft and brittle strands to better reflect their state in life on my father's skull. and while he's up there, it may have even been me who says/ no. not me. his wife drifts up and whispers in his ear, and kevin says right away,

"anybody have some scissors?"

my sister and brother continue to fuss with my dad's hair and exchange looks. my mouth is hanging open like a person watching a mild-to-enormously stunning event; a nude parade, a tightrope walker after a near slip, a fallen eaglet flapping fragile wet wings in the dust…

kevin as i've said, has an autistic son, shane, so handsome at sixteen, mostly joyful, occasionally panicked, exuberant like teenagers everywhere. the genetic sources are supposedly of interest, a sample could be studied and conclusions drawn or future solutions suggested. and kevin could then also establish, presumably, who his father actually was, or at least who he wasn't.

"*i think i have some nail clippers,*" someone says, pretty sure it was jeannette, jerry's bighearted, blonde, no-bullshit wife. and she bustles over to her purse, fussing through the contents.

meanwhile my sister, lou ree, just grabs ahold of the dry dead hair and yanks out big gobs of it. not exactly handfuls, but enough, what anybody would call a lock, out of the corner of my eye i see the evidence, the sample of yellowish white hair, being bagged for later analysis.

i notice now the deceased's falsely inflated chest, suggesting full lungs, but looking more like an overstretched accordion, absolutely tacit, still, propped up from inside, or underneath, by,…what? coat hangers? a fondue stand? then the chest falls off like phillip larkin's coastal shelf. [in '*this be the verse': man hands on misery to man/ it deepens like a coastal shelf*] there is no belly, no discernible legs, not even the withered one, the one he pretended did not exist, at least not in its actual troublesome, endlessly aching way. it did IN FACT serve as the right leg for his body, his strong insistently athletic meatsuit made of bones, muscle and viscera. the leg just had to keep up the best it could, supporting his laboring soul through life. he played short stop. he played tennis, basketball, golf, all ferociously. he did ballroom dancing, not as gracefully as his brother oscar, or as charmingly as his brother art, or as salaciously as his brother gus, but he danced. [i can picture him giving my mother, who took a job teaching at arthur murray dance studio, after their divorce, a whirl around the floor.]

in the end my brother and sister collect enough follicles to establish with certainty that some of us share DNA with the gradually decaying carcass before us, once known familiarly as hal, with newly corrected hair. he does look better within certain criteria. we all begin backing away. its not like we all go up to the bier and bend our knee, sniffle, pay respects. it's more like touching second base and rounding toward third. of course, i always played out in right field. fewer hits come out there, so fewer dropped or wildly thrown balls. [once i was menaced by a tramp from the sidelines during a little league game. that night i dreamt he was there again, trying to grab me again, somehow in my room in right field. i had just begun to sleep naked, like marilyn monroe, and my bed was close to the floor. when my hand dragged on the bedroom floor, i felt the tramp's horned paw and screamed so loud i woke up the whole house.] back in the chapel it got giddy, as if we had all found some small treasure, like at easter, but with less sugar. those who did the deed, kevin and lou ree, are kind of proud at their audacity, and the rest of us feel like we are in this nicely dressed gang of slightly rebellious conspirators out for a stroll. we stride up the aisle, glancing back.

 "i think our job here is done, " i suggest.

 "yes" my sister says, and she hustles us out into the cooling afternoon. the sun hits my brother jerry, so openhearted all through the decades, the tyke scampering back and forth in the murky trailer; the beautiful muscled youth; the graying, tanned, smiling man--in the face of the inevitable disappointments and setbacks, stoic and understanding, resisting embitterment, rueful but accepting, now tooling around in a restored red convertible sports car, he embodies, truly, the redemption and the rebuke to the trap our father laid for us all. we seem to have sidled past the train wreck caused by that long ago afternoon when his stone faced mother dragged him by the EAR from the garage on the corner, his haven, in front of his buddies, his first job, a mechanic, just for pocket money. to have something of his own. disallowed, therefore so disallowing. my mother's mother, granny, told me that story in my twenties, to try to explain why my dad was so angry, always and forever.

 out in the dusk a pink haze has set in. i find myself smiling. heck i'm fullout grinning, regarding my sweet siblings at sunset, the day of my dad's funeral. somehow still holding our own together, like river rocks warmed in our pockets and passed from palm to palm to palm to palm...

AFTERWORD: the DNA test never happened. the sample was never submitted. kevin told me the other day: *"turns out we could have all just spit into a baggie or something. we didn't need hair...not his anyway."* i did not ask what happened to the errant lock of hair. i see it pitched into the trash. and then gone.

further ADDENDUM:
only recently did i realize two odd parallels:
my father, to whom i did not speak, or barely, for many years, from when i was roughly seventeen years old, to the end of his life. and my youngest daughter, lilah, has not spoken to me, mostly, since when she was seventeen. these two, so central to my life, share a birthday, september 27th. and as i've mentioned, my father and i both carried dormant viruses in our bodies for most of our lives. random strands in the **nexus rerum,** rhymes of history. co-incidence. tragedy and misunderstanding echoing through generations.

DORMANT VIRUS exists as PURE INFORMATION

"it is a gift from my father that i see the world in metaphor. it may be his fault. there is a story he told me to describe the damage his father caused him, the story of the horse. in the mid-sixties, in his teenage years, my father's family lived on a range, and my father worked there as a ranch hand during those days. there was a horse that was very wild, and the only one who could ride the animal was my father. no one could break the horse. my father loved that horse. when they gelded the horse my father's father ordered that he be put right back in the pen with all the others. my father protested—he knew that the horses would smell the fresh wound and nip at the animal…it happened anyway, and my father watched it from a nearby hill, watched as all the horses swarm, watched his horse lay down, crumble to the grass, bitten apart from the others. it was my father's job to help bury him. he stood on the tractor-back as they dragged the horse away, and he watched the head be drawn against the mud and rocks. in the end, they could not bury him entirely, he was too immense, and so my father and his cousin dragged him to be left in the empty lakebed."—emma larson, 'in the cornucopia of your ear'

BY DEATH UNTAMED
1.
the horse when he was dead
four legs chained at the hoof
dragged by tractor

to rot
in the dry lakebed
a light rain falls
i'm perched backwards
watching his mournful head
bounce and snag
in the damp dirt road.
i smell the sage and hay
but the horse doesn't.
my jokester cousin
drives the little skip loader
i'm tearful from the long ordeal
holding the horse upright
my puny self under his heavy head
but he'd lost too much blood
after they hacked off his balls
others nipped his rump
to keep him running
and so he bled
in the cropped field
so he laid down
sure sign of death
in a sorrel with a white mane and tail
or any colt
disposed to canter and
leap
as this one had
up and over a ten-foot fence
sudden flight from a standing crouch
straight up and
clean
clear
over!

we all stood astonished
lariats drooping
amazed at the feat

at the desperate effort
defying even gravity
in a mighty surge to survive!
only to find himself in the next corral.
my uncle whooped
my father roped him tight
and tied the exhausted colt
to a solid post.
so began the breaking.
2.
near dusk the next day
i return to the corral
where the horse stands hanging his noble young head,
refusing to eat the dry hay thrown down near him,
not yet a stallion
but ready for some rutting and ranging
picking up the scent
of his rampant future
dreaming of full-tilt gallops.
but now a halter must be placed around his neck.
now he must learn how to work.

i straddle the fence and just
be there in the failing light
after some silence
feeling it out
i hit the turbid mud
thick with shit and straw
and
one step at a time
holding the loop
of the lariat
loose at my side
moving it out in front of me
a peace offering
so he can see it
smell it

occasionally i make a gentle clicking sound
with my tongue.
trying to form
a slight touch
of the ancient secret sympathy
from back when man and horse
lived side by side
in the wild.
he jerks suddenly
and harshly waggles his head
adamant protest and disagreement
emphatically refusing
his blaze of white forelock
his scanning ears laying back flat
his wideset eyes
in a massive skull
developed over centuries
inherited from the dawn horse
eohippus
he paws his bare hooves
fiercely at the ground
he snuffles and snorts.
but he does not retreat.

i take another step
another
one more
i shift the noose back
to my left hand
and offer my right hand to him,
using my teeth to peel off my glove
and put my bare fingers
there between us
to do with what he will
up to the soft
smooth velvet just
above his lips

lightly scratching there
he shows an ugly grin
with spittle spraying
he expels heavy steam from his nostrils
making my hand moist
now i return the tightly woven hemp to my forward hand
with great discretion
smearing it with his spit
let him huff the twisted sissal
and i pass
the noose
with both hands
now,
making sure that not one
bit of it
brushes against his lips,
his nostrils,
his chomping jaw,
and his frightened eyes,
lifting now slightly toward the ears,
and over
as they twitch,
moving slowly down the mighty neck,
resting it now on the bright white mane
and the copper shoulders.
his withers tremble and twitch beneath his deep copper skin
gently caressing the bristly silk between his jaws.
he shifts and paws his heart-shaped hooves
but still he doesn't bolt.
then i put my arm around his flank and lean against him
just for a moment.
i don't cinch up the lasso
i just start to amble around the pen
and he tentatively
follows
as if fundamentally shy
but curious

i take up a bit of slack
without pausing in my circling
he takes more steps
sometimes he hesitates
but then decides to take the next few steps.
i keep up the clicking sound
to urge him on,
and calm 'uhuhs..'
we make a full turn around the corral.
i keep taking up slack imperceptibly
until i am close again
and can murmur in his swiveling ear
"good…good, my friend…thank you".
i hang on him one more time
this time with all my weight.
i grasp a hunk of mane
pull my right leg up
and lay the length of my body where a saddle will go,
feeling his heaving breaths,
his rippling flesh,
just for a moment,
then
i slide back to solid ground.
so began the gentling….

"i dreamed once of the body of a horse. a body i had cut and buried, hidden beneath the ground."—emma larson, 'in the cornucopia of your ear'

"As it was with Icarus
wanting to fly
let ring
from memories of a Minotaur's birth
Away from the mutilated bodies of handsome young men"
—jack larson, 'the relativity of icarus"

SECOND DISQUISITION ON BUSTER
buster:
a **person** who
or **thing** which
breaks
beats
masters
prevents
or eliminates
place
ballbuster
chartbuster
broncobuster
but it was
burster at first
er…
an impressive or startling person
who,
or thing which,
provokes admiration.
a mate
a fellow
a chap
an unusually large person
a guy
especially a wise guy
almost always in direct
address to a stranger
usually
one who has aroused
the speaker's anger
a square
a babbitt
some far-out use
since 1955
a violent gale
buster leaning into a buster

being tossed down main street
summersaulting like yesterday's news
old books blown into confetti
gritty fiendish jetsam
the debris of 3000 autumns
the wreckage of clouds
a storm of such
palpability and purpose it's like fate
or your father debruised
terrified you're sissified
but you are a bustious boy, not massive or bulky,
but fierce, powerful, rough
or the person who
or the thing which
can stand in place
just where the window falls
or ride a flying tree
roots dangling downriver,
you can tumble out of paradise
on the up and up,
not even sightless,
wearing a deepsea diver's suit
with an innate understanding of the mechanisms.
anyone can whistle, sport.
we can all be blown away, buddy.
but who among us
can roll with the bust up
and play all the parts
including the monkey?
BUSTER is that rare person or thing
almost magically
perfectly
in place.
--derived from 'the dictionary of american slang'

TWO LUNCHES IN TWO DAYS

56

it does happen. people who once loved each other, who were once IN love—
as a place, a location, an alternate universe, a state, a zone,—can
sometimes re-enter, revive, reorient, restore—fall back again into that bed of
acceptance, come what may, for better or worse, richer or poorer—

no, wait. no way. if you are seen as unsuccessful, especially to
yourself, perceived as dishonest or worse, see yourself as a victim—you
become in-valid. your visa is cancelled. you're in GONE, a country without
borders and without passports, but with many walls and doors and mirrors
endless littered stairs, a maze, a labyrinth, going precisely nowhere—
although occasionally one finds oneself sitting on hard benches, waiting for
one's garbled name to be shouted, or muttered, and then filed in a pile of lost
notices, pleading for assistance.(and then there was the big black lady in
brooklyn, who saw my distress and shame, and said, *'hey, you are a good
person."* and she got up and walked all the way to the end of the row of
cubicles, came out the door, strode up to me, and hugged me, tight against
her ample body. *"you'll get through this."* and then she made her way back to
the desk where i sat opposite to her, (like those prison deals, but without the
glass,) forms in disarray, astonished and tearful.)

but now, i'm waiting at a safer place, getting cozy after the blustery rain
outside, which prides itself on serving the very tastiest. freshest bread, where
the vegetables are right off the vine, and you can find the ultimate in finger
sandwiches—cucumber and butter, slim and tasty.

when my erstwhile wife arrives she shows me pictures of the garden i
once tended, like a lover. of the bearded irises, flaming orange and deep
purple, sky blue and nearly black, the enormous peonies, the naturalized
daffodils and crocuses, all the rooted jubilation i placed in the earth, following
the pattern of the gardener before me, and the one before him. she shows
me proof of how all the plants, so carefully planted, have proliferated and
thrived. she tells me of the cicadas perched on the hostas (these buzzing
heralds had hatched on our arrival, in our second home together, seventeen
years ago, and now sing their harsh song at my banishment). she speaks of
our daughter, lilah, wearing the frames of the old glasses i wore when we
lived in LA. so now they frame the eyes of the girl who won't look at me. in
the picture susanna shows me, my youngest has her back to the camera.
susanna advises me in the strongest, kindest terms to move back west, and

have the third act of my life in LA, *"where they get you"*. she's says this not without love, not at all. just practical, as always.

the very next day, still rainy, i meet with, at the same franchise, different location, lori swift, my soulful and caring agent, hard by the public library, near her office. it's essentially the same clean, well-lighted room, still the best fresh bread in town. and she tells me exactly what susanna told me. that i should move back to LA, *"where they understand you"*. two women who have believed in me, supported me, even championed me, and still love me, have lost…what? whatever it is, they are throwing up their hands, still with that look in their eyes.
—*2013/ nyc*

SECOND DAY, 70-191—Beaver, Utah to Rock Springs, Wyoming, 1995
breakfast at cottage inn. very well-maintained. immaculate, almost weirdly so. somebody's extensive doll collection, filling every nook and cranny. one human size, to the left as you come in the front door, which gives us all a jolt. dolls for sale, too. one pink bunny, with a human baby's face, with two sparkly tears glued to its cheeks, really freaks tavish out. the conversation we overhear from a corner table is all about shaklee products and the use of alfalfa in them, and hay being used in cereal now, and the one guy, overweight with suspenders cinching up his pale jeans, we figure to be tub, the owner. the food is not great, but elaborately presented.

we drive to moab. the landscape gets increasingly more and more visually stunning. the red earth. the majestic buttes and looming mesas. tav rides with mark, because the sound system is better and i'm not using the air conditioning, as is my wont. i had talked a lot about my dad at breakfast and mormons and such. i got very animated. so now i was thinking about him. as we approached green river i started listening to this local radio station and the commentator was avuncular and kinda homespun, but slightly hysterical, like many of the grown men around me as a kid. he interspersed randomly dire news items, like rottweilers grabbing babies out of their mother's arms, and bus accidents *"because the driver APPARENTLY fell asleep"*, interspersed with sales pitches for allergy cures and improvements on nordic track machines, all of which he hypes as if he were a qualified physician but the guy is essentially a huckster. then he throws in a bit about vince foster, and missing files and then blithely, vituperatively goes on to some air filter that will prevent...i finally lost him. after crossing the river.

we stopped at the rest stop just before the turn to moab to water up and pee and contemplate the prospects. the road to moab, 191, is one of the most beautiful on earth. completely coyote's domain. i could see him dancing, a giant in the sky over the plateaus. i was listening to 'hound dog', both versions. big mama's is way better than elvis; and i yield to no person in being an appreciator, a fan, of elvis presley. his sanctification is entirely deserved. anyway, big mama's is down deep sexual, and the howling is definitely coyotes.

moab is a very cozy town in a magnificent setting. arches . the river. the buttes. we found the production office easily. amy was in the first room we walked into, getting made-up for some tests. she didn't recognize me. i had on eddie bunker's EAST LOST ANGELES hat, which he had bequeathed to me, and sunglasses, looking kinda like a hit-man truck driver. when i spoke she figured it out and jumped up, but she was also clearly, busy busy busy. so i went upstairs on a search for ed and then clambered back down the stairs, and up the hall he came looking like he walked right off the range, long hair weaves, which looked cool, especially coming out from under a big white cowboy hat, like william s. hart's. we all went out on the wide porch and here comes a cowboy, younger, with a short red goatee. damned if it isn't jesse shepard, who is wrangling on the movie. (jesse played the young coyote, the first time we did 7, so did tavish, when we did the all-nighters in LA. and then lilah did it on the vineyard in 2000, that fateful summer.) jesse says, "we were just talking about you this morning." and i tell him about morgan and lola (they moved in together the day we left LA.) and we all smiled and nodded at the memory of the padua kids, and the strange realm they grew up in.

mark, tavish and ed and i go across the street to see brenda and lily, who are having a snack in the shade of a pine tree, on the grass. we talk comfortably and soon ed and lily are making a pinecone mountain. lily is turning that two years old corner and becoming herself. she is playful and very sensitive—especially if she feels crowded. she has a small critical mass. but she is very joyful, we all joined in collecting pinecones and letting her find them. her delight was infectious.

eventually we said goodbye and went to lunch at the jailhouse cafe. excellent hippy food. with an excellent hippy waitress, who it turned out was an actress from new york city. we went back to the cars, behind the production office, and ran into ed and amy and brenda and lily, waved gleefully, said goodbye one more time and drove off honking like migrating geese.

191 just keeps getting better and better as you go north, climbing climbing through amazing vistas. at the summit just before FLAMING GORGE there are ancient groves of aspen and birch trees thirty feet high, with trunks two or three feet thick. i mention that all the aspen trees are actually one tree, they are all shoots from a mother tree, all sharing the same roots, like mushrooms. we see the sunset at the top of the world. tundra at the highest escarpment. deer and antelope.

It's a long drive and we pig out at the golden corral in rock springs while i'm paying the check a heavyset guy with wispy hair asks me if i'm a *"movie star."* I am nonplussed. and then we take a chance on the friendship inn.

SOME SOURCES

alfred lunt, together with his wife and lifelong collaborator, **lynne fontanne**, brought a new kind of naturalism, influenced by the emergence of chekhov and freud at about the same time as the advent of film. the result was a focus on the inner life of a character, which in the nineteen-twenties had a great effect on the american theater. such actresses as helen hayes and katherine cornell, with perhaps the most highly respected being the legendary **laurette taylor**, joined the lunts, in transforming american acting. although all of these popular and successful actors were offered multiple opportunities to make films, by and large they declined. alfred lunt made only four films in a career spanning fifty years as an international star, and three of them were with his wife. his first film, the silent *sally of the sawdust,* was directed by one of the founding father's of film, d.w.griffith and co-starred w.c.fields, a veteran of vaudeville, a top-of-the-bill juggler and comic. so here we see the confluence of this less declamatory style of acting balanced, like a seesaw, or mirror (as in greek tragedies and satyr plays), by the vaudeville style of popular entertainment.

probably the most successful purveyor of this populist style, playwright/performer/songwriter/producer/director, **george m. cohan,** brought a lighter touch of wit and sophistication to what had been a pretty frenzied display. **spencer tracy**, who from the beginning of his career was lauded for the startling naturalism of his performances, was, surprisingly enough, george m. cohan's favorite actor. the famous impresario was instrumental in tracy's launch to stardom, giving him his first featured role on broadway in a melodrama called *yellow.* tracy had performed six cohan plays in stock—and had actually played cohan's parts in two of them. but feeling stuck on the lower rung of the business, spencer had contemplated getting into some "*regular*" trade, according to his wife, louise. but the call came through to audition for cohan. "*the very thought of shaking hands with the greatest living figure in american theater had him terrified....then, said tracy, came the 'terrible moments when they rehearsed for george m. 'i was scared to death. christ, i thought i was going to get canned any minute',* spencer was rehearsing a scene when suddenly george m.,..out of the side of his mouth..barked, "*tracy, you're the best goddamned actor i've ever seen! go ahead!'* ...early in his career cohan had admired **nat goodwin,** whose expressive face and dry manner of delivery had taken him from vaudeville to light comedy and eventually to shakespeare. cohan reported in his memoirs: "*i couldn't imagine any actor better than goodwin, but here he was. the same ease and command of presence that nat had, but something else. a deep reserve.* according to tracy: "'cohan *taught me to keep my hands out of my pockets. oh, yes. don't be a lazy actor. don't start hiding your hands,..(or) you'll never know what to do with them."* of course, **james cagney** played cohan to perfection on screen in *yankee doodle dandy.* tracy couldn't dance like cagney (only cagney could dance like cagney, who's first professional gig was as a chorus "girl" in a very popular drag show called *every sailor,* at b.f.keith's on 86th street.)

cagney and tracy managed to bring a more natural approach to stage acting, exemplified by alfred lunt, in the display of behavior, driven by internal impulse, into movies, as well as a true american panache, derived from cohan and vaudeville. in addition, cagney brought his laser-like attention, with a refusal of all frills. even when dancing, his every move expresses a need from his body and his soul (see *public enemy*, and his little dance of triumph and expectation after picking up jean harlow). and tracy simply could not lie (like gene hackman, who's son I played in *twice in a lifetime*). he carries a truth whenever he is in front of the camera. but he does not strive to *show* it, or really *do* anything at all. he simply *has.* alfred lunt hated filming, refusing to repeat gestures or even bodily positions necessary to match with other takes that were to be intercut. he found the whole process excruciatingly boring and fragmented, and antithetical to his aesthetic, which was to be purely in and of the moment. laurette taylor was filmed only once—for a screen test. she did not get the part. the studio was dismayed to find that this revered actress didn't seem to be acting at all. still, lunt's influence lived on, passing on directly to montgomery clift, who toured as a teenager with lunt and fontanne, in a play called *there shall be no night,* and thereby onto marlon brando, who saw both lunt and clift as heroes and artists to emulate. and then, of course, the baton passed to james dean.

COMPARING BOOMTOWN AND LIBELED LADY,
both were directed by jack conway, and both featured a quartet of leading characters. In both we find spencer tracy providing the bedrock. the others are present as ARTIFICE. (in *boomtown*: tracy, clark gable, claudette colbert and hedy lamarr. in *libeled lady*: tracy, william powell, myrna loy, jean harlow). in both, tracy is almost obsessively focussed on competition with the other male. gable is an amoral oilman and womanizer; powell a rogue reporter and ladies man. both of these male co-stars are versions of the fairbanks persona, powell taking the effete and stylish aspects (adopted later by cary grant); gable the manliness and vigor (adopted by errol flynn and burt lancaster.) tracy is not even in the game with the women. he barely notices the luscious harlow. and although offscreen he admired hedy lamarr and befriended her, onscreen there is less than no spark. his devotion in both films is to his job—and his continued success. nevertheless, tracy has a sense of genuineness—which is his STYLE, as well as his point of view on REALITY, i.e. a PHILOSOPHY, an active, searching intelligence. throughout his career it is this that makes the most improbable hokum—and truly bizarre moral stances—seem evidence of his integrity and the correct position to take, for a thinking person. he is able to be hot while projecting almost no sexual urge. several times he played a very believable priest, first with gable as his best friend, and nearly criminal scamp, in SAN FRANCISCO. but it troubled him to wear the collar. he felt unworthy. in his early years in hollywood (and even before that, when he was working exclusively in theater,) he had many affairs, including with loretta young, (who bore gable's

62

child a few years later,[and in secret]), but once he worked with katherine hepburn, in *woman of the year*, he never strayed again, although they never lived in the same house. (he lived in a cottage in a remote corner of george cukor's beverly hills estate. kate lived around the corner, with her companion-secretary, phyllis wilbourn.) with hepburn he seemed vulnerable in a very masculine way, and sexy. (of course, he was married, through it all, to his loyal wife, louise). fay wray, whom he worked with right after her breakout performance in *king kong*, in a forgettable film called *shanghai madness*, seemed to bring out the carnal in him, with her frank sexuality, but only onscreen. she said of him, "*no nonsense, no pretension, i wanted so to complement his realities that i wore no makeup.*" characteristically, tracy's affair with loretta young was quite public, especially within the business it was well-known. he made no apologies and made no effort to hide his devotion to her. completely up front, just as he was with his commitment to hepburn. for some reason, perhaps the sense of his, and her innate decency, the public never condemned this ongoing, flagrantly 'immoral', adulterous relationship. in fact it was celebrated again and again in very successful films, as a model of a great partnership, mates for life.

ACTING LIKE DOING
JUST **DO** WHO YOU ARE

"*in three words,* just do it. *don't* think *of doing it, or worry about doing it, or hold postmortems on doing it, or stand in front of a mirror, or get out a slide rule to do it. just for christ's sake,* do it. *there. that's my two word theory.*"—james cagney

"*SAY WHAT YOU MEAN, MEAN WHAT YOU SAY*"—james cagney

"…..myself *it speaks and spells,*
crying *what i **do** is me: for that i came.*"
—gerard manley hopkins, '*number 57*'

CLUTCHES AND PURSES.
all of these intricate tremors
queries made with twitches,

screeches and glances
carefully posed
& sighing
sighing
sighing
the stall
and the stare…

i'm heading back.
the lessons in not running
deliver the day.

they strangled satan
and brought me all the way home
just in time to be assassinated.

ALL WE WANTED WAS TO BE TOGETHER
what you needed beyond me
even me i tried
to be beyond me
i tried
we all were
beyond the time to carry
to walk
to say
to do

all i wanted was the truth
or at the very least a shot
at a faint authenticity
but now i just don't want.
i accept.
you must
tell them
nothing
they don't already know

8 DAYS IN RUSSIA, Kaliningrad Hotel, Monday-(2007)
as near as i can figure it, it's about 1 A.M., and **i am** in a hotel room in kaliningrad, in russia, though not connected, by land, to most of russia, the baltic states intervening, and having once been part of poland, occupied by the germans. all these influences to be seen on the streets and byways, ports and parks of this oddball region of the globe), having slept since around 5:00 in the afternoon. i had planned to go to dinner with masha and art, who picked me up at the small, still in construction, (most likely would be for some time) airport, and are the dreamers, planners and tall, attractive, slightly scruffy hipsters behind this whole thing, this vaunted *classic american film festival*, hosted by yours truly, flown in for the occasion from new york city, and the graduate film program of columbia university, actor/director/blahblah, on the state department's dime! (go figger.) both of them are tall and willowy. masha is giggly and enthused, with long dark hair and white pointy boots, (audrey hepburn by modigliani). art is serious, almost handsome and very very knowledgeable, especially for someone who really had to dig for his material. he has a complete collection of buster keaton films, for example. he programs the eclectic art cinema, drawing from filmmakers from all around the world, in the center of town, he is clearly a visionary and somewhat obsessed. he drives a black mini, forcefully. kaliningrad itself is a melange of very old farm houses, just huts really, with steeply pitched roofs, the occasional ruined fort and many senseless soviet buildings (not quite architecture, but imposing)—many with whimsical paint jobs. there's a building in the middle of town—referred to by the locals as 'the monster'—at least twenty stories high, with elaborate antennae and dishes and such on the top, built deep in the soviet time, before gorbachev, the hulking thing is now—and ALWAYS HAS BEEN—entirely empty! they've recently, mercifully, covered its original depressing grey with a hopelessly cheerful sky blue. but no one uses the behemoth for anything, and never have.

the hotel is right across the rotary from the monster and is modern and charmless. in fact, most of the people in 'service roles', such as ticket agents, hotel clerks, etc., are deliberately charmless and truculent. they seem to love saying *'nyet. non. no.'* it may have something to do with me being so blatantly american, but i think its more about a pervasive depression and low-burning rage—these people know they are getting the shit end of the worldwide stick. the room itself is perfectly fine, oddly shaped and shabby, smelling of stale tobacco, and the bottom sheet does not actually cover the mattress, like being short sheeted at summer camp. none of the bedding quite fits, although the pillows are large and adequately soft. susanna would hate this room and this bed.

[for some reason, as i type this seven years later, i am reminded of tavish and i, on our trip through the canyon lands, when he was 11. we left the cabin we took for the night at the grand canyon, and we forgot his pillow the one his mom had given him and which he required for proper sleep, really the most essential part of his kit. it was gone when we circled back, he mourned its loss, and I carryied the responsibility, for his disappointment, with the dangers of depending on me becoming clear. or the beaded coin purse lilah, around the same age, left on a counter, with every dollar and cent she had saved for months, I felt the loss, as again due somehow to my failed diligence. even though i wasn't even there when lilah mislaid her savings, i feel the tug, somewhere inside. that hook in my heart, as denis would say. i felt that I had somehow let them down.]

    anyway, after a lively chat about movies and plans for the week, a brief hello to mary ellen countryman, from the consulate. i slip art copies of *force of evil* and *the misfits,* neither of which he had seen. i think he was pleased, although he maintains a cool, unsurprised, unimpressed mien. i find myself really not wanting to let these people down, to fulfill their expectations, whatever they may be. this is obviously really important to them—they've gotten funding, united states state department, and whatever hundreds of bureaus and committees in their own benighted labyrinthine ultrabeauracratic country, approvals from all those nice folks. and they did all that, and now they've scored, so to speak, this American Film Expert, from a well-known university in nyc—and it's, uh, me—the man behind the curtain, who is a little sick and a lot tired.

    so i retire to my room for a nap—and they are drilling and banging in the room two doors away! a replay of the turks & caicos exactly a week ago, with the hammers and chisels in the room next door. of course the staff in the caribbean resort were entirely solicitous and reassuring and i could stroll down to the beach for a soothing nap. here they are utterly unsympathetic. *"we have no other kind of room." " the kind of room is not the problem—its the location, relative to.."* "we are doing repairs." *"can you put me somewhere a little further from the banging and drilling?"* "we are doing repairs on the

66

sixth floor…and on the second floor…(naturally i am on the fourth floor, getting it from both sides) *come back after twelve tomorrow…we see what we can do."*
i try various methods to muffle the whining sound, with its guttural echoes, and eventually just pass out. at 6:30 masha calls, as arranged, and i say i am just going to crash and i'll see her for breakfast. i'm still feeling sick and stuffy—and when i think about where i am—on the planet—it all seems a little eerie—my identity is elusive to me. they've printed this beautiful catalog for the festival, with a big picture of me along with posters for *gilda* and *rebel without a cause.* it's all in russian, of course, even the quotes from me. so i don't know what i am actually saying, between the quotation marks. could be any damn thing. am i up to this?

ALOHA SUITE/ COYOTE GOES TO KAUAI, Part 2
searching for further verandas
lanais
screened-in porches.
i settle into
slings and arrows and
sentinel frogs in the midnight grass.
one trickster jumps me,
brushing my wounded shin,
without identifying himself.
i smash into the invisible waterlilies.
now i belong here,
in the dripping dark.
tomorrow will be another tomorrow
already imagined and forgotten,
and in between?
each breath
and tumbling clouds
coming to earth as blessed sisters
strumming a thousand ukuleles,
turning lead into gold.

"…for the truth, even if it is inevitable, is not always conceivable as a whole. people who learn some accurate detail of another person's life at once

*deduce consequences which are not accurate and see in the newly
discovered fact an explanation of things that have no connexion with it
whatsoever."—marcel proust, 'remembrance of things past: the captive'
"life is contradiction. contradiction is the appearance of life, is all life. life is
the result of the struggle of forces that oppose…the whole problem is how to
feel more contradictions. there are buffers between contradictions. we say
one thing now, next time another, and we don't see. we read and hear, but
next week we hear the opposite…***what could join the contradictions? only
my ability to be there between them.***"—lord john pentland, 'exchanges
within'*

*"my father laughed and was charming in that scary way he has of laughing
and being charming, as if the truth were not what it is, as if he were perfect
and beautiful in all ways, and in all ways a man full only of love."—emma
larson, 'in the cornucopia of your ear'*

THE LIGHT NEVER DIED
once the dishes were licked clean
and the tapestries beaten from the balconies
the band began
wild people danced on the colonnades
minotaurs pranced
the carpets fit precisely
something of a miracle if you think about it
could it have been that long ago?
was there rain in the streets
peasant fabric
or just a gentle sweeping sound?
the light never died
and the parks continue to thrum.
i'd rather tour than race
a quiet ramble through green neighborhoods
with the cougars
and the quail
a bubble held between the teeth of a dragon.
we ate beneath the pines

68

o our luck!
and the way he runs
bobbing on gravity
like a
small
sturdy
blonde
cloud
—for tavish, and for august

"I am afraid to own a Body--/
i am afraid to own a Soul--/
Profound--precarious Property--/
Possession, not optional--///
Double Estate--entailed at pleasure/
Upon an unsuspecting Heir--/
Duke in a moment of Deathlessness/
and God, for a Frontier."
—Emily Dickinson

3. PERFORMER: EVERYTHING WORKS AND GETS DONE
NATURALLY ACCORDING TO MUTUAL LAWS.
    or what gets done is dependent on each person's mutual effort. people
are rewarded for what they do, not for being who they are.

*"**coyote:** oh, i'm lost and sad! ahhhh! i'm tired of being sad! i'm tired of being
lonely! i can't see! and everything is electrified in this place!"*
—murray mednick, 'the coyote cycle'

"*a **meter**, a **season**, a **priest:** the fire touches them and everything starts to
exist*"—roberto calasso, 'ka'

ALOHA SUITE/ COYOTE GOES TO KAUAI, Part 3:
what fresh paradise is this?

she forgets to say what she has already said.
i look forward to speaking to her
each day.
having been suitably baptized in the sacred spring,
i trudge uphill
to one of her houses
for a shot of fresh mystery juice.
we engage in big talk about small things
with giggles and quiet and a questioning, mirthful, gaze.

her senses are acute.
she can hear the ants getting interested,
she can see double rainbows before they appear,
and place
      each pebble
           perfectly.

we discuss her basket of antique fabrics,
flowered prussian blue, jade green, mellow yellow.
we check out her lucid sewing machine
make her old tools work anew.
premonition or delusion,
it hardly matters.
all is energy
incontrovertible
into the infinite.

*"he [the actor] sees the body as an instrument and temple, a physical and mystic essence, divided and subdivided into various **trinities**."—jean-louis barrault*

SO MANY TRIADS, TRINITIES, TRIANGLES:
time/change/energy (chinese)
mother, father, child
father, son, holy ghost: the three-in-one, the trinity
buddha, jesus, mohammed: founders of the three major religions
minos, aeacus and **rhadamanthus:** sons of zeus who became the three judges of the shades in hades.
cerberus: three-headed guard dog of the underworld
lion (pride**), leopard** (fraudulence) **, she-wolf** (avarice): three beasts prowling through dante's hell.
acheron, styx, phlegethon: three river's leading to hell.
suicide, sodomy, usury: three sins of violence
inferno, purgatorio, paradiso: dante's three afterworlds
terrestrial, telestrial, celestial: three levels of heaven in mormon theology. only those who have achieved the top two tiers become gods of their own worlds. only the highest level permits a man to populate that world with his

own race of worshippers, and then only if he has been married, to a woman, for "*time and all eternity*", in a properly consecrated temple on earth.
agaia (charm), **euphrosyne** (creativity), **thalia** (beauty): the three graces
aello (storm winds), **celeano** (the dark), **ocypete** (the swift wing): three harpies—women with claws and wings, who live in the suicide-trees in the third section of the seventh ring in hell, according to dante's *inferno*
melete (practice), **mneme** (memory), **aoide** (song): three muses, (some say there are nine, but that's for later…)
curly, shemp (or **joe), moe:** three stooges, gods of hilarity and slapstick
…and those damnable **monkeys**, seeing nothing, hearing nothing, saying nothing at all…..

READY/WILLING/ABLE
ARGUMENT/SEDUCTION/NEGOTIATION

PERSON/PLACE/THING: WAY/SHAPE/FORM
        (every dramatic scene is one or another of these…)
and of course: positive/negative/neutral; mind/body/soul; before/during/after; precept/percept/concept; till/sow/reap

i fell for you **hook, line** and **sinker…**

NOTES FROM A WORKSHOP: ROBERT BLY, 1982
THE CASTLE and THE FOREST
(HERA>HEPHAISTOS…technology as a result of women's rage)
STEALING (and keeping) THE KEY
THE FOUR SEASONS OF MALE DEVELOPMENT:
1. BONDING and BREAKING: with mother—1st estate;
2. with father—2nd estate
3. APPEARANCE of/ and LIVING with a MALE MOTHER (Arthur/Merlin)
(Darrell/Harold)
4. MARRIAGE to/ and LIVING with the UNKNOWN BRIDE (the woman with GOLDEN HAIR)(she must be WON)("TRACE of the MOON on the WATER")
Golden Ball (we need an aim…but achieving it is not the point.)
THE GRANDFATHER BEAT.

FEELINGS ARE [BETWEEN] US.

72

INSTITUTIONS are FEMALE

CIRCE (BEATRICE in DANTE) sends ODYSSEUS down to HADES
purpose of GREAT ART (most ceremonies) is to bring you down into HADES
(nourishing, refreshing) (DEATH), a COOL RIVER,
FOREST (**labyrinth**): FEMALE
PLAIN, cleared area: MALE
NATURE doesn't NEED SPRITUAL growth.
SKY GODS disappear. (males leaving the home during the Industrial
Revolution)
WHAT MALE FORCES HELP YOU? (Faithful Henri)

 the CELTIC QUEST:
1. Dream of a UNION with a PURE WOMAN ("where neither death nor
change comes near us.")
2. (a BATTLE) RESCUE the MOTHER from IMPRISONING FORCES
(ANIMUS-DEMON "my angry KING-remembering soul.") SAVIOR<>
MARTYR, DETECTIVE STORIES. INTELLECT. FEAR of the VAGINA.
3. A HUNDRED YEARS SLEEP, inertia and sluggishness after the failure to
save your mother. BEWITCHMENT (6 SWANS). RIGHT-WING
NOSTALGIA. anger against the ORDINARY WORLD. FEAR OF BEING
KILLED BY YOUR FATHER [*my recurring dream: dad sneaking up behind
me, sticking a long thin needle into my ear.*] (reluctance to enter the MALE
WORLD.)
4. SEARCHING for a WOMAN who will REJECT your BODY. self-
CASTRATION. (an angry woman [connected to her FATHER]) "weary-
heartedness". image of the MOTHER is still in the HEART.
the DIVISION of SPIRITUALITY and SEXUALITY. —> the INTERIOR
WOMAN sometimes APPEARS.
5. MAKING A SECRET ALLIANCE with DEATH. "the GREEN HELMET"
anger: want the woman to die, or disappear
6. Sinking into the GREAT MOTHER. **spiral** that goes down. living in an
INVERTED WAY. ALCOHOLISM and ADDICTION. "If the EGO refuses to
accept responsibility for the SOUL LIFE within…that life becomes
MALIGNANT."

The PERSONALITY undermines itself by neglecting to attend to the SOUL's urgent need for TRANSFORMATION.
triangle of EGO (interior organization of the **PSYCHE** (the GATEKEEPER), **SOUL** (longs to grow), Great **MOTHER (Terrible): DEVOURING; (Abundant)**: Life-giving; Transforming (Sophia. MOON),
 HERAKLES—mama's-boy SAVIOUR.

INTERIOR FEMALE BEINGS: shallow interior woman—flatters you.
                                 nourishing woman—you become nurturing. aware of pain in others.
                                 ancient woman (pagan woman)—includes the WITCH. (a gypsy woman)
                                 OLWEN (ELENA) the golden-haired woman, SOFIA, wisdom about the living soul
STEPS IN DEEPENING MALE MODES OF FEELING.
1. superior, tightlipped, controlling and mechanical FALSE PERSONALITY, MILITARY. HERCULEAN. Heart attack is rebellion against this being.
MARINES an EXTENSION of HOSTILITY OF MOTHER.
2. one who clings to a woman. new age male. flying boys. (**puer aeternus**)
3. (manhood begins) the man who can grieve—who can descend. MASCULINE COURAGE.
4. the PIRATE: the one who steals the key. knows what he wants. (LORCA)
5. the man who longs for OLWEN (ELENA) the grail. (HELEN)
6. the man who can do the tasks. the one who can kill the HAG.
7. can join opposites and dissolve opposites.

women put their HERCULES on the men <—> men put their WITCH on women

WILD MAN: is nature. energy that is conscious of the wound. positive sexual energy. guards the spring in the middle of the forest in our psyche.

MALE MODES OF FEELING:
hunter brain—(left brain) mood (feeling in the soul—in the body as mood), language, social norms, FEAR may be a physiological phenomenon
    (right brain) SPACE, geometry, SEARCHING FOR THE OBJECT and SEXUAL SATISFACTION

corpus callosum: **(a broad band of nerve fibers joining the two hemispheres of the brain) is thicker in women. EVOLUTION ([gave us]** (via language) **time to thicken the corpus callosum)**
ANGER must be dealt with. Blocks the grief. SORROW. Depression is involuntary.
THE SECOND PART OF OUR LIFE IS CALLED GATHERING.
the REAL FEELING IN A (HU)MAN IS PAGAN.

WHAT IS THE OTHER WORLD? (not localized in TIME (or the BODY), SEPARATION. the BOY/GIRL, in a slightly different **way, shape** *or* **form)** becomes SACRED. by DYING in this WORLD.
1. the MOUTH of the MONSTER (the WOMB, the HUT)
2. DYING, and the EXPERIENCE of DEATH (how do PEOPLE see you DEAD.)
3. BECOMING a WARRIOR. (how to become a container)
4. the GOLDEN-HAIRED WOMAN (the STONE BRIDE, the ANIMA)
5. SEPARATION from the MOTHER (*i did that at 4*)
6. HIDING and GOING BACK into MYTHICAL TIME.
7. (LEAVING) MOVEMENT from the (PHYSICAL) LITTLE FATHER (JEHOVAH) to the BIG FATHER (the SKY.)
8. CANNIBAL MAN. (socializing the WILD energy—ANGER and RAGE. (*twins who are not twins*)

GIANT: archaic parts of the personality not civilized. Failed evolution. RAGE. undifferentiation. Large and stupid. battle between the CLOWN and the GIANT. gets things done. we give our GIANTS to our parents: must get him back. RECLAIM. what you don't bring in consciously will invade you. (gospel of St. Thomas). BY THE CONFRONTATION WITH THE GIANT YOU RECEIVE TREASURE.

WITCH: cold witch and hot witch (making distinctions). THE SOURCE OF INFORMATION. lives edges of cities, center of deserts. Remote. perverted sexual energy. witches EAT: women FEED. DOES NOT WANT CLOSENESS. (after a distance: THE WITCH IS THERE.) witches hate all intimacy. being close is taunting the witch. KALI—cutting. inside men and women. when you give it to the mother you are a nice boy—she is more witchy. MUST GET IT BACK FROM THE MOTHER. wild man—male form of the hot witch.

wolf—hot witch

"did you come here of your own free will or did someone send you?"

"what is your aim?"

DWARF: from the interface between yourself and objects. KNOWS THE NAMES. very positive (Snow White protected by 7 dwarves). THE OTHER SIDE OF OBJECTS. Underground. (related to PLUTO and wealth.) HEALTH that is inside MATTER. (our culture is anti-dwarf.) GREMLIN (flying boy DWARF). MATERIALISM and CAPITALISM is anti-DWARF.

(Buddhism): 'the temple bell stops, but the sound keeps coming out of the flower."—bash-o

outdoors (in the kitchen) RAISING THE TUNE.

"..you may certainly use the 'teeth mother naked at last 'poem as a one-man show. i think it's intended for some public declamation…and maybe you and i can add a couple of lines that will bring it up to date somewhere in the middle…..it's possible that certain sections of 'the teeth mother 'could be slowed down a lot if one used masks—for example, masks of Kali, perhaps alternating with balinese mask of the ecstatic feminine, and those in turn balanced by a mask of the Negative King, Herod, or the Capitalist Demonic Old Man. you see what i'm thinking….these characters wearing the masks would do short dances or make sounds meant to hit the audience in their stomach place."—robert bly, in a letter, 1990

"…i have been circling for a thousand years,
*and i still don't know if i am a **falcon**, or a **storm**,*
*or a great **song**."—rainer maria rilke, translated by robert bly*

paul auster calls his wife's migraines *"a third shadow walking with us down the street.*

WE THREE
my echo
licked and sucked and gently

chewed on
just like sustenance
sun on the stallion, mare and colt
waiting in the checkered meadow

my shadow
just like all the rest
runs on
senseless through the oscillations
we recall the real lamp habit
a secondhand kiss
& me

threeways sounds soulless and competitive, **threesomes** congenial and
convivial, but **menage a` trois** is simply splendid, a whirlwind, ascending
spiral of constantly regenerating energy.
[deeply struck as we all were by *jules and jim*, 'with the fascinating, slowburn,
sphinxlike sexuality of jeanne moreau as catherine, and her incredibly
fortunate mates, running toward us on that bridge, free as three can be..]

IN THE PARK AT VERSAILLES
wrought-iron gate ajar,
hidden grounds, sunny meadow, shielded by trees,
we spy an imposing group of statues.
larger than life,
poseidon with trident, surrounded by naiads and mermen,
horses with fishtails.
other wonders
positioned within a natural outcropping,
grey rocks with dark caves framing the sculptures
as we approach we see
in the gloom behind the massive figures
flat places shaped smooth
in the polished stone.
what once were scooped pools holding warm water
are now dry
but still inviting, somehow flowing, cool, almost damp...

so we strip down
and set out.
he spreads his navy blue pea coat, she her large french silk scarf, me my
poncho from the andes,
and we emulate those lusty kings and queens
of long ago,
ladies no longer waiting,
rampant noblemen,
bequiling handmaidens and lucky footmen,
kitchen wenches and stableboys,
they'd all fucked merrily
in this secret grotto
now we make love in the present tense

although he snaps pictures of the three of us
in the throes
clicking away at our entwined bodies on the pale marble
our flash
our fervor
does not register
…only that first shot from a distance survives, across the gently rising lawn…,
and the charging steeds and gods beckoning us to the frolic…
framed by the imposing tumble of rocks and the deep caves behind

after the endless moment has past
we return in a slow stroll
back to the walking tour we'd abandoned,
rejoining our ragtag comrades,
all of us in awe
of the hall of mirrors
with infinite reflections of ourselves,
the grandly sculptured gardens,
the immense topiary
the expanse of terrible wealth,

i pause at the reflecting pool to dip her scarf into the cool, greenish, scarcely
rippling water

and douse my head, drenched as it is with her effulgence
all over my face.
she snatches the dripping fabric,
some mysterious turquoise blue,
from my hands,
he chuckles
as she chides me
for lacking the courage to carry her scent
all the way into the crowd.
—*for el and fnw, 1975*

HADES 'LAMENT
i dreamt i saw myself last night
　　　　　lying underground
i dreamt joe hill and saint augustine
　　　　　were nowhere to be found
i dreamt i was in paradise
　　　　　an angel stained by lust
i dreamt i was hades plunging deep
　　　　　into persephone's pomegranacunt

[in 2017, i played hades, god of the underworld, in a mad retelling of the persephone myth, called *ben and liana,* specifically referring to the poor hapless god as a rapist. shit, he asked permission from zeus, persephone's father, and his own brother, to take the nubile young girl as his wife. how is that rape? besides she ate six pomegranate seeds, that was the deal! If she ate something she had to stay in the land of the dead! i played him with an absurdly huge erection, covered by a leopard-skin spandex codpiece, with matching smoking jacket. my reasoning for the outfit was that the poor sap had to wait six months to get laid, every year, for eternity. and even then, when she shows up, she spurns him. she hates hades, the man and the place, because she has been forced to return, over and over. my frustration and rage at being completely misunderstood were quite entertaining, apparently. and my sense of isolation and grief, needless to say, were completely real. in fact, in role after role for a good two years, nonstop, going from play to play, rehearsing one while performing in the other, i just kept poking and jabbing at my wounds. the whole period, which was in a real sense a renaissance for me, at least as an actor, culminated in strindberg's *dance of death,* playing the anguished 'captain'. a play featuring another threesome. a role i specifically chose for myself. not even realizing that the play took place in the twenty-fourth year of the doomed and damaged marriage. yeah, i left susanna in our 24th year. and the dying captain is heartbroken that his beloved daughter won't speak to him. playing the role felt like the culmination of…something. my whole life as an actor? for me it was the ultimate expression of my skills and 'talent', such as they are. along with **coyote** and **pete** (in *mike's murder),* the **captain** was a role i was born to play. for one thing, all three of those characters mistreat women, blindly, unintentionally, and out of desperate love. when i told susanna i was playing hades, she said, without missing a beat, *"who else would they get?"* god, i love her.]

"the broken pomegranate is full of stars"—seferis

'.....without the mirror image, twins whose seams tongue
the ridge of cloud   they are
not angels because angels don't wear out
their high-heeled red, pomegranate's thin skin sex.'
—elena karina byrne, excerpt from 'narcissism: rorschach mask

*"our minds are cunning, compound mechanisms; and one **spring**, or **wheel**, or **axle** wanting, the movement lags, or halts. cerebrum must not overbalance cerebrum; our brains should be round as globes…"—herman melville, 'mardi'* [my favorite book, by the way.]

THE BRAIN IS A PATTERN-MAKING MACHINE
rising up from the belly
tearing the country's heart out,
and
and
somehow i'm assigned
the trick of returning
the palpitating pace
of the rushing blood,

a refreshed and richer organ,
back to its slick place.
the task stays precarious
way beyond my full attention
i couldn't catch a cuttlefish
with a pixie net

THREE TYPES of HINDU POETRY
1. longing for or **separation** from god.
2. **union** with god
3. **falling** away again

THE HITCH
i can't stop staring
while the portly wag
slaughters the blondes
winsome murderous swimmers
arrayed in well-stuffed speedos
permanently forbidden
smicker-smicket
showing their swells
hidden aces
reckless scents
boyishly suggestive
of a quick peak peeking
into the tub of terror.
mostly decent girls
mostly secret caresses to come
killing flies while eagles dare
blizzards in rear projection
those snowy locations
in the semi-serious moonlight

ALL THE DOOMED BLONDES: Part Three
frances farmer must have been a total knockout at eighteen, in 1935, as she
crossed the quad at the university of washington, with her flowing blonde
hair, alabaster skin, a stride in her step which gave her an air of

independence and depth. she labored as an usherette, a waitress, a tutor and in a factory, to work her way through college. while there she became an instant sensation in the theatre department (playing the title role in *helen of troy* and yelena in *uncle vanya)*, but she was equally prominent in the journalism school, earning degrees in both disciplines. she wrote a winning essay for a subscription contest in a leftist magazine, *the voice of action.* first prize was a trip to the soviet union (against her mother's nearly frantic objections), where she visited the moscow art theatre, chekhov's home company. on her return to the states, in 1936, she made a stop in new york, hoping to begin a 'legit 'career. instead, she met a scout for paramount, oscar serlin, who offered her a seven-year contract after a *'stunning screen test, as if she had been in front of the camera all her life. effortlessly.'* she was twenty-two. she quickly made an impression in B-movies, met the handsome, but bland, rising star leif erickson, and married him, perhaps at the behest of the studio. the '*super-fathers*', to use nietzsche's phrase, did not appreciate her uncooperative manner and undisguised contempt for there shallowness and greed. she drove an old green roadster and was indifferent to the clothes she wore in public, refusing to be decked out in the raiment of starlets and rarely attended the glittering parties and premieres, even when provided with such an attractive consort as her new husband. while still in high school, frances had won another essay contest, this time for *scholastic magazine.* she received a $100 for an essay called '*god dies',* influenced by her reading of nietzsche. (in an early **barbra stanwyck** film, the very racy *baby face*, stanwyck's character is similarly emboldened by her exposure to nietzsche. she declares herself independent of men and their power over women. she vows to use them to get what she wants out of life, instead of the other way around. and she succeeds, financially and romantically, something that would become disallowed just a few years later, under the strictures imposed by the hays office. stanwyck, of course, was far from doomed. here's how richard dyer put it in his seminal study, *stars: "…we should not forget that what we are analyzing gains its force and intensity from the way it is experienced, and that ideology shapes the experiential and effective as much as the cognitive. when i see* **marilyn monroe** *i catch my breath; when i see* **montgomery clift** *i sigh over how beautiful he is; when i see* **barbara stanwyck,** *i know that women are strong.".*

frances, at least on the surface, was as strong as they come. she was born in 1913 in seattle, washington. her parents divorced when she was four, and she and her mother, lillian, briefly moved to los angeles. this set-up proved financially unsustainable and mother and daughter moved back to the northwest and back in with the estranged father, although the couple did not reconcile. must have been a cozy home to grow up in, huh? to say that lillian was strong-willed and vengeful is to put the matter very mildly, as we shall see. eventually the uneasy truce between husband and wife broke down and frances and her mother moved to a small-town on the fringe of seattle, when frances was sixteen, and already strikingly beautiful. and then…the essays, the trip to russia, the whirl of incipient hollywood stardom. in 1937, frances bolted back to new york, joined the group theatre, began a very public affair with clifford odets (while still married to erickson), and starred in the premier of *golden boy.* elia kazan was an actor in that production and had this to say about the golden girl: *"a special glow, a skin without flaw, lustrous eyes—a blonde you'd dream about. she also had a wry and, at times, rather disappointed manner, a twist of the mouth, which suited the part."* [stanwyck played the part in the film..]

before her flight from film work, however, frances did act in the only really good film she ever made, *come and get it,* directed by howard hawks and william wyler, two of the best directors in cinema history. hawks was fired from the project, (artistic differences with the studio heads…meaning, money) but he cast her and called her the best actress he ever worked with. she played a challenging dual role, as both mother and daughter, and brought it off with extraordinary wit and sexiness. especially as the saloon singer/mother she is a joy to behold. the veterans edward arnold and walter brennan are obviously in her thrall. as was bing crosby with whom she made a trifle called *rhythm on the range.* unfortunately that film had no script worthy of the chemistry between bing and frances. *"as the only cast member who wasn't called upon to be musical or funny, she brought depth to a shallow role. bing was enchanted by her glimmering frankness, after the wrap he gave her a diamond necklace she treasured all her life."—gary giddens, 'bing crosby: a pocketful of dreams'.*

on her forced return to studio hegemony things quickly unraveled for frances. her marriage was obviously strained, (although she and erickson remained married until 1942), she was labelled a leftist, disturbed, self-destructive, too intimidating to too many people. after her arrest for drunk driving, and the publication of photos taken at the police station as she is dragged in, disheveled, rage burning in her eyes, she was treated as if she was flat-out crazy. her mother took over and had her committed, mostly for the crime of not wanting to be a movie star. she was given shock treatments and eventually lobotomized. nevertheless, in the 1950s, she returned to acting, making several appearances on television, diminished, but unbowed. this whole sad saga, of course, is told very effectively in *frances*, a film starring jessica lange, with **kim stanley** playing the monstrous lillian. although a stunning blonde, with an atmosphere, a faint whiff, of *"victimization and lost greatness"*, [as david thomson puts it in his invaluable '*a biographical dictionary of film*'], jessica lange escaped doomed blonde status. perhaps partially by exorcising those tendencies with this magnificent and fierce performance. rarely have two women blended so effectively and terrifyingly. **kim stanley,** as we shall see, was not so fortunate.

(and i have my own part in this tragic tale. in the film of *frances*, i play a minion of the gossip columnist louella parsons, charged with going to new york, where frances is appearing in *golden boy,* to elicit some quote from the errant beauty expressing her disdain for hollywood. i wait for her outside the stage door, and i convince her that i am a sweet young man who wants to be an actor. but after a few remarks about odets and her husband, she realizes her mistake. in the span of one cutaway the budding artist turns into a snake, right before her eyes. one of my favorite roles, actually. that kind of transformation is firmly in my wheelhouse. once she's back on the west coast, frances is forced by her publicist to attend a party at which she encounters my slime-ball character once more. she nails me with the line, *"you seem to be an intelligent young man, can't you find a decent line of work."* prior to shooting the little scene i approached jessica lange and put out my hand to introduce myself. i knew she knew that i knew sam, and also that i was aware of their burgeoning affair, with the obvious parallels to the film. it was a delicate moment, which she handled by giving me a withering glance and turning away with another priceless line, *"i'm aware of that"*. i realized as she walked away that we had just had a bang-up rehearsal of the scene we were about to shoot. and i was *really* ready. my admiration for this exemplary, courageous actress was firmly established in that moment, and has only grown through the years. after the scene in the film, frances flees the party, quite inebriated, and understandably distressed. driving erratically,

she is pulled over by the cops, leading inexorably to her tabloid crucifixion
and her eventual downfall. and it was all my fault...*again..!*)

momentum error: making assumptions & elaborations which are reasonable
but do not match what is actually happening.

I THINK WE CAN DO BETTER
YOU THINK YOU KNOW WHAT'S BEST
YOU THINK YOU UNDERSTAND
AND I AM WRONG OR WORSE

lonely wreck of folly

WHAT THE RIVER KNOWS
now i know this story
i beg to differ
where there's this enormously pale guy wrapped in a cornflower-blue towel
lolling by the chateau marmont pool
      after days and nights and days and nights bingeing on speedballs
              with a girl named cathy
                    she was the same

cathy
(a witch?)
who sold the smack

that killed tim hardin.
pale as a bucket under a bridge

and now she ministers to jovial john belushi
giving him everything he doesn't need
and then some

lest we forget:

john winthrop never said
"the city on a hill"

at least not out loud. or in public. and those who said it because he said it
don't know what he meant by it because he never said it.

george washington never won a battle
   all his victories were retreats

vincent van gogh did not kill himself
  he was shot in the stomach by a local lout, a giggling galoot, who roamed
  the village costumed like a dime novel cowboy,
      without a thought in his head, loaded six shooter in his hand.

samuel beckett killed the semicolon;
      suspending the penguin parade.

amid exaltations of lies
screams of abnegation
here we find the secrets
    the river knows:
one can be seized on sunset,
tongue defamed
heart exploding
skirtless
shirtless
leaving all your brothers behind.
you can be cannibalized by hawks and crockery
fossil dung
or rogue algorithms
exhibiting your panorama
throughout the panting nation
unsure of your senses
led by blistering lightning
you can unscorch a scar
with expensive cucumber ice
tossed into the astonished cigar box
and put all of that forever
on display.

i pretend for you.
can i make you see you
through my reddened eyes,
after i smeared your lipstick
all over my chest,
stopped the music,
swallowed the phlegm puddled in my throat,
and fucked you good?

"at every single moment of one's life, one is what one is going to be, no less than what one has been. art is a symbol because man is a symbol."—oscar wilde, 'de profundis'

MARVELOUS HONORABLE PEOPLE:
Montreal. December 28, 2001
the room is quiet now while poor sick emma sleeps. we had been listening to music from the harlem renaissance, a boxed set given to her for christmas, i think by tavish and rebecca, following a theme. (i got tav a book by langston hughes called *black magic*, which chronicles black contributions to american culture. i found it at *trevanian bookshop* in nyack). she (emma) also got lots of billie and ella, and some juliette greco from polly, for the french connection. we're in montreal so emma can speak french but so far she's been too sick to go out. last night we ate at a restaurant/bar with a *tintin* theme, which delighted lilah and me. (lilah drew great versions of the *tintin* characters on the table paper, which i saved, despite her protests.) margi picked the restaurant and summoned her friends to welcome us on our first night in town. excellent food, charming people. afterwards emma dosed on dimetapp, but still slept fitfully. the hotel (*auberge du vieux port*) was built in the 1880's, and is beguiling, exposed brick, wooden beams, cozy, commodious. as usual, susanna has done her research well. i went out with lilah for about ten minutes to walk up and down the colonnade. otherwise i've been in the room reading. which is tres okay. i'm fighting the winter cold myself. the sky is a welcoming blue, but it is FRIGID outside.
       susanna and lilah have gone ice-skating in a nifty outdoor rink right across the boulevard. snow started to fall just as i returned from an espresso in a little cafe around the corner. i sat in a seat by the window reading *melville and repose*, and watching the black-lace clouds scud across the full bright

moon, against a dark-blue sky. extremely brisk walk thru the d'eauville district, up into chinatown as far as victoria square, when the arctic wind sent me back to the port. montreal is an absolutely magical city, enchanting buildings going back to the 1600s, mixed with dramatic modern reflections, like the condos across the harbor which resemble an enormous pile of packing crates—a natural extension, visually, of the surviving walls of the deauville chapel. emma is better, her fever has broken, but now her voice comes and goes. on the way back i stopped at a shop i noticed last night which touted *"moccasin indien"*. i found the winter boots i was visualizing, and as i was trying them on (one pair left in my size) the guy said, *'we're you in here yesterday?"*   (appending a total canuck *'eh?'*) *"no"* i said, *"just got to canada."* *"you look so familiar.."* *"do you watch TV?"* *"well, yeah…what would i have seen you in?…i knew it, i knew you were/"* *"maybe* 'law and order'?" I offered, we went through the whole wrist-slitting bit in the bathtub, which most people remember, for some reason, and that seems to satisfy him. the indian moccassins are perfect, i made a quick decision to buy them and wear them out of the store. *"have you been in something more recently?'* thinking there was less than no chance i said, *"well, they played a show on sunday…do you get a&e?"* at which point the guy snapped his fingers and pointed, *'you're the guy who didn't care about anything…the guy who walked in front of the truck! i told my brother about that show! that was deep!"* he was ebullient now, and completely sincere, going on about how most TV was *"absolute shit"*, etc. and how i seemed like a real guy, in real pain. i was very proud, duly credited susanna, for writing and directing so beautifully, and started picking through the coyote teeth they had in a bin by the register. his brother was also beaming and whispering to other customers, which embarrassed my guy. *"i told him not to do that,"* he said apologetically. i did my best to reassure him that his response meant a lot to me, we shook hands and exchanged names (georges), and i left with excellent new boots. he may have been the only guy in montreal who saw that particular episode of *100 centre st.* and he threw in a couple of coyote teeth *"with my compliments."*

HOMO HISTORIOS, man as actor

HUCKLEBERRY *from the 'dictionary of american slang': 'i'm a huckleberry over your persimmon'* the exact kind of man needed for a particular purpose.

sidekick. best man for the job. willing helper or assistant. back-up. old childhood friend.

[as in: val kilmer as doc holliday in *'tombstone'*, that gliding stroll from the deep shade of a tree, sounding lethal and tender: *'i'll be your huckleberry.'* around 2008, i did a one-person show, in los angeles and nyc, called *the confessions of doc holliday,* culled by me from *bucking the tiger,* a novel by bruce olds. in the piece, doc is writing a letter to his cousin, a nun, trying vainly to explain himself, as best he can—how a tubercular dentist from virginia, came to be an outlaw in the old west, a gambler and killer. at the end, doc dies mid-sentence, spewing blood all over the stage, still unable to make his case, or achieve any kind of real redemption. another in the cavalcade of doomed characters i took on through the years. the only run at it that was in any way adequate was in nyc at a space on 24th street called *the cell.* for a time I did a lot of interesting work there, including a series of 'lectures' on film history called *mythic gossip.]* I forced myself, and the director insisted that I try to reach my girls with the performance, making it a supplication, a plea for mercy and forgiveness, maybe even redemption. but they both the piece and the peace, remained out of my reach.]

WAVES OF MUTILATION
this settlement
this encrustation
this barricade
this concrete
this tar
this castle
this plunge
this sinister hearth
this setting sun
this six
six
six
these sunglasses say it all.

THE MAN MIDTOWN
charles mingus, in a buoyant mood, more than willing to be a spectacle, a one-man parade, is dressed in a black, flat-brimmed hat in the spanish

vaquero style, with dangling balls for fringe, and a heavy, swirling black cape. he's here to bestow a visit on paul desmond, to cheer him up. desmond, a charter member of the school of cool, brubeck's alto vox, respected on the charts and in the clubs, is dying of cancer, clinging to life in midtown, keeping his front door open. mingus looms in the doorway, light behind him, enormous, glamorous and sinister. desmond takes one look at him and says:

"to what do i owe the honor? have we arrived at the seventh seal?"

"awright, man, set up the chessboard," mingus enjoins.

"you saw that movie, too?"

"yeah, and that wild strawberries. *thought they were both pretty hip."*

" we in a dream sequence here?"

"directed by bergman's evil twin, irving bergman."

desmond chuckles, then coughs, then he can't stop hacking.

mingus leaps in:

"fuck this. where's the chessboard."

"i'm gonna beat you this time, if you don't cheat again."

"listen, little white boy, the day you beat me at chess there will be a brother in the white house. they'll rename that shit the black house."

"nigger heaven, huh?"

"okay, okay, that van vechten cat, yeah, used to hang with langston. i read that book. not bad...but watch yourself, you little cracker."

"i always do."

"yes, you do, i noticed that right away. unusual for an ofay."

"in what way, precisely?"

"in the way that white people don't have to pay attention. they are attended to. that's why they generally don't make good jazz musicians, whereas you, my brother, are a solid sender, which is precisely why i have delivered my splendid ass to this sad and dank domicile, in the center of the most magnificent ratfuck metropolis on this rollicking planet, in order to visit my FRIEND."

"wow. don't get sentimental on me now."

"who...."

"is dying."

"...needs cheering up, is the scuttlebutt."

desmond lights a cigarette. *"I'd rather play chess."*
"whatever keeps your heart beating, clyde."
"this from the midas of destruction. whatever he destroys turns to legend."
"now that is a good riff."
"you remember that lighting fixture you attacked."
"which one?"
"the sconce...the thing."
"at blue note?"
"yeah."
"vividly. ugly, talkback little pissant lamp."
"still broken all to hell, dangling wires and shit, but they put a little plaque up next to it, instead of repairing it. THIS FIXTURE BEATEN INTO SUBMISSION BY CHARLES MINGUS."
"when was the last time you got laid, you pathetic, hangdog, crippled-looking, brokedown, junky piece of shit?"
"hey man, I think I'm starting to feel much more upbeat, with all this wit floating around."
"yeah? bubbling up into it?"
"yeah, I feel another chuckle coming on."
"don't overexcite yourself, now. i can't stand that coughing shit. can't find the backbeat."
"duly noted. now what's this about hookers?"
"hookers?"
"chicks."
"what chicks?"
"hey man, you're the cat who brought it up. wantin 'to know when was the last time i got laid, wantin 'all the details. you're the one who knows all the chicks. you're the stud who fucked 267 broads in one weekend in acapoke-o Mexico. they lined up down the hall, right? as soon as word got out that the mighty mingus dingus was in deployment."
"where'd you hear all that shit?"
"from you, motherfucker. in your book! "
"first of all—it was a bungalow in cuernavaca."
"cuernalingus?"

"cuernavaginaca. The whole thing started with two impossibly foxy cleaning ladies, a mother and sister team, and they went and got the rest of their sisters, and they called their cousins and they cousins and they sexy mamas and you know i don't like to stop when I get started just can't stop but it shore wasn''t two hundred and sixty seven, that's ridiculous nobody could do for two hundred and sixty seven women in a row. that's plain excessive. it was two hundred and fifty."
"i'm disappointed to hear you say this."
"so when was the last time?"

long pause.

"charles, i don't even remember when the last time was."
"can you get it up?"
"how the fuck would I know?"
"well, I sure as hell don't know."
"i think her name was…nicole."
"a beauty. a real beauty."
"you know her?"
"naw. but i hear it in your voice, man."
"nicky."
"a real sweet piece."
"the very sweetest."

mingus whistles very softly and deliberately.

"so, my good man, you need anything? you got food?"
"i stopped eating weeks ago."
"booze?"
"two and a half bottles of jameson."
"sufficient unto the day. coffin nails?"
"three packs."
"solid. i'll be back, and we'll have that chess match."

*"it's a date. leave the door open on your way out. I don't want to gasp my last
and be rotting in here for days before anybody gets hip. it's just not
neighborly, stinking up the building like that. you never get rid of that smell."*
"yeah, folk often comment on how motherfuckin 'considerate you are."
"thanks for the cheer, charles."
"don't mention it." mingus goes out whistling. from the hall he shouts back:
"STAY ALIVE MOTHERFUCKER!"

desmond is left alone. he whistles weakly, ringing changes on the tune
mingus started, and then trailing off. in a hoarse whisper he speaks to the
empty room:
"hey, nicole. hey, nicky. i miss you, baby."

the lights dim.

COME HOME
bark for a carousel, birch white,
fragrantly floats on the murmuring river of tears
so many sorrows have fed
a human need to secrete
we are what we
are made for
and we follow us
down

i find shelter in a doorway out of the wind
torch a sigh and breathe out easy
this melody of solitudity so low
down
as though the moaning metropolis is throwing itself off two thousand bridges
leaping from crow's nests in truly hopeless wardrobe
to find a home in the lost green sea

i am bewildered by shoulders
sounding the chill winds
of shattered avenues

diamonds powdered in the grooves
hearing necromance in every pilgrim's song
color bleeds out of the tower's while glamour
rides the soul's refusal
and the body leans out *(grooving up slowly)* into solidity
for the beauty others see in us is the cruelest part of us
the torch that lights the nightspots
the smoky rooms the gleaming cabins
curtained by drifting neon clouds.

come into my coat together
press next to my skin
regard my disease as the least and the rest
throw it all away
shake the heavy droplets, the penny candy
flung on the turbid bed, all this confetti confirming canonicity,
frail mistakes in favorite frocks,
all that is left unmade.
one fuck-me heel lying in a damp streetlight
hovering above bleecker
exuding rainsoaked bliss.

the blue shoe
the pale bark
the precious tears
the buildings tell you to stand up straight.
                          i take my usual place against the wall at the end of the bar
nearest the street around the turn. that way, i can see the whole joint. a dark-
eyed bombshell sits in the back in a corner booth, blue light behind her head,
smoking slender white signal fires, nursing a drink. she strolls alone to the
juke box and slides in some coins. *in my solitude.* well, damn. she vows to
never smile again as she crosses languidly back to the shadowed table,
making the merest suggestion of dancing, spinning slowly, swinging down
into her place as sinatra croons. i stare into my fermented agave. a brooke
and dinah duet grooves on and darkhair stands to sway in her snug black
dress, cut low in the back, eyelids shaded blue, smoke a raincloud crown
around her head. i slug the cactus juice and listen as she moans along with

nina simone. out in the wet streets, cars pass sounding like brushed snares.
she runs her hands thru her abundant black hair, her painted nails glinting
purple in the soft bar light. i lean against the paneled wall and whisper
possible names.
—*for nicole, nyc, 2001*

RICHARD MANUEL
"*well we were THE hawks*" —in an interview in *the last waltz*
we hung ourselves with wires
a raptor band
me over the piano,
hung on hooks through my bleeding ankles,
i could barely reach the keys.
gates flew open anyway
walls exploded gratefully
and the prayer
the pleading wound
wound around my vocal cords
could be fiercely grabbed
could be fucked hard
by the girl in the very back row
she
who held my heart in her hands
as i dangled there
tips of my fingers pounded raw
please i said please
set my eyes on fire
shake my sinews
rejoice my skull
hold me
like that.

LITTLE RICHARD IS 80
that's the headline in the *post*
little richard is 80 angels
with demonic tongues
yes!

eighty devils with seraphim cunts
eighty times the man you are
his mercury squealing
is the key to the fortress
to the silence
banging the multiverse
into ecstatic oblivion
octagonally
eighty cocked pistols
blues blam-de-lam right out the back of the barrelhouse wire
and mamas howling
stomp it home, little richard,
show god why he made us
ALL
so beautiful.
but you, you are the emancipator of soul and the king of rock & roll
as for sure the prettiest queen
as long as we got a dime the music will never stop
a wop bop a loo bop a wop bam boom!

ABOUT PHOEBE
there is something impossible
about that perfect clear note she hits on the fadeout of 'time and love',
how can it be real?
way up there in the stars like that.
delicate and indestructible
she named herself after the train that barreled through her backyard every
single day. for real. phoebe snow was a passenger train once operated by
the delaware, lackawanna and western railroad. her given name was phoebe
ann laub. around 1900, the dl&w launched a marketing campaign around the
fictional character of 'phoebe snow' to emphasize how the exhaust from their
stream locomotives was cleaner than the competitor's locomotives. the train
took its name from the character, who was dressed in the ads all in white,
indicating purity, like her voice.
from the beginning, she had somewhere to go....
the first time i heard her was on the radio in my car. tooling around in one of
my long string of vehicles, (maybe mr. hoover, the 53 Chevy station wagon.

just not sure…) i was somewhere in central hollywood, maybe turning left onto vine. at the first touch of her voice i had to pull over to the curb, so as to really listen. i was in a hurry to get to my buddy's house, my jazz mentor, michael. c. gwynne, the first man to mention thelonious monk, charles mingus, ike quebec, herbie nichols, 'salt peanuts…salt peanuts', to me. so i got back into the flow of traffic, to get to his place before this blessed incantation ended. michael c. and i both sailed into his driveway nearly simultaneously and leapt from our cars, "did you hear it?" "listen they're playing it again…people have been calling in." (still possible back then, with live radio, to call the station and make a request.) michael c. actually clambered up onto his car, his hawaiian shirt flapping, and splayed out on the hood, engine ticking in the warm los angeles sun, to contemplate the gift shining down on us, to just listen raptly—for here she was, the brokenhearted angel, the bessie smith, the billie holiday, the dusty springfield, the patsy cline, the anita o'day of our day—the chick singer who gets it all from top to bottom in one sound, the ache of life, the overpowering essentiality of making music, or hearing it, that being the only way to survive the brutality of the beauty of the morning and the desperate dark of night. but this one, she could jump six octaves in a single breath.

she sang for the love of the 'poetry man'.
they played it ten times over. and nobody in los angeles moved a muscle.
but the song was weird, like a mystery or a love affair.
why was it 'you don't have to leave…'?
why was home that 'place where you go'?
the more you listened, the more you wanted to help this painfully lonely girl,
she seemed to cling to the idea that this slick operator 'could make every thing all right.'
when he obviously couldn't or wouldn't or even shouldn't.
anyone could tell that
she was begging him, desperate to beguile.
she had that disease we have all given ourselves,
'the rockin'pneumonia, and the boogie-woogie flu'.

when we did the concert version of 'the wizard of oz', (at lincoln center, a benefit for the children's defense fund, more on that later….)
she sang a medley of all the 'if i only had a…' songs,

with that same yearning, that nearly ecstatic pleading in her voice
for **head, heart, courage,**
with the same celestial flights through the notes,
making it clear that it takes all **three**
to get **home**
whole.

GLIMPSES OF JACKSON/ Part 1
rose bowl at dusk
sometime in the seventies
here to do good for somebody
with the power of our amalgamation
smells like uncountable roses
irreplaceable oranges
suburban revolution
propelled by radical sounds and unfettered music
we are all so beautiful
awkward
cool
jubilant
free
raising money to save the world.

our cheerful mistress of ceremonies
is a strutting sparkplug of a broad
bette
like bette davis
you can bet on her
swinging that stuff
the sophie tucker of our time
not a beauty but hey she knows what it is
'*and now*', she says, '*a man who's heart is as perfect as his hair…*'
and out he ambles
taking it easy
serenely radical
as if he is
hanging out on some arizona country corner

in the shade of that spreading tree
waiting for that girl in the flatbed ford
to slow down
and take a look
  (or that downtown corner in nyc, teenage cute with songs to spare.
along comes a venus in furs, takes a look, and swoops him up. nico, louche
chanteuse looking around for some luscious young consort to present to king
andy, behind darker sunglasses, topped by a terrible blonde bob, and to
show the boy off to the lounging court of genius junkies and super queens:
lou, viva, edie, candy from out on the island, joe never giving it away, jackie
speeding away, snorted up on spoons and slurped into soupcans, boxed and
stamped by ten minutes of fame, in a furious silver foil factory. these days
emerge in permissions he forgot about, in sidewalks of marilyn elvis jackie
and bananas peeling in the backrooms where everybody thought they were
james dean for a day everybody watching giono sleeping for hours and hours
like the empire state building as a screen test.)

and now, in the rose bowl as he strolls to the microphone,
he seems slightly shy and accidentally handsome
he has something to sing about and it is
becoming
i turn to the first woman i will marry,
  [nancy, with the radiant smile and whipsmart mind, with whom i am
making my way through these dark and glittering hollywoods. clever orphans
on our own at 20. both her parents and grandparents had died. leaving her
and her twin brother a small fortune, including the nice little house in
westwood, where a cast party was thrown, sometime in 1969. i walked from
the dorm, made my way through the crowd of mostly strangers, and was
immediately charmed by an olive-skinned young girl, hippieish, but not the
bells and mirrored scarves and long flowy dresses and hair down to here and
no bras and see-through blouses…she was different. natural, easy and
enigmatic. no big show. just a loose t-shirt as i recall. and jeans. no shoes.
shapely. and i sat down near to her, on the floor, as i recall, joints were
passing, people were moving about, standing, sometimes swaying, and we
sat there on the floor, leaning against a wall, we smiled and met eyes and it
seems like we did not actually speak for hours, if not the whole night. til
dawn, for real. we moved around, we danced, we ate, we laughed, we just

sat there, we did not need to speak. it was never awkward. we were being quiet together. as i recall, we did not have sex. i think we kissed. but we did not 'sleep together. '[that phrase has always perplexed me, meaning, as it does, the exact opposite of what it says. typical of our culture...] but the next night i went back and we sure did. we made love. after a formal exchanging of names, we surely did. some kind of agreement was made in that silence that first night, a trust established, that stood its ground for many years. well, at least five. as i say, we held hands and met the storm, with real joy...]

i turn to her now, in the rose bowl, gazing at the brilliant blue california sky, and her open smile, and i believe that maybe, with this guy, and a few others, we could talk the world into saving itself.

MOVING EAST, THIRD DAY, HWY 19—Rock Springs, Montana to Jackson Hole, Wyoming, 1995

house music carries us across the wide open spaces of montana. big sky indeed. the wind river range. crossing the green river again, the third time. into the tetons.

tavish plays me some of his music that he's been making with colman and fremont and joey, with a few drop-ins, apparently. it is *very* good. mellow and musical and the raps are funny. we arrive in jackson hole by 2:30, even though we stopped along the hoback river, at "lower noname" just to look at it. magnificent mountains. the valley where jackson hole sits is surprisingly lush and green, and the town is bristling. we call august from a pay phone. we make our way past a very blustery reenactment. somebody drops off a balcony into a wagon conveniently bearing a bale of hay. dodging the bank robbery,

we find august at the lovely "*snake river grill*", resplendent in the afternoon light, and, naturally, in the very best of taste. august directs us to "shades cafe" for espresso and stuff. on the way, the three of us travelers have a lively conversation about comedy. (lenny bruce, the influence of lord buckley, now forgotten, etc.). we stroll to the music store, where tavish is on his endless search for rare and useful vinyl. we all score at the record store.

august leads us to his place in wilson, idaho. It's a brand new house, a bit impersonal, but chock full of his stuff—art, evocative photos. and it's nestled in a pine grove, with the creek burbling nearby.

we hang around, covering no ground and then mark pulls out an amazing collection of silent-era movie posters and lobby cards and letters from studio execs, wherever he got the stuff, has now been cleared to divest some of it for cash.) i pick out one for a serial called 'son of the border 'to give to august for his birthday on sunday.

at sunset we drive to spring gorge resort, to take in the vista. we smoke a joint and watch the sun settle behind this stunning ragged mountain range. then we proceed to the snake river grill, the finest restaurant in the state, if not the region, for the meal of a lifetime. (i had venison chops.) susanna calls me while i'm there.

we drive back to august's. on the way he and i ride together and he says he has never been happier or more content, and of course it's apparent and very pleasing. what to do with memory? and people dying? live your life.

the next morning on the way into jackson we see the mashed carcass of a coyote. road kill. trying to get to some calves on the other side of the road, make a good dinner. tav and i both make sympathetic mourning sounds.

NOTES FROM A WORKSHOP: JOE CHAIKIN
ornamental words before annihilation
FINDING THE COMPLEXITY OF THE CHARACTER
a relationship with what you're going to repeat
ABSORBING OUR CONSCIENCE
this horrible music
(he fidgets as though he is playing
music on his knee and ankle)
ARCHAIC
(BRECHT: CHOICE [in spite of destiny])
acting out these passions so that the audience
still PARTICIPATES
"often the thing which is most important to do next is hidden under the other things which we are trying to remember to do because they don't matter much. the things that don't matter we work at retaining in memory. the things which matter more are hidden just underneath them."—joseph chaikin, 'presence in time'

"if you want to see it, we can go it, it would be good for me...if you are busy can find plan another dinner, later next."—joseph chaikin, in a letter, after his strokes

8 DAYS IN RUSSIA. Kaliningrad, Day Three, Tuesday. 2007
i wake up at what turns out to be 8 AM, although i believe it to be 9:30. (for some inexplicable reason.) i still feel ill, but i force myself up, after calling masha and rousing her. i wander downstairs and across the street, to the shiny cinema and shopping center which in my fog i have misunderstood to be the location of the festival. much chillier today, especially this early, unforgiving grey. i try to go up the escalator, but i'm stopped by a uniformed guard, um, an armed officer, not particularly threatening, but quite certain i was not to be allowed to enter. so i stand in the outer lobby, across a five street intersection, a turnabout, circling morning traffic, five points on a star, a compass, a mandala, a wheel, a world, a universe, that includes the looming blue monster, and a bridge across the as yet unseen river. i feel utterly, implacably foreign, displaced and therefore suspect. and the shabbiness of everything makes me sad and sullen, just like those trudging to work all around me, puffs of breath clouding their features. i glimpse masha entering the hotel and i hurry across the streets, hopping the meridians, feeling like i'm in an espionage film (monty in *the defector*). my sprits lift a bit at masha's genuinely lovely smile, and we get a cab to the actual location, several blocks away, much cooler than i could have ever imagined. it's actually an arts complex, really, centered around a german-built, oval shaped, very large and now state-of-the-art auditorium for screening films, the whole place carefully redone with exposed brick, sleekly appointed offices, lots of art, classical and modern, an elegant upscale restaurant and comfortable cafe`. and as i would find out later, somewhat to my peril, a disco. (and i do mean *disco*, uhuh, shakeyerbooty and all that. let me just say, russians love to drink. surprise surprise. alert the media.) all of this in the confines of a quite beautiful building, designed and built by, well, the nazis.

art and masha and i talk a bit in art's small office until the cafe` is ready to serve us breakfast. art, actually artem, is shaved and now seems older—in fact i learn that he has two kids, a daughter, 6, lives in germany with her mother, art's first wife, son, age 4, lives here, with a third child on the way, with second wife. art works very hard, programming the films, performers and djs in the night club, and managing several other cultural projects, while writing articles and reviews for several publications, plus writing a new novel, two books have been published, a novel and short stories. he is striving to create a sophisticated audience where one does not really exist. (shades of riverspace back in nyack.) there is a university here in kaliningrad, and an intelligentsia, some bohemian some bourgeois. but there is no core of people who are aware of why old black-and-white movies, from the last century, let alone american films, could possibly mean something to them—or engage them on any level. most american films of the last fifty years are completely unknown in russia, having been banned for most of the century. now the legendary, indeed mythic, treasures they have only read about, or seen as stills, are available for budding russian cinephiles. art and masha must cultivate them. they've had a very successful couple of years, and their combined taste and knowledge, and charm, have led to the active support of the american government and the cooperation of the russians, for this first ever festival of american classics.

the cafe is lovely. they play bird sounds, with an occasional wolf howl, somewhere in the far distance, for background music. we talk about their efforts to shape the audience in other, more basic ways. behaviorally. they've instituted dress codes, insisting that people check their overcasts and not wear gym attire, (kind of the mirror image of the 60's in america, when people dressed down to prove they were hip) —all as a way of taking the artistic aspects of film more seriously. the design of the complex makes the central shrine, the inner sanctum, the temple to cinema, the hub of hip fun and deep culture. i am not allowed in at present, haven't made my proper offerings and ablutions, but as soon as the screening of *letters from iwo jima*, eastwood's film in release worldwide, and up for academy consideration, is done, i'll sneak in. i mention i'm an academy voter and a few minutes later that goes out in a press release and will be constantly referred to from then on, whenever i'm introduced and interviewed. (i give all thanks and obeisance, as well as credit to jeff corey, sylvia sidney and theresa wright, who signed my nomination card. it always takes three friends).

masha and i take a stroll down leninplatz, the main drag, takes about twenty minutes, past buildings in various stages of disrepair, parks with broken down fountains, and listless teens smoking long cigarettes. lots of tobacco and liquor in constant evidence. some kids with dreads and piercings. masha points out one building, now a hotel, which was once some kind of german headquarters, bullet holes still in evidence in its facade, left unfilled, and two rough plaster splotches, haphazardly applied, over the stucco medallions on each side of the main entrance, barely disguising the swastikas beneath. but the town is bustling, chain stores front the west, mingled with street merchants selling dried mushrooms and herbs. lots of amber necklaces in lots of polished windows. and much construction, money has been pouring into the city—not a lot of local benefit, a part from the building trades. apparently there is some talk of giving serious consideration to the notion of legalizing gambling in this region, what with its port, and beaches on the baltic sea, and cosmopolitan air, a touch of casablanca— kaliningrad could be the vegas of russia.

we arrive at a meeting in what i am led to believe is a library. looks more like a community center in akron or maybe cleveland. not a lot of books in sight, but some compelling displays. a chekhov exhibit, quite extensive, with many wonderfully evocative photographs, and documents, letters, journals in his hand. with his leaky pen. the meeting we attend is to commemorate 200 years of diplomatic relations between russia and united states, (which is accurate i guess, if you include the many years that we were emphatically, shoe-thumpingly at war, cold or not. i guess that's diplomatic relations, of a notably childish sort. we were definitely spying on each other and labeling the other guy as evil and demonizing an entire citizenry and way of life, which admittedly we kinda won that horse race, but now we even seem to have given up the space race and the nuclear bomb race, so what race are we gonna run…from, now. besides, who's counting? let's watch some movies.) so various consulate officials, including the previously mentioned mary ellen countryman, mary kruger, and a couple of other consulate types, are present, as well as the ambassador, who is very friendly, personable and, well, diplomatic. three or four people make speeches in russian, and a couple of times my name springs out of the gobbledygook, like a shoe in a stew—and the whole room turns to me and beams and i nod and smile. then the ambassador goes into another room and sits in a circle with former exchange students, and they have a pleasant conversation about cooperation between the two countries—which is only really achieved person-to-person, on a personal level, especially because governments can be so *frustrating*. all in all, i dig the guy. he has a real beating heart and just enough of the diplomat to get by.

all of the exchange students are girls, all are attractive, coltish, calm or classic, and they are all flirting rather openly with me. so is mary ellen coutryman. she refers to my picture in the catalog a couple of times and then says, *"besides marlon brando, he's the sexiest man alive, and brando's dead."* "take it easy," i say. masha grins impishly at me. all in good fun. and then we make our escape. i plead nap time and go up to my hotel room, hook up the portable dvd player art lent me, and after making some notes for tomorrow's lecture at the university, i take an hour or two to snooze. then i watch the beginning of *maltese falcon* for the forty millionth time, i think the first sequence will illustrate very nicely the points i hope to make tomorrow.

masha calls for dinner and we go for japanese—really quite good. it's raining slightly, the streets are slick and shiny, the city looks more european with this added glaze. (and now were in *the third man,* cue the zither.) people are kissing openly in the streets, european style, it's paris everywhere. masha and i have a very lively, borderline cosmic conversation over miso and sushi. the waitress is an adorable girl from the provinces, with braces. she smiles broadly and blushes every time i speak directly to her. of course, she doesn't understand a word i say.

masha's father abandoned her, she's only seen him once, and that was by chance. we talk a lot about family wounds and personal strength, and the importance of art (and artem) and culture…and on and on. i can feel that we both feel that we have found a friend for life. we walk back to the hotel in the light rain. i watch the rest of *falcon* and then to bed. tomorrow is the first big test.

YOUR APPLAUSE
your applause flutters toward me clacketing
a flock of small wooden butterflies
enameled white.
i am crouched on a plank
antlers sprouting from my skull.
in the baying of my dogs
in the snapping of their jaws
now i hear my name

faces lit by campfire
or hearthfire

or moonfire
i leap through the crackling flames
dowsed with sacred water
i am baptized
by your applause

your applause
is the murmur of all the abandoned
is the language of blossoms
is the gilt mirror of pain and terror
is my face as it is
in the full heat of your applause

in the dark lit only by starfire
the melody of your applause
guides me home.

"why not surrender, coyote?
grow fat on love,
eat table scraps, be stroked for no reason,
…………
why not stay alive? '
—shelley m. miller, 'coyote 'excerpt

4. ROMANTIC: AT THE CORE, EVERYONE HAS A DEEP AND COMPLETE CONNECTION TO ALL OTHERS AND ALL THINGS.
        or people experience a painful loss of their original connections, leaving them feeling abandoned and feeling that they are missing something important.

"coyote went running around the whole planet. he could see wonderful things but he preferred to fool around with women!"—murray mednick, 'the coyote cycle'

ADENINE
CYTOSINE
GUANINE
THYMINE
from these four come—all of us.

"urge and urge and urge, always the procreant urge of the world.
out of the dimness opposite equals advance, always substance and increase,
always sex, always a knit of identity, always distinction, always a breed of
life."—walt Whitman

"it started long ago
in the garden of eden
when adam said to eve
baby, you're for me!"
—wayne fontana and the mindbenders, 'the game of love'
*"there are only **four stories** that are told and re-told: the **siege** of the city, the **return** home, the **quest,** the (self-)**sacrifice** of god."—jorge luis borges*

"the ancient rites of male initiation were complicated and subtle experiences
which could be imagined better as a continual spiral than as a walk down a

*road. the spiral could be described as a year which repeats itself in seasons. the **four seasons of development** amount to **four stages**, **four steps** and **four events**, though we all know that seasons run into each other, and repeat."—robert bly*

the SUFIS recognize **four different classes of human beings**, who harmonize with each other in accordance with their stages of evolution: **ANGEL**, seeks heaven; **HUMAN**, struggles with life; **ANIMAL**, revels in earthly pleasures; **DEVILISH**, makes hell for himself and others.

four horsemen of the apocalypse: war, famine, pestilence & death. **four directions, four seasons,** (twelve months divided into four groups of three, like the twelve astrological signs in four groups of three, assigned to each of **four elements** (fire, water, earth, air), **four corners of the earth,** and there are the **four winds of heaven (***'i saw four angels standing at the four corners of the earth, holding back the four winds of the earth to prevent any wind from blowing on the land or on the sea or on any tree."—revelations 7:1*), **four rivers of eden** (prison, gihon, hiddekel, euphrates)**, four humors** (sanguine, phlegmatic, choleric, melancholic), **four evangelists** (matthew, mark, luke, john), **four angels** (michael, raphael, gabriel, phannel), **four alchemical ingredients** (salt, sulphur, mercury, azoth), **four basic geometric figures** (circle, line, square, triangle), **four phases of the moon, four cardinal virtues** (justice, prudence, temperance, fortitude).

in every story of a certain type, the neverending tale, there is always the **one**, our representative, whom we follow on the journey, and identify with, and **three friends,** allies, companions, familiars, who accompany the 'hero(ine)', often finding new aspects of themselves while aiding the protagonist's fulfillment of the quest.
one of the prime contemporary examples, of course, is ***the wizard of oz***: **dorothy** is from the 'real world', [the black-and-white world, where we live] and is transported to the imaginal realm, on a journey of discovery of self and the home in herself. then there is the **scarecrow** who becomes her closest friend and ally, the 'favorite 'because he is the first, empowering her and leading by following. then the **tin man**, a secondary friend, seemingly without a heart, maintaining a distance, but also clearly sensitive and insightful; and the initially forbidding, frightening, even bestial (he is first seen on four legs,

108

growling fiercely…or the best he can do to seem dangerous), **lion**—the last
to join, completing the formation, the foundation of a perfect structure. in fact,
all quartets can be divided into these types, as for instance: **violin** (dorothy),
viola (scarecrow), **cello** (tin man), **bass** (cowardly lion).
and then there are:

the four marx brothers: **zeppo**/dorothy (the 'normal 'one, who *should* be at
the center of the tale, if we were witnessing a standard rendition instead of
the upended, wacky carnival world of the satyrs, the satiric funhouse mirror,
where every aspect of reality is turned on its head, as in mardi gras.) zeppo
and the subsequent string of male ingenues, tenors and such, are no match
for the hijinks of the rustics: **groucho**/scarecrow
(adviser/manipulator/defender, often a shifty lawyer, or quasi-doctor, or fake
explorer); **chico**/tin man (seemingly heartless, or at least guiltless, but
somehow tender); **harpo**/cowardly lion (without language, shocking, but
lovable).
*"the marx brothers, in freudian terms: chico=ego; groucho=superego; silent,
mischievous harpo=id."— slavoj zizek, the perverts guide to cinema'*
the four characters also represent the four major ethnic types thrown together
in new York city: including 'american 'or assimilated [zeppo] ; jewish
[groucho]; Italian [chico, and irish, apparently harpo's irish accent sucked,
thus...he took on the instrument which symbolized irish culture).
So all the 'european 'ethnicities at play in new york city for decadesbbecame
the basis of their entire vaudeville act. and, of course, vaudeville came out of
minstrel shows, and that form of entertainment was birthed by the 'dancing
for eels 'around catherine market near the docks of lower manhattan, in the
mid 1700s. blacks, often escaped slaves, were hired to perform their
exuberant dancing on wooden pallets in front of whatever fishmonger hired
them, as a form of advertisement, attracting customers to witness their antics.
the district surrounding the docks was the only area of the city where the
races were permitted to mix; living, loving and carousing together. eventually
they all *"danced out their regional affiliation and their identity.* [in the
basements of taverns]. *this overlap is first among several that are important
in these early commercial performance of an independent atlantic popular
culture…the dance* [and fashions] *appealed to several* [young] *audiences
who were finding different values..at the same time. it was a yoking across*

perceived differences at least as much as it was a closing out of a separation...an attraction across differences was daily played out. at least some of the whites saw those dancers as their champions."—w.t.lhamon, 'raising cain: blackface performance from jim crow to hiphop'.

the four beatles: **paul**/dorothy (the cute one, most approachable); **john**/scarecrow (closest friend, first collaborator on the quest, the two making the initial pair.); **george**/tin man, (somewhat distant, if not cold, but always soulful): **ringo**/cowardly lion, (obviously. also the fourth to be added, as with the lion.) an alternate view of the beatles is to put john in the dorothy position, and paul as scarecrow. this conflict may have contributed to their breakup, in fact, as both were vying for leadership, to be the center of the story. but paul is inherently conservative and 'normal', whereas john was forever the rebel, the outsider, the wounded one. this volatile dynamic, of course, made them that much more fascinating and effective. *"but although they were a three- and then a four-man band, they were, from the start, a two-man compact— what mattered was their inner twoness, more than their iconic fourness."— adam gopnik, 'new yorker magazine'*
the rolling stones: mick/dorothy; **keith**/scarecrow; **bill**/tin man (later **ron**); **charlie**/ lion. (mick and keith refer to themselves as 'the glimmer twins')
the doors; the who; the velvet underground; csn&y; all fit smoothly into this paradigm. (including the unstable, sometimes antagonistic, often spectacularly creative, rivalry between the 'lead 'pair, often causing conflict and ultimate dissolution—who's the *real* dorothy?).
the four fathers of beat poetry: jack kerouac/dorothy; **neal cassady**/scarecrow (talk about '*inner two-ness*'); **allen ginsberg**/lion; **ferlinghetti**/tin man. (**burroughs,** of course, being the wizard).
the four musketeers: **d`artagnan**/ dorothy (our hero); **athos**/ scarecrow (first to comes to the hero's aid); **aramis**/ tin man (slightly distant, poetic, but essential); **porthos**/lion (bearlike, mighty, jovial, and last to join.) their motto, 'all for one, one for all'.
i could go on...but the important element to remember is that **four** is foundational. stable in a way not possible for one, two or three...
and everything takes shape out of NEED.

110

TOO MUCH MATTER AND ENERGY IN ONE PLACE CAN CAUSE SPACE
TO SAG SO FAR THAT THE MATTER INSIDE CAN DISAPPEAR,
COLLAPSING ENDLESSLY TO A POINT OF INFINITE DENSITY KNOWN
AS /**SINGULARITY**/ OR /A **BLACK HOLE**/.

SPOOKY ACTION AT A DISTANCE
space-time created thusly
it from bit
because ted and bob are the same self
the handsome vagabond turns out to be the prince
but the wormhole hypothesis must ripen on the shelf
black hole horizon is a special place
but then
again…

'*we* are *solitary. we may delude ourselves and act as though this were not
so. that is all. but how much better it is to realize that we are so, yes, even
to begin assuming it. we shall indeed turn dizzy then; for all points upon
which our eye has been accustomed to rest are taken from us, there is
nothing near any more and everything far is infinitely far.'—rilke, 'the dragon-
princess'*

"*…now you are crumpled onto yourself, your back sliding down the wall and it
is now that your heart has been broken…a beam of light pushes and tugs
through the window at the end of the hallway, it pours over you and once
again you see the separate particles of dust, all of the dust that you don't
know what to do with….you are breathless. you are a swirl. maybe it's that
you feel betrayed by yourself, that somehow, it wasn't the plan to end up this
lost, this fallen. it is the morning after all, and you are in your home. louree
still doesn't know you are outside her door, she is on her bed. maybe she is
crying there, maybe she needs you. you, in the honey-colored swirl, stay
crumpled, and you wait. maybe you stay there waiting."—ramona demme,
from 'darrell, upon hearing "just like a woman" for the first time, 1966'*"
[this insightful, lovely story was written in 2006 by ramona demme, my
daughter emma's best friend. i told ramona about first hearing the song, and
sliding down the wall, transfixed…ramona extrapolated all the rest.]

SHIPWRECKED ON YOUR BED
shot
shipwrecked on your bed
surrendering to sound
anticipating the swing of your hips
the swift turn
the languid glance
the dance we will make for sweat and cultivation
the chance
shot
we will take
at salvation
—1974

EPAISSE`
1.Paris, Rosebud Bar et La Coupole, May 22, 1975
six poplars
and the broken hearts
of the women of martinique
rise in your dark robes
and take to the wet streets
we have no hands
no eyes
open mouths
full of roses
and there on the light quiet corner
embroidered blouses
and the yapping of dogs.
go ahead
find what you own
we dare you
dive this way and that in conversation
who feeds you?
who breathes you?
what is your address?
six poplars

on the final avenue.

2.Versailles, May 25, 1975
(le chat du versailles)
o, cool horse of stone
all the fountains are still
but we hear water
running
we can hear bare feet on wild lawn

3. Caen, May 27, 1975
la pluie des etoile
la pluie sans le dommage
and the blue of normandy corridors
and laughter in cubicles
we cannot help the quiet afternoons
the stolen history
the blood and fog
we can only help ourselves
to fruit and cheese et cafe noir
4. Nice, May 28, 1975
le chat du nice
rising late to meals in the sun
le chats du ville-franche
pluie sur l'expression du visage
pluie sur mer
au dessous de mer azur
l'arrivee du soleil
l'arrivee ta mort
a ce` moment
clinging to cutting rocks
and all the cats of france
are survivors
they stand still on flagstones
warmed by the sun.
—*written with elinor, on tour*

8 DAYS IN RUSSIA, Kaliningrad, Wednesday. 2007
i'm awakened by the sound of someone puking in the next room, having what
masha calls 'the russian experience', in our parlance, a hangover. and then
some.now i get why a lot of people look so sullen on the street, especially
before noon. i doze through retching sounds and then rouse myself and beat
on down to the hotel restaurant for breakfast. only one other customer for the
desultory buffet. runny, sunny-side up eggs, partially eclipsed by silver-dollar-
sized disks of something like sausage, or more resembling a hot dog,
plopped on each yolk. other mysterious gruelish mush, vats of guiche-
like…stuff, mini-croissants, and at one end some quite disturbing looking
'prepared 'meats. i spot an espresso machine at the bar and approach the
target. i gesture toward the impressive, samovar-ish machine and the
disgruntled blonde waves me toward the coffee tank near the buffet table.
  "no, i'd like an espresso. preferably a double."
she makes it, each gesture a dance of begrudging. actually the food is not
half bad, if you can get past the visuals.
  i buy some postcards in the lobby shop, and the guy behind the
counter smiles affably, almost friendly. i am duly amazed. i'm sitting in the
lobby, making notes and culling quotes for the first lecture, when i get a call
from masha.
  "here is something funny," she giggles. "there is a strike at the
university."
  "the students?"
  "the teachers!" (shades of the cherry orchard.)
  "what's the issue?"
  "we don't know, but we are trying to find a different place…or maybe
we reschedule."
  "cool…i'll just hang here." i'm relieved. a couple of minutes later she
calls back.
  "okay, we have another place. we pick you up in an hour."
  i'm not sure why i'm so nervous about this—other than the fact that i
have no idea what to expect (a handful of bored twenty-year-olds getting
through another useless hour…unreadable stares…brainlock?), or what they
expect. (button-downed academic, critical nerd, glamorous pal to the stars?).
they may have some equipment to play some clips—or they may not. i think i
have something to say—but can i say it coherently? most of them will speak

114

english, so say masha and art. but i have a feeling i speak something other than the english they've been taught. i am halfway around the world from home. and i feel sick—but i'm used to that. i believe in the material. bogart will see me through.

for one horrible moment i stood in front of a hundred or so russian college students, in a low-ceilinged room, an old german barracks—decrepit from the outside, a maze of long arched hallways inside. jammed, standing-room only—and i was at a complete loss, with no clips to fall back on, or get rolling with. nobody could figure out how to work the equipment, even art, the technical wizard, now sheepish, which saddened me. i had a sheaf of notes in front of me—but no real sense of how to connect them. i start strong, talking about the significance of the invention of the moving picture in human history—but then i just run dry. stand there gaping at these puzzled, intrigued, expectant young folks. i grab a quote from my notes and read it emphatically, look up, *'am i going too fast?'*—i get chuckles and thumbs-up and waves of encouragement, hopeful, gleaming eyes pointed at me, sold just on the presence of this guy from america standing in front of them—and i make a few connections that visibly land. three or four really riveted people ask questions—and they sustain me and keep the whole thing rolling. one especially helpful interlocutor is the dean, a really lovely, middle-aged blonde woman, very bright and easy, she pitches me several intelligent softballs, from way in the back, and i hit them for at least a triple. (we had spent a few moments in her office when we first entered the building. she offered tea and coffee—then tried to give me nescafe`, and grinned conspiratorially when i waved it away, saying to her, *'that's not coffee .'* she mouthed the words" *i agree'* and kind of smirked. we had a secret.). anyway, the kids seemed thrilled for the most part, many of them stopping to express interest and delight and shake my hand on the way out. i go back on friday for a second round, and i'm determined to show clips. for one thing, when i asked for a show of hands of who had seen bogart in a film—exactly two hands went up. one young man had seen what he called *'white house'.* took me a moment to realize he meant *casablanca.* the other hand raised was the hip dean. but *everybody* had seen jean-paul belmondo.

art is sure most of them will be back on friday, and that many of them will come to the festival, which was the whole point of the visit to the school. why should they want to see these fifty-year-old films? how do these artifacts of a bygone era have any relevancy in their lives? how could they possibly matter to them? we zipped over to the theater for a press conference, which was held at a corner table in the café`. four or five journalists, one of whom was at the university earlier, and in fact asked a few questions there. as if that weren't enough of me, he stays after the conference breaks up to do a more extensive interview. turns out his name is vladimir. he has a whole page of questions prepared, based on information he got about me from the internet. he knows about *marcus welby*!—all kinds of details about my life, wife, kids, etc.. it is flat-out bizarre to be known by a total stranger writing for a magazine in baltic russia.

"what was it like working with john schlesinger? UCLA in 1968? why not longer? born in california?"

the press conference itself was good. i felt in control of my attention, focused and occasionally eloquent. i am being frankly political, and it seems okay, so far, even with the consulate people. afterward, masha says she is kind of amazed at how i am the perfect person for this gig—turns out there were several respondents, and she and art just had a feeling about me. my e-mails were engaging and enthusiastic. i had been thinking maybe i was the *only* respondent. (where is it? for how much?) anyway they seem pleased. we had a bite to eat while vladimir was interviewing me, really more of a conversation, and moved on to a diplomatic reception at the *museum of the open ocean*—or something like that. (masha kind of shrugged when i said "*of what*?") modern building right on the river—with a submarine and a bathysphere parked out front and lots of fishlike sculptures inside, floating around with the diplomats and bureaucrats. big spread of russian food, posh version—and a chef wearing an apron emblazoned ***louisiana*** across the bib section, artfully preparing american-style cajun-inflected delicacies—to demonstrate how to utilize american produce and poultry. turns out the guy, the burly chef, is mary kruger's personal cook. he is spieling like a stand-up comic, drolly describing his cooking process as he sautés enormous root vegetables, with visalia onions, and mushrooms from minnesota.

before the cooking show there were speeches in russian, and a moment of silence for people killed in a mining disaster earlier that day. a national day of mourning has been declared, but this brief pause was the only evidence i saw of that. i had a conversation with an affable guy, a russian—igor bolchenko—who runs three automotive plants—they make cadillacs, chevys, cheap chinese cars, SAABS, all at these plants, all for sale in russia. sweet, ingratiating guy, ugly in a typically thick, russian way, bad skin, heavy cologne, but so eager to relate to me, to engage. we had a wide-ranging, thoroughly enjoyable conversation, not without some disagreement. we ended up talking about global warming—and were completely on the same page about it, but speculated on whether we will be able to save the world before we lose it. we made a vow to stay provisionally hopeful, with vigilance. as we were sealing our pact with a drink we were approached by a norwegian diplomat—very polite, who had NEVER SEEN AUDREY HEPBURN, and was *'dreadfully disappointed* not to be able to see *breakfast at tiffany's.* his name was arne gore, the director of the nordic council of ministers. he seemed to be apologizing to me in lieu of personally offering his regrets to miss hepburn. i played along....finally art and masha yanked me out and hustled me back to the hotel, and now i sit in the drab but lively bar in the lobby, sipping a polish beer and writing this report. when i finish i will go upstairs and watch a russian film they want me to see...except i can't find the subtitle command. oh well. and so to sleep.

audrey hepburn's performance incarnating a water sprite, in *ondine*, on broadway, won her the 1954 tony award for best actress. and she never completely lost that air of otherworldliness. in that same year she won the best actress oscar for *roman holiday*, making her one of three actresses in history to receive the oscar and the tony in the same year (the other two were shirley booth and ellen burstyn). a *new york times* critic commented that *"somehow miss hepburn is able to translate [the intangibles of the play] into the language of the theatre without artfulness or precociousness. She gives a pulsing performance that is all grace and enchantment, disciplined by an instinct for the realities of the stage."* as a princess on the run in *roman holiday*, with a stalwart gregory peck, she became international film royalty. but she was already, in fact, the daughter of a baroness. she was often paired, especially early on, with older male stars—gary cooper in *love in the afternoon*, cary grant in *charade,* (after which he said, *"all I want for christmas is another picture with audrey hepburn."*), fred astaire in *funny face*, william holden and humphrey bogart in *sabrina,* (as brothers battling for the charms of the chauffeur's adorable, irresistible daughter). all of these men were at least 20 years older than audrey hepburn. but somehow her girlishness did not seem immature, or fragile, or the affairs in any way unsavory. for one thing, she seemed to be more emotionally, and even intellectually, advanced than the aging lotharios circling her. she felt like the real grownup, waiting for the handsome lunks to catch up with her. in *breakfast at tiffany's* in particular, hepburn is midway between the innocent gamin and the fully sexualized love goddess. holly golightly is a denizen of the new york city demi-monde of kept boys and party girls. the depiction is romanticized, even sanitized, so as to not be entirely credible, but nevertheless, we take hepburn's needs seriously, and we support the attainment of her desires—not just for love, but for a life of fine things and fine thoughts. we even condone her lifestyle—at least to the extent that we believe in her inherent decency. by contrast, rita hayworth in *gilda,* is condemned for, and by, her dangerous eroticism. although at the end of the film she has her johnny, the relationship is clearly doomed, and her relentless pursuit of pleasure in the repressive environment she finds herself in is a kind of martyrdom—for which she insists we *blame* her. ingrid bergman's ilse lund in *casablanca* cannot have her true love because, as bogart's rick famously states: "...*the problems of three little people don't amount to a hill of beans in this crazy world.*"   and marilyn monroe, capote's original model for holly golightly, is, especially in *the seven year itch*, a cartoon of female carnality, whose emotional life is not even a consideration. monroe's joy in her own body, and her obvious delight in the thrill she provides to others, is exemplified, totemized, by the famous scene from this film, of a flushed marilyn, straddling the subway grate as the hot air blows her billowing skirt up to reveal...everything, her head thrown back in nearly orgasmic abandon. the shot became iconic, not least because it was made monumental in a thirty-foot blowup in times square for the films opening, but it also became the emblem of her undoing. her baseball hero husband, jolting joe dimaggio, happened to be on the set when they shot the scene. howling crowds had gathered for the spectacle of the lust goddess on display. he stalked off, disgusted and humiliated. soon afterwards he ended the marriage, but never the love he felt for the goddess he once thought he owned. every year until his death he placed an offering of flowers on her grave.

but audrey hepburn and holly golightly survive, beguiling us into tearful permission for the fulfillment of her dreams. we forgive her for her transgressions, for her trivial life of parties and paramours, for the inferred looseness of her morals, because we feel the innocent heart beating in her experienced body. or, as hepburn put it herself:"*for beautiful eyes, look for the good in others; for beautiful lips, speak only words of kindness; and for poise, walk with the knowledge that you are never alone".*

breakfast at tiffany's marked, probably unintentionally and unconsciously as far as the studio heads or the filmmakers were concerned, an important cultural transition, signifying a more liberated way of looking at feminine desire, and audrey hepburn, with her childlike womanliness, gently led us, quite willingly, out into the rain and the moonlight, and the shimmering moon river of love.

"paris is always a good idea."—audrey hepburn

"—almost the same feeling, if one was alone with her and she restrained and clarified still further the flow of her words, that one has on hearing an old song. then, as i looked,..i could see,..a prisoner in the perpetual and quiet afternoon of her eyes, the sky of the ile de france or of champagne spreading itself, grey-blue, oblique..."—marcel proust, 'remembrance of things past: guermantes way'

HUMAN TORCH
the white trash girl in the black pickup truck
catches fire in the middle of the bridge

i sit here trying to figure out
which way to jump

heard you caught the train in your teeth
shattering your sunglasses

you ask some unfair questions
now you reap what was sown

what is all deliberate speed
anyway?

and how can i get some?
anyway...

have a safe trip up the river

witness for me the achingly slow burning

all around you
and think of me

as i think of the white trash girl
her hair turning from darkened cornsilk to white ash

think of me vaulting over the rail
abandoning my vehicle

think of all of us
annihilating the risk of a total conjunction

resulting in a burned world
my last thought

as i hit the shimmering river
will be of you.
— *for holly*

PRECEPTS FOR ACTING:
ALL I AM IS WHAT I'M GOING AFTER
WHAT DO I WANT?
WHAT CAN I DO TO GET WHAT I WANT?
HOW DO I DO WHAT I NEED TO DO TO GET WHAT I WANT?

MOVING EAST/ FOURTH DAY—Hiways 191-26-20-90-16. Jackson,
Wyoming to Custer, South Dakota
D: There was a corgi in that truck.
T: I knew we were on the right path.
        *de la soul, buckshot lefongue. lightnin hopkins. future sounds of
london*
        crow heart. shoshoni. thermopolis.
        poison creek. bad water creek. wind river
        there is a drive-in espresso stand in riverton, wyoming. (we stop for
caffeination.)

pumpernick's for lunch, in thermopolis, with a yellow-brick building with green brick trim. the obvious point of pride for the town, if not the entire region. we get another espresso at a bakery right on the square.

selena. bob marley. mixes.
tensleep. buffalo.
tensleep creek. no wood creek. trigger lake.
crazywoman canyon.
danny weiszman, wild man. duck's breath mystery theater.
jungle mix.

billowing black clouds over the black hills and distant lightning. we drive right into the storm, heralded first by enormous drops of heavy rain, we drive through it and witness the black hills turn blood red, climbing higher and higher, the lightning now a faraway display.

the sun goes down as we cross into south dakota. roll into custer. eat some very bland mexican food and discuss god and politics. then we take a two-room unit at the rocket inn.

FROM A DISTANCE
i have a picture of you
on my refrigerator
looking adorably snotty
making that insouciant almost grin
challenging in a black leather jacket
demanding occupation
a chuck closeian portrait of elvis
your sympathetic backdrop

i have a picture of you
on my refrigerator
looking french in the snow
or maybe russian
in a bulky handmade scarf
worn for warmth
a modiglianian statue of a soldier/preacher
standing gaunt behind you
holding two halves of the globe

i have a picture of you
an image in my mind
looking suitably solemn
or make that alluring
stretched out on your capacious bed
naked in starlight
one knee raised
a rodinian,
or schieleish,
or klimtesque
sketch of the wonders of bodies afire
calling for an artful
careful
but passionate response
from me
with you
— for karen, in wyoming, 8/9/2018

ALL THE NEW ONES
all the new ones are gone
i used to keep up
by being ahead of the pack
now i just don't know
where to listen
from an inaccessible cloud
way above our threadbare planet
without earshot
lacking sorrow or
perspective
or perceptible melody
all beyond me
unbroken by digital sunlight
i am left bereft
of contemporary comfort
but hey
the past is
there in front of me

our representatives
are serving other customers
and i
contrite and cautious
open my heart
to your imminent storm
and my mind
to your oh so
actual earthquake
my soul to dinner.
—*for karen, 2019*

LAST CHANCE
ashes of stars course through my veins
making me gasp
making me moan
making me weep

are we allowed to utter aloud
the broken precision of our heartlessness
and where is it written that virtuosity
is virtuous or dangerous
or reclining on the sofa?

what are those flaming letters scrawled on the exploding wall?
will we ever stop spinning
or gliding
or spurting on the tattered carpet?
will I ever just hold you
with our breath conjoined
our small murmurs of assurance mingling
with the sweet scent of our calm desire?
no
the pillows are on fire
the ashes of constellations plummet
and roar through my wounded capillaries
and the world is forever at war

123

once I strolled with you in empty pastures
fences long gone
and the truth was our perception
and the sky was our blanket
and the seeds of our surrender
made the world green once more
no
that was our last chance.
—for debbon, 1/11/2010

DON'T GIVE DOWN/ TEAR YOUR PLAYHOUSE UP
i thought i saw you on the street today
and then i did
small rain providing a helpless sheen
of dusk light
just there
        on the edge
            of the park
and i realized that
    if james brown and woody guthrie
    had a lovechild
        she would have to have been adopted
and she would sound like this

i swung by my girlfriend's pad
to give her rats the once over twice
the little fellas love to get high
and of course i always oblige
then they want to touch
nibble my fingertips
cavort all over the shredded light gone bad
how common it is
to do battle
with our beauty
when we have every chance
at shadows beneath the trees
tossed aside with tender deliberation

124

to catch a train
to be caught wanting
to relent
relent
relent
the fluid fragrance seeping into everything
your lost and found eyes
your tongue and the ground beneath your writhing

now we have the torrential incantations
you give yourself an ecstatic gift
including what's missing
as a leap to conclusion
at last.
—*for torey, 2011*

OUCH. An ornament of gold or jewels.
OUNCE. A **lynx**; a **panther**

*"it was like feasting with panthers; the danger was half the excitement. i used
to feel as a snake-charmer must feel when he lures the cobra to stir from the
painted cloth or reed basket that holds it and make it spread its hood at his
bidding and sway to and fro in the air as a plant sways restfully in a stream.
they were to me the brightest of gilded snakes, their poison was part of their
perfection."—oscar wilde, 'de profundis'*

WHAT A LOT OF MOONLIGHT CAN DO
laughter after making love
throaty
hearty
deep
well that's the best song on the immortal hit parade
that's the tune orpheus plucked on the original lyre
that's what robert johnson sold his soul for under that dark bridge
that's what drove tchaikovsky around the portico
and that's why they built venice where they built it
hat's why all the monuments line up in paris

and london is damp with a nightstick fog
that's why rio will never stop dancing
and regret is like a waterfall.
it is that lingering sigh
that made lester young fade into a thick mist of neon tears
and turned john coltrane into a mountain
and made buddy bolden spray his brains
right out of the bell of his cornet.

to hear that expansive sigh is just
why palm trees came to hollywood
& wed the eucalyptus,
that's why a panther stalks down sunset
all the winding way to the sea,
hypnotizing startled hustlers.
that's why miss brown came to town
and I promise you
there will never be enough of that laughter
even for such a one
as artie shaw.

AVA
artie shaw claims that the only time he was thrown out of a high-class hotel
was at the regency in london, when his then wife, ava gardner, took a leak in
a standing ashtray in the lobby, pulling up her skirt and straddling it, while
waiting for the elevator…
ava gardner can piss in my ashtray any time.
she can make those long confident strides
right through my lobby,
in that silvery silk dress,
cut on the bias,
so that her thighs mold the fabric
into undulating landscapes of splendor and promise.
she can muss up my sheets and steal my towels.
she can fuck in my elevator, if she wants to,
and she can piss in my ashtray
any time.

PRIDE, Part 4

i am walking with my friend, margot, who is working as a stripper at *pandora's box,* in union square in san francisco, one of the best of the city's many strip clubs. you must admit that's a great name for a strip club. margot and i first met at an experimental theater conference in ann arbor, michigan. *the provisional* was featured along with *the living theater, iowa theater lab, performing garage*—all major forces in the theater of the 60s and 70s. margot was in the *oberlin dance collective*, and just latched onto me for a couple of days, suddenly striding in step with me as the group walked down the sidewalk—so charming, so buoyant, so naturally sexy, she slipped in with us to watch ric zank and the *iowa theater lab's* version of *moby dick*. [one of the greatest experimenbtal theatre pieces I ever saw. hugely influential for me.] and she was still there, right beside me late into the night. we fall into sex naturally, on the narrow dorm room bed, the next day margot caught her ride back to oberlin. moving on down the road. in *the coyote cycle,* she makes a cameo appearance, when coyote is reminiscing about women he has known, and he fondly mentions '*margot of ann arbor, who could have intercourse while running."* five years later, i found her again, more or less by chance, using burlesque elements in modern dance, for which interest she was booted out of the narrow-minded *oberlin dance collective*, sure, you can be naked, but you can't call attention to it, can't use it to provoke or turn on the audience.

now, it's the middle of the night and we are strolling through north beach. the night is warm and the neon seems to be exploding into the air, sparks glistening on the sidewalks. the street is damp with that mist off the bay, and mingles with the sweat off our bodies. we've been fucking for hours, her slipping in and out of the sky-blue silk corset i bought for her, at her request, with the matching blue panties. on the floor, on the persian rug, on the window ledge—and now we've thrown on some duds, her in jeans, no underwear, and a sleeveless t-shirt, with her hefty, jangly bunch of keys hooked to her belt loop. i can't recall what i'm wearing, but basically the same thing, with cowboy boots, minus the keys.. we're feeling the summer breeze, buzzing with satiation and the expectation of even more fun. we pass a male strip joint. margot pulls me inside, on a whim. unlike me, she'd never been in a place where men tore off their skimpy outfits, down to thongs and posing straps, gridding alluringly, grinding their hips. she's curious. and so we sit, in the back, right on the aisle, and have a shot of tequila and check out the muscled boys getting nekkid. it is a disappointment, to put it bluntly. desultory and disengaged. i am embarrassed for my gender. there is a rowdy table of boisterously drunken women, pushing the jubilation a bit, but dammit they were out on the town, and they wanted to see some undulating dongs. behind them are scattered men, solitary and sullen. margot excuses herself to go to the lady's room. and then i hear a voice on the blower, *"ladies and gentlemen, uh, we have a special guest tonite,...so give a big hand to..MARGOT!"* and boom, margot hits the stage, throws me the possibly lethal ring of keys across the entire room, (fuckin hurts when i catch them, but clearly worth every gouge), and the woman proceeds to work the room. she has three items of clothing, in toto, which she also tosses to me, all the way across the room. now i move down the aisle, to be in catching range. then she's down to nothing and everything. the entire room is on its feet, the bartenders cheering, the lonely men are pumping the air with their fists, the women are whooping like they won the raffle—i'm stamping my feet, too, beaming, and frankly, very turned on. then she flies from the stage, an angel of sex, seeming to float on the luminous high-wire of our adulation, merrily dancing up the aisle, with a look of, *"that's how ya do it, fellas!"*, spread all over her adorable face, her goofy grin, and she capers out the door, absolutely naked. and i, her fortunate consort, as proud as it was possible to be, hasten after her, and stand with the other lucky passersby, witnessing, as she giggles and slips back into her jeans, a goddess come to earth on the corner of powell and union.

OVERHEARD
none of you are my only life
excrescence of flimflam
mine and yours
that champagne slip
delicate strap slipping
taking the buttered biscuit
well
doesn't that put a red dress on it
spreading those silkened legs
like that

what tasty poison laces that bowl?

PARTY GIRL
all these precious party girls

amy on the floor of her mother's kitchen
as dawn softened the dark

that night on the beach, with fanny, redhair so abundant, botticelli beauty, in
the shadowed murk next to the lifeguard station, mist from the moonlit
breakers the only covering for our bodies. her mouth, her freckled skin, the
damp sand coating the blanket we fetched out in the heat of the venice
night…

and then there was that girl i met in minneapolis,
returning from a provisional tour of france,
and those abundant nights of the three of us
sprawled on tumultuous sheets in montparnasse,
once stateside, i split off from the collective consciousness
and thumbed it north from chicago, to hang a bit with my best pal, the red fox,
before the burlington 99 boxcarred me back west,
bobbing in my hammock, tramping it from the twin cities,
across the top of the nation.

i remember that first glance
from a distance
signaling our desire for each other
i remember the park
the late-afternoon light slanting through the trees,

but i have forgotten her name.

i have not forgotten her lips
her quick sad eyes
our agreement made without words.
or the circular scars on the inside
of each knee

the size of a silver dollar
feeling, when touched lightly, like the finest smoothest leather.

> *"i took sleeping pills, a lot of them, and slept for two days without
moving, it was the best nap i ever had, i slept on my side for two days without
moving, and so the place where my legs pressed together just...died. i was
trying to kill all of me, but that's the only place where it worked."*

kissing both places
licking them like a communion wafer

> *"why did you want to die?"*

> *"some stupid guy, of course."*

> *"i'm very grateful that it only worked here."* and i put my lips to each
cinnamon-purple disk, once more.
then i licked her breasts, and lightly chewed her deeppink nipples

> *"and not here"*

then i kissed her eyelids

> *"and not here..."*

i have kept, like plundered pieces of eight,
the memory of those two or three days and nights, in minneapolis/st. paul,
when we clung to each other,
kittens seeking shelter in the rain,
scared
valiant
pirates of love
in mad search for treasure
for the red X so many have sought.
i have saved and burnished what we found there
safe in a small, plush velvet pouch,
for all these years

but i don't remember her name.

(i must ask miriam, who once was susan. or david-michael, the red fox in
pinocchio, one of the first plays I ever did, and who in 1966 was just david,
but at this time in our lives [1975], lived in minneappolis and was known far
and wide as fool moon, the juggler. from these two i learned how much
names matter. and that time passes, but love doesn't.)

130

as it turns out
her name was
jill.
she married a dope dealer
and did hard time.
—*for library girl, david-michael and miriam*

MOTHER TRUCKER
semi-trucks are monk-like, as in thelonius sphere, propulsive and strangely centrifugal, but also a kind of single-cell rolling monastery. not a lot of actual action on those stale sheets, in those cramped bunks. not at all the rollicking porn-enhanced, fuckpads-on-wheels of popular legend. at least, not in my experience.

although once, hitching the highway through hippiedom, there *was* that powder-blue rig, cab chromed and waxed, '*angie* 'inscribed in fancy script, just above the wheelwell, coming to a throbbing pause, looming above me, shiny step sliding out, positioned perfectly for the lift of my right foot, lightly-packed-as-possible backpack my only ballast. door flung magically open.

"hop in, sport".

bless my soul, a lady trucker, loretta lynn-ish, dyed black hair, tanned with freckled cleavage, faint smile pretty much perpetually on her country face. single trailer, but sturdy as all hell. blasting wanda jackson. "*i gotta know.*"

"*where ya headed?*"
"*oh, anywhere the road goes.*"
"*that's a ticket to disaster.*"
"*is that in nebraska?*"
"*cute...you are awful cute, you know that, sport?*"
"*yes, ma'am..um..thank you.*"
"*yer throat dry?*"
"*kinda.*"
"*say what?*"
"*yeah...i guess so..*"
"*am i making you nervous, sweetie?*"
"*kinda...not sure...*"

"well, have a beer. i can't yet, 'cuz i'm driving, but no reason for you not to wet your whistle...right there at yer feet."

under the passenger seat is an ice chest containing a six-pack of corona. i pull out a sweating bottle and make awkward baby-bird movements, searching for a makeshift edge to pry the cap off.

"church key's in the glove".

"gotcha."

i get the damn thing open and take a swig.

"so, what exactly ain't you sure about?"

"sorry?"

"you don't have to apologize."

"yes, ma'am."

"gosh yer polite...how old are you?"

"eighteen."

"that's what i thought. I have a son who's 16."

i kind of gulp my beer.

"no shit?"

"that's right. had him when I was 14...he ain't half as polite as you.

takes after his daddy. he ain't half as cute as you neither."

silence as we barrel along.

"well, my mother can't hold a candle to you...ma'am." [although she could...]

"stop callin 'me ma'am, ya little shit, or i'll paddle yer britches...i might paddle yer britches anyway."

she gives me a sidelong glance. the wanda jackson tape has run out.

"so what kind of music do you like? that bob dylan...that psychedelic stuff?"

"yeah, i dig dylan, a lot. i like jazz, too."

"well, now. how sophisticated of you."

"yes, ma'am."

i smile at her, though.

"yer cruisin 'for a bruisin', buster."

but she smiles, too.

"my dad used to say that sometimes..."

"you got music in that backpack? play me somethin'".

i rummage around and come up with monk, *'criss-cross'*. the tape is stopped on *'rhythm-a-ning'* and starts bang in the middle of it. she clenches the wheel, slightly. when monk goes into *'don't blame me'* she says,

>*"who'didja say this was?"*
>*"thelonius monk."*
>*"thelonius?"*
>*"right. monk."*
>*"have you heard this man play, i mean, seen him, in person?"*
>*"yes, ma'am."*
>*"what's that like?"*
>*"kinda scary. but beautiful. thrilling would be the best way to describe*

it, i guess."
she signals a right turn.

>*"i wanna show you something".*

the truck begins to slow. we are just above san luis obispo. pasture and hills rolling down to the sea. she takes a turnoff and drives right down to a bluff overlooking the ocean. *'crepuscule for nellie'* slides in and emanates its special flow. we watch the sun go down, gold to red to purple, finally to the color some plums get…we slide into the back of the cab, stretch out on the surprisingly roomy bed, and she schools me in her mysteries for awhile, showing me exactly how….by midnight we are back on the road. she gets me all the way to LA, and we say goodbye, at sunset and the PCH. she gives her horn a blast as she pulls away.

"bodily passion, which has been unjustly decried, compels its victims to display every vestige that is in them of unselfishness and generosity, and so effectively that they shine resplendent in the eyes of the beholders."—marcel proust

THE FOUR AGREEMENTS:
1) *be impeccable with your word.*
2) *don't take anything personally.*
3) *don't make assumptions*
4) *always do your best*
—from the toltec

IMAGINING SUSANNA
in that cornfield
slanted like a lovely hip
at the confluence
of a road and a highway
i would wait for her.
ranged in the high grass.
she'd be with her sisters
scuffling in her shorts
and her locket
and we'd go into
that cornfield
with the dangling leaves
rustling
cornsilk
irrigated earth
thighs cool as creek water
and sneak a smoke.
— 1984

[i wrote this poem to be able to experience knowing susanna when she was just coming out of girlhood, into teenagerdom. she showed me a photo of herself from that time, and I yearned to know her back them. I figured the more I read the thing, to more and more people, the more real it would become. and it worked! at least for me. tell a story enough times to enough people, it takes on a truth. and people loved it. I called it my *'hit'*. and most importantly, she loved it.]

PAUSING TO SAY
my one love
beyond imagining
what did i know
thinking myself
able to go
all the way
alone
when there was so much you

134

in so much us
no rain is more right than this rain.
—*read at our wedding, october,1984*

CANYONLANDS
that dipping pool
natural in the shallow river, bryce canyon, just steps from our tent,
arising from it naked,
recreated,
and the way the pores of your horripilating skin became a tender geography,
tiny peaks, each cell a delectable hill rising up to my sky fingers
becoming
rough like wet raw silk
exploring with tender touch
the soft terrain

MY FAVORITE POEM
my wife is a flag
and even she has secret secrets.

JUMPED BY A LOVESONG
sometimes i long
to speak to you in the old way
in that wild calm we had
my hand resting on your hip
after the ardent storm
had past
or
that night early on
out on the midnight beach
in the caribbean
sussurating sand sparkling in the moonlight
my hand firm on your inner thigh
lifting it just right
as another wave
hits

ALOHA SUITE/ COYOTE GOES TO KAUAI/ part 4:
as a child i believed
that dragonflies could sew your lips together,
shutting you down,
if they wanted to.
my daddy told me so.
i pictured brutal stitches,
not fine precise silence,
no
thick as black twine
delivered quick on the flit.

      [it just now occurs to me, half a lifetime later; my forever-wife susanna chose as her totem, at least for a time, the darting dragonfly. was it the silver pin i gave her, with the filigreed wings, and a jewel or two, tourmaline on the torso? or did she discover the connection in a dream?...i recall her saying, one heated day in her attic office, *i'm not into dragonflies any more.*" but for awhile—i was coyote, she was the slender dragonfly, hovering there, above me, dipping swiftly down, to touch my lips...]
miniature copter,
suspended on transparent wings,
iridescent fuselage
flashadelic orange,
whirring there
mere inches from my face,
and then,
in a blink,
away.

immersed in a pool
of undulating liquid,
temperate syrup,
salted for buoyancy.
hockneyed surface dappled
with long strands of flashing lozenges
silver white, crystal blue,
and down in the deep scoop
lightning bubbles embracing themselves, skin to skin.

the whole made up of
twin tubs joined at the lips
shaped like a lazy eight,
reflection of itself,
signpost to infinity,
directed within.

my arms are spread,
a sunburned christ,
floating entirely awake,
rising and falling with
each inspiration
each exhalation
breathing deep
through parted lips.

COMING BACK TO A DREAM

i had a dream not long ago, right after i got back from the island. you and i were at a party. convivial shadowy people hung about. as they are in a dream, not frightening, not in the least. just providing a comforting atmosphere, like essential extras. drinking, laughing…silently. the location for the party has a sort of a caribbean feeling. no walls. open to the beach. i want to say it's jamaica. that place down the beach from our honeymoon room in negril. where you wrote me that check for a million kisses…i still have it…somewhere. [would that I could still cash it.] blazing sun on the white beach, but under this capacious thatched roof the light does not penetrate the pleasant murk.

ace is there. you and i are standing very still, close, together. then i am standing at a distance away, watching the two of you, talking easily. lightly, and i'm feeling a kind of swelling in my heart. you two are essentially silhouettes, but i can see shaded details, deep purple, midnight blue highlights, shifting, on your clothes, your hair. and your expressions are…nearly visible.

ace reaches out to you, tentative fingertips, approaching slow, as if not to startle you. he gently unbuttons the front of your dress. one of those drapey, beach dresses you favor, sheer, loose, subtly patterned. he takes the hem of your dress and slowly lifts it, gathering the fabric in his fingers as he moves up your body, revealing the perfect contours of your perfect ass. he lets the dress fall and puddle at your feet. he cups your breasts with the palms of both hands. he leans in and kisses you. like elvis kissed that girl in that photo, taken backstage in natchez. [the one sam used for the cover of 'fool for love.']

i am not aware of gaping, or leering, [as you referred to my gaze at you *"sometimes"*, when you undressed.] i am simply looking. aching with desire, yes. but not in anger or any judgment at all. and then i wake up. i wake up, feeling hopeless. envious, maybe, but not jealous, no, truly. something much more lost. just left out. always and forever. left out. and the loss, the mystery, has followed me for days.

i thought of the asian girl, who approached me in a bar in nyc, across the street from a play i was seeing. ' *'fool for love'* as it happens. robert and gilbert had purchased the tickets when they heard i was coming to nyc on a quick visit, knowing i couldn't afford the ticket price.
she said i *'emitted light'.*
which had been what drew her to me. i was reading a book of some substantial girth, standing at the bar. [*the underground city,* h.l. (doc) humes. old friend of bill styron's, never got his due.] first i heard her voice, quiet, as if to not startle me.
"what are you reading?"
i turn to see one of the most beautiful young women i have ever laid eyes on. almost blindingly so. and i tell her—after we have discussed poetry and paris and who reads in a crowded bar at happy hour in nyc—or anywhere else, especially such a massive tome to boot—
i offer, fairly blurting it out, but maintaining some level of cool; i guess because of the softness and acceptance in her eyes, deep and kind. i say to her,
"do you know how absolutely beautiful you are? you do realize that, right?"
i glance over to the gaggle of nattily suited young men she had just recently left. they are looking at us with some perplexity.
"it is you who is beautiful, because you are beautiful from the inside.
she has the very slightest accent. which kills me.] *you do realize that, of course?"* she says, smiling, without a tinge of false flirting.

it's around this time that i realize i am in the midst of a moment unlike any other that i can remember, certainly not a conversation in a bar, in new york city, with a strange woman, immersed in a near cacophony of chatter.
"well, why did you feel safe approaching me like that?"
"i knew you would be who you are. simple as that."

now i realize i have to move on. the show is starting. i can see people bustling into the theater.
[as i said, the show is *fool for love.* how perfect is that? this version is on broadway, with sam rockwell and nina arianda. i had been present at the first performance ever, in san francisco, with ed harris and kathy baker and sam directing. i'll never forget the boom of the slamming doors, hitting you in the chest, like a blow to the heart. and the glowing feeling of sitting around the table after the performance, in some all-night joint in san francisco, with sam and ed and all of them. the sheer luck of having a place at the table, but also the vague, sick ache of feeling fundamentally left out, really, always and everywhere.]

i start to step away from the asian girl, but the bubble around us stays firm and unbroken. so i hold my ground.
how many gifts can you be presented with, in a lifetime of such good fortune? the trick is not letting them pass without honoring them.
so i kiss her, i put my right hand on her neck, gently, and we kiss. we hold the kiss for a long moment. before we part, she puts her hand on my neck. we stay within the cone of light as long as we can sustain it. then we say goodbye. and i wend my way to the street, without a backward glance.

later when i've told the tale, or tried to, of this magic interlude, i can tell it plays as fantasy, nothing but a dream [about my shining cool]. i can hardly believe she's real myself. but the truth, the actual truth is—moments of grace just like *that* one happen pretty regularly to me. here lately, they've been increasing, in point of fact. i honestly don't know why...

HOW IT HAPPENED

(a riff on *fool for love,* with apologies to sam shepard)

i would see her in the hallways. clutching her books and binder close to her chest. moving faster than most of the other kids, like she was in a big hurry. sometimes she would stop and giggle with some dumb chick, and then move on, her face returning to her usual expression: solemn, proud, a little scared.

i'd scope her hair, blonde with a mist of red you noticed when she stepped through a blast of sunlight, and, man, i would go after that flag of her hair like she was a calf bolting from the chute. i knew it was stupid, but sometimes i'd even kind of make a lariat gesture, just for myself, a little spin by my head, and toss that rope over the heads of all the shuffling kids milling around, and that noose would settle right over her head and her shoulders, settling just below her breasts, and i'd cinch it up good. but, of course, she'd just keep moving, slipping into science class.

later, after we had kissed by her locker, after we had groped all over each other's bodies, thrashing like two trout tossed into one of those wicker baskets fishermen use to hold their catch, but long before we found out.....well, she put her hands on my shoulders, me kneeling in front of her, after sipping iridescent droplets of water off the reddish thatch crowning her pussy, both of us still dripping from a dip in the icy pond, still sweating from our ecstatic exertions, naked as jaybirds, as my dad would say, my hands cupping her ass, the skin rough with goosebumps, but smooth as silk. precious rain dripped from her hair, splashing on my upturned face like a benediction, water made holy by blending with her juices. and she dove into my eyes, with that look of gratitude and fury she always carried around, and whispered, *"never put a girl on a pedestal. it makes it too easy for her to kick you in the teeth."* and i gave her my snaggletoothed grin, her hair a halo, and said, simply, *"when it comes to you, baby, i'm just a fool for your love."*

but like i said, i took to following her. got so i was always late to my own classes. i was like a ranch dog, busy getting the prize filly fully into the corral. even though i kept a certain distance, it was a matter of time before she came to notice me, and one day she just turned around, and walked back to me where i had stalled out, holding my breath. she thrust her books and stuff into my hands and said, *"might as well make yourself useful."*

and from then on, i'd be there, waiting when she came out of every class, and i'd escort her through the hustling mob, right up to the door of her next location, and transfer her belongings back into her custody. even gym class. a couple of times i made like i was going to stroll right into the locker room, and she'd give me a little slap on my chest, and push me back. and her friends would giggle, and one of them would say, *"well, you gotta give him points for persistence."*

the first time our lips touched, just a week or so after we first spoke, was by her locker, way back in a dark corner of the maze of metal cabinets. it was after last period, around dusk. she dawdled with her friends, sensing my impatience, knowing i had made up my mind to make my move. i don't know how she knew, but she did. she always seemed to be able to see the truth of me, inside, in my heart or soul or whatever you want to call it.

anyway, i had seen this picture of elvis, kissing a girl in a dress with thin straps, baring her shoulders, not a girl, a woman, with clip-on earrings, (found out later it was backstage in biloxi or somewhere, before a show. she was a fan who managed to get back stage. elvis is looking slick in a dark jacket, white shirt, white tie. but what got me was—he had her backed up against a metal railing, she's got her right hand on the pipe, kind of bracing herself. he has his hands on her waist, gently but firmly, and they're kissing, but really they're just touching the tips of their tongues—delicately, like butterflies.

so that's what i did. i held her like that, my hands firmly, carefully, on her narrow waist, and i pressed against her, pushing my hips against hers. but i didn't rush. i moved in slow and smiled. and she smiled. and i slid my tongue out between my lips, still smiling, and she took the hint, and peeked the end of her tongue out. then i moved in closer—and it was like a spark jumped between us—our tongues were twisting and turning around each other—you ever seen snakes fuck? like that—and then we were swirling and falling and soaring all at once. and we were grinding our molten bodies against each other and i took both of her hands in mine, entwining our fingers, and raised our arms above our heads, forming two X's, melded, conjoined, on fire.

from then on, we were pretty much…doomed. blissfully doomed. if i got ten feet from her i'd get such a hard-on,so quick, i'd almost pass out from the rush of blood to my dick. and when i came, i'd come like a river. and she—well, she'd climb on top of me and ride me like a bronco buster, grab my hair with her left hand, like it was reins, wound around her fingers, lashed in her grip, spurring me on to a gallop. with her right hand she'd stick four fingers in my mouth and her thumb under my chin and use my skull like the pommel of a saddle, pounding it into the mattress, or floor, or dirt, bucking her hips and butt at about a million miles a minute.

we got so crazy we'd cut class and climb into the back seat of some random car in the school parking lot and just go at each other like there was no tomorrow.

then came the night when i followed my dad. i don't remember any more why i did that, that particular night. i guess i just had to. but it had nothing to do with her. she was from a different planet, as far as i knew. a place where everything was right, where i was kind of a king, as long as she was queen. (just the other day i heard a song on the radio, one of those hiphop deals, with the line: *i could feel your energy from two planets away".* yeah, that was the way it was.) and besides, we really didn't talk that much. we already knew all the answers to the questions we cared about.

but my dad and me—we were always at war. and he would get all liquored up, and come at my mom, and i would step in, and the battle was on. one night he broke every window in the place. methodically. and then he upended the fridge to block the door, so i went out the shattered window of my room, cutting my hand on the jagged shards. one time he threw a lamp at the television set, which didn't work anyway and was only a black-and-white set to boot. something was tearing him up, something more than just us, more than just the rocks and garbage and sheer helplessness of being poor and trapped.

there was the time, before all this, when he challenged me to a foot race. i was maybe sixteen, not that long before i met her, i guess. my dad and me used to race all the time, just for fun, to blow off steam, and he always beat me.   something was bugging him that day, though. he wasn't drunk yet—just a little buzzed. and he came up to me grinning, loose and friendly. *"you think you can beat me now, boy? those legs long enough yet? what's say we race to that oak tree?"*

I was mad that day, too. he was pissing me off fairly regular. so we both ran it to win. and i was way ahead for most of the dash. both of us in boots and jeans, shirtless, (although he wore one of those 'wife-beaters', like clark gable in 'it happened one night'). about thirty feet from the finish line i heard him huffing and puffing, coming up behind me, making this high-pitched moan and hissing like one of those old steam engines. then with an agonized, ragged roar, he passed me, his limbs pinwheeling like a cartoon. i reached down inside for a burst of speed and came up short. he beat me, leaving me gasping, bent over, completely depleted, and i looked over at him, kind of proud of him, actually. then i saw his face, scarlet and pale at the same time. he was puking his guts up, hawking long strings of brownish phlegm and greenish bile, stinking of tobacco and rancid whiskey. fear, hate, and disgust with himself, glistening in his eyes. from then on, we were pretty much lost to each other. he would rarely even glance my way. and he mostly stayed stewed all the time.

so one night, months after i'd met her, he got all cleaned up, like he did sometimes. even combed his hair, splashed himself with cologne, never looking in my mom's direction. and she just ignored him as he strolled out into the sultry night, whistling.

i followed him, all the way to the other side of town, keeping my distance, but never losing sight of him. shit, i could've followed him just from the fumes of old spice coming off of him. he stopped to get a bottle of cheap whiskey, while i lurked in the alley next to the liquor store, norteno` music blaring from the bar across the street.

eventually he came to a small house, way past needing a new paint job. he strode right up to the front door, wide open, but with the screen door closed. he tapped lightly, standing there like a returning war hero. two women came to the door, one hanging back while the other one, my mom's age, with radiant auburn hair, clad in a simple summer dress, showing some cleavage, threw her arms around my dad, and gave him a righteous kiss. then she mussed up his careful comb job. they both laughed, and then turned to the other woman, who was standing back and holding the screen door open. she moved into my dad's arms, too, and he gave her a kiss on the top of her head. as she stepped into the porchlight i could see her clearly, the shine of her hair, blonde with a mist of red.

may. the other woman was a girl, and the girl was may. and i knew right away. i knew for certain sure, and my cock got as hard as it had ever been. ever. and then it was like i was hypnotized, or under a black magic spell, some juju. i stumbled toward the sad little house, out of the shadows across the street, and into the dusty, bereft yard, into the yellow light from the porch, and i said her name and they all turned to look at me. each of them had such different expressions: the woman with auburn hair looked puzzled, perplexed, but not unwelcoming; my dad was more furious than i had ever seen him, murderous, betrayed; and there was may, looking like she had always known, and now i did, and hating me, and loving me, and sad as hell, and wanting me so much she could barely keep herself from leaping off the porch and straddling me right there on the dead grass, right in front of them, showing the whole world.

so i ran. and i kept running all the way across the bedraggled town, to the outskirts, where our own woeful house still stood, emitting the blue light of the replacement tv, where my mom sat watching some western, all alone. i slipped in through my bedroom window, silently, grabbed some stuff—t-shirts, socks, a few books—and i lit out. and i never went back to that house, or that town, except when i was searching for may, and she fled soon after that night herself, although sometimes she'd drift back home. i just stayed on the circuit, shacked up in cheap motels, except for that interlude when the countess kept me up in her penthouse, in new york city, and fucked me for a solid month—otherwise i stayed on the ramble. and i'd track may down, when i could. we'd be right back to that moment, pressed against that locker, right as rain. no, i never got shot of may, and i never will. i don't care about the right or the wrong or the sideways. i don't exist without her. without her i don't want to exist. she is my everything. and that's exactly how it happened.
--*for carl*

MEETING MARY COOL/ TEQUILA FOR BREAKFAST
[written in the notebook she left behind]
everytime i think
that i'm the only one who's lonely
someone calls on me...
and then along comes mary
she was downstairs at the gate
a ram's skull tattooed
on her décolletage
spiralling horns
tracing her scapula
like ancient wings
some species of radiant smile on her face
recent tears in her eyes

i say
i have a buffalo skull upstairs.
wanna see it?
i know.
what a ridiculous line.
especially coming from some sleazy older guy
to a lost young lady.
i might as well have mentioned my etchings…
but now her beguiling smile spreads
with a broader question
around the eyes
sure…but..uh…um….i should take these…
indicating the bags and a bedraggled piñata
you don't really have anything you **must** *do right now.*
i have no idea how i knew that
something about her bravery
and the way she tilted her head as she looked at me…

that's true, she says
after a beat
an intake
and she giggles as i lead her up the stairs
lugging her soft bags, which i help her with,
long
flimsy
flowered
summer dress
and boots
as we enter my place
and the white of the buffalo on my wall
and the bright light of los angeles
all over the books
she does a step or two
a skip of uplift
laughing because of and beyond
her self
but the anxiety lingers

so i offer
*you made a joke about renting my couch, when you first came in. but the
thing is, you really can. i don't mean rent it. you can use it. so take that off the
list of your worries. you have a safe place to stay tonight. okay? you can have
your own room, see, the doors slide shut. you'll be safe. so, that problem is
solved for now.*

when do i start thinking…?
no it's not thinking
its something else than thinking
something the body just does
the ego does?
the dick does?
her breasts do,
when she pulls open her dress and offers them?
her mournful eyes do?
our lips do?

but that is much much further on
hours and hours pass
before we even exchange names
no need, really,
is that trust?
is that need?
and,
for what,
exactly?

she plucks my given name out of an anecdote
about how my life was saved
elinor, i want to live alone
darrell, i'm pregnant
and there you have it
fatherhood.

bestowal of her cool surname comes later
after many clever giggling evasions on her part;

i tell her; on my way out the door to do a favor,
you know, you are beautiful, smart and cool.
downstairs, after helping him out, i plot with mark to pry it out of her
this woman has been here all afternoon, and i still don't know her name
just put your hand out and introduce yourself
and he does, he puts out his hand, *i'm mark'*
but she simply answers, with that wide grin,
i'm cool.
and it sticks.
but still
her first name eludes me

entwined snakes are tattooed
on her right thigh

now sadness pools
her eyes glisten
she stares into the impossible hurt
under her breath
i was just being honest…trying to be myself
i say, *that's all we can do*
she murmurs, *i told her i didn't trust her and she told me, take your*
daughter…but…
hunching her skittish shoulders
gasping helpless with the fear of being
terrifyingly misunderstood
left hopelessly out.
i ask specific questions,
making her talk about the details
and then the cloud passes

her honeyed laugh
bursts out
i make her laugh
hours and hours before
we make love

we sprawl on the couch
all over each other
playful animals of different breeds
chimp and lynx
rabbit and wolf
at ease
amused with our differences
mesmerized by what we share
i ask without asking
so, looking at me straight in the eyes
from mere inches
she says
i know you want to
so i kiss her.

i want the laughing and the fucking
to help her
i do
i mean it all to
assist her in taking the next breath,
help her face all of what
she turns away from,
let her sing that cole porter song she loves
      love me or leave me
      you can take this heart
      heal it or break it all apart
or
      how deep is the ocean
      how can i tell you
      what's in my heart?
      how can i measure
      each and every part?

or pink floyd *us and them*
      black (black, black, black)
        and blue (blue, blue)
        and who knows which is which and who is who

148

up (up, up, up, up)
and down (down, down, down, down)
and in the end it's only round 'n round (round, round, round)
   haven't you heard
   it's a battle of words
she knows **all** the words
it's very impressive
in one so young
   that's why
   the lady is a tramp
   i love the free fresh wind in my hair
   life without care
   i'm broke, it's ok

human skull impaled on a sword tattooed on her left thigh

yes i want to be inside her
sure
to be up to it for one thing
and once i see her whole body
naked
stretched out on my bed
floating on light
having brought her there in a lunge
spreading her legs wide
i dive
in

i learn her first name when she murmurs it in my ear
over and over
mary mary mary
so i call her mary cool

in the morning, she can't find the coffee, so she has tequila for breakfast. just
a shot. she asks first, standing by the tall table. *do you mind?*, she says,
lifting the bottle. staring into the cold metal sky of a new day. then she's
standing next to my bed while i stubbornly slumber. once again she is lost in

the great distant plain of her sorrow…and…desperate dislocation. her heart drifts in the breeze, a silver balloon losing air. i force my eyes open. i reach over and hold the hem of the same dress. *i have to move my things,* she says, flat voice, trying to get used to her losses…*will you be back?* i manage. *i don't know….*and i hear her boots scuff down the hall, i hear her flip the lock, swing open the door and close it with a ringing of coyote's bells. i dream of snakes and skulls and…

the second time she comes over, bringing her frazzled mom, all trailer park bitterness, but somehow plucky and upfront, we played a ribald madlibs-in-a-box game, which they brought with them, for some reason. it was a blast for all, but i won, and then they left. in a few minutes mary called to ask, *what are you doing?* i tell her to return. she does and stays to watch *to have and have not.* she loves bogart and bacall.
she brought along her sextoys that vibrate and make her throw her head back in crazy wet jubilance. out of simple gratitude? desire to go deeper? in the morning, before she leaves, she crawls back into my bed and spoons with me for a brief endless flight. she kisses me a million times, forcefully, with affection, on my neck, my shoulders, the back of my skull; and then she slips away.

in a text some days later, after saying some things to her she didn't want to hear; about sharing her little kids with their dad:
don't talk to me again. why is my name in everyone's phone 'cool'? why do you want to help me? why did you have sex with me even though i was so clearly distraught? i don't want to hurt anyone but i hurt myself and it sucks that has to hurt other people. then that makes me want to be completely alone. but It's too late for that…..i don't feel that you did anything wrong I'm just very confused by which peoples advice, peoples place in my life…
i know exactly how she feels.
and then a few days after that:
you didn't hurt me. i was already hurt. you made me feel better. about myself but i don't know if i should….i want everything and i hate that people want to be cheap and bullshit all the time.

by the third tryst

we are past all the formalities
we do wait for the soup to be sipped
some sewing to be done
some philosophizing
her brunette hair picking up highlights
from another stunning sunset
ordered up special
she gets impatient for me to make my move
so i throw down the yes
for the future

i ask by text
after listing the moments i cannot escape in my mind
driving around overcome by desire
what's one of yours?
well when you devoured me of course
when you presented yourself to me
i resisted resisting
it was too hard
literally
and I'm throbbing while driving
all over again

fourth time around
her sad eyes drive me wild;
in the late heat of the day;
mary cool splays her legs
      i've got a sweet angel/ i love the way she spread her wings
like a gymnast or a pole dancer
leaning back
in the corner of my kitchen counter
displaying herself full pure slut;
next time, and there will definitely be a next time, i'll move the toaster oven,
the spatula and stuff in the silver ice bucket, the coyote cookie jar, the brown
ceramic mezcal jug, the black plastic dish drainer, so she can brace her foot
against the aluminum sink to assist her in keeping herself so so so open so
wide, yes, like that, oh fuck…

i fall to my knees before her
in supplication and avarice and mouth and tongue and fingers and nose and
slickened chin.
unable to wait another moment
i rise up,
slide my hands beneath her knees,
and lift her onto myself
swinging her around,
impaled,
onto the kitchen table;
jars and plates and various swans,
spent negra modelos,
sections of the crumpled *times*,
various crayons, limes
and ripe dragon fruit
her wanton hair just missing the mild green salsa
all of it clattering in syncopation,
onto the marvelously cluttered floor.

as the horizon seen from my window
becomes burnished gold
as the clouds turn dark periwinkle,
i turn her over to fate.
i drop her off to whatever
i can help her with
as if i am up to it.

ALL THE DOOMED BLONDES: Part Four

veronica lake began her movie career in a hit film called *i wanted wings*,
which proved prophetic. in her forties she became a licensed aviatrix, and
frequently went flying, to find serenity, solace, and eventually to escape from
what had become a chaotic life. (in one of her most iconic films, *i married a
witch,* she flies on a broomstick—at least in publicity shots.) it was also while
filming *i wanted wings* that she found her famous hairstyle—long, straight,
silken, blonde hair covering half her face, a come-hither look that made her a
star. as she described it: *"i was playing a sympathetic drunk,* [another
foreshadowing] *i had my arms on a table…it slipped…and my hair—it was*

152

always baby fine and had this natural break—fell over my face...it became my trademark and purely by accident." when she tried to drop the look a few years later, her popularity faded. (in fact, the war office asked her to change her hairstyle to encourage women working in the factories to adopt more practical, safer hairdos. turns out there were a lot of accidents involving women getting their hair caught in machinery. veronica complied—but it damaged her career.) of course, a string of stinkers also contributed to her plummet from the stratosphere. not that she had any choice in the matter of material. she did whatever project the studio put her in. after the success of *i wanted wings*, it was announced that she would be starring in *blonde venus*—but that direct reference to our subject matter, was never filmed. instead she was cast in *sullivan's travels*, written and directed by preston sturges. the script is full of actual *wise*cracks, delivered at the speed of fun, and directed to a fare-thee-well, with a host of legendary character actors, and an exuberant energy. it has become a classic of populist comedy, in the capra vein, (with a definite sturges twist), not least because of the combination of mccrea's cornfed huskiness and lake's slinky, wry, soulful, little girl lost. dressed as a fragile boy-tramp, going undercover to find out what it's really like to be poor in america, clinging to the sleeve of the hulking mccrea, she is sincere and sexy. for her next film, to capitalize on the chemistry, she was to be reunited with mccrea, in rene clair's *i married a witch,* in which a beguiling wisp of a woman magically materializes, out of the historical mist, to enchant a handsome mortal. but joel mccrea declined the part, saying, *'life's two short for two movies with veronica lake."* fredric march was game for the honor of marrying this luscious witch, ethereal, ever evanescent, and yet so so carnal. this time it was veronica who was not so wild about her co-star. *"he treated me like dirt under his talented feet. of all actors to end up under the covers with. that happened in one scene and mr. march is lucky he didn't get a knee in his groin."* the director of the film, the sophisticated rene clair, said of her, *"she was a very gifted girl, but she didn't believe she was gifted."*

the path that brought constance frances marie ockleman, born in 1922 in brooklyn, to the valhalla of hollywood, has some familiar signposts—her father, german/irish dockworker, died in an explosion on an oil ship, when connie was twelve. a year later her domineering mother, also named constance, remarried, and the girl took her step-father's name, becoming connie keane. in 1936 the family moved to miami. although connie did well in school, graduating in 1938, possessing a natural beauty and easy charm, and a marked talent for acting, she was also diagnosed as a paranoid schizophrenic. [at least that's what her mother said in a scurrilous biography of lake, *peekaboo,* claiming veronica's mental illness caused her *"alcoholism, numerous infidelities, mood swings and vindictiveness".* apparently, the mother knew from vindictive. in the late 40s she sued her daughter for non-support.] her parent's solution to her mental problems was to move to beverly hills and enroll their winsome daughter at the *'bliss hayden school of acting'*, in hollywood. they saw acting as an apt treatment for her condition. her mother, particularly, thought it was a wonderful idea. and connie did what her mother told her to do...and who's to say? the lovely young girl, billed as constance keane, did well as a starlet, almost immediately snagging a series of bit parts. then in 1941 she got the wings she wanted, changed her name—and soared for a time, as **veronica lake.** but even at her apex, she was...wary and disgruntled. *"you could put all the talent i had into your left eye and still not suffer from impaired vision."* or this: *"there's no doubt i was a bit of a misfit in the hollywood of the forties. the race for glamor left me far behind. i didn't really want to keep up. i wanted my stardom without the usual trimmings. because of this, i was branded a rebel at the very least. but i don't regret that for a minute. my appetite was my own and i simply wouldn't have it another way."* and to put it most succinctly: *"i wasn't a sex symbol, i was a sex zombie."* but she was also very, very good. in *hold that blonde,* she holds her own with a veteran comic, the frantic eddie bracken, and said, *"it's a comedy, rather like what **carole lombard** used to do...[for me] it represents a real change of pace."* she was highly praised for her compassionate performance as a suicidal nurse in *so proudly we hail!.* and opposite the taciturn alan ladd in several hardboiled noir films, especially *this gun for hire, the blue dahlia* and *the glass key,* she is simply extraordinary. she embodies, in these seemingly effortless performances, the eternal femme fatale, our flickering lady of the shadows. and, indeed, there were plenty of shadows in her own life. the premature birth of her first son, anthony, in the sixth month of her pregnancy, was brought on when she tripped on a cable on the set of *so proudly we hail!* the baby died a week later, and her marriage to the baby's father, john dettie, did not survive the year. in 1944 she married the director andre de toth, with whom she had two more children. [it was just days before the birth of their daughter, diana, in 1948, that the suit for support was filed by mother constance.] she and de toth made a couple of films together, one a successful western, *ramrod*, but by 1951 the two had to file for bankruptcy, and the IRS seized their home for unpaid taxes. on the brink of a nervous breakdown, **veronica lake** took to the skies—she flew herself solo all the way across the country to new york city. as for hollywood: *"they said, 'she'll be back in a couple of months'…well, i never returned. enough was enough already. did i want to be one of the walking dead or a real person?"*

      as it turned out, for much of the next decade, **veronica lake** drifted from cheap hotels to cheaper hotels. she was arrested several times for public drunkenness and disorderly conduct. in1962 the *new york post* reported that she was living in the all-women's *martha washington hotel* in manhattan, working as a waitress/bartender downstairs in the cocktail lounge. and her name was now connie de toth. she told the reporter that she took the job because, *"i like people. i like to talk to them."* when **marlon brando** read the story, he told his accountant to send her a check for a thousand dollars. seems they had been lovers. as she described the affair in her autobiography: *"our romance was short but sweet. he was at the dawn of a brilliant career, and i was in the twilight of one. of course, my career could never compare with his."* out of pride, she never cashed the check. she kept it framed in the living room of her last home, in miami. she showed it off to visitors and friends. in fact, her autobiography, published in 1969, brought her back into the public eye, with appearances and signings and tours. the book described her guilt and regret for neglecting her children, her erstwhile career, as well as love affairs with howard hughes, aristotle onassis, and, of course, brando. she went to england to promote the book and was asked to appear in a play called *madame chairman.* she jumped at the chance, and followed it up with an acclaimed performance as blanche dubois in tennessee williams '*streetcar named desire.* [blanche is a prototypical doomed blonde, of course.]

"i was never psychologically meant to be a picture star. i never took it seriously.i couldn't live 'being a 'movie star'and i couldn't 'camp 'it up, and i hated being something i wasn't….hollywood gives a young girl the aura of one giant, self-contained orgy farm, its inhabitants dedicated to crawling into every pair of pants they can find."

"even though you ate your own heart long ago to survive,
you have known a little pain, coyote,
and you want more."
—shelley m. miller, 'coyote 'excerpt

HYDROGEN
OXYGEN
CARBON
NITROGEN
from these four, come all of us.

5. **OBSERVER**: THERE IS AN AMPLE SUPPLY OF ALL THE KNOWLEDGE AND ENERGY EVERYONE NEEDS.

     or the world demands too much from people and/or gives them too little, potentially leaving them depleted.

**"*coyote:* **okay. i realized that i didn't have to be me, because i could just as easily be somebody else. i could be almost anybody. i could even be you."— 'the coyote cycle'*

"the air itself sees together with us."—cicero

"it is a joy to be hidden but disaster to not be found."—charles winnicott

SCOPOPHOBIA: fear of seeing and being seen.

NOTES on NATALIE WOOD, GODDESS OF SADNESS
i'm on the set of *brainstorm*, early in the day, about 9AM. people are bustling around in a far corner of the soundstage, lighting and pounding and getting ready. but here, behind a maze of flats and doorways to nowhere, she sits, in a tall director's chair, a glass of white wine in her right hand. in her left hand she holds a hand mirror. in front of her, stands one of those rolling vanities, consisting of a large mirror, surrounded by light bulbs, attached to a cabinet, a set of drawers. she is looking intently at her reflection. she is breathtakingly beautiful, with her pale skin and thoughtful, pained eyes, petite and casually sensual. it's just she and i, although i am standing at a slight remove, not lurking exactly, but i have found myself drawn to her vicinity all through the shoot, and she has noticed, used to it, as if people had stared at her all of her life, which, of course, they had. but sometimes she nodded to me, occasionally passing close and smiling at me, to let me know she was comfortable with my presence in her zone. once she even touched my arm

as she moved past me, leaving the set after a rehearsal, wearing a white, very plush, terrycloth robe.

now i stand in the shadows, thinking what a lucky sonofabitch i am to be standing in any proximity at all to natalie wood, my ultimate pubescent wetdream. but she was more than that to me—she was the embodiment, the personification of an inchoate desire that i could not as yet name. there was a look in her eyes, not quite despair, a plucky melancholy, and a little twist to her mouth, a skepticism, a hurt, which made me ache.

as i watch her, she suddenly, and quite violently, throws the hand mirror into the larger mirror, dismantling her image, making a sound like a gunshot, and a cacophony of shattering glass, large heavy shards hitting the floor at her feet. through the chaos, she does not move a muscle. she takes a sip of wine.

very quickly we are surrounded by startled people, all of them voicing concern, questions, cautions. still she does not move or speak. then, pushing through the muttering group, comes chris walken, (known familiarly as 'ronnie', it was his birthday a few days earlier) her co-star in the picture (*brainstorm*). he and natalie have a special bond, not just the white wine which they both sip all day, but also something deeper, perhaps due to the fact that they were both child actors, an exclusive club, comprised of many wounded adults—if, that is, they even survived into maturity. but chris obviously cares for natalie, and they have established a kind of bell jar in the last month or so in which they feel safe and faintly romantic. now, he encircles her with his arms, giving her a small kiss on her head, easing her gently from the chair, murmuring softly in her ear, '*watch the glass, baby.*' he leads her through the crew, who step out of the way, the makeup woman says, '*it's okay, sweetie...i'm right behind you.*" and the three of them leave the soundstage.

two weeks later, or maybe less, natalie wood drowned in catalina bay, stumbling, a bit tipsy, from the yacht belonging to her husband, robert wagner, who was in deep discussion—politics? business? fidelity? her?— with chris walken. neither one of them noticed the splash as she slipped into the chilly water, as she slipped through all our fingers, natalie wood, our goddess of sadness.

158

CLUTCH HAND

sometime in the week of september 18, 2009. fort tryon park, nyc:
as the squabbling pair drew nearer to me, where i sat on a park bench; beneath the bluff on which stood the cloisters, in the area i call my living room; i noticed something beyond the obvious hostility they felt for each other. the old man in the wheelchair was even more the ancient baby bird he seemed in the far distance; in a black-and-white herringbone sport coat that looked at least two sizes too large for him. the caregiver, a late middle-aged black man, wearing a scarf on a warm day, had a malformed left hand. it looked as if all the fingers, even the thumb, had melded together, with the index finger the sole survivor, writhing from the nub. with this hook he conducted his argument, waving the mangled appendage up and down, rapidly and with insistent regularity, as if conducting a recalcitrant, rhythmless orchestra. he stopped the rolling chair and spoke directly to me.

"he keep sayin we lost." then he leaned over to address the old man, *"WE AIN'T LOST?"*

the old man looked imploringly at me. *"i don't know where we are."*
"that don't mean we lost, fool. we in the park. we come here every day."

and they moved on, the paid companion repeatedly poking his gnarled hand into the older man's face, to make an unmakeable point.

i turned the page on *this week;* a news sheet culled from various liberal sources, from around the world. in the book section there was a review of a new history of the early days of the mafia in america, beginning in the early 1900s. the article was illustrated by photos of blood on the sidewalks and hard men with harder eyes, and featured a daguerreotype of giuseppe morello, the first 'boss of bosses'; known as 'the clutch hand', he was afflicted with the exact same deformity as that attendant who had just passed me; locked in endless squabbles with his bewildered charge. a compression of the hand, causing constant pain, bones and ligaments gnarled all the way to the heart, shackling the maddened mind to revenge and resentment. both of these poor souls, in different centuries, doomed from the get-go to predation. and somehow, at this particular moment, they both passed through my bleary field of attention; as i sat there, spaced-out after a frantic weekend, on my favorite park bench, in some kind of synchronous…what? and how do i figure into it at all? as observer of the conjoinment; because i was presented with this coincidence? one which only exists in my jaundiced gaze? i had been given…what exactly? another rhyme of history? once more, the *nexus rerum*?

SPORTS
meaningless action assigned value
by entranced non-competitors
subsequently taken as much more than real
more value as a pastime then simply passing the
abandoned service station
dead center of the
desiccated prairie
and we are windblown
dustwracked
gritblasted
we
in our sputtering pickup
so low on fuel
parched of all liquid
blood boiling

SUBWAY THRENODY
      mucal hocking from a woman wrapped in rags
      back of the throat brutal gargle or shred or
      willful rending of muscles & ripping of membranes
      so loud she leans out into the rushing air
      to accomplish it.
      she in her black coat and knit cap
      growling up her viscous spit
      clearing her clogged throat with the devil's vacuum cleaner
spectacular raptor
hawking her wares
making lazy circles
in the heat.
      she scurries through the chrome grove
      rumbling her backpacks
      angry at all the obstructions
      consuming all her energy
      like scalding rain.
my hide of concern

worn like bloodied pelt
vestige of carcass
ravaged skull intact
or lolling maybe
on my impeccable head
my crippled cavort in anxious firelight
re
re
re
enacting
hunted down
i lay trembling
lay awaiting
thrust to my obsequious knees
terrible arrows
occur like clockwork
want them or not.
even with my stiff leather armor
i am pierced and painted
irregular like rain
cold spears
chafed elbows
swallowing blind

comes another derelict
so toothless so shoeless so face like a clenched fist
bodybent in ragged rags
bleating and keening
highly birdlike
with the voice of a drunken infant
sweet and quavery
as if begging for a bit of worm
        that's the time...that's the time...that's the time..that i love the best
he makes his way,
shuddering south
feeling the subway sway,
spasmodically north

with third leg of aluminum
young man comes
preachrapping his pleas
abjectly proud
proudly abject
i pity his soft sneakers stomping
so two illicit quarters
flip from my pocket
somersaulting into his pale wounded palm
a private showing
under the bridge
of all my masterpieces .

the story comes down to the store
to buy some unnamed nothing
sleep hard
for the buckets are filling up with rain.
    "you see,"
    the smudged woman says,
glancing my way,
    "i cried like an animal...i'm sure that phrase sounds beautiful in french."

BODY SURFING/ THE SUMMER WE WENT BLONDE
he perceives the seas sinews so
    he gives the perfect bend to his arm
        permitting the embrace of wave after wave

achieving with each ecstatic ride
    a poem of surrender and skill
        signaled like an urgent hermes willing
            to plummet poised in the froth of the ocean's nape
                one limb hidden close to the body
                    one hand pointing to the snared nick in physical law
                        pulling him hurtling through wet space and just in time
                          stroking both arms like a hawk leaving a high branch
                      to remain on the roaring crest
                        where balance becomes release

162

even then he disappears into the turbulent mortal clutter
        the foamy breakage of pebbles and sand
                and returns to us shining.
—for peter sacks

"read it at my funeral..."—peter sacks, in a letter

VINEYARD RAIN
i protected your book from the rainfall
holding it under the seat of the folding chair
while the fine drops fell on me
i broke
from the revelation in the poems
sun broke
from behind the clouds
my son
came striding into view
round the corner of the little house
saying in a voice so startlingly deep
"drizzle drizzle"
how does this love work
going deep into the ~~ground~~ like a tree into green ground
in no visible way   earth
in natural time
growing in the harvested meaning
in every word
reaped from repeated
and repeated
and repeated
rereadings
—for peter sacks

THAT FEEL/ INWOOD, NYC, 2011
i'm strolling to the market, to pick up a six-pack of dogfish raison d'etre ale,
currently my favorite beer; maybe some new flavor of ice cream. getting
bored with rum raisin.

larry comes running up the middle of the street, flat-out escape in flipflops, grasping at his black shorts like he hastily tossed those bitches on and hit it. clutching a teeshirt and cellphone, trying to punch in the number on the run. barreling past me and the domino players on the corner. fucking hottest day in the hottest summer after the hellishly hottest spring in recorded history. we're talking 1875 (no shit!) and motherfuckers are still saying it's FINE and here comes the crew chief of the cagey but open, almost friendly, pot dealers on the corner, a true leader, smart and intuitive and attentive and deep. larry running for his life, eyes ablaze. all heads turn and watch him bolt across nagle avenue. i blurt out *"do you need help?"* he doesn't have time to respond, and i keep moving down the block toward the market.

now larry is out in the four-lane street trying to flag down a gypsy cab, hundreds of which, like battle-scarred sharks, roam the neighborhood. he is gasping in the humidity, pouring sweat, and feeling exposed, he retreats to the far corner, standing slightly hunched behind a parked SUV, holding his phone to his ear. i decide to cross the street. but i don't want to blow his cover, if what he's doing now is hiding. i can't tell if he's still being pursued, or how to defend him if it comes to that. nor do i want to intrude. i'm one of the few, if not the only, 'americano' out of hundreds of people on the street, at this moment, and i sometimes feel like an interloper, or guest, in the neighborhood, unfamiliar with the intricacies of the culture. in this case, i just don't want to leave this guy without backup. we have a mutual respect for each other, developed over the last year of street corner negotiations and philosophical conversations. this kid is smart, entrepreneurial and a natural leader. he knows I see that.

i walk past him as he bends over, panting behind the vehicle. i say loud enough for him to hear, but without really looking at him, as if i'm going somewhere else, *"if i can help in any way, do not hesitate to ask."* i stop then, as if reconsidering my destination and cross back toward the market on the other side of the street. as i pass, he looks at me kind of blankly and then vomits into the gutter, copiously, pale green, torrents of it. i keep moving across the avenue. two guys i think are allied with him pass me. one of them mutters, out of the side of his mouth, *"does he need help?"* i nod and proceed to go get groceries.

164

when i come out larry is gone. i round the corner of my block, sickles street, and see blinking red lights down at the end of the street. turns out to be a FDNY ambulance. lots of people milling around, but no larry.   then I see li'l mike doing his pimp stroll, on the other side of the street, his face swollen and bruised. a kind of whimper escapes my throat. i keep moving to the mom-and-pop bodega on the corner. i forgot tomatoes at the bigger market, and they might have fresh bread pudding, a staple of my diet. they save a piece for me every day, in case they run low, before i can make it in.

next morning i'm glancing around for information. i head for my preferred sunday brunch spot, the parkside diner. i buy the sunday nytimes, at the yemenite bodega near the park. a whole group of families from yemen seem to have incorporated and bought a lot of the small markets in the neighborhood. this branch of the clan have built-out this particular place with care and pride, and they are maintaining it nicely. they usually save me a copy of the paper. armed with reading material, I proceed to the bustling diner, and my usual brunch of french toast with bananas, and a big double espresso. in fact, they start the espresso as soon as they see me come in the door.
'

but I'm worried about larry and mike. i don't know how to find out what actually happened. not even sure how to broach the subject with anyone. i don't really *know* anyone in the neighborhood, and no one knows me. basically, my existence is completely solitary. i have very cordial conversations, sometimes even deep ones, but basically they remain polite and distanced. i don't speak spanish, and i sure as shit don't understand *dominican* spanish, which seems to be ten times faster than any other version i have ever heard. they love the rhythm, and they like their music LOUD. i just swim in it. i find it restful not to understand most of what i hear.

li'l mike is obviously in trouble, though. the last few times we have had dealings he has been curt and distracted. but a month or so ago he approached me, after hearing about a favor i had done someone else I knew from the street, and gave me a slap and pound, his face all lit up. the kid has a teardrop tattoo under his left eye, but he's slight, sometimes frail, and he has that tail-wagging thing runts have. he's funny, even when i don't get his jokes, i see his buddies breaking up delightedly. but last time i tried to score something, he left me hanging at my door. everybody's got different procedures, and his is to bring it to you, while you wait on your stoop. finally, that particular night, i gave up and went upstairs. later he admitted he forgot all about me.

i take an amble through the sunlit park on the way home from breakfast. still worrying, and wondering how i can find out what went down. i'm coming up to my corner, and there's larry on the opposite corner, looking fine, his boyz with him in the sun. he sees me and beams. i gesture a general inquiry as to status and he indicates all good. i do a discreet thumbs up and round my corner. but he indicates *'hold up'*, starts to cross to me, doing that forearm pull-in gesture. so i stop and step into the street, saying, "*i didn't know what to do, i just wanted to make the offer…*"
"*i know, man. it meant a lot to me.*" and we hug in the middle of the street we take a step back to the curb and he speaks more quietly. "*what happened was…this kid, mike…he is so fucked up…he's like trying to rob people…he tried to rob ME…*"
"*but he's a good kid…he's just been fucked up lately….spaced out…*"
"*i know i know, he gets to doing the drugs, the coke…*"
"*i saw he got popped in the eye…but he's not a bad kid…he's got a good heart.*"
"*i know…i know,*" he nods, pursing his lips, considering.
"*man, any way i can help…,*" and i walk away, provisionally relieved.

an hour or so later i glance down to the street, from my fourth floor window, and here comes li'l mike, furtive and hurting. minus his usual jaunty cap, now he's redshirted and sunglassed. a sympathetic lieutenant of larry's, wayne, steps up and tries to reason with him, but also snaps his cellphone open in an obvious call to larry. mike starts to get heated in his own defense, "*fuck that motherfucker*" and so on, i scramble into my shoes and hurry downstairs, buttoning my shirt as i go. i go into my bread-pudding bodega, on the corner. I see lieutenant wayne, lead li'l mike across sherman, right into the blazing sun and hold him against a big brown town car. i grab three rolls of recycled paper towels, because they have no bread pudding, and step outside.

166

lieutenant wayne is being firm and relentless. mike is trying to work himself into some kind of reckless state where he can do whatever it takes to push back hard, and then i become aware, from his stance, that he is probably armed in some way. i go across to the other market, the people who own it are related to that same yemenite crew, and are good folks, especially one very hip guy who calls himself 'bob', as a kind of drollery. i grab a six-pack of summer wheat ale and set it on the counter, but when i glance out the door, i can see bad feelings rising up in waves from the interrogation zone. i quickly go outside and join the crowd of onlookers, along with bob. lots of people of all ages, are openly gawking at the drama unfolding. way down sickles, larry arrives, and he's carrying something in one hand, wrapped in a white teeshirt, cradling it. he's coming fast, furious and determined. mike moves to the middle of the street. it is definitely 'high noon 'time. i blurt out, with a conciliatory tone, *"take it easy now. easy, larry."*

people in the crowd glance at me, but it doesn't stop me.

"take it easy," i say a few more times, again, not shouting, just insistent, projecting. a young girl next to me says, *"that kid, mike, he's always fucking up."*
"but he's not a bad guy."
"no, no, he's sweet," she says. *"he's just a fuckup. he probably owes somebody money so he did something stupid."*
"he just got scared."
the guy from yemen, bob, looks at me with a friendly squint and nods, *"he's a good kid."*
i yell out, a little louder, *"easy, larry. you can do this.."*
as they move around the brown car and onto the opposite sidewalk, larry steps up his intensity. he gestures vehemently and points under the car, as though instructing mike to put something there. mike pulls an enormous blade, a small machete, like landscapers use, out of his pants and carefully puts it under the passenger-side wheel of the car.

"good, good," i say. and one of the taller boys in larry's crew, standing on the other side of bob the yemenite, gives me a smile.
"larry's a good leader," i say, and the guy nods.

across the street, larry insists now, to li'l mike, "*let's book. come on, let's book.*" and the three of them, larry, lieutenant wayne, and li'l mike, trudge off down the block, and around the corner. i think about going down to the park and walking in the fountain, just to cool off, but then i think i've pushed my presence far enough. i go inside to pay for the beer, but bob the yemenite jumps behind the counter. he bags the beer in a black plastic bag, and hands it to me, waving his palm, no charge, and nodding at me with a light solemnity.

coda: LT. WAYNE DID TIME
    short stretch
    six months
    leaving his high forehead
    smooth as a river stone
    eyes a slightly lighter shade of gray.
    out now, he basks in the sun
    with his slim wife (the tensile strength of fresh steel)
    and their rambunctious infant

    police walk the streets thick as drifting pollen
    in the blued air.

    when i flee new york, i give wayne my king-sized bed. his wife is overwhelmed. she has never slept in anything so capacious. it takes up pretty much their entire bedroom.

WHAT I LEARNED FROM THE DOMINICAN CHILDREN OF INWOOD
the entire point of
a vehicle, be it bike
trike
or
skateboard
is to withhold it from other children.
run for the joy of it.
the whole point of
screaming
is the announcing

168

of a total lack of restraint.
be patient with your parents
        until you need them
        then let it rip.
carry one dollar at a time
only.
when you have two quarters,
clack them together for all they're worth in a hasty rhythm.
        climb on everything

IN KEY LARGO
the plump, sunburned, ginger-haired, twelve-year-old; whose name seems to
be ariel, bearing a float and bright-orange leash attached to her snorkel,
paddles around in the shallow water, trying to get her officious mother to look
at the cool shells she's found, "*at least hold them, mom,*" she exhorts,
breathing apparatus in place, snuffling, like the blowhole of a small whale;
then she beaches herself on the rocky shore and calls out. she bleats like a
dolphin, to no avail.
        a naked toddler wobbles by, wearing only his water shoes, all limbs
flapping, to catch up with his feet. his mother exhorts him to put his wings on.
he declines and hurries on, as if the sea will run away if he doesn't catch it.
mom comes along slow and steady, barefoot, stepping carefully on the
granulated coral path. she is more than a lot pregnant. she captures him,
slides bright orange pillows just above his elbows, he scurries off to discover
an important stick.
        as i leave my spot on the jagged seawall i scope an ancient cannon,
imbedded in it. i am drawn to it, compelled to get a closer look. the antiquity
fascinates me. the way the rust announces the inexorable passage of time.
along comes another small boy, moving toward me, pulling a rope. he is
moving with absolute confidence, exuding knowhow. but still he moves oddly,
scuttling like a crab. now i realize that he has only one leg, but he is so
tanned and capable, pure boy, he does not seem in the least bit misshapen.
our eyes briefly meet. i attempt to make it a simple hello, between friendly
strangers, nothing irregular at all. but in his eyes, the set of his face, he does
not believe that i am not staring, not for one second. he does not pause in his
passing. he's getting his job done with that rope, whatever it might be,
scampering deftly back down to the pier.

he is a member of the family staying in the bungalow attached to mine. a large family, who are roasting their catch of the day, and teeming about in the packed dirt yard. so many in one room, which is not much larger than mine. i'm all alone. the boy could be more than ten, but not by much. one of his legs ends just above the knee, but he still uses it for balance and propulsion. the other complete leg seems to be hinged in a way that allows him to move more like a dog—on all three-and halfs, so to speak, counting his strong arms—completely naturally and unapologetically. not that he has anything to apologize for. and he has no observable rancor. i have never seen someone so malformed seem so uncrippled. i credit his family. and him, especially. his equanimity. his ability to accept reality as it is.

[i realize now, all these years after I wrote this, that what i was really noting, somehow, and puzzled by, is the contrast between this noble kid and my father and his withered leg, his rage at fate—meaning god. therefore his desperation to not blame the 'lord'. and so much flowed from that fury.]

after dinner i stroll down to the water and watch the distant lightning pulsate and flash in the charcoal sky. will it be different when he gets older? as gertrude stein said: *"what's the point of being a boy if one becomes a man."* brutal as it is, there's truth in that, for sure. but i'm in a kind of reverie—of satisfaction, loneliness and contentment all at once. a bogart moment, so to speak. the mood is broken by the grating voice of a woman nearby. i can't actually hear her words, but the sound penetrates, even from several yards away. she's trying hard to make a point, dammit. the tone is unpleasantly, wistfully, familiar. i miss susanna, simple as that, but often, these days, i miss her more when i'm with her…the lightning has no discernible pattern. it simply happens.

the little seizures that are occurring in lilah's brain are like electrical storms in the grey cloud of her brain. a lightning storm that transfixes my dear little girl's attention. like me on the pier, my last night in key largo, watching the distant flashes over the gulf. the capacity for these small explosions is in the code of her cells, part of how she is built. what's to be done? can i fix her? can i protect her? from what just…happens?

now i am chilled to the bone. i go inside…past the rambunctious bunch, shouting and chowing down. the boy is laughing, joyful and open, chasing his siblings all around the yard, catching them easily while they squeal with delight…

MOVING EAST. Day Five—Highway 16-90, Custer, South Dakota to Chicago, Illinois, 1995

we understand south dakota as a ramp out of the rockies and into chicago.

mark (on seeing mt. rushmore): *"i thought it would be bigger."*

me: *"that's what she said."*

we had espressos at the chief restaurant, right across the street from the rocket motel, in custer, south dakota.

we went to mount rushmore with thousands of bikers and their significant others

lots of NPR. across minnesota. barns and silos. samuel barber. bartok. aaron copland, naturally..

distant lightning. then smack into the storm, again. and all the bikers are huddled under the overpasses, like wet cats and just as pissed. we keep up our pace but the storm is relentless and getting more so and perseveres all the way across minnesota. we cross the mississippi as the sky goes coal black. the rain has stopped. we go down by the river and then on into downtown la crosse and cruise on to madison. thinking we will get a room and sack out. no rooms in madison. no rooms in the entire state of wisconsin. and then on into illinois. in fact we are forced to go all the way into chicago. nineteen straight hours of driving. in and out of fog and all kinds of precipitation. i am delirious and so aggravated that i scream at tavish, riding shotgun about how highway 90, traps you into entering the fucking toll road, into the domain of the chicago mob, every ten miles they charge another 40cents (*exact change please!*) and there is no way off, so even when we see a motel—we can't get off the fucking road, a prison of a freeway. i am vituperative to my very patient son. again. finally we make a break for it near the airport and get a room at an enormous ramada, (bigger then many of the towns we've passed through. a sprawling dorm for tourists and airline personnel. we get two rooms. i take the one alone. age before beauty, i have behaved badly, i'm the wagon master…take your pick. and sleep like the dead. all told we drove 913 miles in one swell foop.

HE HAS REMEMBERED EVERYTHING AND LEARNED NOTHING.

CIRCLE OF FRIENDS
i dreamt last night…
i look outside my window
and there i see phil ochs
alive as you or me
leading some massive demonstration
marching through the streets.
and then, in a flash,
i am marching right beside him, arm in arm
i turn to him and say
«phil
i thought you died"
"naw, i never died" says he
"i never died of envy
i never died of despair
i never hung myself
or drank myself to death"
says phil
"i aint dead"

in 1968 i am seventeen, sitting on the floor, in a dark apartment in westwood, at a party thrown by another student at UCLA, whom i barely know. on the turntable (remember those?) spins a disk, from which comes a high, but somehow sonorous, voice, floating through the room, challenging comforting clarion. the young man assures us smoking pot is more fun than drinking beer. he sings of terrible incidents of no interest to anybody—outside of a small circle of friends. my heart swells, i yearn to be included in that circle. then i realize—i already am. just like that. so are all of us in this room, within earshot of his songs. we join that circle just by hearing him. his voice, the melodies, the poetry, they do that for us. we care beyond ourselves. because he does. because we must. because now is the time.

"i never died" he says,
"look around you".
"but phil,"
i say

"i saw you there at the frichtman auditorium, around 1975, a few months before you died. my friends and i helped to organize a concert for something or other, protesting against some atrocity, some war, some injustice. mimi farina opened for you. you didn't look so good. your skin was sallow. your face as pale as a prisoner. you had a metal splint, webbed in soiled gauze, on your right arm. backstage the bandage began to unravel, and mimi tried to wrap it back up for you, as you grumbled under your whiskey breath, yanking your hand away. but she spoke softly, coaxing you to let her help you. then you went on, to enthusiastic applause, welcoming you back. we hadn't seen you for awhile. since the 'war is over 'concert. since they cut off victor jara's hands. you were sweating. you strummed your guitar with your broken wing, for way too long. as if you had forgotten your own words. you seemed exhausted—by the music business, by the FBI harassment, by all the lies and apathy. but then, when you sang, your voice was young again and clear, still reaching out for connection, your lyrics just as eloquent and potent, just as brave as ever. there but for fortune...""

'*well*," says phil,
"there you go,
i aint dead
fuck the music business fuck fucking robert christgau fuck the FBI
they cannot kill what they could not compromise
i never compromised
and the songs i sang
are just as true today
as they were then
the struggle carries on
our struggle carries on
where people stand up for their rights
i am with you still"

so let the songs of freedom ring
from the valleys and the hills
say the names
fill the streets
phil ochs is with us still
—*for library girl, june 30, 2020, with apologies to billy bragg*

"it's the very last line that joe hill wrote
when he knew that his days were through
"boys this is my last and final will
good luck to all of you
good luck to all of you"
—phil ochs, 'joe hill'

BART
bart is under the overpass
another rider in a different storm
in the rain and two flannel shirts
and he is beaming on the road
hitching, with a sixties spirit, to get
home for thanksgiving
a surplus backpack neatly stuffed
with clean socks and all he owns.
can't afford a bus ticket

when i offer him twenty bucks he says
"naw, man, barter is better…
let's trade…
got some great homegrown…
d'ya like the doors?…got some doors cds,
never been opened…"

by all means
i'll take the doors
"yeah, you said you like LA woman"
when i tell him i know the drummer, and saw them at the whiskey,
he straightens his spine, leaning slightly back
to get a better look at me.
"who else didja see?"
"well, at the whiskey—flying burrito brothers, joe cocker, john mayall, almost
saw x…up the street at the roxy i saw lou reed, bob marley…and springsteen
the week when he was on the cover of time and newsweek."
"damn."

174

he tells me he met the bass player for the meat puppets
"cleaning up after woodstock 2...
they paid me $6.50 an hour...
the bass player was just hanging around...
he was on all kinds of pills...really cool guy...
my mom had a volvo...my mom had like seven volvos...they're great
cars...really comfortable..
i hated them when i was little...
they weren't cool at all...i wanted like..a sports car...but volvos...
too boxy...they're really safe...
so, what kind of music do you like...i guess all kinds?..."
so i slip in a mix, and we smoke a joint of mine
and the rain doubles down.
looking through the windshield with furrowed brow,
bart will not be drenched
he will persevere
"naw, i hate busses...i'll just keep rolling...i'll get there by easter."
and he flashes me a peace sign as i drive away.

i move along the river
musing on how each moment
emanates in endless variations, timeless ripples
each small gesture toward grace
and how each season
each storm
each absentmindedly whistled note
born along the parched or rainslicked roadside
o each caress
is shared and shared
and shared some more.
—november, 1998, somewhere in connecticut

EIGHT DAYS IN RUSSIA, Kaliningrad, Thursday, 2007
again, with the retching. each morning around 8AM, the sound of someone
puking. i realized yesterday morning that the vomiter is a woman, and she is
really hurling up her guts. is she bulemic/anorexic or just really, and with
regularity, way hungover? whatever, she's thorough and consistent. i'll give

her that. i doze off and then about a half hour later LOUD rap music ensues, old school, from another room, vibrating the walls. an extremely effective radio alarm. amazingly, i doze more, then the workmen start up, with the sawing and the hammering and the drilling. usually, by 10AM i give up and get up.

last night would have to be called a triumph. completely sold out, in fact they had to turn people away. i was so happy for art and masha. the whole idea of the festival seems to be working, and i realize as i'm basking in the glow, that there were a whole passel of gambles at stake here for both of them. masha was very nervous about translating in front of such a large audience, *"i am not professional"*. she says, winsomely. and she's not a showoff either, but she is very charismatic. she can lead. she was grateful that i had written out what i was going to say. and i had gotten kind of inspired thinking about audrey hepburn and why she remains so irresistibly beguiling. it was wonderful to sit in a room with a packed, rapt crowd, the majority of whom were seeing her for the first time, and feel them palpably fall for her, taken by her, absorbed into her aura. once the movie started they hustled me out to do more interviews, but i insisted on seeing the opening shots of holly in front of tiffany's at dawn. (so evocative of what i imagined life in manhattan would be, as i put *moon river* on the jukebox, to cheer up my desolated sister, after some humiliation or other had been brought down on her by our rageful, single dad, the two of us left for a moment alone at the formica table in some cheaply paneled truckstop diner, outside of yreka, or worse. i knew at that moment that i would have to leave her behind, eventually, abandon her, to make my own escape). i needed to hear them, feel them, hear that intake of breath, the realization of just how much we want…her.

masha did an excellent job translating, (as far as i could tell) and managed to soften the blow when i said the size of the crowd was a tribute to, and an indication of, how the people around the world want to connect, even when the government obstructs that contact. i didn't mean it quite so starkly—and i apologized to mary kruger afterward. she admitted that she found the comment *"ironic, since we paid to bring you here"*. anyway, art and masha assured me that it was completely appropriate—and true, as well, and merely an extension of what the ambassador himself said in the meeting with the exchange students.

176

after the film i did a few more interviews and managed not to insult any governments. art, masha and i had a bite and a toast to the whole enterprise. then art announced that he had just found out that the new baby was going to be a GIRL, and he was quite obviously delighted. then we went to the after-party in the night club attached to the theater. great space, okay party. they imported an 'american 'DJ, very nice guy but strung out on disco. i didn't have enough energy to dance, especially to the uninviting thump that was being provided, but art prevailed upon me to have a vodka, for medicinal purposes, and it actually did me good! perked me right up. when we went to get our coats back in the office, there was an email for me from seth bauer! i have no idea how he found masha's email address. i imagine susanna overheard him leaving a phone message, or something like that. i answered back at 1AM, and apparently i will be directing a backer's reading at the signature theater, for *early in the mourning,* with estelle parsons and jerry stiller, while simultaneously directing *lie of the mind* at the actor's center.

earlier in the day i took a walk by myself to the ancient cathedral, which is situated on an island in the middle of the river which runs through the center of the city. It's just a short walk from the hotel, past the blue monstrosity, and down to the medieval bridge. as i crossed the bridge a very fresh faced young man, with bright blue eyes, talking on a cellphone, looked at me with surprise and delight and blurted out *it's you hello!* 'i said *'hi'* and kept walking, for one thing, although the sky was assertively blue and clear, the wind was polar, damned cold, and i needed to keep moving. i circled the cathedral, handsome and squat in a stern, germanic way, and was headed back out of the park, having done my tourist duty, when i paused to checkout the statue to immanuel kant, not my favorite philosopher, but here he is, looking mean. he was born here…etc. and then around the corner of the church comes the blue-eyed boy, semaphoring his arms. he trots up, beaming. turns out his name is misha, he was at the lecture at the university, to which he gives a quick two thumbs up. he's a physics student, interested in film, and music, and…everything! his english is rudimentary but he is really trying—and i keep saying, *it's okay…take your time.'* and we stand there shivering while he kind of pours out all his aspirations. i give him my email, and take his, and his cell number so that art and masha can contact him. he wants to write reviews, among other things, and i figure *they* can understand him. he walks me back across the bridge and then to the hotel and then bolts across two streets to catch the bus back to his hometown, on the coast, about an hour away. i do another visit to the university tomorrow, hopefully not so jammed. i've got some choice bogart to lay on them.

ALL THE DOOMED BLONDES, Part Five
...and so, we come to **HER**: **MARILYN MONROE**
"marilyn monroe was a legend. in her own lifetime she created a myth of what a poor girl from a deprived background could attain. for the entire world she became a symbol of the eternal feminine."—lee strasberg

*"people create me. so who i really am is of no importance. it's so easy to forget that, and to begin thinking that you are what you are up on the screen and carry that notion over into life. that was **marilyn monroe's** mistake."—* ***marlon brando***

no love goddess of the last century and a half wielded more pure power than **she**—the most doomed, most blonde, most incandescent:
marilyn monroe: she was born norma jean mortenson, in 1926, to gladys pearl baker, a negative cutter at columbia and rko. gladys was unmarried and mentally unstable. she was committed to an institution when norma jean was still a toddler. the high-spirited girl grew up, from the age of five, in a series of foster homes, where she was neglected, humiliated and, at least once, raped. she dropped out of high school at 16 to marry a 21-year-old aircraft plant worker, jim dougherty. in fact, they first met when she was 15, and began living together almost immediately. when she applied for a marriage certificate, her illegitimacy was revealed, along with the identity of her father, edward mortenson, listed on the document as an 'itinerant baker'. turned out ed wiped out on a motorcycle when norma jean was three. not that he was ever in the picture.

[even my dad loved **marilyn monroe**. i have a fleeting memory, an image really: there's a magazine open on a table, it may be that picture of marilyn in korea, singing to the troops, arms thrown into the air, as if on a cross of adulation, offering herself for worship. you can feel her palpable joy in **their** joy, all those soldiers, those sweet boys, feeling more alive, more invulnerable, indestructible just being in her presence, breathing the same air...somehow, we, my dad and i, seemed to acknowledge in the same moment our admiration for this woman, of her womanliness, of, yes, her sex, before i really knew the word, or knew what it meant, as something you do

178

and something you are. it may have been a more overt pose, a clinging white dress, her breasts presented by bending over, toward the lens, smiling brilliantly, her smoky eyes, an overt display of the reality of sex. i think he's standing on my left side, looking down, about to go through a door, we're in a waiting room. i'm not more than six or seven. he may have chuckled a bit, or even pointed his finger. or made a sound in his throat that meant *"she's bad...but she's good."* a fleeting, errant moment with my anhedonic dad, never to be repeated, but the flash, the shard of recollection, demonstrates the power of her emanation, the irresistible glow, the indelibility of her image—and the shadow inside of it.]

in one of those startling *chiasms* that mysteriously occur in the *nexus rerum* [*"the word* 'chiasm' *or* 'chiasmus '*comes from the greek letter* chi, *written* x, *and it denotes exactly that crossed intertwining shape. in biology, it refers to the crossing of two nerves or ligaments. in language, it is the rhetorical device in which one phrase is countered by another, inverting the same words, as when* **john f. kennedy** *said, 'ask not what your country can do for you, but what you can do for your country', or when mae west said, 'it's not the men in my life, it's the life in my men.' the interwoven figure calls to mind two hands grasping each other, or the way a woolen thread loops back to grip itself in a knitting stitch. as {the existentialist philosopher} merleau-ponty put it, 'the hold is held.' for him, this was the perfect way of making sense of the connection between consciousness and the world. each clasps the other, as if by criss-crossed, knitted links."—sarah bakewell, 'at the existentialist cafe*], the man who worked next to jim dougherty on the assembly line at lockheed was a strapping, free-spirited, *'very easygoing'* young man named bob mitchum. dougherty and his teenaged bride took a liking to him, and, at least according to mitchum, spent a lot of time socializing with him. doughtery told a slightly different story: *"yeah, i'd hear him on television saying how back then we all went dancing and saw frank sinatra and all this. it didn't hurt anybody if he wanted to say it, but bob never did meet norma jean when i was married to her. the closest he came was to eat some of her sandwiches. he never had any lunch to bring to work, and i'd give him one of norma jean's, tuna salad or bologna. and i'd tell her my buddy didn't have anything to eat, and she started putting in an extra sandwich for bob."* in later years, of course, when they were two of the most famous people on earth, robert mitchum and marilyn monroe did actually meet, in a movie called *river of no return…*

norma jean and jim didn't talk much. as she put it: *"we hardly spoke to each other…we had nothing to say."* after about a year of this she made a first fling at suicide. (that we know of..). it was halfhearted, but when jim shipped out with the merchant marine, she divorced him. norma jean, with a rita hayworth-like mane of light brown hair, a fulsome body, and a ready-for-anything-smile (masking her despondency), got a job as a paint sprayer in a defense plant. it didn't take long for an army photographer to notice her, toiling on the assembly line. he took some exuberant, morale-boosting pinups of her, and they were an instant smash. the seventh division medical corps voted her the girl they would like most to examine. soon, another photographer introduced her to a modeling agency, where they cut her hair and bleached it blonde. she was sent to a 'charm school '[to learn 'charm'? *"…the indefinable power of delighting…work charms, use spells, practice magic,…an incantation; any action, process, verse, etc. credited with such properties…bewitch."—excerpts from the oxford english dictionary*]. by 1946, she was divorced, on the covers of men's magazines, and attracting attention in hollywood. fox signed her at $125 a week, changed her name to **marilyn monroe**, gave her acting, singing and dancing lessons, and proceeded to give her the starlet buildup. she was on her way…seemingly.

unfortunately by 1948 she had been dropped by two studios, fox and columbia, and she was going nowhere fast. she took a gig posing in the nude. she was paid $50. of posing naked, marilyn later explained: *"i was hungry."* [here's a first person account of the photo session: *"…in 1949…desperate for cash, norma jean baker called photographer tom kelley, who had once offered to pay her fifty dollars to pose nude. she had turned him down but now said she would do it. that night, kelley covered the floor of his pink-stucco hollywood cottage with a red-velvet drape; he put on some music, and his wife, natalie, assisted him in loading and unloading film plates as a naked norma jean lay on the velvet, 'graceful as an otter, turning sinuously with utter naturalness, 'striking pose after perfect pose. the experience, kelley said, was 'extraordinary in its intensity.' a year later, the first of kelley's pictures of a nude marilyn was printed on a calendar, 'golden dreams. 'more calendars would be published through the decade. monroe feared that being revealed as the 'golden dreams 'girl would hurt her career, but in fact it increased her popularity. in a later interview, marilyn was asked, "was it true you really had nothing on when you posed?" she said, 'oh, i had something on. the radio. 'it wasn't the radio,' tom kelley said. "it was a phonograph.' and it was playing* begin the beguine', *the artie shaw version".—tom nolan, 'three chords for beauty's sake: the life of artie shaw'*] eventually the calendar company realized a profit of $750,000. this attitude, innocent and bawdy all at once, made her very popular with the press. as for example: *"what do i wear in bed? "why, chanel no.5, of course."*

in 1952, fox signed her, again. she had made an indelible impact in two classic films, *all about eve,* gleaming cluelessly on george sanders arm, a nearly nude descending the stairs, heralding the *'bumpy night'* ahead. sanders, the ultra-suave older man, an acerbic theatre critic, introduces her as *'a graduate of the copacabana school of dramatic art',* and says to her, *"i can see your career rising in the east like the sun."* she smiles and stares vacantly. she is just as guileless, and bursting with sensuality, as a kept woman in *the asphalt jungle,* reclining voluptuously on louis calhern's couch. (another suave and corrupt older man). john huston directed *'asphalt jungle'.* he describes the casting session thusly: *"..little johnny hyde of the william morris agency called and said he had a girl just right for the part of angela— might she read for me? and few days later johnny brought the girl around. the scene she was to read called for angela to be stretched out on a divan; there was no divan in my office, so marilyn said, 'i'd like to do the scene on the floor." 'of course my dear, any way it feels right to you.' and that's the way she did it. she kicked off her shoes, lay down on the floor and read for us...i later discovered that johnny hyde was in love with her. johnny was a very reliable agent, and we were friends, but marilyn didn't get the part because of johnny. she got it because she was damned good. that role was the beginning for marilyn, and she was always grateful to me. it started her on her way to fame..."*
anita loos, the writer who had been so key to the image and popularity of jean harlow (with *redheaded woman*), and was the creator of *gentlemen prefer blondes,* one of marilyn's early triumphs, gives us another example of her auditioning technique: *"it was surprising that a girl so intensely shy would want to be an actress...she spoke so seldom and in such muted tones that conversation languished. but she radiated a childlike sweetness that was*

disarming. marilyn knew how to communicate without language. evidently she felt no shyness when she approached 20th century-fox boss joe schenck for a job. while he concentrated on her fabulous face, marilyn shook her torso free of a flimsy shirtwaist, and bare to the waistline, asked in her girlish whisper, 'do you think you can use me in a picture, mr. schenck?' joe took a long look at her delectable torso. 'not unless we get a board of censors to come up from mozambique,' said joe. marilyn squealed a dainty giggle and got the job."

"there was another girl in the band [in some like it hot'] who had blonde hair. and she said to me, 'no other blonde. i'm the only blonde.'—billy wilder

simone signoret, the soulful, sad-eyed french actress, herself a bottle blonde, got to know marilyn while she was working with signoret's husband, yves montand, on *let's make love.* as with every man to come within marilyn's vicinity, there were rumors of an affair. but if the smooth, rakish montand and monroe did in fact 'make love', it didn't seem to interfere with a warm friendship between the two blondes. in her autobiography, *'nostalgia isn't what it used to be'*, signoret offers this insight: *"every saturday morning the hair colorist of the late **jean harlow**, pearl porterfield, would board a plane in san diego and arrive in los angeles, where marilyn's car would be waiting for her at the airport and would bring her to the kitchenette of bungalow number 21 [at the beverly hills hotel]. before allowing her to remove the bottles from her old carrying bag, marilyn would ply her with food from a buffet—a combination of brunch and cocktail party ingredients—she had carefully prepared. the old lady would indulge with gusto. marilyn would knock on my door, telling me to bring my towels, and then the hair-dyeing party would begin. now the old lady began to relive her life. while making the two of us blonde, she would tell all about the color she had concocted for jean harlow's head thirty years earlier, which had been the secret of harlow's success. her tales were full of silk dresses, white foxes, lame` shoes, and parties…listening to her, you might come to the conclusion that jean harlow had her hair dyed twenty-four hours out of the day, since it would appear that this lady had never been absent for a minute of the daily, conjugal, and amorous life of her star…it amused me enormously to have my hair tinted by the lady who pretended to have created the myth who was splashed across* *the newspaper pages of my adolescence. but it did not amuse marilyn. it was no accident that she had tracked down the address of this retired lady. she believed in her. she liked her and respected her. she was perfectly willing to pay for her round trips from the mexican border, her limousine rides, and her caviar. it was a kind of association through a third person between the premier blonde and the blonde she turned into."* marilyn herself once said: *"i used to look at movie magazines and cut out the pictures of jean harlow. that's what i wanted to be one day—a **jean harlow**."* late in her life, marilyn posed as harlow in *life* magazine. photographed by richard avedon. she also expressed interest in starring in *the jean harlow story.* after reading the maudlin treatment for the film, however, she rejected the idea, saying, *"i hope they don't do that to me after i'm gone."*

*"**marilyn monroe** shows, besides her charms, the gifts of the great comedienne she now is, the definitive substitute for **carole lombard** in the american comedy."—g. cabrera infante, 'twentieth century job'*

*"she was never vulgar in a role that could have become vulgar, and somehow you felt good when you saw her on the screen. to put it briefly, she had a quality no one else ever had on the screen except **garbo**."—billy wilder*

constance collier was a revered english actress, already established as one of the greatest tragediennes of her time, who came to tour the states with beerbohm tree and stayed to make silent films. she became the vocal and acting coach of some of the greatest performers of the 20th century, from eva le gallienne to colleen moore to greta garbo to vivien leigh to **katherine hepburn** (they met on *stage door* and remained lifelong friends), to audrey hepburn to **marilyn monroe.** she provides this incomparable insight into marilyn's special magic: *"i don't think she is an actress at all, not in any traditional sense. what she has - this presence, this luminosity, this flickering intelligence - could never surface on the stage. it's so fragile and subtle, it can only be caught by the camera. it's like a hummingbird in flight; only a camera can freeze the poetry of it. but anyone who thinks this girl is simply another **harlow** or harlot or whatever is mad. speaking of mad, that's what we've been working on together: ophelia. i suppose people would chuckle at the notion, but really, she could be the most exquisite ophelia. i was talking to* *garbo last week, and i told her about marilyn's ophelia, and greta said yes, she could believe that because she had seen two of her films, very bad and vulgar stuff, but nevertheless she had glimpsed marilyn's possibilities. actually greta has an amusing idea. you know that she wants to make a film of dorian gray? with her playing dorian, of course. well, she said she would like to have marilyn opposite her as one of the girls dorian seduces and destroys. greta! so unused! such a gift—rather like marilyn's, if you consider it. of course, greta is a consummate artist, an artist of the utmost control. this beautiful child is without any concept of discipline or sacrifice. somehow i don't think she'll make old bones. absurd of me to say, but somehow i feel she'll go young. i hope, i really pray, that she survives long enough to free the strange, lovely talent that's wandering through her like a jailed spirit."—constance collier*

john huston echoed collier's estimation of marilyn's acting: *"she wasn't acting—i mean she wasn't pretending to an emotion. it was the real thing. she would go deep within herself and find it and bring it up into consciousness. but maybe that's what all truly good acting consists of."* and, of course, john huston directed monroe in her final film, *the misfits*. as fate would have it, *the misfits* was clark gable's last film, too. (also the final film of one of the greatest actresses to ever grace a screen—thelma ritter. hollywood deaths always come in threes...) it was not montgomery clift's valedictory, but nearly, and he was certainly never again to have a role that allowed him to express so much of himself. this is especially true in a wrenching scene in which we hear monty, as the aging rodeo rider, perce, in a phone booth, pleading to his mother, almost wailing, that despite his head injuries, *"you would to recognize me!"*. marilyn adored monty, they were clearly two kindred souls. she said of him, *"he's the only person i know who's in worse shape than i am."* and in reference to the powers-that-be's disdain for him, she whispered, *"they aren't fit to open the door for him."* [even the super-macho gable, after watching monty do the scene in the phone booth in one superb take, was protective and respectful and kind.] the role of roslyn was written for marilyn by her third husband, the esteemed playwright, arthur miller, and the script is a magnificent tribute to her. but by the time the film was before the cameras their marriage was a shambles. marilyn was addicted to pills, and had to be hospitalized twice during the shooting. she was always late, sometimes not even able to show up on set at all, for days at a time. huston was frantic. the budget exploded. gable was not well, and in pain himself. nevertheless, both of the old hollywood stalwarts, although frustrated, evidenced great patience and compassion for their star. gable, particularly, gives one of his very finest and deepest performances, capping a career of four decades as the beloved king of hollywood, as a kind of love song to this glorious blonde goddess next to him, decidedly in the flesh, so like **harlow** and **lombard**, whose skin he had also touched. there are many memorable scenes and moments in *the misfits*, not only because of its seemingly doomed nature, and its pure excellence as art, but also because so many narratives and mythologies cross in it—so many chiasms in the *nexus rerum*. but the scene that moves me the most is one in which gay (gable) and roslyn (monroe) are driving through the moonlit desert. as he gazes at her, gable blurts out, *'roslyn, you just shine in my eyes.'* some say the line was improvised. to me it doesn't matter. the man we see means it down to his bones, and he is speaking for all of us.

after one of the most publicly chaotic filmings in hollywood history, the movie was already despised, before it was released, partly because the film was exactly like it's title—a downbeat neo-western about losers, in a time of 'camelot 'and cool, with john f. kennedy leading the nation.—and especially because marilyn's behavior during shooting, was deemed to be the cause of the king's demise, two weeks after the wrap, and just a week before the birth of his only child, a son. marilyn was excoriated in the press, widely condemned as a depraved slut, who through her indulgences had killed **clark gable,** the king of hollywood.

and then, she did this, as told, once again, by anita loos : *"few normal men could have coped with the extravagant daydreams that obsessed marilyn. she was always convinced that any affair, no matter how casual, would end in marriage. when it failed, she was well into her next romance with the same unreal expectations....she was at MGM in the midst of filming a picture called* let's make love *at a time when president kennedy was due to have a birthday. marilyn concocted the idea of flying to washington and making a surprise appearance at his birthday celebration. "have you been invited?" asked her skeptical agent. "oh no," marilyn replied. "but we're engaged to be married". her agent reminded her that the president was already married and, as an ardent catholic, would never divorce his wife, jackie. evidently this made no difference to marilyn who's answer was: "i was*

185

born to be mrs. jack kennedy." at the studio, news of her 'engagement' provoked laugher and also the sad remark that poor marilyn had gone around the bend. with a secrecy typical of the obsessed, she arranged a flight to washington, where she checked into a hotel and proceeded to cram her swollen body [she was bloated from drugs and alcohol] *into a tight satin evening gown. (ultimately she had to be sewn into it backstage. the dress sold at auction in 1999 for $1,250,000.) then she made her way to the white house and through the amazed throng that surrounded kennedy".*

a special show had been arranged for the celebration, by JFK's brother-in-law, peter lawford, charter member of sinatra's rat pack, and many show biz greats were performing and/or in attendance. the master of ceremonies was mike nichols. once, in conversation, mike gave me this insider's view of what took place onstage: *"i don't remember who was actually performing next on the bill, but i was stage right near the microphone and suddenly stage left, where peter stood, became an instant ratfuck. a scrum. chaos. peter started waving at me like one of those airport guys. and suddenly, there beside him, seemingly rising from the sea, appeared marilyn, in that glittering dress. peter rushed over to the microphone and kind of gulped, "mr. president...marilyn monroe." and out she came, undulating across the stage. we moved the microphone to center and i stepped back, but not offstage, just upstage right. and as she...um, sang, or sort of moaned, the song, the dress, in the back, began to open, stitch by stitch—and i was presented with the most beautiful moon i have ever seen, ever, in my life."*

back to anita loos: *"a seemingly delighted JFK referred to her version of happy birthday, mr. president 'as the 'most wholesome 'he'd ever heard. a group of MGM public relations people took marilyn in charge and got her back to hollywood. before long marilyn was gone, a victim of sleeping pills that couldn't quite quell her lethal daydreams..."* marilyn's 'wholesome' rendition of a song sung by millions of people every day, is probably the most listened to, most remarked upon, by more people, than any other in the history of the western world...

for the last few months of her life, marilyn barely left her bed, or got dressed in more than her bathrobe. jack larson once described to me an encounter he had with marilyn around this time. he was strolling down camden drive in beverly hills, when a limo pulled over a few feet ahead of him, the back window on the passenger side slid down and a familiar blonde head leaned out and called to him in her whispery voice, waving her hand. *"hi, jack, hi…how's monty?"* jack chuckled as he approached her, leaning in to see that she was dressed in a white, plush, terrycloth dressing gown. *"he's fine, kiddo. ralph takes good care of him."* she took his hand gently and gave it a little jiggle. *"i think you and i love him more than anybody else does."* *"well, elizabeth would strongly dispute that. so would ralph."* *"yes, but we know the truth."* jack saw that the backseat was littered with flotsam—fast food boxes and candy wrappers, empty pill bottles, magazines, an open make-up case, spilling its contents. marilyn appeared to be wearing her usual bedtime apparel, chanel #5, under the dressing gown. *"what's going on, sweetheart,"* jack said, leaning further in and speaking softly. he glanced over at claude, her driver and masseuse. (he's the one who said that in the dark, marilyn's body would glow like moonlight. her skin emitted light.) *"is she okay, claude?"* *"oh, i'm fine,"* marilyn murmured. *"i just don't feel like going home. it's so empty…i feel too alone..you know…so we just keep riding around."* *"well, but, how long have you been..?"* *"just a few days…right, claude?"* *"six, baby…"* *"well, but listen, kiddo, why don't you come up and stay with us for a few days? jim would absolutely love that. we'll cook you a swell dinner…you can't just…"* *"i know…i know..but i feel like i'm..sinking…and claude has been so sweet about it.."* *"whatever you need, baby, you know that."* now there were tears in her eyes. *"monty would really hate this, marilyn. he would never forgive me for leaving you like this…"* *"well, then, you better not tell him. i just can't seem to sleep in my own bed, that's all. even when i…"* now her words went even breathier, and got a little slurry. *"i can fall asleep when we're driving around. i feel safe. isn't that what mom's do to get their babies to go to sleep? it works!"* and she giggled. *"i always love seeing you, jack. always. always…"* *"i love seeing you, too, kiddo. sleep well…"* and the limo pulled away, her hand fluttering a goodbye, as the window slid shut.

and then, last night, i caught the end of BUS STOP on TMC. there's a moment when she is totally defeated, her head down on the counter, then beau approaches her and she feels a glimmer of hope, she raises her head, and a thin strand of spittle is in the corner of her mouth, clinging to her hand. every time i even think about that i tear up. the whole scene just floors me. last night i was weeping by the end. i wanted so much for her to get what she wanted. what many people don't realize is that she *produced* that movie. she was in charge. any other *star,* would have *demanded* that they use a different take, one that did not reveal the extremity of her vulnerability, both in the character and personally. she was a great great artist. all most of us think about are her body parts. which are magnificent, don't get me wrong.

i picture her, at the end, languishing in the soiled sheets, in solitary anguish, her naked body still aglow, so alone, so alone, spending nights on end on the phone with former lovers: sinatra, brando, both of the kennedy brothers, the always faithful joe dimaggio, reaching out for a love that was lost at birth, one of the most adored women of all time, still worshipped around the world, and yet—eternally unreachable, especially to herself.

"although in herself she transcended americans 'fantasies by a constant effort of self-protection, marilyn simultaneously represented those fantasies. she was the postwar ideal of the american girl, soft, transparently needy, worshipful of men, naive, offering sex without demands."—donald spoto

"someone i've always admired is **marilyn monroe**. *she died young but remains one of my favorite actresses. she did comedies, dramas; she was funny, moving, seductive. i found her incredible. she embodied beauty and cinema at the same time."—catherine deneuve* [who also embodied beauty and cinema, although she was never doomed, even in the harrowing *repulsion,* directed by roman polanski, whose blonde and gorgeous wife was **sharon tate**, who was oh so doomed...]

"whenever i saw her, i forgave her."—*billy wilder*

THE PORTRAIT
will my background be the blue the famous blue
of the blue shutters on adelaide?
even hermes the thief knew of them
the blue of krishna's skin
the blue of pennants in the land of the dead
blue of permitted stillness
an exercise in concentration
intimacy thru observation
the blue of sequoia skies
to be seen

not for value but for simple appreciation
restful burning which is to be
my background after all
deliberately shifted gaze
glance not to snare but to see
more thoroughly
his mouth purses rhythmically
til deep lines mark the tanned face
sometimes the lips hold a brush
so delicately so firmly
especially if more than one color is in play

those who pose
cannot control the attitude displayed
(although they think they do)
beatific
grieving
seductive
or is this all reductive
poised to swell to enormous size
inside my eyes
behind my gaze
beneath the art.
— *for don bachardy, 1993*

ALOHA SUITE/ COYOTE GOES TO KAUAI, Part 5
she spends some time
each day
knitting a gift for me,
so soft around my neck,
with threads of various magentas.
seven careful stitches and then
nine the other way,
as per my specifications.
the gentle clicking of her clever needles
marking time's passage
and its stillness.

the woven present
accumulates the shape
she will send my way.
this dawn mighty clouds, edged with pink,
beckoned me out of dreams
of loping over prairie turf,
making me marvel once more
and affirm belief
in hallelujah
and beyond.
yes.
love is not some victory march,
but done *quite rightly*,
provides perpetual comfort,
a deeper beguilement,
perseverance in the face
of incremental loss.
what good is counting?
always answer with a question?
what should we expect from romance?
spirits full of exhaltation?
bodies filled with light?
sons of adam,
daughters of eve,
all foregather at the immense and melodramatic ocean,
voicing our mutual devotion
weaving that indestructible net
of all possible noise
starting now.

I GAVE FIVE RIBS AND ALL I GOT WERE THESE SILLY WOMEN
clucking around the yard
rejecting the all purpose grain
giving me the opposite of sympathy
like kicking a guy when he's down
bleeding on the bathroom floor
or throwing a bucket of water on a drowning man,

as he gulps and thrashes, lost at sea.

o they circle around.
like taxi's with their out of service lights teasing
in their kimonos and bikinis, unitards and caftans
some of them even show me their breasts
or their underwear
or playfully muss with my hair
but the real bitch is
every breath every chuckle every whistle every sigh
brings down a ton of pain on my sorry sorry ass
like a piano falling from outer space and landing square on my gut
the agony echoes in my skull
pounding like panicked buffalo stampeding
across the prairie
or a heavy-booted cain stomping at the front of a headlong mob
thundering toward the east of eden.
in the swamp near the wasteland at the backside of the garden
near the poisoned pond and the scorched pasture
i hang in my hammock
strung between the bleached spires of enormous primeval trees sunk deep
a thatched contrivance gives me what little shade there is
banished adam
balls sagging
sheaves of papyrus, bark, hides, some crumpled, some bundled with hemp
twine
litter the whole area
some special stacks i have forbidden the women to touch
any approach to those piles will cause brutal retaliation
i have made that clear
all of these materials are covered with scribbles and etched
in a rudimentary alphabet full of pictographs and symbols
i no longer remember the meaning of
but I write it down anyway
a man's gotta do something in 600 years.

my chest is horribly scarred

the removal ceremony has become downright savage
first of all
to have an entirely separate body
shaped from one of your own bones
from the very cage of my heart
plus some miscellaneous sinew and viscera
formed in these beastly agonizing rites
days of chanting and panting and incantation
relentless throbbing thudding and banging
it's the phantom limb in reverse
every time they lower the squirming caterwauling thing into the cauldron
then to see these persons sashaying around
consorting with snakes and such, and popping out progeny
A MAN COULD GO MAD WITH FURY!

so i try to write it down
everything
as exhausted as i am after giving names to all the animals
and keep in mind the original deal, after the carnage i mean,
called for a cutoff point on the creation of new creatures
but its all a joke to…somebody.
and still i scribble away
hoping to keep a record

they bustle in
a covey of fussing, jiggling, fragrant beings
and i submit
not without pleasure
not without pain
one of them
the daughter of the daughter of the daughter
i believe
whispers in my ear
"is a kiwi an animal or a fruit?"
and then she flits away.
then one of the riper ones
bountiful in fact so full and undulating i am mesmerized

a thread of drool connecting my chin and chest
she announces in a delicate and modulated voice
that makes me contort with desire
"the tuatara is here again."
"what?"
"the tuatara wants to speak to you."
"the lizard?"
*"actually, as you well know, he is a reptile but he is not a lizard, nor is he
crocodilian. the tuataras are their own order. i think that's part of his
complaint."*
"complaint? he's complaining to me?"
"somebody…doesn't seem to care."
"so what am i supposed to do about it?"
"i'm fed up i tell you," the tuatara screeches, barging into my presence,
approaching with his peculiar froggy hop
*"sure i've got a third eye on the top of my skull, and who needs periodontal
ligaments, besides we got a special hemoglobin, i'd like to see a damn
iguana survive the kind of cold your average tuatara can skate right through,
but that don't mean"/*
"you're henry, right?
"okay, yeah…"
"did't you and mildred just deliver a brood?
"okay, yeah…"
"how old are you, henry?"
"111."
"and this is your first brood?"
"what's your point?"
*"well, henry, you've been a pretty nasty character for years, kind of a local
celebrity for being such a total pain in the ass"*
"now wait a damn minute, i had a MALIGNANCY on my genitals"
"and we took care of it. we removed it, or one of the girls did, right?"
"well, sure, but…"
*"and then you got together with mildred and now you're a father. what are
you complaining about."*

"you ever seen a weta?"
"not since i named it. a cricket, right?"
*"it's a cricket as big as yer damn HAND, its hind legs are like TWO HUGE
SAWS, and i'm expected to EAT this thing. i'm crunching on these damn
critters all night, you know how much actual juice is in these cracklers?"*
*"henry. HENRY. i have absolutely nothing to do with food supply. you know
that."*
"what do you have to do with?"
"naming."
"rats. you named them, right? and pigs. and stoats."
"look, i don't MAKE them. i name them."
"who decided not to give me a dick?"
"what?"
*"I DON'T HAVE A PENIS! I DON'T HAVE A MALE INTROMISSION
ORGAN! I HAVE A CLOACAL OPENING!"*
"okay, henry, calm down."

but the tuatara is gone
as though his rage has vaporized him
he is gone from my clearing

he doesn't know how lucky he is not to have a dick.

i go back to dipping my sharpened stick into a pulpy pomegranate
making my marks
skritch skritch skritch
i'm thinking of calling it poetry.

GOING OUT TO WATER THE LAWN
having crawled up my pant leg
the lizard now lies with its spine broken
there on the front lawn
the hose clenches for no apparent reason
a cacophony of birds
and yesterday a man left blood on the sidewalk
my breath shudders in and out

the cartilage where my jaw meets my skull
is sore.
will everyone be all right?
no.
the lizard has not moved in some time.
i still feel him there
squirming at my cuff.

"...of the **lacrimae rerum**, *of the tears of which the world is made, and of the sadness of all human things..."—oscar wilde, 'de profundis'*

"there is pain ahead, coyote.
muscle, cunning, speed*? these will never set you free.*
you will lay your foot in the trap again and again
and howl at the pain the trap brings;
and then you will want that pain
every night for the rest of your life."
                    —shelley m. miller 'coyote', excerpt

6. **LOYAL SKEPTIC**: WE ALL BEGIN WITH FAITH IN OURSELVES, IN OTHERS, AND IN THE UNIVERSE.

   or the world is unpredictable and hazardous, hence people often can't trust one another.

*"**coyote:** ...i need to give my pain room to stretch...pain is a vessel, and you hold on to it in order to float...?"—murray mednick, 'the coyote cycle'*

in greek mythology, time (**kronos**) and necessity (**ananke**) made the world. 'ananke 'is the etymological source of the word 'anxiety '.

*"...when man is capable of being in **uncertainties, mysteries, doubts**, without any irritable reaching after fact and reason."—john keats*

MASLOW'S HIERARCHY OF NEEDS
1. physiological needs
2. safety needs
3. social belonging
4. esteem
5. self-actualization
6. self-transcendence

EMERGING
grasshopper legs and the trolleys creaking
just coming from the sky
that metal *is* the music, and the music is crumbling,
as music dies, it emerges.

NAKE: to make naked
RECREANT: 1. cowardly; mean spirited; subdued; crying out for mercy; recanting out of fear.
   thou must, as a foreign recreant, be led

with manacles along our street.—shake-speare(de vere)
    2. apostate; false.
RECREATION: to refresh after toil; to amuse or divert in weariness.—Samuel
Johnson's Dictionary

MOVING EAST, DAY SIX, Chicago
we get up after eleven. i call susanna feeling spaced out and empty and
inexplicably ashamed. we can't get breakfast in the restaurant in the lobby of
this labyrinthine hotel, which seems harsh and shabby, even for chicago. we
split after i cop a cup of coffee you're supposed to pay $1 for. we use the
express checkout box and move on without a backward glance. we head on
into chicago proper and i find the exact street (by happenstance) that leads to
the art institute (monroe), park the car, and find the place mobbed, but we
(maybe me, more probably susanna) have made reservations, so we slide in
pretty easily, stand in a disneyland-style maze line (for a painter!) (monet) to
get into eighteen medium-sized galleries chock full of glowing, pulsating,
glorious, sedate, passionate, reflective, deep and exhilarating paintings. but
packed with people! (with little murmuring voices emanating from the general
area of their ears, small boxes seemingly embedded in their chests. looking
dazed by the docent audio tour...) WE UNDERSTAND MONET AS A
CREATOR OF LIGHT. only GOD CREATES LIGHT!
    we take a walk to the lake and around the park. drive up lakeshore
drive. get gas and drive back down clark to halsted to steppenwolf. score the
tickets. back up halsted to some music stores tav had scoped earlier. (happily
all three of us are music freaks—in overlapping genres. tavish is amazing at
finding the 'spot 'as he calls the hippest record store in any town or city. he's
like a vinyl dowser.) we all get things we've been looking for. buzz back
down halsted to the theater to see frank galati's adaptation of faulkner's *as i
lay dying.* we are all very moved and transported. jeff perry is magnificent and
the physical production is grand—with real rain and a fantastic scene when
the wagon is overturned in a roaring river. (marilyn dodds-frank is in it and is
very fine and funny and quirky, as always. she seems to have worked really
hard and done well in chicago. LA wasn't her place. at the curtain call she
sees me from the stage and is really pleased and surprised and she yells out
to me *i'll see you later* as she exits down the vom. and we do have a nice
talk afterwards. warm and pleased for each other.) jeff is also delighted that

we made it and as a bonus, linda is in town. we go up the street to *vinci* .
although they say they're just going to have drinks, we all have full meals,
including dessert. mark and tavish really enjoyed the play and linda says
several times to me, " *it's so good that you saw it—especially you. you can
really appreciate it".* which i surely do. they insist on paying for dinner, and
also point us to the cheapest, but still reputable, hotel. a ramada/days inn in
one sprawling building on michigan avenue, across from grant park. (they
seem to go in for hotels designed by daedulus here in chicago. endless
hallways leading to…a murky future, with no escape. where's ariadne when
you need her?) most definitely a weird place, semi-well-maintained, one big
section of it was once considered well-appointed, known as the congress (!?)
hotel but now the whole deal is quite tawdry. we have to change rooms and
then wait for none-too-clean bedding. we watch some lame TV. smoke a
joint. write these words. and now to sleep. goodnight chicago.

*"notes is good enough for you people, but us likes a mixtery.'—an ex-slave
from the georgia sea islands, quoted by nathaniel mackey*

THE MIX(TERY)
allison miller is the ballsiest drummer since john densmore as dave tough,
even gene krupa in his pot-charged reveries,
maybe ginger baker, reassembled and lubricious,
poor buddy rich could not even imagine, in his wildest dreams
> (so when flash buddy opened for dusty springfield,
> [something of a doomed blonde herself] bouffant of
> goldflecked snow, cornered raccoon eyes, the woman was
> forced to bust the bozo in his finely shaved chops for his
> opening night androcentric devouring of time, his
> machismotic posturing, all the kowtowing to the pallys,
> banging on his cans for hours, while she, the headliner,
> stood offstage steaming. so on the second night, in white
> vinyl high-heeled boots, she strides into his blazed-up
> dressing closet, and honest-to-god slugs the dipshit on his
> powdered jaw. the next night, the boys in his band
> bestowed a pair of red-leather boxing gloves on the
> battling blonde, signed by each and every player *"in*

admiration". but buddy's finger snapping rigamarole rattled
her. she came out hoarse and forced and fluttery. another
chorus of the same sad song...)
allison miller can soar swell tumble and strut
she can conjure conjugation
complete with punctuation
and elucidate regret
as deft as jack dejohnette.

short exchange on 6th avenue:
"hey buddy, gotta quarter?....I'm a brooklyn dodger and I'll be a
brooklyn dodger until this country gets its share."
i shake my head, pat my pockets and mutter
"no change"
"doesn't matter. you don't need a quarter."
and he strolls away...

allison miller permits us to believe
in the beat
with untrammeled primitivistic maneuvers,
bouncing off back alleys
beating on the balustrades
knocking the pilgrims home
while the physician mist announces
anguish on the shrieking waterfront
wharves ablaze
dice on fire.
yes the mix is crazy beautiful
the mix is worlds aspin
the mix is words awhirl
the mix is killer
listen
i have never heard before now
i have not yet been graceful
only i knew what i meant
and i still don't
so, yeah

let's go get triumphant
and otherwise
let's go get a lack of ambition
real fast
with the knowledge
that we are water
or *ki* tumbling through handmade locks

the mix is a maze
flurries and fates
beyond the blanket ghost
keeping score in a naïve manner
dazzled by the sunlight through winter trees
or that thrill you get on bridges
that the girl just can't help
the mix is eroticizing the hump of the saxophone
and may the pilgrim's bless
our labile parade

i am an abject object
i can raise no preconditions
like geese migrating in the wrong direction

truly a bigger mix
than any of us can ever traverse
shouldshouldshouldshouldshouldshouldshouldshouldshouldshouldsho
uldshouldsh
shhhhhhhhh
there, where the ice is thinnest,
that's the spot
where my girl read me
and wrote me off.
still
allison miller keeps time
safe in her secret pocket.
—*2010, after the deluge...*

200

KALYGONOMIA; the laws of female beauty

ALL THE DOOMED BLONDES: Part Six
jean seberg was burned at the stake, literally, on the screen, and figuratively, by critics and audiences alike, for her performance in her film debut, *joan of arc*, directed by otto preminger, with a script by george bernard shaw, no less. she had been cast, at 17, after a nationwide talent search that included 1,800 hopefuls. jean, who had done nothing but amateur theatricals in her hometown in iowa, was submitted by an admiring neighbor. the film, featuring a spectacular performance by richard widmark, playing very much against type. [widmark was most famous for his indelible psychokiller, tommy udo, in *kiss of death,* in which he shoves an old lady in a wheelchair down a flight of stairs to her death, all the while giggling hysterically. but he is also very good as a callous lothario whose heart is opened by a dazed and troubled **marilyn monroe**, in *don't bother to knock,* a sort of psychological noir, made early in her career. although she was ridiculed, then and now, for this performance, it remains one of her most vulnerable and personal roles. she plays a traumatized young woman, still really a girl, new to the city, with dreams of glamour, trapped by her fantasies of undying love, having attempted suicide after the death of her aviator boyfriend. she is freshly out of an institution, and so shy it hurts to watch her. wearing very little makeup and a plain dress, she is pure norma jean, distracted and troubled. using another woman's jewelry and negligee, she attempts to transform into the 'marilyn 'we will come to know and adore, but the cost is a desperate madness and delusion. widmark's character is saved from terminal cynicism by interacting with this damaged girl's innocent soul. he is moved beyond himself to care for her. and marilyn as an actress is completely committed and selfless. she makes no attempt to woo the audience, in fact she is deliberately cruel to the child she is supposed to be looking after, using a deep, flat, cruel voice we would never hear again. something is revealed in this film that no other role would provide or require]. but back to **jean seberg**. *joan of arc* is now considered a classic rendition of the oft-told tale of the girl whom god selects for sainthood. the time it outraged the religious community and movie critics alike, especially for the natural and sincere performance of the fresh-faced, insouciant, jean seberg. she was considered not 'pious 'enough in her attitude, not sufficiently in awe of the voice of god, too certain of her own strength, and woefully inadequate as an actress. despite her lack of piety, or

perhaps because of it, preminger cast her again in *bonjour tristesse,* to play a spoiled adolescent. again, seberg is self-possessed and straightforward, refusing to indulge in histrionics, or false drama, despite preminger's tendency to overheat the images. the film was only a modest success. the combative nature of her allure, the rebellious charge in her beauty, the sphinxish smile, is pure love goddess, but seberg brought her own personal and political element to the task. after two more middling american films, and perhaps as a gesture of disdain, she took the role of patricia, a free-spirited american girl in paris, in jean-luc godard's *breathless.* overnight, she became an international sensation, and the first notable american actress to work in the french film industry. she returned to hollywood in 1963 to star in robert rossen's *lilith,* as another otherworldly woman. her co-star is warren beatty, befuddled and sexy as ever, and a callow peter fonda, in a daze. as with joan, she brought an earthiness to a mythical character, lilith, said to be adam's first wife, made from the same clay. and although the film is ambitious beyond the writer/director's talent, seberg proves the depth and wit of her poetic imagination. she was never to be tested to that degree, again. at the height of her fame, she stopped working in films. on september 8, 1979, two french policemen looked into a white renault that had been parked for ten days on a quiet street in paris. they found the decomposing body of jean seberg, with a bottle of barbiturates. she had, since the late sixties, been involved with the black panthers, the NAACP, and native american activists, and other political causes. in 1970, the FBI, which had been harassing her for decades, spread the false assertion that the child seberg was carrying was not fathered by her husband, romain gary, but by raymond hewitt, a member of the black panthers. the story was reported by the gossip columnist joyce haber in the *los angeles times, and* was also printed by *newsweek,* consequently being picked up by many other news outlets and spread widely. seberg went into premature labor and, on august 23, 1970, gave birth to a baby girl. the child died two days later. seberg held a funeral in her hometown with an open casket allowing reporters to see the infant's white skin, a heartbreaking and humiliating display. and still the rumors persisted. she attempted suicide on each subsequent august 23rd, surviving each time, even after flinging herself under a train in 1978. finally, in 1979, she succeeded in her escape.

here's an anecdote that gives a great sense of the spirit of jean seberg: shortly after the assassination of martin luther king, a fundraiser was held in hollywood for the *poor people's campaign,* an organization started by king right before his death. the party was in the home of the producer ed lewis. nearly everyone of a liberal persuasion in the industry showed up, including **marlon brando**, the writer and producer abby mann, and jean seberg. brando was holding forth in angry, radical, terms saying, "*now's the time to DO something…i want the names of everybody who isn't here and i'm going to put them in the trades.*" he kept referring to the no-shows as shallow and hypocritical. the whole time brando was ranting, seberg was whispering in mann's ear, "*what is this, a take-a-negro-to-lunch meeting? he's the biggest piece of shit i've ever heard.*" marlon had announced in *newsweek* that he was leaving acting to dedicate his life to civil rights—and that he was going to dye his skin and live like a black man. gradually, other conversations began bubbling up, until brando finally exploded, "*who's that talking in the bar? i want him HERE.*" and out from the bar, bemused and smirking strolled the guilty party: james baldwin, saying "*i'm sorry marlon, did i miss something?*" seberg laughed and whooped. brando was not amused. "*marlon just glared at jean,*" said mann. "*he was so pissed off that he wasn't being taken seriously.*" as always, jean seberg refused to be intimidated.

"*the important thing…is that you must have, deep down as the deepest thing in you, a sense of equality. then anybody will do anything for you.*"—gertrude stein

ATROCIOUS CITIES
just tell me the story
holding an awareness of why you want to tell it
think of it as an object inside yourself you very much want
to examine more closely
look at with more than reaction
without the filter of your viscera
come around the corner to meet yourself

yes an awful lightness
up into a golden evening
no result without desire
no belief without despair

no faith without trembling
only instantaneous truth
atrocities occur
work goes on in the burbling crematorium
atrocious cities sprawl across the continent

and still we canter along the river
unaware of our oblivion
blaming the rider for the horse's stumble
smothered by patricide
brought low by sibling crush
stridulations spring forth not without impact
mice babies scrambled by ultrasound
all manner of horror leaving something to be
desired. fuming in the drizzle of this blighted bread
hair trigger tempers jumping the gun
leaping from trees
falling from the sky
each snowflake a new mechanism
on the theme of dissolution

"INSIDE ANY DEEP ASKING IS THE ANSWERING"—Rumi

WHAT WE FORGET
we have forgotten the first time
we chanced to hear
the coast is clear
we have forgotten that people are
luminous beings
or the joy of going over the speed limit in a 2-tone sedan
the significance of the path through the sea
and that the highest good
is usefulness

WITHOUT SHOES
and so the shoes we wear are weapons
snakeskin ostrich vinyl or canvas

not just a volcano
but a god.
barbaric yawp
in sequent toil.
my short crawl to the open hole
slight tumble
brief escape
how guilty will this winter be
do you suppose?
if empty broken shells
with all dust views
peeling the sills down to bare wood
too many layers
exposing faded patterns
maddening to strangers
and intolerable to all
crossing jagged mysteries
without shoes.

ALOHA SUITE/ COYOTE GOES TO KAUAI/ Part 6
there is no way around
the historicity of shoes
repudiated
by an extraordinary variety of browns.

she has a cadre of loyal young men
ready for work, C-Bo and J-Toe, Tony from next door,
and one sturdy filipino, about this high,
of indeterminate age or name.
even she cannot understand a word he says,
but he makes it beautiful anyway,
he gets the good job done,
like the time he hefted a ton of stone cupola,
all by himself,
that one she had shipped from bali,
hoisted up to the steeply slanted roof,
red clay quadrants,

to the pyramidal pinnacle.

    jimmy yancey tickles the ivories, somewhere in the air, moaning low:
        now the sheriff come and got me
        he handcuffed me right and down

        i was a poor poor prisoner
        carried off all by myself

she has an eye
for the perfect length
of vines grown thick as anacondas,
vegetation sculpted by geologic time
festooned with pendulous blossoms astoundingly turquoise,
pistil stamens carpels
filaments fused and the anthers free
dripping stigma
attached by compact anther cap of dusty grey mauve,
all of it draping the grandfather tree,
dead since the last century
still standing sentinel
up behind the main house,
his mighty limbs drooping with long
heavy
strands
of waxy leaves,
and of course the multitudinous blooms,
the whole cloak
on his sturdy shoulders,
on his massive head,
sure to withstand
any hurricane at all.

COYOTE ANGEL LISTENS TO THE RADIO
lassoer in lingerie told me
she was in a place called misery
maybe she meant missouri

i'm in a blizzard in hartsville
icy bridges span the cumberland
it's a storm in tennessee's heart
even the transvestites of nashville
are having trouble with the boss
kind hatmen defer to the salted roofs
atom bombs in the mouth
steel guitars ring out
remember
the night
has a thousand frozen tears.

and still the snow comes down
blinding the fire
and still the coyote angel
spreads his influence
sends messengers to retrieve his snakeskin boots
slings wings on his spurs
vinegar pepper on his beans
limping dogs cower in the wind

and still the snow comes down
scrapings from the whitest sky
courthouse bricks standing here
for centuries and then some
topped by a squat cupola
empty worlds have come and gone
and still the new snow comes down
mama said there'd be cafes like this
mashed potatoes drift against the bricks
old man winter has sure set in

      got to dance dance dance
      right here on the spot

i seem to be
what i am not

you see there
a god of thieves
a great pretender
a head and a dick
garlanded by the pitiful river
wilted shoebox full of snow
on the encrusted riverbank
and still it flows
in flight
melting.
old man winter has surely kicked in.
last time this happened it was a hundred years from now
when they laid off those fallen shoes
shops closed
towns moved on
just like the river
even the postman split
the judge has left the courthouse
even the worn carpets have been ripped
from the upstairs gallery
and smoked for fuel
two hills over they have abandoned the atomic energy
planted on the crest
supposed to be bulldozed
or bushhogged
or some dang thing…
old man winter pleads for mercy
doctor doctor
please don't leave
all i really need
is bushhoggin 'work
to clear the land of poverty
let me play my organ
on the frigid river.
you won't hang up…
willya?

he may be cooler than james dean in *giant*
even steve mcqueen in *the getaway*
or monty in *red river*
marked by an elaborate spirit tattoo
of a voodoo indian *san miquel* and his bone, held at his crotch,
inches from the fangs of a snarling wolf
infertile women line up to touch his meteorites
glad all over
elixir for the demiurge
flows more phallic than testicular
aprons billowing
women wipe their hands
dishing up the green beans and corn
arousing a contagious joy.

gowns more encrustations than sewn
evoking what we permit ourselves to see
our sorry shameful selves
with thirty-two pairs of eyes
and seven impossible wings
we preen

the rod of truth goes both ways
life from one end death from the other
dendrite and axon
bipolar straight up to the brain
daddy who will not let you down
pillar of fire more resplendent than the sun
it seems

then the moment passes
the costume is revealed aromatic
of the wrong sensations
tinkling sound of a girl on a dromedary
plummeting away
thirty-six pairs of wings or whatever
useless to us

that magic moment has aged indeed
when we took our time growing up
singing old and new songs in rooms
without names.
now we mock what moves us
give secret love to our cartoons
our pallid faces smeared with the shades of deepest night
playing at boogie-man
with girls of flaxen hair
make a clown of loneliness
above what's below
in your room the color has faded
where once your very skin was aflame
where you danced the unknowable steps
in mirrors without frames
now we worship what frightens us
destroying what we adore

whose name is in us?
if at all
can that infernal region be finally found
that we call
home
where we are new
every morning

ME AND GARY BUSEY ROB A BANK
we come out with six-guns blazing
with a definite kick
and we hop on our horses and gallop on out of there…
it's 1972
and we're acting in the third sequel to *the magnificent 7*
the *magnificent 7 ride..!*
shades of steve mcqueen
james coburn
both of them the essence of cool
charles bronson

yul brynner
robert vaughan
not as cool, but still pretty slick,
eli wallach as the vicious mexican bandit, caldera,
basically the same part he played in *the good, the bad and the ugly*
he's the **ugly,** tuco,
(they wouldn't do that anymore..cast a jew as a mexican. and a good thing,
too.)
and speaking of which
this sequel of the *7* features lee van cleef
in a departure from his character in *the good, the bad, and the ugly*
he's definitely the **bad** in that one, indelibly,
here he's **good,** steadfast u.s.marshal, chris adams,
backed up by a cohort of characters from the dusty streets of the hollywood
west:
lethal-looking luke askew
big bill lucking
the great leering ed lauter
crafty pedro almendariz jr.
(why isn't he playing tuco?)
anachronistic michael callen, late of elvis 'posse,
playing the hip newspaperman from the east, noah hayes,
riding with a very different posse
(or maybe not so different. a few years later i worked with red allen, elvis '
right hand man in everything. he would fit right in with this gang.)
and oh yeah, ralph waite, as the decent rancher, jim.

on the distaff side, there's the flirty, sultry, stefanie powers, as the cantina
girl, laurie gunn, with her blouse off her shoulders and her smoky eyes.
and especially, mariette hartley plays the marshal's brand new bride, arrila,
wholesome but hot, who can clearly hold her own.

i play the good kid, sliding into badness, shelly donovan.
seems i've robbed something or other,
and in my first scene i'm confined to a cell,

with my tearful mom, played by allyn-ann mclerie, prim redhead, pleading for
me, asking me *"why?"*
i have my contrite face on, grasping the bars, puppy-eyed.
strong-willed arrila hears my mother's cries
and pleads my case to her hard-nosed spouse.

    *...chris refuses his new wife arilla's request to release teenager shelly
donovan, jailed for robbery.*
he says no, with that stern squint.

> *the kid committed a crime,* he declares,
> *simple as that.*
> *he needs to be punished.*

but

> *...the next morning, loading prisoners onto the tucson prison
> wagon chris decides to free donovan.*

he lets me go!
after all,
i've just fallen in with the wrong guys
i'm in cahoots with the bad boys,
the rapscallion allen brothers,
played with a sneer by gary busey, as hank allen,
along with the producer's son, bob jaffe, giving us the callow younger brother,
bob allen.
here's the weird thing...that's the way i remember the story.
but the truth, the real plot is...

>   *...donovan celebrates his release with hank and bob allen.*
> **donovan** *leads the brothers in a bank robbery...*

i'm candlewick!
just as i had been all those years before,
in *pinocchio* at the eaglet theater,
leading the poor puppet astray.
singing gleefully,

> *"hi-diddle-dee-dee/ an actor's life for me/ hi-diddle-dee-day/ an
> actor's life is gay/ it's great to be a celebrity/ an actor's life for
> me/ hi-diddle-dee-dum/ an actor's life is fun...!*

braying desperately while transforming into a donkey,

212

trapped forever on pleasure island.
i'm the troublemaker
the wastrel
the curious cat
          ...wounding chris, donovan abducts arilla and escapes with the
     allens..
except i thought it was gary who did all that cool shit.
shot the sheriff,
stole the bride.
but now it comes back to me,
naw, it's me!
now i see
myself
charging out of the bank's facade with pistols flaring,
smoke and sparks spewing from the long barrels of our weighty revolvers
i remember my bold run
out the doors,
flanked by flimsy pillars
scrambling down the steps
taking a wide stance,
pointing my gun
right arm stretched out full length,
just like steve mcqueen, gary cooper, clint eastwood,
and plugging lee van cleef!
i do a running mount onto my spooked horse,
pumping stirrups, urging the animal on
as i thunder past her i seize mariette/arilla (a lithe stuntman) around the waist
and swing her up onto the pommel of my saddle.
hightailing out on the packed dirt of the town square, in a cloud of dust.

now this part i have always vividly recalled, down through the years, because
as soon as we galloped behind the unconvincing fronts of the backlot town—
we hit paved road! [this particular element of the trick was not made clear to
me by the laconic wrangler who sidled up to me that morning, and mumbled
from the side of his mouth, "*are ya 'handy?*" in stuntman lingo that means,
"*are you capable. can you ride? can you fall? can you take a punch? can you
throw a punch? can you ride a motorcycle? are you handy?*"

well, yeah, i could ride a horse, and…most of that other stuff…i couldn't make a motorcycle fly…but i'd give it a shot]. however…when the horses hit the pavement of that road they start sliding and scuffling around like drunks on ice. the bewigged stuntman doubling marriette hastily slips off from in front of me; grabbing the reins, yanking down hard and forcing the bit back at the same time. the horse squeals and twists but finds his footing. i hang on like a baby chimp, my arms clinging to the horse's lathered neck. meanwhile, gary's mount seems to go airborne, scrabbling his front hooves over to the nearby dirt. and bucking nearly in half. gary is whooping and hollering like a rodeo star. we are both laughing maniacally as we leap off our ponies. *"man, that was some shit! what a trip!"* gary shouts out. i heartily concur, tossing my hat in the air as he punches my shoulder. and we dance in a circle, whooping.and hollering.

the thing is, gary and i had smoked a fat doobie right before the scene, in his narrow room in the honey wagon. or maybe it was my cubicle. maybe i brought the pot. that would certainly fit the pattern, huh?
anyway, gary and i were bouncing with joy to be playing cowboys for REAL, which is how it felt, because the camera made the whole thing ACTUAL.
with the deafening blast of the bullets,
leaping onto the backs of real bucking broncos!
the surprising weight of the hot guns,
the outfits!
the hats!
the boots!
all so dusty and aged and authentic looking,
i mean, fuck man, what FUN!
just like when we were ten and had gunfights, with carved pieces of wood sufficing as six-guns, ducking behind rocks, making that *"pchew! pchew!"* sound of firing, that *'ping! ping!* marking ricochets,
and, especially, emulating *high noon,* fiercely disputing who got who first, what a fantasy come utterly true on a sensorial level…
when the A.D. rapped on the door,
we took one last toke and hit the ground grinning.

but things did not go so smoothly in the real story

...revived two days later, chris sets off in search of arilla, accompanied by noah...in the desert, noah and chris find arilla dead. chris tracks down the allens and demands donovan's whereabouts....hank reveals that donovan has fled to mexico, and admits that arilla was raped and tortured before her murder. chris shoots hank, and bob pleads for his life, insisting he did not join in the assault, but chris shoots bob anyway, as noah looks on in shock and horror.

so that means...my character did join in the torturing and raping and murdering of arrilla. i did not remember that at all. I thought I was a good boy gone bad—but not that bad. eventually chris does track down sly shelly donovan. but i'm already dead, my head stoved in, killed by the marauding bandits; along with jim, the noble farmer, and most of the women of the town, who had been left unprotected because the marshal was busy tracking me down to exact his revenge. so those needless deaths were my fault. i do recall vividly the slab of plastic gore slapped and glued onto my forehead; and i remember lee and michael callen turning me over, and their looks of disgust on their faces. now i see that my perfidy drove the whole twisted plot—infecting even the best of the men; and causing carnage and death everywhere.

not to put too fine a point on it, but, let's at least admit, there is a pattern here...a motif, found in a dream, a fantasy; yes, a made-up story, nothing but movie magic; telling a tale about a lost boy, bleating his heart out on some lost island of pleasure; having committed real crimes, some of which he barely recalls, but guilty as all hell, nonetheless.

Hi Son,

Just a quick note to say hello! I had another weird happening in Willits—i told you that about a year ago i turned on the T.V. and stood there and waited for the picture to come on & the first face i see was you face to face—well it happened again. i turned the set on and i layed down on the floor waiting for the set to come in and there you were—in Jail—both times were closeup shots of you. i couldn't believe it would happen twice—

well anyway—how are you—Hope you are doing your exercises—we have gone out and played golf the last couple of days—teed off at 7:00 AM. it is really nice that time of the morning—

Morine is not feeling well. i am worried about her—she won't go to the doctor—
We both send our love—
Dad & Morine
(a letter from my father—from 1973 or 4)

"taking humankind as a whole, the incidence of the virtues shared by all is no more remarkable than the multiplicity of defects peculiar to each. it is probably true to say that it is not common sense that is the commonest thing in the world but common kindness....even if this kindness is so paralyzed by self-interest as to be in abeyance, it still exists."—marcel proust, 'in search of lost time: in the shadow of young girls in flower'

LET IT BURN
turning my back on the beast highway
clothed in nothing but scathing sunlight
to leave unreadable tracks in parched loam
some vulpine yearning
stained like old boots
spurs me on
much obliged
la la how the life goes on
how quick we come to cedar grove
and the terminal obligations
sure i see the hope in your backyard eyes
while my fingers abrade your tear-slicked lips
i see the fawn in the meridian
where the lawn grows lush
i see the falling poplar tree

fort trash is in flames.

8 DAYS IN RUSSIA, Kaliningrad, Friday, 2007
once again a packed lecture at the university. i was more prepared in terms of my subject matter—but we were still totally unprepared technically. fortuitously, one of the more resourceful students led us to a room with a monitor and deck and i was able to show the beginning of *high sierra*, and the

whole first act of *the maltese falcon*. only one person out of the group of 40 or so had ever seen bogart before. no one in the class had ever seen steve mcqueen! this is really hard for me to absorb. to me that's like never having seen a tree, or the ocean. that two cultures could be cut off from each other so utterly, is just stunning, especially when one of them is so ubiquitous and influential—and now the russians are hungry for everything they can get. (would that the curiosity went both ways. when i leave art gives me some russian films from the silent era, and some excellent contemporary films, none of which have gotten any exposure in america.) anyway, i did manage to give them some idea of what this particular film, *the maltese falcon*, and this meeting of actor and role, signified.

i put together three pages on clift/brando/dean for the screening of *the wild one* tonight, and masha set about translating it. turns out there's no microphone tonight, and art is worried that she won't be heard in the auditorium, so she is to do it from the booth, where the mike is functioning. trouble is she can't actually hear me in the booth, so we mark the breaks, but then we don't have time to rehearse, or even try it out before the audience is in the room. we start out fine, but then she gets ahead of me, and then as i try to catch up, she interrupts me, TWICE, and finally i hold up my hand and yell, *'stop!'*, which gets a big laugh and applause. i conclude, to very warm clapping. now the problem is the film is not subtitled, or even dubbed. it's shown in this odd, only-in-russia manner, with a simultaneous translation shouted in the background as the original soundtrack can be faintly heard. there is a man voicing all the male characters, and a woman doing all the females. It's like someone talking, no, yelling, in your ear all the way through the film, in gibberish (at least to me.) it's impossible to enter the story, and since this is not a strong film anyway, it doesn't play too well. but brando comes through very effectively, and so does lee marvin as his nemesis. the last scene is very stirring. and the scene in the park with the woman spread at his feet as he leans on the gleaming motorcycle, causes sighs to waft through the room. brando's famous response to the question, *'what are you rebelling against so hard?'*—*'whaddya got?'*—raises a few cheers.

afterwards, art, masha and i, and roman, a longtime friend of masha's, in town for a week, and a very fine fellow, go to a club called *dreadnought*, for some beers. i have a 'baltic eel', which is surprisingly good, and an enormous tankard of russian white beer. art has to leave early, his wife had some sort of operation today and is depressed. roman and masha want to go club hopping, but i beg off. still subpar health-wise and TIRED. tomorrow they are taking me to the seashore.

MONTGOMERY CLIFT, MARLON BRANDO and JAMES DEAN were, without doubt, the three most influential, and most gifted, male movie stars of the 1950s. with their quicksilver intensity and unconventional eroticism, clift, brando and dean seemed to herald a revolution in acting style as well as in sensibility. shredding accepted notions of actorly behavior, (and wardrobe), they caught their audiences by surprise, they were self-consciously extraordinary: they were considered neither innocent youths nor conventional adults; they were strikingly handsome men yet they were unsure of their masculinity; they were fascinated by american culture, and its fascination with them, they considered themselves 'indigenous émigre's'. they were highly aware of the sense in which they all shared a set of basic values and concerns; indeed in both their private and their professional lives, the number of similarities between them was remarkable. all three were products of the american midwest: clift and brando were both born in omaha, nebraska, the very navel of the nation. dean was born in marion, indiana. all three clashed with their fathers when it became known that they were set on pursuing a career as 'effeminate 'and 'frivolous 'as acting. all three were profoundly obsessed with their mothers. all three began their careers, learned their craft and became stars in the post-war years, the era of mccarthyism and the cold war. all three were heavily influenced by the theories and discoveries of stanislavski and anton chekhov, especially as interpreted by lee strasberg and the actor's studio, (with freud as the man behind the curtain). although monty, who was a few years older than brando and dean, was always suspicious of the method, especially its more cultish aspects. he learned more from alfred lunt and michael chekhov. all three felt themselves to be bisexual and therefore well suited to roles which expressed an erotic quality bereft of rigid gender identity. as each man reached adulthood, he was confronted by a daunting array of social, sexual, cultural and political problems. it seemed as though society was unusually anxious for its young citizens to conform to traditional values and familiar types. as did many others of their generation, clift, brando and dean rebelled against this climate of conformity. the difference was that they rebelled in the most sharply self-aware manner, in the most powerful medium for communicating to large

218

numbers of other humans ever known, generating the most memorable of images. marlon brando in full regalia as johnny, leader of the *"black rebel motorcycle club"* in *the wild one*, is an extraordinary sight. while presenting the tough surface of the adolescent male, brando permits us to see precarious this image really is and how tormented and anguished he is, afraid as any child, the real person is beneath the superficial machismo. making johnny even sexier. (indeed, the reason brando signed on to the project [it was a distinct step down at this early point in his career.] was to bring a level of compassion and understanding to the problems of disaffected youth in america after the war. the film was based on two journalistic reports of actual incidents of towns being occupied by roving gangs of frustrated young men, traumatized by war and severely underemployed. however, production codes mandated cutting out any reasons that might be cited to justify rebellion, unemployment, as for instance, or a repressive society. brando was bitterly disappointed with the result,and railed against the script while shooting the film. the gangs are made to seem inexplicably irresponsible; all possible societal explanations are ignored and consequently the movie becomes a display of violence for its own sake. setting a pattern that would be exploited for decades. on its truest, most beautiful level, the film becomes a veritable ballet, [reminiscent of douglas fairbanks in *'thief of baghdad*], featuring a fleeing woman, and half-man/half-motorcycles, pursuing and being pursued through slick streets and turbulent trees. the film was banned in britain until 1969, for fear it would incite random acts of mayhem. brando characterization contradicts the movie's general, garish tone. but you have to be looking at him clear-eyed and openhearted to see it. if you let him, he will draw you in, intrigue you, he's so seductive, physically imposing but oddly insecure and unsure. he rarely instigates anything, usually he just reacts. when at the end of the film, he rides back into town, alone, he takes his first steps toward controlling his own life.

but there is no doubt that he is still wild. still the wild **one.** untamed, just as holly golightly describes herself in *breakfast at tiffany's*. brando in every role exemplifies this comment by richard dyer: "*one of the types that stars embody is the type of 'individual 'itself: they embody that particular conception of what it is to be human that characterizes our culture.*"

"simply put, the more brando disappeared into a role, the more he became himself, the more the film became a brando film, his acting a tour de force bigger than anything else on screen. this was the trap he set for himself with his great films of the 1950s, a streetcar named desire *and* on the *waterfront, where his performances are so convincing as to seem menacingly, dangerously 'real'…he is radically singular: a man alone, isolated by his madness or his anachronistic code or his class or his explosiveness, in addition to his dazzling beauty, his face unrivaled in film history."—dan chiasson, new york review of books*

MY DINNER WITH HENRY MILLER, Pacific Palisades
he's in his walker, grumbling his way to the door, shouting through it, *"yeah, yeah, hang on for chrissakes..oh, it's yo u,thought it was my girl-friend."*

    "no, it's us," lorinne says. *"we've brought you your dinner."*

    lorinne is part of a loose cohort of approximately twenty people formed for the sole purpose of bringing henry miller dinner, on a rotating basis. each person brings a meal and an interesting guest, capable of providing intelligent conversation with one of the ages' great raconteurs. on this night i have the extreme good fortune, if somewhat dubious credentials, to play the part of the evening's entertainment. i'm in my twenties, a voracious reader, and can basically talk to anybody.

    "sure, kiddo, sure. whadja bring me?" he flings the door open, and scuttles backwards in his walker, like a very agile crab.

    "roast duck with truffles," lorinne says as she moves into the kitchen. i squeeze in behind, carrying two brown shopping bags brimming with tupperware containers and two bottles of vintage french wine. *"garlic mashed potatoes, and green beans with almonds."*

    "as the french do."

    "oui, a la francais, and cheesecake for dessert."

    "well, i can always use a little cheesecake." and he pinches her on the butt, i swear to god. lorinne appears delighted, (although years later, reading this, she denies this outrageous gesture ever occurred. no one ever pinched her ass, she majestically declared), and giggles as she unpacks what turns out to a really delicious repast, and says *"this is darrell".*

as she bustles around unpacking bags, i become mesmerized by a stack of paintings, tempura i think, on rough sketch paper, neatly piled at the end of a long high table covered with paint and brushes and artist's paraphernalia. the entire wall behind the table is glass, as is half the ceiling, kind of a solarium in lieu of a living room. the art is something like picasso's black and white erotic sketches, in chagall's colors. wild, exuberant, chock full of life. apparently you can judge henry's vitality on any given day by how many paintings he has produced. by the looks of it, today he feels very fine indeed.

"go ahead, take a look, i just do it to keep the sap oozing, if you know what i mean…whaddya think, any good? say whatever you want, i can take it. also i don't give a shit."

"no, man….i dig them….they exude, um…joy and.."

"exude? jesus christ, lorinne, you brought me a fuckin wordsmith…where'd you go to school, kid, yale?"

"oh, henry stop teasing..," lorinne calls from the kitchen.

"it's okay…completely pretentious choice of..uh, i dropped out of ucla…i'm just..man, i'm intimidated. i mean you're one of my favorites.."

he kinda leers at me like the wolf in little red riding hood. *"nonsense. of course i am. take it easy, kid. i'm just rattling your chain. banging on your cage. testing your mettle, huh? good decision to drop out, by the way.."*

and he whirls his aluminum contraption, his portable half-cage, around in a sweeping circle, like a mansatyr with six legs, and stomps right up to me, and gives my shoulder a jab. *"i'll tell you what, my intimidated pal, I'm plenty pissed off. these cocksuckers, these american nazis, there's an oxymoron for you, emphasis on the moron, say what you will about america, and i WILL, they got nothin on the germans when it comes to complete and utter idiocy, and my people, to my lifelong dismay come from german stock, sauerkraut for brains, and now these popinjays in there silly little uniforms and boots and buckles and suspenders and fuckin armbands are at it again, can't kill enough of the poor yids, nothin but class in that race, nothin but art and music and joy, so of course these slugs these insects, lower than insects, grubs, feeding off the teat of the planet, deluded to the point of believing somehow they are superior in their pastiness and perversion, superior to ALL of us to the point that they must MARCH down the middle of the street in fuckin SKOKIE, illinois, eighty percent jewish, eighty five, and these assholes want to march through this perfectly lovely neighborhood, to what? flaunt the absolute bankruptcy of their pathetic...concepts, notions, one must not deign to label this drivel they spout and spew as a philosophy, or even a bestial reaction to their own craven terrors! do they want to gloat over the deaths of SIX MILLION human beings? damn these motherfuckers, damn them to the hell of their own devising!"*

he pauses and glares at me, as if it's clearly at least partially my fault, and i had better get my ass together and do something about it.

"yeah, but you gotta let them march. it's free speech." i offer this up expecting, even hoping, to draw his ire.

"those thugs can kiss my ass," and he grabs his crotch. *"i got their free speech right here."*

i must admit i am absolutely delighted with this diatribe, with his stupendously high dudgeon. the old rapscallion is still in the game. ready to cause a riot, or at least a disturbance, of the nonexistent peace.

"i'll tell you what, henry, if you lead a counter-demonstration, just plant yourself in the middle of the street, on your mighty steed there, hundreds, maybe thousands of people will fill in beside you and behind you, i'm sure of it. just fill the streets of skokie so there's nowhere for them to march."

"goddamit, that is an excellent suggestion, i like this kid, lorinne, LET'S DO IT! lorinne you hear that? we're going to skokie. helluva a good idea. get me a plane ticket!"

lorinne comes in from the kitchen to calm the boys down. *"henry, you know you can't fly."*

"bullshit, the kid here will carry me on board. right, me bucko?"
"you can count on me."
"show him around, henry, dinner's almost ready."

so he leads me on a tour of his pacific palisades digs, from the outside, a blandly normal, upper-middle class residence, in a nice neighborhood. inside—light-filled, no air conditioning as far as i could tell—that would have been a disappointment, if not quite a nightmare, but the place was given unmistakable character by the hundreds of images, most of them carefully cut from newspapers or magazines, and taped to the walls, along with several framed photographs of a beautiful asian woman, about thirty-five years old.

"who's this, man? such a beauty."

"i'll say. you have good taste, sir. that's my girlfriend, believe it or not. never met a better woman. she says she loves me, but i don't know why. she could do a helluva lot better. she should, in fact, i tell her every damn day. i'm a disgruntled sonofabitch most of the time. and i can't really fuck her…but, i'll tell you what, eating pussy was always one of my spec-i-al-i-ties. i'm quite dextrous, but of course i was very well trained. strenuously and strictly. so that's my ace in the hole…so to speak." he chuckles sardonically, as do i, in a higher register. i have a moment, a bubble of awareness, of how enormously fortunate, indeed blessed, i am to be here in this home with this cultural hero, this personal saint, from whom i had gathered, faintly, but now coming, in the flesh, into finer and finer focus, the wondrous varieties of mortal, carnal, spiritual, experience available to the sincere seeker. i notice a photo, cameo shaped, clipped from a newspaper now yellowed to brown. its a shot of joan baez and bob dylan snuggling at the apex of their love affair. dylan especially looks quite cuddly. so i inquire, *'you dig bob dylan?'*

"sure. the music's simplistic, but he's a good writer. flights of fancy that will cut your throat. he can't hold a candle to his namesake, naturally, a bit of a joker and a thief, just to paraphrase, and he's a rude little shit, i'll give him that. fucking guy comes over, joannie brings him over, now there's a broad i admire the shit out of. that babe's got balls. the joan of arc of the twentieth century, not that we deserve one, but she's swell, that joannie, and funny as only really smart women can be. beats hell out of all the supposedly amusing wits of the male persuasion. women know the fuckin 'TRUTH, and they know exactly why men are hopeless goons. still, they tolerate us. god knows why, cuz i sure don't. but yeah, she brings this little shrimp over and he skulks around…lurks in the corner like a..i don't know, a scared little ferret. you know, like the kind of guy, if you approach him, he folds in. fuckin 'unnerving. then he kinda snarls, under his breath, so i can't hear a word of it. fuck that. i threw him out."

"wait, you bounced bob dylan?"

"fuck, yes!" he fairly crows. *"it's my house, my very castle, he could at least speak!"*

"i'll bet he was intimidated.."

and he gives my shoulder a jab. *'thereyago…i like this kid, lorinne…"*

lorinne approaches, platter in hand, *"i knew you would.."* she winks at me. I fairly beam.

we sit down to dinner by candlelight. i have done my homework and i bring out the big guns straight away.

"so henry, i know you revere the russian writers...who do you...or what books...do you consider essential for..."

"for anybody who touts himself as a reader," and he glares at me. *"i got three words for you, punk, dostoyevsky, dostoyevsky, and dostoyevsky, and when you finish every jot and tittle he ever scratched out in blood on rough paper, read it all again. slower. then cleanse your palate with gorky and take a shot at tolstoy, although let's face it, his enlightenment came too late to do anybody any fuckin good in his lifetime, but we here in the future we have a lot to thank him for, not least his little talk with chekhov, you know the old man summoned our anton, more or less demanding that the good doctor get down to business. anton chekhov is absolutely, incorrigibly, profoundly human, implacable in his searching, his exploration, his heartbreaking discoveries, and his brilliant, cellular understanding of the pathos, the hilarious, rapturous tragedy of life, for want of a better word."*

mind spinning a bit i offer, *"what about turgenev?"*

"you can skip turgenev," he says with a brusque wave of the back of his hand. *"he just circles around it, hemming and hawing. although there are moments in 'a month in the country', asides really. chekhov dissects it, but gently, carefully, so we get the whole picture. he throws back the blanket, where lawrence and i tear the clothes right off the broad."*

lorinne clears her throat and gives our host a sidelong glance. i wonder if he means d.h. or durrell, or both, but the moment passes before i can muster the nerve.

"sorry, my dear. got all het up. it's his fault," and he waves a fork at me. *"i meant no disrespect. the gruel is consummate, by the way. fresh, just the way i like it. real vegetables. haricot vertes` with the almonds sautéed to perfection. where'd you get this bread?"*

"henry," she asks, *"did you ever see chekhov well-acted?"*

"coupla times. in london. i thought the french did the atmosphere well, if you know what i mean. the germans are...let's just say, i ran for the exits. they can't do it here in america, in my experience. far too psychological and

emotionally indulgent. have you done it, baby? i bet you would be sensational."

"well, yes, i think i got a handle on it. his through-line of action is so vivid. it can be done."

"but's it's the stories. the short stories. reading them is like reading the sonnets. i need to read it, lick it off the page. that's my metier. and, of course, despite what you theatah folk might say, his short fiction is the apex of his gifts to us."

i make note of this guidance. must get right on the complete chekhov short stories.

henry pours us all more wine.

there is a lull while we all bask.

"so what about american writers," i say.

"you mean besides me?" he glowers at me, looking fierce, then, his eyes sparkling, he chuckles. *"had you going there didn't i? scared ya, you little shit...well, i'll tell ya, all of these cocksucking critics always cite the same three assholes: faulkner, fitzgerald and hemingway. as if those three bastards INVENTED THE WRITTEN WORD, american-style. have these pompous blowhards never heard of SHERWOOD ANDERSEN, one of the greatest storytellers who ever lived, DREISER, DOS PASSOS, (and the beats!? well, the beats can and did kiss my ass.) how about fuckin MELVILLE? he writes from life, ever read TYPEE?, PIERRE? MELVILLE is as modern, today, this minute, and will remain modern, which is to say original, which is to say IMMORTAL, until the churning cosmos evaporates into mist and we transmute into stardust. or, alternatively, and far more likely, the whole rotten putrid sinkhole of what we call being, the supposedly HUMAN being, is reduced to slurry and flushed down the toilet of the universe, like a giant turd, into the blackest of black holes!"* and he chuckles again, merrily. *"kid, you got me all wound up."* and he slaps the table, hard. *"let's have some more of this excellent vino. thank you, madame lorinne, you are a veritable goddess. thank you for your care."* now he has a tear, just one, in the corner of each eye.

"i cannot thank you enough." he puts his hand on hers, both palms down. and once again we have one of those pauses. they used to call it grace.

"stop flirting, henry. you're incorrigible' , but she smiles shyly, and lowers her gaze. she may even be blushing. it's hard to tell in the candlelight.

WITH BILL AT ELAINE'S/ WALLPAPER SKY/1997
clad in the best goods
engaged in
a glorious mortality
full of words
like giant luscious pears
even in his gray eminence
a giddy youth
given to quick dashes uptown
for latenight saloon reveries
and whatever fine ripened cheese
they happen to have around
only parmesan and goat?
oh, good enough!

the proprietress is
just the right size for her establishment
and there's always room for him
given the splendid architecture of his mind
his table checkered with mirth and mystery and warm bread
shots of gleeful ike and grinning bogie
just over his shoulder
with this year's ritas
hovering
perched on bentwood chairs
pulled up close.

the discussion turns
to religion
how to beat the traffic
criticism of rhapsody
in which he sips iced rain
and commits opinion
to oblivion and more

somewhere a trumpet floats on smoke
giving the lie to anyone who wants it
saving the truth for him
basking in refined progeny (only slightly scarred)
noting the delicate resemblances
exact proportions of inner spaces
elegant structure of bones
his glow of satisfaction
becoming the actual light of this bustling space
lending a freshness free of charge to the air
and a lilt to the background din
yes this is the city of life
yes this is the night of all nights
neverending repast
candles burning brightly at both ends
and somewhere a drum is pulsing,
somewhere a clock is ticking,
but not here
at this safe table,
in her commodious room.

"it is a poem that has both tenderness and mirth—besides wit—and i'm
making a copy for elaine, who i'm sure will love it, commodiously."—william
styron, in a letter

TO BE MADE FUN OF
by one's children
not mocked exactly
more like
massaged by sharp affection.
the entire proceedings incited often by the practiced older brother,
he with the more extensive overview, and material amassed over the
decades,
and thereby given the license for overreach,
his presence ensuring maximum hilarity.
then the giggling girls leap in

amazed as they are by the depths of my dumbness
my total lack of any
even the faintest
the slightest
like, zero
as in none
completely *nolo contendre, of a clue.*
a fog of unknowing clouding around my hopelessly silly head…
and how can i argue?
why would i want to?
with these balmy gales of laughter?
these peals, these trills,
falling upon me like warmest rain…
i was never more proud of myself
than in those shining hours,
never felt more useful,
or more loved.

PRIDE, Part 1
there is the time we told my children that i was HIV positive. each displayed
their own kind of love and support. emma said later that it felt like the other
shoe had finally dropped, and that she had felt as a child that she could lose
me at any moment. my son had been seventeen when we told him. he
hugged me to confirm my solidity, with tears in his eyes. lilah never spoke
about it. the girls were younger than tavish was when we told him, but times
had changed, and they were ready for it, at least we hoped they were. the
next day they went to school, and with some other friends, organized an
AIDS awareness club, and brought me to the school, several times over the
next couple of years, to speak to the entire student body, in small groups of
50 or so at a time, to answer any question any one of them needed to ask. i
was as proud then, of my children, as of any moment in my entire life.

HEBRON: JUST ANOTHER JOURNAL ENTRY/1997
listening to '*rubber soul*'on the third of july. sun is setting on a day full of rain
and thunder, sheet lightning breaking through the scudding grey clouds and
soft bright sunlight. forgot to shower but feel romantically extravagantly
beautiful, in the same way the guitars on '*rubber soul*'are complete and

inevitable and jubilantly seductive. the way our four kids are perfectly balanced like the beatles. the wonder of the quartet energy which just goes on and on and on in an appreciation of the steady rain, the rightness of random structure, the making of lasting friendships. old barns and filigree fiddles. here strolls a rain-splashed, beaming, banjo player, proprietor of the property, lending a jaunty atmosphere, to the reenactments on the lawn, of favorite childhood stories, rendered with perfect poise. like ringo's drumming on 'michelle', or the loose patter of raindrops on the porch. "i love you i love you i loooooove you/ that's all i've got to say". the soft air just like that slight intake, that succulent, almost sung sip in 'girl'. just like that. and i make dinner for the little ones, the boy and the girl, so close so respectful such good friends as they make small intricate clay pipes to be utilized in their popeye imitations, kept safe and close for the rest of their lives.

IMAGINATION'S SISTER
is it just my imagination
or are there ponds of blood
glowing on the linoleum
surrounding the nativity bed?
consciousness lost
(the doctor emphatically states your name)
and the consciousness gained
just shivering in my arms.
this is what we do for bodies
this deliberate dismantling
panthers prowling
on the border between death and life.
both are irrepressible and constant.
we count the breaths
the pains
the thrum of the heart
we become more material than ever
our attention paid in full
signaling to some
one
struggling to be some
body

one composed of a substance beyond words.
imagination's sister.
this is a poem about nothing.
this is a poem about you laboring upright
in a rocking chair
like mingus composing
in his rolling chair
like a poem hovering…
and me gripping your ankle
and squeezing til the bones of my forearms
burn like molten steel
focussing
like the lens in a light house
beaming out over the uncrossable ocean
just where we are
just who we are
just how hard we will try.
—*for susanna and lilah,1990*

POLLEN/ FATHER AND DAUGHTER
both of us struggling to breathe
inspiralling
our chromosomes in common
both loving and hating the fluidium
drifting in the thickness
pistils and stamens seeking
and finding instead our besieged vents
hopelessly clogged
her tender weight
leaving a small circle of saliva on my shoulder
she gives in at last
to sleep
slurping in green and golden air
her cheeks flushed tulip pink
lilac veins in her delicate forehead
her small blossoming face
a mask of fever's buzzing

with the fecundity of dreams
where time is made palpable
as flowers
her opening eyes
revealing the person she is
and is becoming.
she is learning she is not god
gently lowered into fringed carnations.

my *imago dei*
limbwrapped with yours
napping in the slanting sun
after lovemaking
then sliding into the springfed pond.

LULLABY
you sang *child of mine*
i sang *all i have to do is dream*
or sometimes *golden slumbers*
we took turns
child to child

you sang *you belong to me*
i sang *lullaby of broadway*
or sometimes *hit the road to dreamland*
with each in their turn
girl to girl

then we would carefully slip
from the darkened rooms
gently closing the doors
standing quietly on the landing
and give each other a nod and a smile

good job

then we would ease down the stairs

to watch something
side by side
on the handpainted couch
while i gave you a foot massage

my specialty

without ceremony
you would flop your feet
onto my lap
sandals and all
and i would set to work
easing the strain of the day

my pleasure

going easy on the ankles
where the skin was so smooth

and you
—*another one for susanna, 2020*

EARTHQUAKE
i save every little scribble my youngest girl makes,
(just as i had with her brother, and her older sister, i still have all the precious materials),
i assemble a calm portfolio
i conceal the astonishment
under a collapsing porch
porte-cochere
portcullis
(say it)
home
crushing uncounted children
a simple case of ramshackle maintenance.

232

"we live in our own souls as in an unmapped region, a few acres of which we have cleared for our habitation; while of the nature of those nearest us we know but the boundaries that match with ours."—edith wharton,'the tombstone'

AFTER READING DE MAUPPASANT'S *AFLOAT/* 4th OF JULY, 2010
those same savage rocks
cutting and sad.
on one such outcropping
paganini's son found a shallow home
for his papa's ripening corpse
as it was refused entry from port to port
for so many sunstroked transgressions.

i found those lost pictures
you left for me
concealed in the forbidden files
those you uncovered in the hidden drawer
of the secret desk.

fireworks of tragedy ignite
in slow motion
in your aching eyes
i heave a heavy sigh.
at last
the question is stated plainly
in your wounded gaze:

how could you?
how could you be you
and be you?

i found the partially erased
the crumpled
the carefully crafted
sketch
torn to shreds

now i have hidden myself in an ornate box
in the improper city
or rather
i live in a darkly magic chest
constructed from discarded parts
assembled according to lost instructions
composed in an unknown tongue
while investigating my own crimes
evidence i keep in moldy-green folders crammed with musty clippings.
it was on that mournful search that i found the final evidence of your grief
staring me in the face.
there are three of them,
three screen shots,
desolate and spent.

and now it's the fourth of july
and i have walked down to the river in search of driftwood.
people are taking up positions
in the park
while the particular panic of infants
sizzles like sparklers in the charged air.
i find a useful bleached plank
wedged between boulders

but what shall i do about that look
in your eyes?
—*for lilah*

"where'd you go?
where you been?
what'd you see?
did you look at what you did to me?
doesn't matter much to me
…..if i say that you could see me, too
would that mean that we were born again?
tell me what good would that really do?

234

you really want to do it all again?"—
lilah larson, from the song, 'father, daughter, ghost"

yes, i do. I want to change it. although I know it can't be done.

"fatherhood kills fathers...i wanted you to see me. just open your eyes,
i would think. just enough to know it's me. this is what i would think. just open
your eyes long enough to know it's me.'—dave eggers, 'hologram for the
king'

A PARENT
not in ruins crumbling
but left
to grow as it strives
above the trampling
boots and scorn,
up toward the sun.
see those petals reaching
opening
to a crocus blue beyond all evil
to hands which hold
fragile treasures,
periwinkle mist,
deep in their palms.
—for emma, 1997

"i lived in fear of losing him, because he was so easy to lose. i could feel him
falling through my fingers all the time, even if sometimes i could only
understand it in my dreams."—emma larson, 'in the cornucopia of your ear'

"no doubt it happens at times that people, even those whom we love best,
become saturated with the melancholy or irritation that emanates from us."—
marcel proust, 'remembrance of things past; cities of the plain

"cross i am sometimes with my little daughter:
fill her eyes with tears. forgive me, lord.

unite my various soul,
sole watchman of the wide and single star"
—rilke

"they fuck you up, your mum and dad
they do not mean to, but they do.
they fill you with the faults they had
and add some extra, just for you
………..
man hands on misery to man
It deepers like a coastal shelf.
et out as early as you can,
and don't have any kids yourself"
--phillip larkin, 'this be the verse'

7. **EPICURE**: LIFE IS A FULL SPECTRUM OF POSSIBILITIES TO BE EXPERIENCED FREELY AND WITH SUSTAINED CONCENTRATION.

or the world limits people, frustrates them, and causes them pain that can be avoided.

"coyote: i sing my song! it penetrates all thickets! and not only that—i will mate with my own!...i am a fine thing! i display myself!...my life is devoted to dancing! i am coyote!"—murray mednick, 'the coyote cycle'

"...that its bouquet might the better be savored by the true epicures of what was really exquisite in life..."—oscar wilde, 'de profundis'

"my old daddy used to say: it's some comfort to a man if he must be an ass anyhow to be his own kind of an ass."—walt whitman, july 26, 1888

LIBERTINE: one unconfined; one at liberty.
to LIE: to lie at. to importune; to tease.
　　　　to lie with. to converse in bed.
　　　　　　pardon me, bassanio
　　　　for by this ring she lay with me.' —shake-speare (devere), 'othello'

OVERHEARD
none of you are my only life
excrescence of flimflam
gimme a pig foot and a bottle of beer
that champagne slip
slipping
that one sure takes the biscuit
doesn't that just put a red dress on it

spread your silken legs
yeah, like that
sugar bowl laced with cheap mezcal
p' is a labial consonant
formed by a slight compression
of the anterior lip
send me
cuz i'm on my sin.
—*2/15/2019*

TALKING ABOUT SEX
thousands of impaled bats,
skewered to the walls
frantically flapping in the bedroom,
terrify my dreaming wife.
although diminutive
even winsome
furry like fresh almonds still on the tree
in their fruit disguise.
my disguised spouse
is not really sleeping
she is in flames
or sequins
she is in a guise
not in service to the ego
or the superego
or the sequence on the street
she is in a negligee
     sewn by bold spiders
     spun by bees
     from threads of rainwater
which evaporates with sighs

MOVING EAST/Day Seven—Highway 80-81, Chicago to Scranton,1995
this congress hotel/ramada/days inn is "*messed-up*" in tav's phrase. seems
to be staffed by bored and bitter pakistanis. when we found no bedding on
the fold-out couch, they brought the haphazardly folded sheets and tossed

them on the bed, turning to leave. when i said, "*no, the couch.*" she went in and threw them on the couch and hurried out. they charge $17 dollars per car to valet park the vehicles, there being no other parking of any kind for blocks around—then they try to charge $5 more to bring the car *back!* mark and i just hike over to the cars and get them ourselves.

at breakfast i am served '*stuffed french toast* (which is essentially a giant donut, encrusted with powdered sugar, stuffed with bananas. disgusting and irresistible, as it turns out. *"no greater beauty than a conquered repugnance."—norman mailer*]. kinda like chicago. my kind of town.

julius hemphill. coltrane. holiday 'tatum/pres young/gillespie. louis armstrong. terry riley (in c). pick up 'the river '(93.9) out of detroit. smoke a cigar through indiana and into ohio, while tav stretches out in the back and reads *another roadside attractio.*

we stop in ellyria, ohio for dinner at *michael's*—a turquoise building which may have once been a chain of some kind, but is now privately operated by some very friendly and open african-american folks. the waitress is very bright and engaged and she keeps calling tavish *"honey"*. reasonably fresh food (for fried) and a lot of it. cherry pie for dessert.we strike up a conversation with an older black man, who tells us a couple of politically incorrect jokes, does funny voices, tells us he's an *"ex-undercover cop, preacher and gospel organist."* and assures us he can play *"twenty-five"* musical instruments, and counting. I did not doubt him for a second. he rocked just sitting at the counter.

the rest of this leg of the journey turns into another marathon drive. tav plays some more fine new mixes (*dirty old bastard. freestyle fellowship.* his own) and we get all the way to scranton. no room at the lackawanna station. we get two rooms at the best western. it's 3AM or so. tomorrow: NYACK!

SEVEN VIRTUES/ SEVEN SINS:
    diligence/ sloth
    liberality/ greed
    patience/ anger
    chastity/ lust
  abstinence/ gluttony
    kindness/ envy
    humility/ pride

SEVEN HUMAN NEEDS (according to **kim stanley**):
     to celebrate
     to charm
     to plead
     to accuse
     to seduce
     to destroy
     to entice

ALL THE DOOMED BLONDES: Part Seven
kim stanley was a sixteen-year-old high school student in san antonio, texas when **katharine hepburn** came to town in a touring production of *the philadelphia story,* recreating her role in the movie that made her a genuine, honest-to-goddess, movie star. the young girl was overwhelmed by the performance, moved to the point of tears. she didn't want it to end. and she desperately wanted to do what she had seen hepburn do. in 1947, with $21 in her pocket, she went to manhattan, to join the actor's studio, and study with elia kazan and lee strasberg. 'the method 'had taken american acting by storm: brando, dean, paul newman, lee j. cobb, anne bancroft, eva marie saint and **marilyn monroe** all were acolytes. **kim stanley** appeared in a play by gertrude stein called *yes is for a very young man,* and was singled out by the *times* critic, brooks atkinson. in 1952, at the age of 27, she played the pre-pubescent millie owens in *picnic,* by william inge. paul newman made his broadway debut in this same production, in a supporting role, eventually taking over the lead. the playwright was so impressed with kim's dedication and skill, that he contrived a vehicle especially for her, the starry-eyed chanteuse, cherie, in *bus stop,* which opened in 1954, and promptly made **kim stanley** a broadway star. when it came time to make the film, however, the role went to marilyn monroe, who had optioned the play, and yearned to be taken seriously as an actress, especially after having worked with lee strasberg, who had become her mentor, just as he had been kim stanley's. marilyn had many coaches through the years, but strasberg, and his wife, paula, became her constant companions, especially on set. and it paid off. marilyn's performance in *bus stop* is her apotheosis, just as indeed, kim stanley's performance in *goddess*, a thinly-veiled cautionary portrait of marilyn, released in 1958, further confirmed kim as *"the female brando"*. [in

fact that's the title of a biography of stanley, by jon kramptner]. as rita shawn she achieved mythic status with a bravura performance directed by john cromwell, who had also directed **frances farmer.**

[when i asked meryl streep to name the performers who impressed and influenced her the most, in all film history, she cited kim stanley in *goddess* and garbo in *camille*, as well as montgomery clift in *the misfits,* and paul newman in *cool hand luke.* she also cited barbara stanwyck in *double indemnity,* although she said, *"I don't really do this kind of acting. I don't know how."*]

stanley's next great performance wasn't until 1964, as an unhinged medium who has kidnapped a child, in *seance on a wet afternoon,* for which she was nominated for an oscar. [the film had been a hit in england, but could find no american distributor willing to take on such a downbeat subject. and kim stanley was hardly a marquee name. by another of those fateful accidents, one of the producers happened to run into an old friend, artie shaw, the genius of jazz clarinet. [once married to **lana turner,** who could be included in this list of doomed blondes—but I have to stop somewhere. not to mention **ava gardner,** certainly a *femme fatale,* but not blonde, and definietely not doomed. although she did break sinatra's heart.]. shaw had retired from music at the height of his fame, to focus on writing prose. he went along with the producer's pal to the screening and immediately after seeing the film, somewhat impulsively, to put it mildly, instantly formed a distribution company and took the film in hand. powered by kim stanley's electrifying performance the film was a major art-house hit, returning artie's investment many times over. [typically, he never distributed another film. quit while your ahead was always his motto.] although the performance was widely acclaimed, and richly rewarded with multiple nominations by various critic's associations, in america and europe, she went into a tailspin, leading to a total nervous breakdown. she was in and out of institutions and didn't work again for many years. but she was nominated for an oscar a second time in 1982, in her return to the screen, for her terrifying performance as **frances farmer's** devouring mother in *frances.* in the intervening years, stanley had become a revered teacher, and jessica lange had been one of her star pupils. she personally requested that kim take on the harrowing role of the monster mother. together they created perhaps the most indelible depiction of mother/daughter dysfunction ever committed to celluloid. the only comparable combination is in *goddess,* in which rita's endlessly disapproving, despicably pious mother [played by betty lou holland], is a major element in the star's ultimate downfall, just as with frances farmer.

mother issues seem inherent in the love goddess archetype. hera, zeus 'wife', and venus, were in constant conflict and competition. these elements are also evident in kim stanley's life and career. marilyn's mother was committed to an institution early in her life, and was never a part of her childhood. while married to arthur miller, she endured at least two miscarriages and an ectopic pregnancy. kim did have three children, with various husbands, including curt conway. however, her second child, born while married to conway, was fathered by brooks clift, the brother of montgomery clift. she suffered a miscarriage in 1957 while rehearsing the broadway production of *two for the seesaw.* anne bancroft replaced her. in 1964, she had an abortion just before filming began on *the idol,* opposite michael parks, [one of a legion of film actors heavily influenced by dean and, therefore, brando and therefore clift. in fact, parks replaced brando in a film produced by brando's father, *wild seed*]. as shooting began on *the idol,* kim began drinking so heavily on set that she had to be replaced by jennifer jones. she died of uterine cancer in 2001, in santa fe, new mexico.

it does seem a bit incomprehensible that this toweringly talented artist, the female brando, appeared in only five films. even so, she garnered two oscar nominations, a golden globe and bafta nomination, and best actress from the national board of review and new york film critics. not to mention two emmys, one for big mama in a television version of tennessee williams' *'cat on a hot tin roof',* and another for a guest shot on the series *ben casey.* from 1949 to 1964 she was in only 12 major productions on broadway. still she was awarded two tonys. although she loved acting on stage—she is quoted as saying. "*i was happy on stage; it was my home really.*"—after the harsh reception of the actor's studio production of *the three sisters* in london, in which she played the morose masha, she vowed to never act onstage again. and she never did.

on the road across america with the provisional theatre, we have a gig at the university of new mexico, santa fe. the day after our show, a largely abstract endeavor called, solemnly, *the america piece*, comprised entirely of sound and movement, no words, we gave a workshop to the students in the theater department. as we cavorted around, doing theater exercises with the

242

students, it was hard to miss a woman spread out in the corner, as if enthroned, the light from the large window giving her backlight, dressed all in black, her blonde hair gone white. when i realized who she was i bolted from the group scrum, dashed across the room, and went down on my knee to her.

"*yes,*" she said, seeming to confirm her identity, without fuss, lowering her glasses to look me in the eye.

"*miss stanley…we're so honored to have you here.*"

"*now, now, sweetie.*"

me: (gulp)"…*did you see our show?*"

with a slight smile, she gazed even more directly at me, as if to say, "*i wouldn't be sitting here if i had found it intolerable.*" and then she spoke, husky, slightly southern, "*oh yes, i enjoyed it a lot. i had no idea at all of what …happened, if you know what i mean..*"

"*absolutely.*"

"*but it's an interesting way of working. very now, huh? very of the moment. in the way that the studio could only have happened when it did. the way you strip the expression of the need down to the absolute essentials…underneath the words…i love that. i used to do something like that in my classes. i'd make them improvise the scene, entirely, without using any of the lines. very informative, especially with chekhov. but you all take it further, just the basic sounds, the barest gesture. without subtracting the…well, everything that we really need to know, the nuance..the..ummm* (rubbing her fingers and thumb together), '*particularities*' . (eyebrow raise, smile, sigh) *my my my, listen to me. how i do go on. but i must say, the characters aren't really…well, they aren't what i would have thought would have been really actable. i mean in the traditional sense. but they moved me. i felt i knew them. so interesting.*" she did that glasses trick again. "*do you understand, darling? well, of course you do…you're doing it.*"

i glanced back at the ongoing exercise, the earnest frolic. "*you want to join in?*"

she gave a slightly scandalized bark. "*for goodness sakes NO, you don't want to see me rolling around out there. at this point it's just fun to be able to be here and watch, and take it all in…now you should go back to it. you've been a perfect gentleman. good luck with your endeavors and tell your colleagues i admire them all.*"

i repressed an impulse to kiss her hand. now, i wish i hadn't held back.

WHOLE
put a picture
of a river
and the entire meaning shifts
or lightning
or a snake
put it in front
like that
and a vacancy
an emptiness
fills up with
all and everything
canyon becomes plain.

"now you must go out into your own heart
as onto a vast plain. now
the immense loneliness begins..."—rilke

"i'm on a plain
i can't complain
i'm on a plain

my mother died
every night
it's safe to say
don't quote me on that
love myself
better than you
i know it's wrong
so what should i do..."
—kurt cobain, 'i'm on a plain'

THAT CERTAIN BODY
somewhere in there
something dead

remains
and something very much alive
sensing the sacred as the nipple
of the text
an area of erogeny
the next chasm or lover's lips
pressed to peak or ridge,
furrow or plain
pleasure in following contours
with tongue to the fulcrum

TOUGH GUY
he knows what he's doing
he's smoking a cigarette
and feeling a whole lot better
death floats in the room
leaving dust on the lampshades.
saint in soiled trench coat
sliver of soul surviving on
what grows in poisoned air

through the window the sea
glistens pink and gold, pink and gold…
final drowning of the fire
o these tough guy themes
this body and soul
this stardust
pillow red lips
honey blonde mane
creamy thighs
patent leather pumps
finger to clit
hammer to bullet
slug and skull
blood and wall
bare bulb
rancid air

she's kneeling there on the stained
and worn linoleum
frenzy
and stillness
in his uneasy chair
throbbing in the veins
there's that fat vein on the right side of his dick there's the tip
of her tongue tracing it leaving the thinnest filament of spit gleaming in the
neon blinking pink and gold
pink and gold…

the door explodes in splinters
it's a shitstorm of fedoras and gats
a cyclone of cops
the tough guy grabs her golden hair
and the black silk strap of her negligee
ash from his cigarette
falls on his shirt
he's blown
away
*"what does physical eroticism signify if not a violation of the very being of its
practitioners?—a violation bordering on death, bordering on murder?"—
george bataille, 'erotism: death and sensuality'*
AUDACITY OF FLOWERS
music dark and sundown
requests of me a poem
now and rouge
lipstick smeared from motel frenzy
and the audacity of flowers

now i stand here deaf
no i stride
into the enveloping fog
where they are gunning for me
all those dames i let down
not in the sack, buddy

trust me
it's when standing up i am a stumblebum
a cheap lamster
a bruised and hammered angel
an all-thumbs demon
a smoking gun
outmanned acid of distraction
scarring the light
splayed facedown on the slick cobblestones.
is that the
click of her stilettos?
is that the sound that could save me?
is that the melody that never comes?

i dreamt it snowed in los angeles
soft powder settling on me
lying there in my lost alley
where he sprung me three slops
giving me the pally act
i figured i'd find you birds here
bawling me out
nothing a guy can do about the real mccoy, is there?
how about slipping into something more comfortable…
like a coupla drinks?
can i get high on one of these.
cool winds cross coral reefs
enforcing a mermaid's downfall

women always surprise me when they take off their shoes
but now that he's been murdered—
it makes a man so romantic
don't ya think?

coyote: *"i'll tell a coyote tale!…one morning coyote woke up, and his blanket was gone. then he looked into the sky and he saw a banner in the sky, , "oh boy, must be feast day! they only fly a banner when its feast day!" so he jumped to his feet, and it was then he realized it wasn't a banner at all: it was his blanket on the end of his penis! so he said to his penis, " little brothers, if you keep this up, we're gonna lose the blanket!" and he rolled his penis up and put it in a box on his back, and he went on his way. and he came to the shore of a lake, and there, on the other side of the lake, were women...swimming, and one of the women was the chief's daughter! coyote said, "now is the opportune time, i will have intercourse!" so he sent his penis across the lake, but as it went it hit the top of the water and made waves! so coyote reeled it back in, and he said, "no no, little brother, if you do it like that, you'll scare them!" and he took a fine rock and he put on the head of his penis and he sent his penis across the lake, but the rock was too heavy, and his penis hit the bottom of the lake, and got stuck! so he brought his penis back again, and he took that rock off and put another rock on, and this rock was just right, and he sent his penis across the lake and it went so fast that it hit some of the women and upset them! so they swam for the shore, but the chief's daughter was too slow, and the penis went right in her! now all the women were frightened and ran to get the men! who are strong! but they couldn't get the penis out! they had to find the old woman who knew what to do in matters of this kind. and she came and recognized coyote. she yelled right across the lake, "first-born, come out of there!" but of course, he wouldn't! they had to hire a chipmunk to come and take care of it. the chipmunk went right in there and chewed the penis into little pieces. and coyote came and he gathered up all the pieces and he went running through the forest throwing pieces around and wherever they landed was food! one piece was potato and one piece was artichoke and one piece was sharp-claw berry and one piece was rice. and that is why our penis is shaped the way it is!"—adapted from the winnebago by murray mednick, 'the coyote cycle'*

[it strikes me now, all these decades later, after having performed this story hundreds of times, that, for one thing, it depicts a rape. it also makes explicit the connection of coyote to the *puer aeternus* figures, like osiris, and attis and adonis and odin, whose dismemberment provides sustenance for the human race. as for the rape—doesn't it model a male prerogative, to spread his seed where he will?...forcing his organ of desire into whatever receptacle is around, regardless of the female's willingness? seemed funny back in the day...and was met with much hilarity and delight. and, of course, it was

248

delivered, and taken, as a demonstration, an advertisement, for my personal
potency and allure...]

corpus cavernosum: either of two masses of erectile tissue forming the bulk
of the penis and the clitoris.
corpus delicti: concrete evidence of a crime, *esp.* a corpse.
corpus luteum: a hormone secreting body that develops in the ovary after the
ovum is discharged, degenerating after a few days unless pregnancy has
begun.
corpus sponglosum: a mass of erectile tissue alongside the
corpus cavernosum of the penis and terminating in the glans.
corpus striatum: part of the basal ganglia of the brain, comprising the caudate
and lentiform nuclei.

*"welcome is every organ and attribute of me, and of any person hearty and
clean, not an inch or a particle of an inch is vile,
and none shall be less familiar than the rest."—walt whitman*

*"our desires interweave with each other; and in the confusion of existence, it
is seldom that a joy is promptly paired with the desire that longed for it."—
marcel proust, 'remembrance of things past:'in the shadow of young girls in
flower'*

*'it is better to murder an infant in its cradle than to nurse desires unacted
upon.'—william blake*

OSCAR WILDE came to america on a personal mission. it was not, as was
supposed by the producing company, d'oyly carte, who paid his passage, to
make a prominent fool of himself. he was often ridiculed at home, with his
fulsome personality, and his flamboyant style. the producers expected the
american citizenry, especially the press, to react with derision, so as to pave
the way for their latest gilbert and sullivan trifle, a lampoon of our oscar, and
his ilk, called *patience.* the producers were concerned that the show wouldn't
work without some direct knowledge of wilde's, well...WILDeness, so they
offered to pay him handsomely for a tour of the colonies, with the joke on
him, of course. instead, oscar triumphed, all across the nation, on the stage,

and in the drawing rooms of america's best connected writers, scholars, salonistas and politicians, extolling the adoration of the beautiful, in all and everything, to all and sundry. and as he traveled across the nation, all the way to the gold rush country, he proved just as comfortable and scintillating, and popular, with cowboys, farmers or miners. he once descended to the depths of a coal mine, in leadville, colorado, to converse with the laboring miners. by all accounts it was quite a convivial gathering. the stories and the liquor flowed. he had the men, covered with sweat and black dust, slapping their thighs and bending over with laughter.

In 1869 an austrian litterateur named karl maria kertbeny coined the term *'homosexuality'.* the trial of oscar wilde popularized the use of the word to refer to a wide-range of (banned) sexual practices, in particular those between people of the same gender. (of course, wilde did have sex with the other gender. he may have preferred young men, but he had passionate and quite public affairs with many women—including the international star, lillie langtry. he fathered two sons with a woman he adored, constance, and remained married to her until he died. which makes him bisexual. i insist on it.). while on the american tour, oscar was invited by walt whitman, in his dotage, to come out to camden, new jersey, for a glass of elderberry wine and friendly advice. "*you are young and ardent.*" proclaimed uncle walt, *"the field is wide and if you want my advice, go ahead!"*

"listening to his mother reciting walt whitman, and often embellishing the lyrics, had created in the child oscar a visceral bond between the maternal and the word, a place of storied memories, of desire, loss, and sensual pleasure."—emer o'sullivan, new york times book review: 'the fall of the house of wilde'

"all women become like their mothers, that is their tragedy. no man does. that's his."—oscar wilde

oscar wilde garnered more american press coverage, all of it positive, in the year of his tour, 1882, then any other british person—including queen victoria.

250

SAM AND SAL

sam steward knew what the fuck he was talking about, and he took notes. each sexual encounter he had throughout his lifetime had its own 3X5 card, kept in hundreds of file boxes, numbering upwards of four thousand by the end of his long and lusty life.

he was there when it was illegal to have in one's possession any erotic representations of ANY kind, but gay would get you prison time. sam steward had hundreds of photos, drawings, and fictional depictions of depraved acts, non-fiction accounts of depraved acts, all carefully filed and ready for instant access. he decorated his apartment in frescoes painted by himself, right on the bare walls, sprawling gorgeous murals celebrating mansex.

sam steward taught english for twenty years at a catholic university in the midwest. he had sex with men from all walks of life, from priests to policemen, from very young to very old.

he wrote a poetic, comic novel in the late 20s, *angels on the bough,* and achieved notoriety and acclaim among bohemian artists around the world, particularly those who shared his predilictions, becoming particularly close to gertrude stein and alice b. toklas, thornton wilder and jean cocteau. after gertrude died sam steward was hired to edit her letters and wrote an eloquent introductory essay that was subsequently published separately, again to much acclaim.

in the 1960s he wrote a series of sensational pornographic novels under the pen name phil andros. (read them. they are impossibly hot.) his publisher was arrested multiple times and served time in jail. two phil andros films were made, the producer of which was duly arrested and also went to prison for a long stretch.

by then sam steward had given up teaching english to beautiful college boys and become a tattooist, known far and wide for his elegantly earthy designs. he taught cliff raven, ed hardy and many other artists who were later to popularize body decoration in the united states. when sam first became obsessed with tattooing it was still illegal in most states, and the instruments of application were very hard to find. sam tracked down an old and much utilized kit, and set up shop near the wharves and naval bases in chicago. only sailors and convicts had tattoos in those days. of course, sam knew many convicts and sailors. when steward started hanging out with the founders of the nascent leather culture in chicago,(which was heavily influenced by the kenneth anger films, *scorpio rising* and *invitation to the pleasure dome*, and, therefore, marlon brando in *the wild one*), they all lined up so that he could emblazon their muscular bodies with soaring eagles, noble snakes, hearts aflame skewered on crossed swords and endowed with angel's wings.

he was one of alfred kinsey's favorite research subjects, partly because sam was so organized in his recollections. he and kinsey became very close, although just how close is a mystery. sam's jam-packed card files and other memorabilia, were given to the kinsey archives and are now sealed.

in the nicholas ray film 'rebel without a cause' we see sam steward's name and [actual] phone number written in plato's little red address book, on the page directly before jim stark's. [dean's character]. the name and number was slipped in there by the screenwriter, stewart stern, who was a regular member of sam's circle of lovers. sam's name is spoken aloud by one of the thugs menacing plato, [vic morrow] just to make sure we don't miss it. plato is played to perfection by sal mineo, and was one of the first clearly gay leading characters depicted in a mainstream film. the look in sal's eyes when he gazes on jimmy dean is very clear in its content and intent.

as it happens, sal mineo was the first movie star i ever met. i responded to a casting notice in drama-logue, for a play to be directed by SAL MINEO himself. the play was a controversial prison drama, *fortune and men's eyes*. auditions were to be held at the [original] MET theatre on poinsettia, just off melrose. when i arrived, the tiny, shadowy lobby was chock full of aspirants from everywhere, most of us drawn, on some level, to the chance for a direct connection, in the flesh, to **james byron dean**.

and then in walks **sal**.

sal, silhouetted in the doorway, shirt open to the navel, skin the color of chocolate milk, cool bandito moustache, like the beatles in *sergeant pepper*. i was stunned at everything about him. all the childishness, the pubescent fleshiness, was gone. he was a full grown man, tight muscles and tousseled hair. his smile was still a little guileless and innocent, but also openly flirtatious. i just grinned back at him, pretty much unable to speak. but i did manage to make it through the first scene, and then sal stepped in to read the second scene, vaulting up onto the slightly elevated stage. as we went through it, i could see in his eyes that he was impressed. i held my own, but barely. i kept getting lost in flashes of *rebel*, especially the scene with plato being cradled by dean and wood, as if he has finally found the family, the parents, he has yearned for...but better, more intimate and accepting. all three of the kids finally have found a home, a shelter from the storm of adolescence, a circle, a triangle, of safety. the tragedy ensues when the couple go off to be alone together, and poor little plato is abandoned, and he panics...but, back on the stage at the MET, looking into the eyes of SAL MINEO, the actual person, i tried to concentrate on the task at hand. my first professional audition.

after several callbacks, in which sal kept saying, "*so **what** have you done?*" i kept shrugging and answering, "*well,...i did plays in high school...and in a children's theater..*" sal would give that big, almost goofy, plato grin, and chuckle. *"no shit...well, okay, let's try this one, again."* i was gaining confidence with each round. one particular scene was particularly intense and physical. we did it several times, each time with more abandon. then he asked me to come back in a couple of hours. for reasons unclear to me now, i was dispatched in the interim to accompany sal's giraffish manager, in his little sports car...

sal had temporary digs at the cherokee hotel on franklin avenue, a block from hollywood boulevard, while his mulholland home was being redecorated, as the manager explained. i didn't actually know what a manager was, but he told me he also handled a vocal quartet. it turned out various members of said quartet could be seen lolling around, half-naked on the pleather couches of sal's suite of rooms. i no longer recall by what pretext i was accompanying this effortlessly elegant man, towering above me like a masai warrior, to the tenth floor of this louche dwelling. or if i even knew then what was up, in general. some errand or other....? and i cared not...i was ready and willing to be carried away.

ultimately, sal asked me to understudy the nubile don johnson, who was coming right off a hit musical version of *as you like it,* which had set san francisco on fire. don had way more experience than me, on and off the stage. he was brash and confident as the fresh meat, raped by sal's convict character. [originally another actor was cast as the heavy, but at some point in the rehearsal, sal replaced him.] backstage, as i stood wide-eyed at the opening party, at the coronet theatre on la cienega, i saw sal glancing over at me, several times. finally he made his way over to me, through the throng of well-wishers. he pulled me aside and kindly but firmly withdrew his offer, because, as he said, *"you're just not ready for this scene…i see it in your eyes, baby."* and i knew exactly what he meant. after all, i had done nothing, nothing at all. i was 17. this was all happening in my very first weeks in LA, in Hollywood, out in the wide wild world. i was a film student at UCLA, with inchoate dreams of…directing? acting?, maybe stardom, a life of being seen, recognized. at the very least, unfettered, as much as i could manage. *"this scene…will eat you up…you'll be swallowed whole…you are not prepared to decide to be devoured…not yet."* even then, in the throes of my first of many, painful disappointments, i knew how kind he was being. then he put his warm hand on my cheek, his brown eyes glittering, and said, *"you will go far."* *"i was really looking forward to working with you.."* *"we will. we will. i promise."* of course we never did. just a few years later, his life was taken by a lowlife thief, in the parking lot of his apartment in west hollywood. but the whole experience was my first touch of that magic realm, that i determined to make real.

james dean once said, when asked if he was bisexual, *"what do you want me to do, go through life with one hand tied behind my back?"*

personally, that made perfect sense to me. i never did decide on one team or another. didn't seem to be necessary. certainly to myself.
and sal was right, i did go far…

*"every man has some reminiscences which he would not tell to everyone, but only to his friends. he has others which he would not reveal even to his friends, but only to himself, and that in secret. but finally there are still others which a man is even afraid to tell himself, and every decent man has a considerable number of such things stored away…**man is bound to lie about himself.**"*—fyodor dostoyevsky, 'notes from underground'

"the greatest sources of our suffering are the lies we tell ourselves."
—elvin semrad, quoted in ''the body keeps the score' by bessel van der kolk

254

WHAT TO CALL IT
of course all labels are onerous, simpleminded, incomplete.
the accepted categories are absolute:
heterosexual
homosexual
just announce what you want with your presentation
style as essence,
and play on one team or another.

but as for what bodies do,
the meshing, for an ecstatic intimate instant,
of two facets of the infinite soul,
have sex
get laid
make love
or just righteously fuck,
i suppose
i'll go with
bisexual
as good a word as any.

because for me there had been:
levada rasmussen, who kept giving me that look in the halls at las palmas
junior high, bold and secretive all at once, like she knew something about me
nobody else did. she was a bad girl, who spent time at lunch period, and
before home room, in the grassy area across the street from school. off the
grounds. smoking cigarettes and looking sulky and sexy as all hell. i was the
good kid, president of the student council, straight As, mormon boy, and all
that. but i was also a border animal, and levada rasmussen could see it. at a
party in junior high, levada came right up to me, real close. she took me out
behind the garage, where the lights couldn't reach us, the record player
spinning 'everybody's doin '/a brand new dance now/ come on baby/do the
locomotion'…she opened her blouse, unhooked her bra, and let me hold her
bare breasts in my trembling hands, and then she kneeled down in front of
me and put my cock into her mouth. just practicing…after a moment or two,
she darted off, pleased with herself, and left me there, hung up, as it were. all

it took was a couple of strokes, barely touching myself, really, and i was back dancing the locomotion…

and then, right around that time, there was:
the very first full-out blow job i ever received. it was from an elegant, well-groomed, older man, in downtown sacramento. i was killing time, wandering around the darkened streets, and i noticed the man noticing me, subtly moving closer. my friend, alan, had driven us across the river to the art house in town to see peter brook's film of '*marat/sade*'. they wouldn't let me in because i was very clearly under eighteen. they didn't even bother to check my ID. in fact i was just sixteen, but alan passed muster.

so i ambled right into a nearly overwhelming fireworks explosion of humming bliss.

how did he know i wanted it? how did i?

after some preliminary glances and gestures, the older man led me down an alley, got on his knees and unbuttoned my pants. i was the hardest i'd ever been, clinging to the damp brick wall behind me, jeans around my ankles, so grateful i could not speak. after what seemed to me an eternity of paroxysmal explosions, he stood up, placing a crumpled twenty dollar bill in my hand. and off he went. my first taste and i got paid for it!
who can blame me for loving it?

well, as it turned out, many people found reasons to blame me…and so did i, for that matter, from time to time.

there was a guy in venice, in the 80s, who promoted his own label:
"*trisexual*". it had a ring. a ding ding.
and and of course, now we speak of non-binary, gender fluid, demisexual, pansexual, polyamory…and so on and on…

"*we simply will do things or let things be done to ourselves in love and sex that violate all norms, the violation of which would trigger disgust if unprivileged, if coerced, or even if witnessed. and to do such and to have*

*such done to us is much of what sexual intimacy is."—william ian miller,
'anatomy of disgust'*

*"to drown my sorrow there is no abyss,
however deep, that can compare to your bed."
—baudelaire*

TRANSILIENT, TRANSILIENCE: abrupt transition; leaping from one thing to another.

GENDER IS A <u>BEING</u> THING NOT A BODY THING. and it modulates. it's a MIXTURE, a MIXTERY, determined by desire.

*Q: What are souls like?
    Jesus: Nursing babies are like souls entering the matrix.
  Q: How can we enter too?
    Jesus: If you can make a double into a single; and if you can make the
outside the same as the inside; and the upper the same as the lower; and if
you can make yourselves both male and female, so that you aren't one or the
other; and if you can make your eyes function as EYES, and your foot
function as a FOOT, if you can see images solely as images—then you, too,
can enter heaven."—fanny howe, questions: interpreted; responses: from
coptic, greek, english versions, 'gospel of st. thomas'*

*"i have heard nothing but expurgate, expurgate, expurgate, from the day i
started. everybody wants to expurgate something—**this**, **that,** the other
thing. if i accepted all the suggestions there wouldn't be one leaf of the
Leaves left…expurgation is apology—yes, surrender—yes, an admission that
something or other was wrong….expurgate, expurgate—apologize,
apologize: get down on your knees…i must expurgate, expurgate, pick up my
skirts and run back to nature: beg nature's pardon and be good hereafter."—
walt whitman, may 14, 1888*

no apologies, indeed:

PLUSH HYMENS
"plush hymens on your eyeballs"—samuel beckett, 'serena 3'
my whole face as deep into her as i can urge it,
determinedly, deferentially but insistently,
wriggling her open as wide as possible,
my breathing channels blocked with her writhing body and her way in
tongue fluttering in a mad cadence
nibbling on luscious labial wings, layered like peonies,
delicately o so delicately
sucking that clit like a muscular carp, with uncanny accuracy,
engorged nub swelling deliciously
no thought of surfacing
to avoid suffocation
not now not never
her scent is the only air i need
she begins to cry out in wails of pleasure,
sensing the electric emission to come
a charge a bolt courses through me
then i'm choking on spraying oceans of ecstasy
all over my face and chest,
and she,
is left trembling
on the soaked sheets.

i love the squirting SPENDINGS, the CUNT-JUICE, CONCOMITANT OF
DESIRE, VAGINA-JUICE, PROSTATIC SPECIFIC ANTIGEN emanating
from the CLITOROURETHAVAGINAL COMPLEX…you name it, I dig it.

and furthermore::

COCKSUCKING HERO
as for penilingus:
i am a cocksucking hero.
ask anybody…
BLOW JOB, HOOVERISM, HEAD, SUCK THE SUGAR-STICK,
that abandonment on my knees, or lying side by side

i love that ecstatic CUM, the SPEW, the thick hot SPEND splattering my face
and chest,
being become fluid
all over me.
and besides:
*"...what goes into a man's mouth cannot make him unclean...what comes out
of a man's mouth* IS *unclean, for it comes from the heart where evil
lurks..."—matthew 15:11*
[these lines were declaimed by me, without knowing their source, as the
'street preacher my character in an episode of *law and order:SVU.* i was
decked out in an enormous mohawk, bleached platinum. i wore soiled white
raiment, including the linen pants i wore when I married susanna, the same
formal shirt, now hopelessly sullied, the sleeve artfully rolled up to reveal the
coyote tattoo on my left arm, right above the wrist. the display of the tat was a
special request from the director, helen shaver. i had first met helen when i
directed her, with ed harris, in a play by murray mednick, *are you lookin?,* of
course he was the writer/director of *the coyote cycle...*full circle, wheels
within wheels, rolling on. in fact the scene took place on an actual bus,
lurching down broadway, around 116th street, just across the road from
columbia university, wherein i taught *'directing actors for film* for a dozen
years. while the company was busy setting up the shot, i wandered the
sidewalks, dipping into stores, in my full madman regalia, clutching my floppy
red bible. the hardware store, where i had often shopped, kicked me out
immediately, the guard waving me away with the back of his hand as soon as
i came in the door, physically blocking my way. a former student saw me on
the street and stopped in her tracks. i could see in her eyes that she was truly
concerned, although not entirely surprised that i had come to be in this
shattered condition. she approached me, wide-eyed and careful.
"darrell?...are you okay...?" i assured her, dropping my wild, wounded
demeanor as much as i could manage, that i was *'acting'.* we both laughed
and i pointed to the crew, rigging the bus, and then i hopped aboard as helen
called *'action'!*]

GRAVIORA DELICTA
clandestine ecstasy
on every street corner

to the left
of the laughter in shadows.
or is that slaughter in the neorgasmic moon on moon,
making a steady drip
of scaffolded regret?
o shut the door
shut the damned door
dowse the blazing arcade
this is the winter for it
now is not
a spell for giving so much more
now is graviora delicta
and fear is compass true
skin is certain true
the sunset tilt is simply a matter of noticing
the signs have been exploded.

*"it's a profound problem: teaching morals; they should be taught—yet also
not taught: sometimes i say one shouldn't teach morals to anybody: when i
see the harm that morals do. i almost hate seeing people good: then there's
another side to it: then i see how necessary it is that we should have a code,
live with it, die for it."—walt whitman, january 27, 1889*

EIGHT DAYS IN RUSSIA, Saturday, 2007
once more the morning puker heralds the dawn. i put together some notes
on james dean during breakfast...but by 11:00 i haven't heard from masha. i
call her and she is pretty distraught. seems the hot water heater in her
building burst. happens regularly around here, people die from the
explosions. i tell her not to concern herself with me. i'm having a bad
reaction this morning anyway. really nauseous so i go lay down. about 2:00
she shows. roman snaps pictures as i emerge unsteadily through the glass
doors of the hotela ghost behind glass. (meanwhile *the wizard of oz* is
unspooling at the theater to a full house of delighted russian kids. we had all
decided the children needed no comments from the aficionado from
america.) masha, lovely and slightly frazzled, is driving a sleek silver car that

is apparently owned by the guy riding shotgun, who announces with a wide smile, that he is drunk. not that this fact needs any announcement, beyond the obvious manifestations. roman and i clamber into the back seat, and i see some upchucking of my own in the near future. (all the basic requirements are in place. as a kid, on any long trip, two stops would be required for me to stumble out onto the shoulder of some twisty highway for puking purposes. and yet, i was always assigned the back seat, as a kind of preemptive punishment, [or just plain cruelty].)

but i stabilize as we creep through sunny kaliningrad and make our way out of town. beautiful balmy day. art and his curly-headed and adorably pregnant wife are ahead of us in art's car. the air is redolent with the tang of burning grass, a slight, sweetly pungent, haze in the air. andrej (our drunken passenger, and the owner of the car), mans the music, mostly loud russian pop, but he rarely lets a whole track play, or even get past the opening verse, phrase or riff before clicking on to the next song. finally he settles on radiohead, lending a certain grandeur to the passing farmhouses, which look like accretions risen up over centuries right from the soil, with sloping tin roofs, various shades of rust and grey, with blotches of damp purple in the walls, and ancient peasants, right out of millet, sitting stoically in the packed dirt yards. and splashes of colorfully bedecked graveyards.

we enter the national park that surrounds acres of pure white dunes, the largest in all of europe, (as white as the sand at alamagordo.) first we pass through the forest of pine and birch, centuries deep with moss. every once in a while andrej, turns around and gives me a conspiratorial smile, shrugs and chuckles, "*I'm drunk.*" the road through the woods is winding, masha drives fast and sometimes she brakes abruptly, for no apparent reason—all the things that make me carsick—but not this time. maybe its the longitude. the sun slants in cathedral beams through the great gray birches.

we arrive at the main parking area. under some traditional huts people are selling amber jewelry, and i solve my gift problems. this area is the main source, the chief exporter, of amber to the WORLD. then we amble through the woods, eventually emerging at a truly glorious prospect—miles of pure, blazing, white sand, wind-sculpted into graceful, undulant shapes, the whole immense plateau at least a hundred feet above the baltic, on the left side, and the bay of kaliningrad on the right, eventually tapering to nothing, leaving a mouth for the enormous bay. we climb to the highest point. so now i see the portal nature of this cosmopolitan city at the crossroads, the market realm of hermes the thief, the place where tribes came to trade. compact as it is, the feisty little city contains multitudes. multiple cross cultures, like san miquel in mexico, or casablanca. expats and exiles, rovers and traders. artists and criminals. women and men on the run...to or from. when we turn around we can see lithuania, and the last village in russia, situated in the woods on the edge of the dunes. we move over to the steep cliff down to the sea.art says, *"usually we run down the cliff, me and andrej...it's exciting, but it's a bitch getting back up."* like i said, my kind of folks.

the six of us are the only people in sight. they've brought a soccer ball. every once in a while, somebody gives it a swift nudge, but mostly we just meander on the bright hills of sand. underlit by purity. its a bit like flying. at one juncture art says to andrej, *"we brought you along just to prove the cliche` about drunken russians."* andrej seems shamed, and a few minutes later, as we start back, he has disappeared. we call his name but he does not emerge. eventually he trudges out from behind a scrub-covered drift and catches up to us as we enter the woods again. i duck behind a stunted pine to take a leak. the group pauses in a glade while roman fashions a pipe out of a soda can, very deftly, so that we can smoke a little excellent pot that roman brought. at least roman, andrej (who needs it like a hole in the head) and i toke on the can. the others demur. after a few minutes it becomes clear that the pot is extremely good. once more roman and i lead the delegation through the dappled woods, falling into a conversation about women, specifically the girl who taught him english— *"sara from san francisco"*— *"that's definitely the best way to learn a language,"* i say. *"for sure,"* he says, chuckling. i really like this guy. we are instantly in cahoots. wonderful slavic face, prince valiant haircut (or david crosby in the early byrds), delightful, open grin. i have the thought as we stroll along that i would love him to meet emma.

now we head down to the beach, on the baltic sea, which is magnificently deep-green and majestic. it strikes me that i have been to two different *seas* in less than two weeks. (after the quick hop last weekend to turks & caicos in the Caribbean, for r&r with rose.) the water is not prohibitively cold, not swimmable, but not polar, and apparently quite popular in the summer. one cool thing is that they construct these sapling grids, (reminiscent of coyote fences in the southwest) to stabilize the dunes, with bulwarks out of rough pine planks. all these constructions look natural, like they belong here, happened without humans. in america we used concrete, cement, treated timber, emphasizing the imposition of man.

before going to the beach we took a pause at a picnic table and shared a couple of delectable oranges. we would have had chocolate, but art's wife entrusted it to andrej, who proceeded to eat it all. andrej asks me if i have a family. naturally i say yes, three children, a son and two daughters. *"two daughters!"* he crows, *"you are a happy man."*

"well, i'm certainly lucky…you mean LUCKY, i think."

"yes, yes…LUCKY!"

"sometimes i'm happy. standing here with all of you, i am. in this beautiful place. i am very happy."

and we all bask in a moment of contentment, beaming at each other.

down at the beach andrej is noticeably drunker, he's been sipping cheap vodka every ten minutes or so, and there's some fear, as we negotiate the steep stairs, that he won't make it down. the last few steps have washed away. some sandbags and the metal frame remain, but the boards themselves are long gone. andrej gets down okay, but now, after watching the soccer ball drift out to sea, and talking philosophy, andrej insists that i sit down on the beach and *contemplate.* so i do. *"it's nice,"* he declares. and it is.

well, we just can't get him moving. it's getting late. we have a screening at 7, and its already around 5. art and i have a quick sidebar about andrej, his childhood friend who has basically become a hopeless drunk. he's a fairly successful business man with a partner who drinks a little less and trusted employees who keep the enterprise running. used auto parts, always a good business in russia. he even drinks quite openly at work, but the thing is, he's sweet and affable and smart under the vodka fog.

he manages the steps back up quite well, to everyone's surprise, including his own. in fact as i come to the steps he warns *me. "careful— watch me,"* and he scampers up quite gracefully. however, on the path which is bordered by a low, stacked-sapling fence, he turns slightly and says to me, *"two daughters…"* and falls flat on his face. which he gets a big kick out of, of course. literally guffaws with his face in the dirt. doesn't even turn over. art is chagrined, but his wife is visibly pissed. i get the strong feeling that she is fed up with old pal, andrej. roman and i get him to his feet, chortling as he rises, and we proceed. after a few steps he says again, *"two daughters..."* and i turn and put out a hand, *"don't fall down again,"* i exhort, which he finds really hilarious. *"that's pretty funny...good one,"* and he giggles us onward.

but now we're really late, and we have to get back to the hotel to pick up my notes, and even then masha won't have time to translate them as she did last night—and she really doesn't want to be onstage with me. she's afraid she won't be heard. her voice is very soft and light—and they just rented the microphones for opening night. she's going to try it from the booth again. so we speed home, making roman very nervous. masha is far from an experienced driver, and on one turn she actually goes off the road a bit, onto the shoulder, spraying pebbles. *"mash....mash..."* roman blurts, and adds a stream of urgent imprecations i can't understand, but thoroughly agree with. here we are rushing down a country road, (in,...um, russia!) hellbent on making a screening of a film starring JAMES DEAN. ironies could abound.

its dusk, golden light glints on the wetlands, the fields are lit with patches of fires, little tongues of flame, with the smoke making the air a lavender haze. andrej inserts the soundtrack of a russian film, heavy with lyrical piano, and passes peacefully out. it's a beautiful ride.

we swing swiftly by the hotel, i dash up, we get to the show with five minutes to spare. we decide to try it with no translation upfront. i have given masha a general rundown as we raced into town, but she is tense about it, and understandably distracted, as she was steering the hurtling vehicle. she decides it will be better to not translate at all. just me muttering in english. when i mention, or sheepishly announce, our plans for tonight's sermon to the assembled multitudes, some people laugh and clap. apparently they were here last night. anyway, i plow through the prepared material, with people murmuring to their neighbors who have less english. (i flash back to the performances of *xa: a vietnam primer* with the proVisional theater, at the international theatre festival in nancy, france, in 1975. i had seven different languages represented in my 'village', including a deaf person, between us we could all understand one or two others, and we managed to pass the information around to everyone else. each cast member would, at semi-regular intervals, take a small section of the audience and 'make a village'. in this way we told the whole history of viet nam in a couple of hours.) to this crowd of hopeful residents of the new russia, in a building erected by the

264

nazis, i stress the fact that j.edgar hoover ranked the *"teenage jungle"* as exemplified in *rebel without a cause*, as second only to communism as a *"threat to american freedom."* (irony indeed.) some folks in the audience really get a kick out of that. i know i do.

unfortunately, the film is another of those simultaneous translation deals, and especially in this case, it just doesn't work. you can't enter the movie. the story is constantly undercut, and the dated behavior is even more risible than it seems at home. the truth is, natalie wood and sal mineo are working too hard. they seem stilted and oversold, but dean is still simply miraculous, achingly beautiful and completely alive. he's undeniable. but people chuckle and titter through the entire picture—especially the young men in the restive crowd. they find sal's plato funny in all the wrong ways. for some inexplicable reason, when jim and judy run into the observatory to join the terrified plato, something about their scampering gets a big, knee-slapping howl. really pisses me off. after the lights come up i just sit there and wait for everyone to leave. i feel like you do when you know a show, or a performance, just did not work. then, when i finally groan to my feet and decide to face the music, out in the bar it's shoulder pats all around. several people approach me, visibly moved, including vladimir, the guy from the magazine and the bridge, who has tears in his eyes, and says, *"i waited so long to see this film...i was not disappointed...james dean is not dead...he will always be alive."* so i feel a little bit better.

but masha is despondent. she and roman and i go up to the office and she talks to art on the phone and then she gets REALLY sad. i ask her what's wrong and she just stares silently. finally i insist that she tell me what is upsetting her, and she nearly cries as she says, *"i let you down. i should have done better."*

"but i let you down, i'm the one who didn't bring the notes. i just didn't think it through. i didn't think you would want to translate while we walked on the dunes."

"i should have reminded you."

"look, everybody wants to do better all the time with everything. the thing is what it is, to quote hunter thompson."

but she won't be cheered. roman and i share a look and a shrug, devoted knights of a mournful princess.

"well, listen, roman and i are starving. and you deserve a drink."

we go to the pizza place around the corner. its quite ritzy, actually, and packed. masha sees some friends at a table and we join them. people throughout the restaurant hold up their glasses to toast to a job well done as we wend our way to the table. We join three sprightly young folks, who turn out to be dancers, although they don't look like the typical dancer where i come from. the young man is slight and delicately blonde, one woman is plump but firm, robust, curly, reddish-brown hair, so pretty and exuding health. the other woman is darker in every way, hair, style and vibe. a vincent gallo fan who didn't like *breakfast at tiffany's* because it was so unrealistic. (can't argue with that, and i don't.) we have a very lively, very wide-ranging discussion, mostly movie-based, but including literature, music, politics, drugs—the entire table squeals with delight when *tropic of cancer* comes up and i mention that i had dinner with henry miller, so i regale them with the entire tale, over thin crust pizza and an excellent caprese`.

afterwards we go to art's apartment, right across the street. the entrance to the building, and the staircase up to his place, looks as bad as any tenement/bombed-out project/dystopian city-in-ruins anywhere, busted light bulbs, moldering trash, graffiti warping the walls. SPLAYWASHERE, spraypainted (whatever the fuck that means…)—chipped railings trudging up concrete steps to?…all of kaliningrad appears unfinished or crumbling (not unlike mexico), even the newest buildings look like the workmen walked away before finishing. (the exception is the theatre complex. unusually well-maintained.) however, as it turns out, in these apparently desolate towers are some very DONE environments. art's place is just like him—sophisticated technology, mysteriously installed, deeply cultured, thoroughly bohemian, a circular, spiraling layout. the wall you face on entering is covered with framed postcards of the pantheon of modern geniuses. furthering art in all its forms, areas or disciplines: films, music, literature, painting, science, all the various and abundant heroes and saints. (i fail to identify mayakovsky, to my shame, even though art gives me a solid hint: *"the first suicide of the 20th century."*) the ceilings are very high, jazz is playing and russian films from the 1890s are on the plasma screen. art serves an extremely potent german liquour as he finishes burning some dvds of russian films he wants me to have. after awhile i start to fade. masha is still melancholy. art and roman are going clubbing, so she and i take a cab. i drop her and she apologizes again.

"its been a very emotional day…and the movie was so beautiful."

"and so fuckin 'sad," i say.

i'm a little shocked to find its 2AM when i walk into the hotel. i had agreed to teach a class of kids, 9-15, at 10:30 in the morning—and tonight is the russian daylight savings, so we're losing an hour. (i'm getting this thing coming and going.) and, needless to say, inevitably, its saturday night at party central, the kaliningrad hotel, and revelers are laughing heartily and singing their lungs out and shouting at maximum decibels and bumping into each other for several more dismantling hours. but at last...i drift..off.

JAMES DEAN was the ultimate teenage rebel, the definitive neurotic boy outsider. his career was over almost before it had begun. he spent less than two years in hollywood, and when he died in 1955, at the age of 24, only one of his three movies had been seen by the public. his image, more than forty years after his death, seems richly symbolic of the culture of the 1950s: youthful, anxious and angry, insolent yet innocent, a narcissus in denim, forever young. andy warhol described dean's image as *'the damaged but beautiful soul of our time.'*

his films show him coping with the perennial teenage problems: coming to terms with sexuality, establishing a working relationship with parents and trying to find a place out in the world, all against a background of a vague and generalized air of discontent with the family, authority and the status quo. more than any other actor, dean distilled the essence of youthful non-belonging for teenagers in the *"free world."* (especially *east of eden* and *rebel,* in *giant* we get a glimpse of how or what the gone-to-seed dean may have looked like. would he have gone the way of the burnt-out but still blazing but.wounded clift [" *longest suicide in show business history* " some wag is supposed to have wagged] or the bloated brando, bludgeoned hero abandoned by his devouring audience? dean's life was as alienated as that of his characters. his mother was dead. [john lennon, and his lost mama, rise up on the icon horizon] his father didn't understand him. he spent time back in the heartland, specifically Indiana, with his uncle and aunt [shades of dorothy, and john's aunt mimi]. his appeal was not so much to a sex or gender, but to an age group. what he offered was a rallying-point against the adult world of corruption and disenchantment.

"in james dean today's youth discovers itself. less for the reasons usually advanced: violence, sadism, hysteria, pessimism, cruelty and filth,

*than for others infinitely more simple and commonplace: modesty of feeling, continual fantasy life, moral purity without relation to everyday morality but all the more rigorous, eternal adolescent love of tests and trials, **intoxication**, **pride**, and **regret** at feeling oneself 'outside 'society, refusal and desire to become integrated and, finally, acceptance—or refusal—of the world as it is."—francois truffault*

in america, the mccarthyite reign of terror during the first half of the 1950s fostered a social climate which demanded the enforcement of conformity. where men were concerned, the 1950s movie turned inwards. indeed, in a society where dissent meant the loss of one's job and severe alienation, it seemed there was nowhere else to turn but inside. alone in the privacy of one's consciousness, individuality and integrity might survive. the 50s movies reveal the psychic price american culture paid for repression: of the right to disagree with social and political policy. this repression led to an outpouring of frustration and rage, depression and confusion, which could not help but surface in popular culture. america has always been obsessed with the individual's relationship to the law, even when its culture glamorizes, glorifies or even condones certain instances of lawlessness. whereas in wartime there seemed to be clearly defined heroes and villains, the post-war generation found that its enemies were not so easy to identify. the rebel now appeared as a particularly positive male role model in the american movie: the anti-hero as hero, the one guy who refused to be *'one of the guys'.*

what gave 50s teenagers a sense of group identity both peculiarly intense and historically new was that their generational status, their social position, was given the name of 'teenagers', a nomenclature never used before. sheer numbers and the group proximity caused by the population shift from rural to urban and suburban areas, encouraged a collective and standardized response—in how they dressed and danced to a new kind of music—rock and roll, rhythm and blues. [jack kerouac referred to james dean, marlon brando and **elvis** as 'the new american trinity".] the cultural guardians likened american teenagers to barbaric hordes descending on a city under siege. at the same time the business community was welcoming the arrival of the barbarians at the gates: a fortune was to be made selling trinkets to the invaders. hollywood, with typically mixed feelings, started catering to the teenage audience. clift, brando and dean, became possibly the most influential actors in film history, their cohort came to included dennis hopper, [who appeared in two of dean's films, *rebel* and *giant* and auditioned for *east of eden*], nick adams also in *rebel*, the aforementioned michael parks, paul newman (especially in *the lefthanded gun),* and of course, steve mcqueen. *rebel without a cause* was, and still is, the touchstone for a generational strife that lasted most overtly for the next two decades. [in fact leading directly, through the beats, to the hippy 'revolution'.] from dean's opening sequence, in fetal position on a cobbled street, playing with a mechanical drumming monkey, to his opening cry of anguish, like a siren, the stumbling destruction of his dad's portrait, the terrible apron, to the thunderstruck anguish at his friend's sacrificial death, the movie is shot through with archetypal images of teenage angst. in this film, and in this performance, inarticulateness is a virtue, his moaned and mumbled incantation of confusions, doubts, fears—is the song of adolescents. *rebel* opened on october 3, 1955—three days after dean's death, thereby achieving his oft-stated goal: *"live fast, die young, leave a beautiful corpse."*

A NOTE ON NICK ADAMS

in the array of james dean's cohort, nick adams was a standout. he probably met dean in december, 1950, in griffith park, jitterbugging in a television commercial, but they became fast friends during the filming of *rebel without a cause* [later, adams starred in a TV series called *the rebel,* as an ex-confederate soldier, what the publicity referred to as a" *'reconstruction beatnik"* wandering the wild west. warner brothers had a whole passle of half-hour tv westerns in the late 50s, including a show called *wanted:dead or alive,* starring steve mcqueen (my favorite show, although i watched them all] and *rawhide,* starring clint eastwood as a dean avatar, trailhand rowdy yates. [adams was also a standout in a film starring steve mcqueen, *hell is for heroes,* in 1962.] on the set of *rebel without a cause,* jimmy and nick entertained the entire company with imitations of brando and elia kazan. here's what dean, sounding a bit tongue-in-cheek, said, according to a warner brothers' press release, during the filming: *"i shall be busy for the rest of 1955 [* [the year he died] *and nick will be doing film work for the next six months. come 1956, however, i wouldn't be surprised to find myself with adams doing a two-a-night nightclub routine, or acting in a comedy by william shakespeare."* once the movie wrapped, dean was quoted, in another press release: *"i now regard natalie, nick, and sal not just as co-workers. i regard* *them as friends, about the only friends i have in this town."* after dean's death, nick overdubbed some of dean's lines for the film *giant*. [the film also starred dennis hopper and sal mineo.] adams capitalized on dean's fame with various publicity stunts, including posing for photographs at dean's grave, holding flowers, surrounded by grieving girls. he told a reporter that he had adopted dean's obsession with fast cars, bragging, *"i was arrested nine times in one year. they put me on probation, but i kept racing...to nowhere."*

adams then set his sights on another doomed icon, elvis presley. knowing of elvis 'admiration for james dean, on the set of *love me tender* he loudly boasted of his connection to dean, getting the attention of tom parker, elvis 'domineering manager. sensing the brash young actor could be of use, major parker made sure nick became a member of an entourage of paid companions, actors on the rise, surrounding the rock king. in the press, nick was referred to as the closest of these new friends. elvis would ask him to stay the night, and they'd go motorcycle riding, blasting the whole length of mulholland drive, high on prescription drugs. In that period , nick was roommates with the ubiquitous dennis hopper. both adams and hopper urged elvis to date natalie wood, extolling her beauty and hipness. [dewey phillips, elvis first record producer, along with his brother sam, tells a story about how elvis was introduced to 'going down' on a woman. elvis had been a bit squeamish up to then. dewey quotes him as saying, *"mister sam, you remember when y'all used to make me sick talking about eatin' pussy? well, i eat me some the other night. but man, now i'm in trouble."* *"who was it you eat?"* sam asked, because he thought right off that elvis had eat somebody's wife and got caught. but he says, *"natalie wood"*, and sam says, *"hellfire boy, what's your trouble?"* and elvis said, *"damn if i didn't fall in love with it."*]

nick published an account of his friendship with elvis in a fan magazine in 1957. years later, in 2012, his daughter found a much more intimate and extensive manuscript that he had written in 1956, called *the rebel and the king*. she saw to its publication, fifty-four years after his death, in 1968, of an overdose of paraledehyde and promazine. the coroner called it *"either an accident or a suicide."* nick adams was 37 years old.

THE FULL MCQUEEN

1.

punishment serves glamor
imprisonment asserts freedom
elegance of gesture is a stillness
revenge is reason enough
when motorcycles can fly
intimacy is the ultimate kindness.
find amusement in barbed wire
wear the crown, play the fool
lose yourself in the imperative rain
attain the full mcqueen
orphaned towel boy
in a turbulent cathouse,
he offers me this advice, murmuring into the mouthpiece:
gentle your killer horse
torch two houses out of heartbreak
be reticent on the issue of innocence
and airborne on supercharged mustangs.
in the face of sawed-off love
keep your heart open
never bet blind
you'll find the full mcqueen

2.

in the summer after my freshman year at UCLA, 1969, i plucked a card from
the bulletin board at the student center calling for someone who could write
short articles, on various subjects, with some photography skills, and editing
abilities…none of which i possessed as far as i knew. i went on down to
meet the outfit—three leos, a tall commanding woman, eve, her latino
husband, carlos, and a growling, balding, overweight, garrulous guy smoking
a cigarette with a battered remington typewriter on a littered desk, by the
name of gus. united features syndicate. being a sagittarius with scorpio
rising i fit right in. there was a vibe. they said they'd teach me how to get
good shots, at openings and funerals and celebrity golf tourneys and such.
and how to develop them and print them. they had a dark room right there,
the place kinda smelled of chemicals and cigarettes and a whiff of perfume.
they dug me. i found them fascinating, and hip. or at least savvy. i did learn

how to do most of the things necessary for the job. basically, we were sent photographs of, for instance, ice-fishing in minnesota, or throwing your own backyard luaus, and wrote copy to accompany them. (we sold the luau to an airline magazine and the ice-fishing to *field and stream*.) as for as the photos generated by us—that was almost entirely paparazzi kind of stuff. one memorable event involved sally field leaving the hospital after having a baby. i got in a bit of a scuffle with ron galella, the most prominent and despised of the hollywood regulars, roundly disliked by the stars, and those fellas trying to capture their light in the form of salable images. the last thing you want, naturally, is the back of some kid's head when you're about to get a shot of the flying nun looking blissful in a wheelchair. so the guy literally shoved me down from behind, knocking me into a couple of other guys, to clear his lens. none of us got that special shot and this dude comes up to me after. i have no notion of who he was or what the fuck was his problem. but i was a hippy and a kid and intimidated by all these adults who were *really* doing this job. an older guy stepped in, in fact, and told mr. galella to back off. called him a *"grandstander and a fucking bully."* but most of the assignments were fairly peaceful, at least not violent. kind of like driving in rome, or pogoing around in a mosh pit. basically all bets are off and try not to hurt yourself or others. it was actually kind of fun, and eventually i was considered in the club. we all approached one particular event with trepidation. that was the funeral of jay sebring, one of the people killed by manson and his girls. one guy said to me as we were walking up to the chapel at forest lawn, *"this is so fucked up…sharon tate is one of the most beautiful women i've ever seen in person. always nice to all the photographers, having a good time, you know what i mean? i don't even want to do this. seems ghoulish, but you could get a shot from a mile away and sell it on this one. shitload of stars gonna be here."* he kept talking as we positioned ourselves. everybody kept their distance from each other. and then people started coming out—every single one of them looked devastated. some had to be held up they were so distraught. men openly crying, some women sobbing. a particularly distressed couple were steve and neile mcqueen. she had big, jackie-o sunglasses on, clutching a purse. mcqueen, mr. cool, was clearly shaken, lost, utterly bereft. and he was doing nothing to cover it. naked anguish. and the crowd of people recording this sad parade on film was completely silent. never happened before in my experience. no shouts of *"over here!" "mia, give us a smile." "frank, how'd ya like the picture?"* none of that. we were at a funeral that had sent shock waves way beyond show business. some line had been crossed. the country would never be the same. the kennedys, martin luther king…altamont was just a few months later. the world was going mad.

someone to my left said, *"you know, mcqueen was supposed to be there. he was sebring's pal, and was on his way to polanski's house that night. got curtailed somehow or other, probably some chick. man, this would be an even bigger story!"* i split right then. i'd had enough. i had natalie wood and robert wagner. not to mention warren beatty, looking lost, shellshocked. when i developed the roll and printed some up, one of my pictures of mcqueen revealed his devastation to an almost shocking degree. i didn't even show it to my bosses. i just trashed it. and scratched the negative, so it would never see the light of day.

3.

the other night, i caught most of *bullitt* on tcm. i recalled how about 15 years ago, while still living in nyack with my family, i had stumbled on a documentary about steve mcqueen on the biography channel. it reminded me of all that i had gotten from watching him as a kid. i would never miss *wanted dead or alive.* so cool with his sawed-off shotgun (his own idea) and his unforced masculinity and easy physicality. he stood apart from all the other posturing and preening male stars of that era from john wayne to chuck connors. they all made a big show of how tough and macho they were. somehow i felt at home when i watched mcqueen as if i was a better, cooler, version of myself—or my aspirations for myself. i was reminded of that feeling as i watched the bio, in 2006, or so. in the next two weeks i tracked down every film of his i could find. the complete *wanted dead or alive, the blob, the st. louis bank robbery,* early comedies in which he tried too hard, silly stuff like *the honeymoon game* as well as heartbreaking films such as *baby, the rain must fall.* and work that combined them both as in *soldier in the rain.* i was impressed by his versatility and his depth and solemnity in *bullitt*, and *the getaway.* he communicated without much effort from his soul. but what i noticed most was how he handled the anger of the women in his life. (ann-margret and tuesday weld in the same movie! *the cincinnatti kid.*) in film after film there is a scene in which they pretty much excoriate him—for being a bad man, withholding and haunted, impossible to really know. they all say a variation of, *"i thought i knew you, but you won't let me into your world."* *"half of it is in the sewer,"* he says in *bullitt,* to a stunned and tearful jackie bisset. through it all, he maintains a look of love and a glimmer of hope in his eyes.

he presents a poker face full of yearning. he does not argue or defend himself but neither does he stonewall. he listens. carefully. he holds his ground but he does not try to talk them out of anything. by then, in our marriage i was stirring up a fair amount of anger and disappointment in susanna on a pretty regular basis. or at least that's what i experienced.

i could feel her backing away from me, figuratively and literally. so i would challenge her perceptions, try to argue her out of her dismay. of course, my perceived failings were not always the topics of the discussion but i would make them so. simple domestic matters felt like reprimands. and on topics anywhere near money or sex, i would often panic and she would throw up her hands, *"i can't have this conversation now,"* she would say and that would be that.

but now, here in the tv room, watching mcqueen I see that in nearly every movie allow those women the right to their frustration and confusion and yes, their anger, in some cases even rage. something clicked. he was not acquiescent, at all. he was entirely sympathetic. *"yeah, i am a pain in the ass,"* he seemed to be saying, without rancor. *"i always have been. that's my nature."* it was like a light went on inside my head. from then on when talking with my loving, irritated wife, i started focussing my efforts on simply letting her have her feelings, without resistance, or excuses. and i hung onto that strategy, pretty well there for awhile. i learned from observing mcqueen and his calm, engaged acceptance of his own flaws, expressed simply in his eyes, no words, no weak assurances. i found i could take in susanna's fervent, sometimes brutal, critiques and complaints and she would come to feel a little safer. she felt husbanded, I think. and i could believe that a chasm was not going to open up underneath me, casting me into the pit of abandonment. we got another five or so precious years more of relative harmony— even passion. and i owed it all to steve mcqueen. of course, soon enough the train of my life, stoked by endless neediness and fear of failure (not to mention huge doses of testosterone, administered every few weeks, meant to keep me alive in the face of HIV. more on that later...) went careening right off the tracks, squealing and reeling onto the *'vast plain of my immense loneliness'*...

4.

here comes the part that i have been ambivalent about including, in the fullness of this tribute.

something vestigial troubles me.
a tabloid ache.
a secret that plain decency forbids exposure,
should be hidden from the daylight of normalcy.
or else face rejection and mockery.
but then i think,
why should you find this aspect of the man shameful?
to be denied or ignored or locked away?
is it because this is the part of my nature
that i believe drove them, especially them, so far away?
or is that just a weird kind of justification for my actions, even in their
extremity?
or perhaps a condemnation of *them*, not of me, for their intolerance, prudery,
punitive lack of compassion and seemingly endless cruelty?

is this shit actually what i feel?
how can that be, at this late date?
(bill styron once told me, as we drove through the halcyon connecticut
countryside, "*once that sense of being a sinner is inserted in you, you can
never extract it.*")

but i know the reluctance is real, no matter what.
as real as anything else...

so, jack once told me that jim told him
about a time when jim was still an actor and got a job in an early television
show called *west point story*
it was shot at the real west point. the actors were billeted in the actual dorms
for the cadets.
jim and steve mcqueen were playing small roles in the show, and were given
the same room
jack said jim said that one night steve came on to him.
but he turned him down.
he'd already met jack and wanted to stay true to what was developing
between them.
jack was furious when he heard!

as he told me, giving that wonderful chuckle of his,*"heh-heh-heh…i told him, are you nuts! you can't turn down a guy that cute! you fool! heh-heh-heh…"*
jim said, *"he scared me. and on the set he hissed into my ear, 'i'm gonna be a movie star..so stay out of my way.'"*
at one point in nyc i saw a therapist who was the therapist of a therapist, that therapist being the wife of one of susanna's best childhood friends.
the woman was much older than her husband, michael.
she had been a friend of his mother's.
she was very hip and on the level.
she figured frank Donnelly and i could relate to each other.
frank worked out of his house in chelsea.
after months of sessions we had gotten to know each other pretty well. frank was the kind of therapist who shared a lot of his life, his own sexual nature and his adventures and heartbreaks as a technique for leveling the playing field, in terms of revealing oneself. (not unlike the way i direct and teach). the method worked.
he referred to blow jobs as the worshipping of maleness, kneeling at the altar. honoring. celebrating.
i dug that.
during one session, steve mcqueen came up.
i have no idea why.
perhaps it was during the time that i was watching all his movies and getting as much as i could from his style and substance, the way he carried himself, especially with wome. to find a stance for myself again.
i spoke specifically of his indisputable masculinity,
and how as a kid
i felt it was in my range, somehow.
and that it was precisely the 'me 'i wanted the world to see.
"well, you have a lot in common—you and mcqueen. in many ways. profound mother issues, feelings of abandonment, and all that…but more specifically—
i took a trip to provincetown one summer, just for the weekend, with these two lesbians. they had this great old station wagon. beat-up rusty chevy.
they brought along this utterly beautiful young stud with a goofy smile, frisky.
they folded down the seats and we stretched out in the back.
i must have sucked his cock all the way to p-town."

276

"*wait a minute…*" i was literally sputtering. "*you…you…sucked..wait a minute…*"
"*yes i did. obviously, he wasn't* steve mcqueen *then he was just this kid who wanted to be an actor, who rumbled around the village shirtless…*"
"*well this just..*"
"*so, his masculinity is indisputable, absolutely without doubt, but not uncomplicated.'*
certainly was one of the most therapeutic fifty minutes i ever experienced.
hands down.
5.
crowded into jimmy dean's digs in the iroquois hotel,
after a rollicking binge at jerry's bar uptown,
all liquored up,
dean asks mcqueen
"*like to do my hair?*"
drawing his mane back from his forehead
as if clearing his mind
and helpfully producing a brush.
steve sits down behind jim,
patiently backcombing all that hair
thick and shiny as a mink
breathing
or perhaps
chuckling down the back of dean's neck.
"*wanna do mine?*"
"*drop dead.*"
"*come on, JD, don't you dig my fur…*"
"*naw. your hair's impossible, man.*"
then they kiss souls
to the buzz of being bent
dismissing the distinction
between epicene and alpha male
exquisite designer crumpet
body perfectly honed
a wild one in short shorts.

on some frantic automat night
off times square
eating as if he is on fire
writhing in his seat
going into a slump
acting the neglected child
slouched there alone
shoulders hunched
he shook her when he said,
"how would you treat a suicidal nut? just the same as any other guy, or make an exception?"
so they walked down 7th avenue to sheridan square, where he bounced off his bleak walls,
begging for mother's milk.
yearning to suckle.
later she said,
"steve loved anything with wheels or tits, probably in that order...all in all, a very torn-up guy."

he arrived at a meeting with agents at MCA,
seeking representation,
by roaring right through the marbled lobby
on his deep-throated harley
right into the elevator
straight up to the eleventh floor.
they took him.
in his immaculate black denim
*"this lean, tense boy
you felt could slug you as fast as smile at you."*

jack told me that when he was in nyc, (visiting monty), he ran into alan pakula, (closeted) producer of *love with a proper stranger.*
"well, its going great. just great. the dailies are superb. talk about chemistry...but i have a star who likes to go to the baths..."

there was a small bathhouse in LA, at fountain and van ness. (i went there more than once, myself.) a friend, a screenwriter, told me this:

"he was the biggest star in the world…this would've been the late 60s.
we were in a couple of meetings together, with the studio heads, on a script
of mine, and he kept talking right to me..
these guys would ask a question and he'd look at me when he answered…
so i used to run away to this little place to smoke dope
and one day there was steve!
in a towel..
he reached his arm out from a room as i passed
and pulled me in with a grin on his face..
from then on we'd meet there occasionally
we'd signal through secretaries..
he was really nice to me.
he admired me because i went to yale..
he told me
'i really like you..and that's not good.'
then i didn't hear from him for awhile
we ran into each other at a party.
i went up to him and said hi
he turned around without a word and walked away…"
6.
so, some months after the sebring funeral, we got some pictures of a
motocross race in baja. mcqueen had come in second. the shots were just
spectacular, with mcqueen cresting a hill, splattered with mud, and looking
impossibly cool, joyously engaged. but we had no details. we didn't really
know where or when. and that mcqueen had come in second, which was a
story in and of itself. no written reports anywhere. the stupid photographer,
supposedly a professional, had taken no notes. when i got ahold of him he
was enthusiastic but clueless. *"yes it was a blast, man. how much do you*
think i can make on them." *"nothin 'if we can't have some background. like,*
why'd he come in second. and do you have a release from him?"
"uhhhhhhhh…" *"thought so. well you can just try to sell them, sure. it is*
steve mcqueen. but that means nothing to us, really. we sell articles. that's
where we make our money." *"can you give me. like, cash for them? i'm kind*
of strapped.." *"talk to eve, man. but i doubt it."* eve says to me, *"listen you*
little shit, get out there and find some info on this. our commission if we just
sell these for him is bupkis. it's fuckin steve mcqueen on a motorcycle, in

mid-air, then he's covered with mud, with his shirt off and totally cracking up. are you kidding me? carlos, why'd we hire this kid? i thought you said he was smart?" "because you wanted to fuck him!" "what? he's an infant." then carlos says, *"why don't you try calling mcqueen's production company? he's gotta have an office there. somebody must answer the phone."*

i do some detective work. i call solar productions. i explain to the receptionist what i'm calling about. a guy named bob relyea comes on the phone. i tell him i'm working my way through college, i'm a theater major, we have these great pictures and i'm supposed to write a little piece to go along with them. but we have no information at all. i have the temerity to ask, *"why'd he come in second?" "hang on a minute,"* mr. relyea says. *"i think there's a guy here who can explain that to you."*

and a familiar voice comes on the line. speaking softly into the mouthpiece. *"yeah. i understand you're working your way through college. whaddya wanna know?"* to say this situation was not the one i expected to be in is—like describing death as a little nap. but, incredibly, i just went with my real question, *"why'd you come in second?"* i really had nothing else— which is to say, i had so many questions for this man, so much i wanted to say to him, and ask, and learn, and get advice on, and absorb, and become…all of it like a shout from my soul. so i kept it simple.

"well, i made a miscalculation. i underestimated this guy that i should have paid a little more attention to. you know what i mean?"

"no."

he chuckled, in that way he had. like we were both in on it now.

"good answer…..well, because i tend to overestimate myself."

now i was plain astonished.

"how is that possible?"

"okay, none of that. so, what do you have shots of?"

"uh…well, one is you coming up over this hill, and you get air…like in the great escape."

"right." and i describe all the images we have in detail. and he talks me through the race. moment by moment. with great humor and delight. i tell him one shot is him going into a slide, with a spray of mud coming right at the camera.

"really? that's cool. that's the moment. that's when i lost. there's a guy blasting past me, on the right, right? now, that guy can hold his mud. he'd been dogging me the whole damn run. i had him coming up to the line, but he just came right up at me and got a wheel on me and i spun right out." surprisingly, i actually knew what he meant. *"got it?"*

"i think so…"

"the important thing is, i let down my guard. i thought i had him so i lost my concentration…gotta be vigilant, especially with yourself….so, bob says you're an actor?"

"well, i want to be."

"you either are or you're not."

"i guess so."

"don't guess, man. or they'll roll right over you. life will."

"i'm getting that sense."

"good..quite a job you got there…must be interesting. do you know what one of my first job's was? the first job i actually got paid for? towel boy in a cat house. seriously, the girls need clean towels between tricks. just stands to reason, right? i learned a lot of very useful information on that gig. i moved up from there, in terms of salary, anyway. out of persistence and panic. i said that to some press guy the other day. he didn't have a clue as to what i was talking about."

"i completely understand it."

"i figured you would."

we went on from there. for quite awhile. he was curious and engaged, moment to moment. where'd i come from? why acting? i guess it was a slow day. or maybe he was just an incredibly kind person. eventually we got around to what he was looking to do in the future. here he surprised me, again.

"you know what i really want to do?"

"well, you can do whatever you want to do, i would think…"

"maybe. but the ante keeps being raised, right? you get nominated and then you want to fuckin'win. you want to prove something else than what you've already proven. mostly to yourself."

"you should have won. for sand pebbles. *if for nothing else than your death scene."*

"really..why do say that?"

"the way you do that last line. 'i was home…something happened…what happened?' *and then you just slowly tip over…"*

"interesting you should pick out that moment…i had to fight for that, actually. talk about rolling over you. the whole thing was written like a war movie. you know, blaze of glory.."

"like hell is for heroes.."

"shit, kid, you know your stuff…yeah, it was bullshit. i came up with that line about home. that's my life story, right there. or it was. i think i've found a pretty solid home for myself now. but then, no matter what, you do the ultimate rollover, right."

"yeah. i get it."

"already? i doubt it, but listen to me, you don't have time to fuck around. time is awasting. so, you know what i'm into at the moment? i want to do ibsen, man. enemy of the people. my wife gave it to me. she knew i would dig it. it would make a helluva movie. but it is fucking with these money people's heads, big time. so, yeah, theoretically i can do whatever i want…"

"man, that is just mind-blowing!…i mean…"

"yeah, that's what they think. the suits. but fuck 'em. i get that guy. he knows the fucking truth, and nobody wants to listen. but hey, i gotta split. they're waving their hands at me. nice talking to you, kid."

"uh, yeah…really nice talking to you…"

"best of luck, buddy. hope this helped."

and then he was gone. i took a long moment to just sit there and bask in the…magic of what had just really, actually, truly happened—in *reality*. i had just spoken to **steve mcqueen**. we had talked, at some length and depth. but still i didn't quite believe it. i walked up to eve's desk, in a daze, playing the whole conversation back in my mind. laughing out loud.

'what the hell are you laughing about? are you high?' eve said, considerably annoyed, frazzled and distracted, as usual.

"i don't think so…but…i got the story on the motocross race. i just talked to steve mcqueen. for a half an hour."

"you are obviously high. fuck off. and get to work. we don't pay you to smoke dope."

"no, seriously. i got through to him. i called his production office. and…he just…came on the line and ran me through the whole thing. i'll have the story for you in an hour."

she sat there stunned, looking at me as if i had just pulled a frog out of my mouth. i hustled over to my corner and wrote the whole race up, more or less as mcqueen had described it. and it was great. we made a shitload of money on it from some motorcycle magazine or other. there are quite a few of them, and all of them bid on it.

it took mcqueen ten years to finally get *enemy of the people* done, in 1978, with charles durning as his bourgeois brother, directed by lamont johnson. he does a massive speech, directly from the play—probably more words than he spoke in all of *bullitt.* he is magnificent in the film. of course, nobody saw it. it was barely released. by then, he had more or less dropped out. he was almost unrecognizable in full beard and long hair, living at the beverly wilshire hotel. two years later he died of cancer. he was 50 years old.

"time starts now."—steve mcqueen in *bullitt.*

'come to my arms, cruel and sullen thing;
indolent beast, come to my arms again,
for i would plunge my fingers in your mane
and be a long time unremembering—'
—baudelaire

THE MONTIFICATION OF THE FLESH, excerpt from a threnody
like insects
as he sprawled
in the back room
passed out on the table
in his soiled grey suit
flannel
and wasted face
like insects in a bonfire
in a frenzy to infest him
they lick beneath his eyelids
tug harshly at his sweat-soaked scalp
invading every orifice

a man should be what he can do

nobody lies about being lonely

he would run
lean and naked
into the cool night air
craving starlight on his skin
bones in the torque of dreams
guilt addled
his irises the exact color of the sky at dusk
he's got the world on the thinnest thread of beauty
encased in his mother's sunny bubble
those were the days when the door to the attic was double bolted
when he scratched his way out with bleeding fingernails
when he dangled from the dormer window
aloft and carefree

marilyn whispers, *"they aren't fit to open the door for him."*
she longs to cradle his head in her lap
we all do
but he's slouching tight
in some misfit phone booth
bright white light glaring
door shoved open
exposed, like a wounded bird
trying to reach his mother
gravel crunches under the tires
"yes you would too recognize me"
he beseeches
as his bandages unravel
busted skull
skin and bone
bessie keens like a mother bird
cradling his head in her lap,
reaching past his ruined jawbone
scooping out shards of his splintered teeth
his shattered face
stains her gown

bits of glass diamonds in his hair
monty stares into the last remaining mirror
reflecting himself into eternity
he is engulfed by cataracts of loss
waterfalls of shame
rain pelting the proud trees
and they pull monty dripping,
out of the polluted river,
with a hook.

his drug dealer, BIRD, saw him come into a bar in Harlem, very late, about 3:30 in the morning. *"monty looked terrible. unshaven, dirty—he asked if he could buy heroin from me for some friends. i was going to go out and get it for him, when all of a sudden there's a fuckin 'murder at the bar. one guy shoots another guy in the gut—blood spurts out, there's all sorts of screamin' and yellin'—the murdered guy was a pimp. his girl starts keenin 'over him. monty just stands there in the midst of the noise, the confusion, watching the whole scene. he's hanging there like a ghost, and then he glides out the door into the night...now, i'm not sure he was even there..."*

"they receive from me but do i touch their souls?...a hunger grows out of my beauty: i should like to hurt those for whom i shine; i should like to rob those to whom i give; thus do i hunger for malice...oh, the loneliness of all givers! o the taciturnity of all who shine!...light am i; ah, that i were night! but this is my loneliness that i am girt with light. ah, that i were dark and nocturnal! how i would suck at the breasts of light!...this is my poverty, that my hand never rests from giving; this is my envy, that i see waiting eyes and the lit-up nights of longing. o wretchedness of all givers! o darkening of my sun! o craving to crave! o ravenous hunger in satiation! —nietzsche, 'night song'

ALOHA SUITE/ COYOTE GOES TO KAUAI, part 7
recon
ciliation
with self (or other)
one more time.

papaya: a soft skinned melon

she said so little
he heard so much

soul: sum total of one person''s affect in the mind of another

she never raises her voice

shame: outline of shadow
where did you go?
into a mineral fog?
>	*let me hear your soul,*
>	*sister*

grit of dreams
under the sign of monstrosity
anxiety in the costume of contempt
>	*come on, baby, let's do the twist*

father sleeps
mother gone
>	*round and round and round and round*

our spirit ripens
just like this
love for a lifetime
and then some
desire in tower breezes
afternoon embraces
moving ever nearer
to eternal truth
radiating from that mystery
>	*radio tuned to rock and roll*

'blind loving wrestling touch, sheath'd hooded sharp-tooth'd touch!
did it make you ache so, leaving me?'—walt whitman, 'song of myself'

"coyote: *no one is going anywhere. no one is coming from*
anywhere…everything has already happened…all i see is movement. nothing
else is happening…i am nothing at all."—murray mednick, 'the coyote cycle'

286

*"i got to keep movin'/ i got to keep movin'/ blues fallin 'down like hail/...
as the day keeps on 'hind me/ theres a hellhound on my trail..."—robert
johnson, 'hellhound on my trail'*

8. **PROTECTOR**: EVERYONE BEGINS IN INNOCENCE, COMING FRESHLY TO EACH MOMENT, AND EVERYONE CAN SENSE THE TRUTH.

or it is a hard and unjust world in which the powerful take advantage of others, which must be resisted.

"know what is in front of your face, and what is hidden from you will be disclosed to you. for there is nothing hidden that won't be revealed."—gospel of st. thomas

*"***coyote:*** *when i was a child everything was familiar to me and had power. the air had power, the earth had power, the sky had power. the power was the spirit in all things and i knew it personally—me, coyote!"—murray mednick, 'the coyote cycle'*

*"much is said of what is spiritual, and of spirituality, in this, that or the other— in objects, expressions.—for me, i see no object, no expression, no animal, no tree, no art, no book, but i see, from morning to night, and from night to morning, the spiritual.—bodies are all spiritual.—**all words are spiritual.— nothing is more spiritual than words.**—whence are they? along how many thousands and tens of thousand of years have they come? those eluding, fluid, beautiful, fleshless, realities, mother, father, water, earth, me, this, soul, tongue, house, fire."—walt whitman*

*"**as it was with icarus,***
*****even the clouds mushroom in echoes of thunderous shrouds*****
*****and tho 'he flies straight as light,*****
*****like light he'll curve—near the moon,*****
*****and return to the labyrinth a trillion light-years too soon."*****
*****—jack larson, 'the relativity of icarus'*****

ALOHA SUITE/ COYOTE GOES TO KAUAI/ Part 8
he calls for a revolution
ten silver saxes
having the balls for retribution
alone in the night
extra violence in anticipation
i'm drifting back
of desperate conflagration
dreamer of pictures
and cataclysmic lack of action.
alone in the night
she whispers to the ocean
we catch the wind
melody of motion
mad about saffron
tender consolation
yellow is the color
'make a contribution
sunlight came softly
to a peaceable solution'
yonder misty mountains
see the trees dance
hung with tears
rainclouds advance
caterpillar sheds his skin
sunlight entrance
to find the butterfly within
she speaks to the plants
that's the time
he fumbles the chance
that's the time
all our dreams converge
that's the time
he and she and us and them
merge
surge
always on the verge...

and there we rest.
we contemplate
    why wait
they ask?
we answer with a question.

CUPIDITY. Concupiscence; unlawful or unreasonable longing.
CURIOSITY. Nicety; delicacy.
    When thou was in thy gilt, and thy perfume, they mock thee for too
much curiosity;
    in thy rags thou knowest none, but are despised for the contrary.
    —shake-speare's 'timon of athens'
CUTTLE. A foul mouthed fellow; a fellow who blackens the character of
others.
    away, you cutpurse rascal; you filthy bung, away: by this wine i'll thrust
my knife in your moldy chaps,
    if you play the saucy cuttle with me.
    —shake-speare's 'henry, IV, pt. 2'

BODY TALK
in the language of muscle
in the language of posture
in the language of the way we carry ourselves
we want to
get it over
with
we want to be born
to be lifted
and soon
only the ramifications will remain
the fortifications
in the language of the way we carry the body
we want the body to carry itself
we want it all
to carry itself
we want to be borne.

290

GLIMPSES OF JACKSON/Part 2
you better bring your own redemption when you come
for there are barricades
running out of empty love
pretenders pretending to pretend
just like me.

a bunch of us take a long lease on the old oxford theatre, one block east of western, just off santa monica. it is to be the new home of a company once housed in a little spot off melrose, a storefront playhouse known as the MET Theater (nobody could remember why. this earlier venue was the location of my meeting with sal mineo in 1968). the first MET had been run by jimmy gammon, a face like forty miles of bad road, with a guttural growl and a sideways smile, and tim scott, tall, laconic, wise and droll. both of them had been kicking around hollywood for decades, and had earned the respect, almost awe, of the entire show biz community. (jimmy was sam shepard's favorite actor. he played every dad sam ever wrote). for the rebirth of the MET, jimmy and tim invited artists they admired and trusted: ed harris, amy madigan, holly hunter, arliss howard, alfre woodard, beth henley, alan vint, laura owens, paul koslo, marty kove, joe cortese. we've had several rambunctious meetings to discuss how to run a space with no one in charge (*"NO ARTISTIC DIRECTORS!"* cool…then what?*). to be in cahoots with these folks, to be included in this circle of friends and colleagues, means everything to me. i am not left out. emphatically. to be invited into this particular group of artists is one of the first times i am convinced that i have come to be included in the show business/theater community, that i am respected and valued, whether or not i have achieved fame, or even wealth. i get busy making myself useful. and in the nearly five years that we are in operation that feeling grew and grew. so as to beat an immediate path to our door, even before we get a play up, i throw together what we call *"the great writers series."* twelve weeks of twice-weekly readings, with the writers present if possible, and it turned out to be more than possible—some of the greatest writers alive showed up—denis johnson, louise erdrich, bill styron, eddie bunker, james ellroy, fannie flagg, peter matthiessen, joy harjo, budd schulberg…and many more. instead of being relegated to reading between the shelves of bookstores, now they're center stage and they are thrilled. with readers such as dustin hoffman, roddie macdowall, bill pullman, fionnula flanagan, eva marie saint, dermot mulroney, raquel welch (reading *myra breckinridge*!). the thing was an instant and sustained success.

i also produced a similar reading series with poetry as the focus—with actors and poets combined, '*the act of the poet*': james merrill/tim curry; james tate/ andrea marcovicci; carolyn kizer/ blythe danner; michael ryan/ julia louis/dreyfus; sharon olds/me. it took place in the elegant lobby of the legendary chateau marmont, one sunday a month at four o'clock in the golden afternoon. in fact, the two projects overlapped for a couple of years. for me, all of it is the gift that keeps on giving, in terms of a sense of belonging.

turns out the guy with the perfect hair is a regular at the monthly poetry events. by now we have become more than acquaintances. susanna had worked with him on the *no nukes* concerts in the early 80s, so the rapport was easy to find. he and his statuesque, platinum-blonde girlfriend, are serious poetry fans, especially darryl hannah. (she referred to herself as my 'other sister darryl') she was very well-read and actually a very canny, deep chick. plus jackson and i had been on the serving line of a celebrity thanksgiving dinner, given as a benefit for *oxfam*. (he did sweet potatoes, i did dressing.)

one night i arrived at the MET theater, and there, sitting disconsolately in the lobby, was the crack sound guy, theo mondle, sent each week by the local NPR station, KCRW, to record the readings for later broadcast on the radio. theo had demonstrated such wizardry and inventiveness when he'd been swooped up by an NPR team doing a story in dubai. [here's how theo described it, in 2020: *"johnny fodor was visiting dubai radio, saw and heard about my work and the same evening offered to bring me to KCRW."* and no wonder, theo was such a fine fellow, always upbeat, always enthusiastic, that they essentially let him stow away on the boat back to America, and on arrival, arranged a green card for him. now he sat there with tears in his eyes. a piece of paper in one trembling hand and a torn envelope in the other, staring at the carpet like it would open up beneath him at any moment. i asked him what could possibly bring him to this totally un-theo like state.

"i've lost my status…i've been denied…if i go back, i will be killed."

"whaaaat?…NPR will take care of it, man."

"they can't do anything…i've stayed too long…and they say somebody else can do my job."

"well, that's bullshit…there's gotta be something we can do!"

" i need to get a different job, that nobody else could do, no american, anyway.."

*"**nobody** can do what you are doing… "*

"…like some kind of musician gig…somebody who needs a tabla player..maybe.."

now, people are arriving for the show. i reassure theo and then hit the microphone with some high dudgeon going. i am righteously pissed off.

"folks, before we get into the literature, we have a problem. some of you know theo. he records all of these readings impeccably and edits them and makes them pristine for broadcast on KCRW. let me make it clear that nobody can do what theo does, with this kind of care and joy in his work. now, the bottom line is that they want to throw him out of this country, because an american can do his job just as well. or so they say. obviously nothing could be further from the truth. so…he needs a gig only he can do. please give this some serious thought. if theo goes home he will not survive. bad people are angry at him. so, if anybody has any ideas, see me afterward."

and we get on with it. but as i stride away from the podium an idea comes to me: JACKSON!

i rush to the office and call buddha, jackson's manager and in general a completely right-on guy. nothing throws buddha. he had been jackson's roadie, then road manager, then everything manager. i tell him the situation. he tells me to call the studio the next morning at 10 sharp. at a break, i hand theo a scrap of paper with a phone number on it and the name: jackson browne.

"call him…he needs a tabla player.."

"you're kidding!?"

"he does now."

the next morning, when theo calls, a light, almost teenagery voice, comes on the line:

"hey, so this is the famous theo, right? hear you are a fantastic tabla player—and you do electronic stuff, right? live?…i could really use that texture.what time is the hearing?"

"thank you so much, sir, um, mister browne."

"call me that again and the whole gig is off. sounds like your talking to my dad. so, what time is the hearing?"

"8 o'clock.."

"fuck. these guys are brutal. okay, see you there…you gave buddha the details, right?"

"yes, sir, i did. well, not yet, but i will…"

" yeah, cool. looking forward to working with you,. looking forward to **meeting** *you, brother…"*

and that was that. jackson showed up and stood in the back, causing murmurs throughout the courtroom until they asked him to step forward and state his purpose.

"your honor, i just can't make the sound i want to make without theo mondle. i have recently interviewed him and we are about to go on tour and do some recording before we leave. so i need theo immediately. i ask that you renew his status and in fact, accelerate the process of citizenship, if that is possible…"

to this day, theo credits me with saving his life. he went on to become a crucial member of beck's band, as well, and toured the world. since then he has been a chief sound editor for NPR on the west coast. (he has since retired, very happily and comfortably.) but as for saving his life—it was really mr. browne that carried that ball across the goal line. i just knew where to toss it.

ALL THE DOOMED BLONDES, Part Eight

barbara loden was mrs. elia kazan, much to her peril, and the first woman to write, direct and star in her own feature film, *wanda.* [if you don't count mary pickford who never took a directing credit but who directed everything she was ever in, really, possibly excepting the shorts with griffith and oversaw every script, after moving on from d.w. griffith. even with him, the stories were always conceived by her.] loden's innovative and accomplished work displays a genuine feeling for wayward, disordered lives, and for an off-center, unsentimental pathos, characteristics sorely missing from her husband's work. *wanda* did not go without notice or praise. it was the american entry at cannes in 1971, winning the critics prize at the venice film festival and making many critics' top ten lists for that year. sadly, there were no more films from barbara loden. in the wake of the success of *wanda,* she sought financing for several other scripts, but was not successful. earlier she had appeared in two of kazan's films—as the sour secretary in *wild river* with montgomery clift and as the sexually rapacious, bleached-blonde sister in *splendor in the grass* with natalie wood [the sight of the nubile natalie soaking dreamily in a steaming bathtub in this film, her body barely concealed by bubbles, marked the first screen-induced hard-on of my young life] and an almost callow warren beatty. loden also played the fragile laura in a television version of tennessee williams '*the glass menagerie,* with shirley booth as the suffocating mother. perhaps most significantly, she played the '**marilyn monroe** 'character in arthur miller's finest play, *after the fall,* written after marilyn's death. loden won a tony award for her intense performance and her identification with marilyn was almost eerie. she was called the "*new **jean harlow**"* and dubbed a *"blonde bombshell",* a phrase first coined to describe marilyn.

she was born in a small town in north carolina. when her parents divorced, her mother went to another town to find work, leaving barbara with her very religious maternal grandparents. at 16, she left for new york and worked as a pin-up girl, model, and dancer at the famed copacabana nightclub. (the very same *"school of dramatic arts"* marilyn is said to have graduated from in *all about eve).* in kazan's self-serving autobiography [*elia kazan: a life.* need i say more?), he bemoans his inability to control loden and her dependence on her "*sexual appeal",* and yet he speaks of her, according to the *new york times* with a "*mix of affection and patronization, emphasizing her sexuality and her backcountry feistiness."* although proud of her accomplishments, (*"I realized I was losing her",* kazan wrote in the aftermath of the success of her film) she irritated him by dressing in a more-masculine fashion in boots and trousers, perhaps in an effort to gain respect on the set. the mixed messages took its toll, and although the two remained married, kazan and loden grew apart emotionally, even through loden's later breast cancer crisis. according to kazan, she blamed him for the "*negativity*" that she thought had caused her stress and thus her cancer. she died in 1980 while preparing what would have been her second directorial effort, an adaptation of the feminist classic, kate chopin's novella, *the awakening.* describing the source for the character of wanda, she referred to the role as semi-autobiographical. *"i used to be a lot like that. i had no identity of my own. i just became whatever i thought people wanted me to become."* a few years after her death, kazan claimed to have written the script for *wanda* himself, "*to give her something to do."* by all accounts, including that of the cinematographer on the film, nicholas proferes, this claim is utter bilge. despite her work in several monumental films and stage plays and her relationship with kazan (or more than likely, because of it), she "*found most doors closed to me,*" in the film business, and like her character in *wanda*, was shunned by society, her talent sadly neglected.

NIGHT RIDE HOME
October 23, 1995, NYC

i get a call at the office (for the production of *the wizard of oz in concert,* one of my few 'office jobs') around 6:00 PM, saying rose is hung-up at the UN listening to arafat. i imagine him in his keffiyeh droning on in palestinian. i'm supposed to get to the ziegfield by 6:45 to pick up some tickets as rose and i are going to the premiere of *cry, the beloved country*. nelson mandela will be present at the screening. so will hillary clinton. i don't get out of the office til 7 and the city is tumultuous with many streets blocked off. lots of fire engines and rumbling motorcycles and madly flashing lights. i bop uptown, staying mid-block from around 46th, feeling *slightly* at-home because i now know these passages through the city like i know backroads in LA. every head of state in the world is in nyc and i guess they're all staying between 6th and 7th in the lower fifties—because that's where i need to go and its impenetrable. finally i get to 57th, which is one block past the ziegfield, as it turns out, and i'm stopped on the sidewalk in my near-frantic rush, head down and barging along, by a guy with a cord coming out of his head.

he holds up a calming, but commanding, hand.

"*how can i get to the front of the ziegfield,*" i pant.

"*hang on a minute,*" he says gently. "*the first lady is getting out of her car.*"

then i notice the stretch limo, parked to my left, door open. then i see all the other guys with cords looped behind their ears.

oh, these fellas are secret service.

"*i know who you are,*" he says with the faintest smile, mostly to let me know it's okay. "*all you have to do is go through the alley here, and you're there. just hang on a minute.*"

he glances back at the limo, shoots a look at the guy nearest the car and then says into his tiny mic, "*i got the styron son-in-law here, i'm gonna let him through.*" he wags his head at me. "*its okay, you can go through now.*" i am so stunned that the guy knows exactly who i am that i stand there for a beat kinda gobsmacked. then hillary clinton exits the limo and hustles into the theatre. the agent does a small thrust of his chin and i get a move on. rapidly. past the agents and the crowds into the lobby where rose is waiting, smiling as always, tickets in hand.

the movie is suitably moving. the dinner kind of strange, with alfre hosting and reciting a truly gorgeous poem beautifully read (found out later, she wrote it herself!), while people ate stuffed chicken breast and mashed potatoes, warmish. at least they waited to serve the food until after mandela spoke. he'd said a few words right after the film as well. he told the same story twice. (i'm sure it was a mainstay in his repertoire everywhere he spoke.) about street kids whom he met at midnight outside a hotel in johannesburg, i think. the security guys held the children back but Mandela said, "let the children through," (*suffer the little children to come unto me*) and the first thing they asked was "*why do you love us?*" and he said "*how do you know that i love you?*" and they said "*because when you got the money from overseas* (the nobel prize money) *you gave some to us.*" and he said, "*many people, if not most, including your parents, love you as much as i do, if not more, but they do not have the luxury of being given money without working for it. i have been fortunate in that way, so i share it with you.*"

after the dinner i walk to grand central and get a ticket. the desiccated guy behind the counter tells me that the train i need leaves at 1:30. he names the track of the last train out. i walk hastily to the office, change clothes, walk briskly back. it's 1:15. i get on the train as the conductor announces the destinations. it does not include tarrytown. that train left at 1:20 on another track. i'm fucked.

i fluster back into the main concourse and one or two other people are standing there. one says, not unkindly, "*miss your train?*"

"*yeah. no. the fucking guy told me the wrong platform number.*"

"*well, ya wanna cab?*"

i storm up and get my 5 bucks back from the barely sentient corpse behind the counter. try to get cash from the citibank at grand central. not open. finally i make a deal with the guy for $60 to tarrytown. the guy takes me up through the bronx, which i have never actually laid eyes on before. at one point i say, somewhat wistfully, "*are we lost?*" and he chuckles, "*no, i know just where we are.*" comforted, we start to talk. he's been driving for fifteen years. he's from the dominican republic. he lives in jersey, with a backyard and a couple of kids. *"i have picnics every year."* drivers are an oppressed lot, with no benefits, basically on their own in a harsh city, but this guy makes it clear that he will take *any* amount of bullshit for his kids. by the time we get to tarrytown and my car, i feel blessed to have met him. i give him $70. we drive along together to the bridge entrance and wave goodbye, honking. i'm in my bed in nyack by 3AM.

GLIMPSES OF JACKSON/Part 3
in 1995, having newly moved east, i am immediately immersed in mounting a concert version of *the wizard of oz,* a benefit for the *children's defense fund,* in avery fisher hall, lincoln center, new york city. i have a lot riding on it. mostly in not wanting to let the *cdf* down. this is to be their main fundraiser for the year. so first I have to assemble a crackerjack cast.
i am in desperate need of a person who fails to scare crows.
knows how to fend off flying monkeys
and elude jitterbugs
not to mention melt witches.
after losing my way in some dark woods among talking trees and other showbiz shenanigans,
i call jackson and he says
    "what a perfect song for me: 'if i only had a brain'…listen to this.."
and he moves to the piano and plays the changes
just like that.
he joins a cast including natalie cole as glinda, roger daltrey as the tinman, nathan lane as the cowardly lion, debra winger as the wicked witch of the upper west side, joel grey as the wizard and jewel, newly arrived on the scene, as dorothy. so the cast thing worked out pretty well. the band included ry cooder on guitar, dr.john on piano, and david sanborn on sax. we raised what was eventually 3.5 million dollars in one night. a high point of my life, so far. and an especially pleasing aspect of the whole thing was working with jackson who threw himself into the whole thing with uncommon grace and courage. he'd rarely if ever sung someone else's song in public. except *stay,* i guess, which he definitely made his own. at least, that's what he told me. i heard him sing plenty of other people's songs in the coming years. but come to think of it, those are recordings, not live performances…). he'd certainly never done choreography like a chorus boy in front of millions, let

alone move like his arms and legs were made of straw. and do hat tricks joel grey taught him. the rehearsal period for this project was another time when I felt right where i should be, at home and belonging there.

GLIMPSES OF JACKSON/ Part 4
in 2006, i am summoned back to LA to stage the program for a celebration of desmond tutu's 75th birthday, a benefit for *artists for a new south africa,*(an organization i had helped found, in the days before nelson mandela was released from prison. when mandela came to los angeles on his worldwide victory lap, we were his hosts. and thus, i was in the room when nelson mandela and muhammad ali met for the very first time!) ANSA is using the occasion to throw a benefit dinner in a giant banquet room at the beverly wilshire hotel. activists and performers, will sing and make heartfelt speeches and toasts: samuel m. jackson, alfre woodard, cch pounder, don cheadle, and so on. when jackson shows up for sound check early in the afternoon the organizers, roderick spencer and sharon gelman and i are all there to meet him to make sure the process goes smoothly. because mr. browne can be tetchy. to say he is a perfectionist is to put it mildly.

[in the aftermath of the oz concert, ten years before, i got a glimpse of this aspect of his talent. the concert was filmed live with many many cameras including one on a crane which would swoop in and grab close-ups and get right up into the action. one particular glide-in coincided with the scarecrow strolling out from behind his music stand and moving down to do a little soft shoe step or two, coming down to the lip of the stage..it was pretty adorable, actually. unfortunately the camera barged in too close and it momentarily threw jackson off. he sang a note slightly off key....not so i could really hear it of course, but i could see him do a slight duck and cover move, just instinctively, so as to avoid the bulky contraption lurching toward his head. it all corrected itself and most people in the audience wouldn't even have noticed it. but *we* sure did. in the after-show flurry of congratulations, relief, amazement, triumph and glee, jackson and i had a quick sidebar. we pledged to *"fix it in post".* i swore i would cut away so the tv audience wouldn't even know the semi-collision had occurred. *"no it's the note...we gotta drop in the right note!"* i had no idea what he was talking about...how do you just record one note and insert it into the vocal track? well, with computers for one thing. plus otherworldly patience and persistence. it took hours...and hours..to get it *just* right. it was truly amazing to behold. FOR ONE NOTE!]

anyway, here we are at jackson's soundcheck. we get a little hung-up when his guy forgets to bring along a particular foot pedal—or some kind of gizmo. nothing lesser will do. jackson wants it right. really really really right. he strums, he talks to his guy, he fiddles with the magic box and meanwhile people are bustling about setting the tables and so on for the hundreds of people who will show up in a couple of hours to pay tribute to one of the truly spiritual men of our troubled times. a man who commands nearly universal respect and affection—just through the power of his humanity. most of the people working bustling about quietly are latinx, possibly illegal, all are absorbed in their various tasks. jackson starts singing quietly, 'redemption song', by bob marley. he does not raise his voice or demand attention. nevertheless the entire room goes silent. seems like the whole hotel holds its breath. maybe all of beverly hills. who knows. but in this banquet hall, stupidly ornate, we are all transfixed. because he means it. now. right now. he is seeking redemption for himself and for all the rest of us. these men, carefully setting down plates and placing silverware, the people bringing in the flowers, the videographer setting up lights—they all hear it. loud and strong. and they honor it. the simple tone of it, the insistence. many of us, certainly me and roderick and sharon, have tears running down our cheeks. he can feel our concentration and so redoubles his efforts. not louder. deeper. more emphatic. a prayer if i have ever heard one. then he plucks the last few notes, lovingly, to hear *exactly* how it sounds. he lets it ring into silence then he glances up and sees us all gaping at him. he looks around the room and he chuckles.

"that went well…that's gonna be nice."

at the end of the tutu show, after cutting a rug with the 'arch 'and his ebullient family, we were saying our goodbyes, waiting for the elevator to take him down to the valet parking. he had heard something about my health and the ongoing challenges to it. he got into the elevator and then turned back, to look me directly in my eyes and simply said,

"stay healthy, brother. and call me any time."

EIGHT DAYS IN RUSSIA, Sunday, 2007
(i'm writing this last bit in the warsaw airport. the plane to newark has been delayed at least until 7PM. supposed to leave at 5:30. i'm going to go back through security as there are no provisions to be had in the waiting area.)

300

masha wakes me up, both of us pretty dragged but we push through. i'm all packed, i check out, make it to the school on time. the kids could not be kinder. ages 8 to 13 and incredibly soulful and open, they ask a lot of questions ("*what's angelina jolie like*?") and i try to steer them away from STARS and that part of the equation. we do the 'faces 'exercise with shots culled from the whole history of film acting—the one-eyed pickford, lorre in '*m* ', stewart in *vertigo* , fonda in *the grapes of wrath*. it's so moving how much they intuit from these pictures of faces having feelings, so long ago, how much of the essential situations they can perceive and how sincerely they give themselves to the exercise. after all these years, having done this exercise in many many classes with hundreds of people, this was the most amazing occasion, particularly the 9 year old boy who said of fonda, *"he misses his mommy."* the shot is from *grapes of wrath*, a closeup of tom joad getting prepared to say goodbye to his mother, forever. anatoly, their teacher, speaks no english, but is so buoyant and enthusiastic that i understand him before masha needs to explain. they show me a five-minute news program they all make together each week. this episode is about a local ballroom-dancing contest. then they present me with a book that *they* had won in some..uh, competition..? (masha was a little confused about the re-gifting element) they all sign it and want me to have it, so i gratefully accept. then they all ask me for my autograph and i can't do that paul newman thing of having a beer with them, so i sign whatever each of them hands me. we do some group photos and then anatoly gives us a ride to the theater. we have a quick lunch in the cafe` (the delicious duck salad) then art and masha take me to the airport. on the way, anatoly calls to say the kids were still "trembling" with excitement. we get stuck behind a ridiculously slow car and just cannot get around it—so at the airport it's just too quick, as though life has suddenly accelerated and we can't keep up. art and masha follow me into the restricted area, art giving the uniformed official squinting at us an airy wave. we hug. i say, "god bless you—and i don't even believe in god." then they're gone and i'm on my way back home.

NIGHTFALL
nightfall is standing by
your godmother is the president
who took that faded photo?

(was it me?)
what bad dog won't make small talk?
or gnaw on some exposition?
somehow my love
my love
has exploded
deepened into nowhere

anatoly means sunrise,
i never knew that
did you?

MOVING EAST, DAY EIGHT—Scranton, Penn. to S. Nyack, New York,1995
up late. breakfast at best western. beautiful, balmy drive. listening to "*over
the rainbow, volume*', a mix i made of dozens of versions of the song, just to
get into it; then to the actual radio, start programming the nyc stations. get
psycho killer right after middletown (where dennis sweeney lives now) and
then '*end of the line*', by the traveling wilbury's as we take the nyack exit.
(somebody is doing some uncanny programming.)
　　　follow main street right through the heart of the town almost to the
river. turn right on piermont. see the trucks. park.
　　　give susanna a big long hug.
　　　all of our stuff fits (just) into the garage. the house is really looking
good in mid-construction. we walk across the street down to the river then
into town to get sandwiches and my first espresso in nyack. susanna goes
back to sign the final papers and write big checks. i amble down sunlit
sidewalks, the hudson on my left. back at the house, i try to make myself
useful by checking off the last few items on the truck. i am stunned at my
plain luck, this moment, this life.
　　　we are home.

[in 1955 I saw a picture of dennis sweeney in a magazine showing him
immediately after he had assassinated allard lowenstein, a protégé of eleanor
roosevelt's and a very prominent liberal in the mid-60s. (he convinced bobby
kennedy to run against lbj.) I was riveted by the madness and pain in his
eyes. dennis was an acolyte of allard's and an avid activist. he had yanked
out his upper teeth with pliers, because he believed allard and the fbi were

302

broadcasting into his brain through his teeth implants, telling him to do awful things, like shit on his stepfather's grave. he begged allard to stop torturing him, and when allard explained that he was doing no such thing and that dennis should get help, dennis shot him, several times. then he sat down in the outer office and waited for the authorities to arrive. the picture I saw was taken while he sat there. I knew I had to play him. It turned out to be the last play i did in los angeles, until I moved back in 2013, having escaped from new york. the play was called *dreams die hard,* written and co-directed by john binder and produced by jeanne field and veronica brady. the play told the story of allard and dennis, and included david harris, the stanford university student president, also heavily influenced by allard, who founded the draft resistance movement (of which I was a member) and married joan baez. in fact the play was based on harris' book, also called *dreams die hard.* the story seemed to encapsulate to all of us the disillusionment with the hopes and dreams of the 60s. dennis was found not guilty by reason of insanity and permanently institutionalized. he was living in an outpatient facility in middletown when we passed through, just an hour or so from my new hometown. the show was controversial, especially in the press. the *los angeles times* critic asked, somewhat plaintively, *"who cares about the 60s?"* despite the notices, it drew big audiences.

ELEGY FOR MR. EARLE
about six months ago, in november of 2014, one of my favorite teachers died. norman earle taught senior year english and was one of the first adults i ever knew who really 'got' me completely. with clear eyes and warm heart and a subtle sense of support, he watched and coaxed and sometimes scolded me into close reading and careful writing. he urged me to grow my vocabulary and utilize it even when i was met with eyerolls from some of my classmates, who accused me of showing off or putting them down as clearly not as smart as me. mr. earle essentially said, '*fuck them. be yourself as completely as you can.'* mr. earle was gay and even in our naivete, (this was 1968) we all knew and had absolutely no problem with it. even the macho element, the football players, the athletes, dug mr. earle, and would often hang out in his room after school trying to squeeze out an essay or an assignment just out of reach. mr. earle would be patient and supportive without condescension. after we all left norte del rio high school dispersed into our various roads, in the mid-to-late seventies as increased awareness of homosexuality filtered

into the culture what with stonewall and such, a group of parents complained about mr. earle to the superintendent of schools. he was summarily dismissed. he never taught again. he settled into a long-term relationship, bought a house on a hill and planted a garden which ranged up the hill like a verdant labyrinth. he had some wild parties up there, you bet, lots of nooks and benches under arbors. and he kept growing as a man. he contacted me on facebook when i first jumped on and we were able to say all those things i was not ready to say back then, or in fact simply did not consciously perceive. the last time i went to sacramento, i visited mr. earle and toured his garden. i told him it was *'effusive and ramshackle'* and he patted my shoulder. *"still up to your old tricks,"* he chuckled. now he has moved on to a larger garden, acres and acres benefitting from his attentions and bigots don't make it through the gate.

"as it was with Icarus
out of the labyrinth in wings of things of feathers and wax straining free of gravity into air currents that relax
he took flight into the transforming softness of the clouds"
--jack larson, 'the relativity of icarus"

"coyote: when i became a human being, i fell out of the womb of a woman. i had been implanted there. i fell out of a hole in the sky into the body of a woman, like a seed. i was an egg in the body of a woman..."—murray mednick, 'the coyote cycle'

RECIPROCAL AFFECTION, ITS CRUCIALITY
1. Mother's Day, 2010
one night, not long after i wore them all out and had washed-up, shipwrecked on manhattan island, i was cast by an old friend in a small festival of one-acts. the play was about a man who has lost the bond he once had with his daughter and therefore his entire family, and thus his supposed life. in a void of misinterpretation, he lashes in. notwithstanding the rather glaring similarities to my own woeful situation, i wasn't bad in the piece, just a little erratic. i would often cry too soon, knowing so so surely what was coming, what freefall rockslide of the irresistible gravity of anguish was coming my hapless way (hopeless would have been too wise).

304

rehearsals were like a sandblast on my skin. the deeper we went, the more i pitied the three noblewomen, young and old, bravely sitting down to dinner with my male hysteria, and the more i realized that stirring this particular pot was not necessarily yielding a palatable stew, heavily seasoned as it was with undissolvable gobs of floating rage. purgative perhaps, but not palliative. the proverbial scab scraped off to draw fresh blood. then again, compared to the contortions i would soon assume, this little play was keeping me occupied in some meaningful, if completely desperate, activity, something like art.

but one night i just sat in my kitchen, staring into space, instead of getting ready to go out to do the show. i literally could not rouse my SELF, the one who could ACT, to saddle up for another tearful roundup. the moments crept by, but since the piece i was in was late in the program after the intermission, i was sure i could get there in time…even if i missed the first call. suddenly, with a start, i bolted to my feet, threw on my coat and ran to the subway. mounting the stairs of the theatre on 78th street, i stepped stealthily, as the show had already commenced. in the hushed, small, close lobby, the other waiting actors stood like inanimate animatrons. mostly staring at the floor, straining to hear snatches of dialogue from the stage, blocked from view by the ubiquitous black curtain.

the stern stage manager approached me and whispered gruffly in my ear, *"we cancelled your play, because you missed the call."*

"but we don't go on for another half hour…i just…"

"you should have called me…i sent the others home." and he turned his back on me and walked away.

i stood there, purposeless, once more a disappointment—to different women, different children, different loves entirely, but i felt once more that feeling of falling, invisible, unusable, permanently dormant, twisting in the wind.

and it was mother's day.

i stumbled down the stairs, dialing my phone as i hit the street. it rang. i heard the familiar strains of roger miller's *'king of the road'*. *'i'm a man of means by no means'*. my mother's answering jingle, and then the brash beep. i said the following word: *"mommy.."*

i shocked myself.

i had not spoken that word since i was a four year old boy, weeping into an embroidered throw pillow on the daybed on the landing in my uncle oscar's and aunt alice's house. this area between two other rooms would be my 'room' for the next year or so. my kind uncle oscar, my angelic aunt alice, both caring so carefully for me and my two cousins, candy and karen, older girls who seemed to adore me almost as much as my own sister. and thus began a whole cavalcade of sympathetic women who saved me, almost, providing protection as best they could. but then, on that dappled afternoon, no one else would do, i wailed for the loss of the one person whom i could call *'mommy'*.

now i blurted the word into her machine. just saying it, heard or unheard, was some kind of comfort…

2. The Times We Talked, New Year's, 2013

that talk we had when meggan, my niece, left us so young. taking her own life in her early 20s.

her bewilderment at such despair.

that talk we had stretching through so many mother's days over so many years
so dark so light
she a constant ballroom dancer
always with the right white shoes, just enough lift
to dance through the pain.

those years she raised worms
or drank herself to sleep
or pounded up some abalone, for me and nancy, freshly pried from tide pools
on the shore of half moon bay, sautéed in lemon and garlic

or when she came to my graduation from high school, at my special invitation, effusive in her affection,
(and that she picked up some man in a bar after the ceremony, or so said my dad, telling me many years later, saying he had to go out to del paso heights to get her, too drunk to drive, something like that, the whole tale delivered to me like a malignant patriarch, to splatter her memory with mud.)
still she showed up that day gleeful and glamorous, a smiling spark plug, ready to cut a rug.
we danced a lot over the decades, energetically jitterbugged at various weddings & even a few funerals.

so proud to surprise her with my prowess, she so pleased and flirty, delighted with my footwork, and that twirling up trick, curling up the leading partner's arm, rollup into a side by side embrace, two steps than spin out, arms crossing over our heads, up and ducking under, sliding down to reclasp hands, right on the beat. (susanna and i delighted in the same move. but she loved the stroll better. that was her step.)

the time we talked on new year's eve 2013. jubilant. tearful. me stalking up and down the sidewalks of sunset boulevard, silverlake section, an amalgam of laundromats, sex shops, mexican restaurants, high-end cafes, breakfast joints, indy garb outlets. i seemed to have landed here from outer space, spit from a black hole.
and she makes me laugh, as always. she makes me throw my head back and roar with belly laughs. she is so damn right on, so loose and so accepting unconditionally, the exact opposite of my traumatized dad.

or that time we talked of everything and she told me she allowed as how she had loved a woman once, soul and body, yearning to press next to another woman's comforting warmth, and the other woman knew, they were best friends, and still are, they have given to each other the gift of acknowledged desire, one for another. for them that was enough to last a lifetime. and my mother insists, emphatically, in her smoker's contralto, *"there's no way there can be ANYTHING WRONG with those feelings. no way in hell,"* and she laughs, with pleased surprise at herself.
there is a picture, two pictures, actually. yellowed early kodachrome. my mom in a reindeer sweater and semi-pleated skirt, cut mid-calf. bobby-sox and loafers. posed on the wing-shaped fender of a teal green dodge coupe. one leg up to show the shape of her gams, breasts thrust forward like lana turner, burst of auburn hair framing a movie-star smile, like rita hayworth in *gilda*, ready, willing and able.
the other picture is of my dad standing in front of the same vehicle, in a matching sweater and slacks, big grin on his face, gleeful in a way i never saw him, not once, for all the years i lived in the shadow of his rage.

and back on sunset, new years eve, she, my dear brave mother, keeps me laughing, even through my tears, she coos in my ear lightly, as she must have done when i was just a baby. as i close my coat to the LA chill, she sings love at me and we dance in the streets.

"in order to survive mentally, i had to find a place within myself where plague couldn't get me, where success or failure in such a battle were of equal consequence. this was not an easy task. it required resisting the emotional satisfaction of being cured and the emotional closure of death itself. but in that, of course, it resembled merely what we all go through every day. living..is not about resolutions; it is about the place where plague can't get you."—andrew sullivan

PLAGUE CAN'T GET ME
1.
the first single i ever bought,
my very own 45,
was *'all day and all of the night'*
by the kinks.
i'd play it on the turntable
Lift the lid on the family console
which also contained the precious TV screen
hidden by sliding doors
i'd play it LOUD
rattling speakers concealed behind gold-flecked cloth.
beating the air with my hands my fists
spiraling my arms as if working up
to a mighty leap
rock on into that other place
where i could be with *her*
all day and all of the night
that place where i could dance on the ceiling and move with perfect grace
where i could be home.
that's the screen where i first saw *la strada*
and james dean, newborn on asphalt, cackling at the wind-up monkey, still beating on its side,
having fallen from rhythm.
and fred astaire, defying all the rules of gravity,

spencer, seemingly so assured in his assurance,
kate just as certain,
of her dominion.
monty, spellbinding like no other man i'd ever seen,
steve mcqueen and the pegasus cycle, reaching for the full mcqueen,
all the glowing grey gods,
light emanating through their silver skin,
for we were a black and white household
pork chops and canned peas, iceberg lettuce, dressed in mayo, ketchup,
relish, whirled together in a perennially descending whip called ' thousand
island'
and some pale tasteless tomatoes.

i pictured a train
coming toward me
crossing the great salt lake at sunset
and then i'm on it, hurtling over ancient ice
i'm on it with *her*
the girl
her knowledge of me
and the rhythm of our connexion
i knew they'd never catch me now
in fact
they could no longer even see me, i had the *fever down in my pocket*
i'm INVISIBLE now, got no secrets to conceal
a train of blossoms rolls on
across the plain
thru the jungle wet with rain
i belong to her
we let the river be the answer
she and i
2.
in the swell of belonging
you once told me
as though your very blood
was cheering

the clouds drift slowly by
in their infinite shades of grey
all the way to white
no matter how long we must wait to turn
we must have the patience of saints.
3.
faith and patience
when my arms go around you
i can't help wondering
can they give you comfort shelter solace
wound so tight
boulder after boulder rounded by the flow
let the river reply.
—*for susanna, always*

MISSING THE ANGELS

"the only thing we are missing is angels. in this world there's no place for them. and anyway would our eyes recognize them? perhaps we are surrounded by angels without knowing it."—henry miller

i'm sitting in the dark, wood-paneled, beverly hills office of frank sinatra's doctor who is, unexpectedly, a well-groomed, middle-aged woman, dr. maxine ostrum, quite motherly if your mother is a stern, slightly sympathetic, junior high school principal, faintly judgmental around the eyes. it's 1987. there's an autographed picture of the chairman, old blue-eyes himself, over her left shoulder, having it his way. the doctor is fumbling with her papers, my HIV test results, and she gives me that 'this-is-gonna-hurt-me-etc 'look.

"*i have to tell you, ahem,..that you, uh, have tested…positive for…ahem…HIV…you're a time bomb waiting to go off…you probably have five years to live…at the most..*"

well. it is early in the game, she can be forgiven for being somewhat unprepared to deliver such a message. imminent demise and so on. not to mention, no known cure or even an ameliorative response. in the intervening years when i have told this tale such as right now, i always include the same line in response to her abject failure to come up with even a vaguely encouraging remark; or at the very least, a measured tone, thusly:

"don't say that.." with a wry chuckle, suggesting preternatural
confidence and élan.
for the next three decades i dined out on this imaginary bravado. unless i
really did say it…?

naw, i'm pretty sure in actuality i did not say a single word.

i do know that, at that very moment, i saw my son's face in my mind. he
was 9 years old. that little guy was and remains as a strapping 43 year old
man, the light, the lodestar, the lodgepole of my life. i did say to myself, *"well,
i might deserves this, but he sure doesn't. he does not deserve to lose his
dad."* that part is absolutely true. i said it like a vow…like a prayer.

but mostly i just had that harsh, metallic taste of terror in my mouth.

whiff of shame in my nostrils,

nausea, roiling deep in my gut.

i am as uncomfortable as i have ever been. ever. sitting across the
desk from doctor ostrum, i felt utterly disclosed.

i went directly from her office to see jeff rochford, chiropractor extraordinaire.
just a few blocks away, in beverly hills.
jeff was a true healer,
you could see it in his clear blue eyes.
you could feel it in his hands.
he always spoke quietly, directly, without false assurances.
i had no appointment, but he waved me back into his office anyway.
he could see my stricken state.
he listened to my 'results', then he said to me,
*"these are all just numbers. you are healthy and very strong, and you will stay
that way."*

then i went straight home to tell susanna, an angel if there ever was one. i'd
had the test so we could be sure it was safe, given my history, to get
pregnant. at the time, if either partner tested positive, that was deemed
impossible. but we did, safely, twice. but that's another story with a whole
other set of angels…

a few days after my initial diagnosis, i went to see another angel, a holistic
healer by the name of bob jacobs. bob was a nice jewish boy making his

mother happy by becoming a doctor. however, he quickly became disgusted with the close-mindedness of western alloppathic medicine. so had i, hippy that i was, long before HIV came into our lives, i used homeopathic remedies for everything from poison oak to herpes. i had already been seeing bob for a couple of years. after bailing on med school, bob had lit out for the territories with adventurous notions including crystals, magnets and the computer, as a diagnostic tool and to tap into the network of the most significant research and experimentation all over the world. he missed nothing, and therefore neither did i. using all of his discoveries he constructed a table which, while laying on it for an hour, one came into perfect balance. sounds goofy but even super-skeptic susanna bought into it. in short, the fucking guy was a visionary and something of a genius. and he flat-out saved my life. and in 1997, bob called me from london where he was then living and said, 'they're ready for you. they've found something called protease inhibitors and it's going to work."

so, that means from 1987 to 1997, at the height of the plague, in the face of the incessant headlines telling me i would die any minute, i declined to avail myself of allopathic medicine of any kind. i took a pass on the most poisonous substance ever given to human beings as a remedy—AZT. to this day i believe that shit killed more of my beautiful friends than the virus itself. this was a drug the medical professionals already had laying around on some back shelf,
having failed miserably as a cancer cure. it proved too lethal.
they apparently thought, well, why not give it a try on these desperate faggots?
after all glaxosmithkline had spent so much money developing it…
turned out it killed the virus, more or less, mostly less,
but, at the same time it annihilated whatever personal immune system the victims had left,
making a battleground out of their beleaguered bodies,
while the men in white coats dropped their big bombs.

when i first met my third healer/angel, doctor paul bellman, we had moved to nyack, new york, two beautiful daughters in tow, while tavish attended NYU. paul perused my medical records carefully and intently and then he looked up

at me and said, very matter of factly, *"well, you're a hero. how did you find the courage?"*
after tearing up a bit, mostly from just being seen. i told him that i was surrounded by angels who had given me unfailing support, wisdom, and love, heroic amounts of love. that was how.

so, i did survive that plague.
with intrepid trail guides showing me the path through the wilderness…
you could certainly call them angels.
and the upshot is, i never got sick.
now they can't find the virus in me at all.
and while it is true that sometimes i became terrified, felt despair and regret, shame and all the rest of it,
mostly i kept that stuff to myself.
when i really needed it, some angel would touch my shoulder and i'd get back on track.

so, yeah, i agree with henry.
i believe we are surrounded by angels,
without even knowing it most of the time.
what's that jackson browne song?
too many angels
have seen me crying.
well, let's let them see us.
maybe then we'll recognize them
make a place for them, let them hold us close..

it sure worked for me.

THE WEDDING, 1992
we're at a wedding in Washington, D.C. susanna, emma, 4, and lilah, 2. the girls are serving as flower girls. lilah, still willing to wear a dress, leads the procession. she's the spreading-the-rose-petals girl. it's the wedding of two friends. actually they are two of the legion of susanna's friends, but after nearly 5 years living amongst the east-coast intelligentsia, i had been warmly welcomed into the tribe, despite, or perhaps, because of the full disclosure of

my whole self, out in the open. i had made the decision to be honest with myself and others about my sexuality and everything else when i was around 13, and i have managed to stick with that right up to this minute.

the reception took place in a bright, high-ceilinged room, full to the brim with ebullient celebrants. both the bride and the groom had lost a parent when they were quite young. many of the toasts from their friends and relations made reference to this sad fact. there were lots of very sincere exclamations like, "*he would have been so proud*", "*she would have been so overjoyed*". when the couple took their turns, they both spoke of the missing parent, the pain of their loss so young and each shared some moment they had grasped close to their hearts and kept through the years, their eyes glistening at the retelling.

this was in the days before protease inhibitors. my t-cells had fallen well below 200 and though i felt just fine, i also often felt that terrible vertiginous chill that taste like cold iron in my mouth as when i was first told that i was HIV positive. i knew with certainty that i had brought this calamity on myself and more shamefully, into the lives of my dearest ones.

i looked over at my indomitable, stubbornly-loving wife—and she was looking right at me! i had thought she would be completely absorbed in the proceedings—the stories, the laughter,—but no, she was searching for my gaze. i instantly had tears pooling in my eyes and then running in rivulets down my cheeks. she put her hand on top of mine. she leaned toward me, tilting just a few degrees. she knew—almost before i did—that a question was looming in my mind, throwing a shadow on my heart.

would i survive to attend my daughters 'weddings?
would i walk them down the aisle?
would i give them away?
would they lose their dad?

as i looked into her eyes, i thought of the lou reed song: '*i'll be your mirror— reflect what you are/ in case you don't know..*'
and then she nodded, firmly. and i pulled myself together.

IF IT'S CALLED SOMETHING IT'S OVER
but the truth was
as the years were turning
the dream was fading
for both of us.
the sag was setting in.

she is not the wife i expected
     and i am not the husband she deserves

whose thought is this?
     or maybe
not a thought at all
     who lives with this description
          no
          conception
     follow the fragments
          coyote's trick
          god's trap
     the greatest discipline must be exercised
     in the telling to yourself the story of your
          self. the race is a collaboration of stories, our
     VERSIONS
our stories of our selves.
     OUR INDIVIDUAL BURDEN
with such a fla
     OF HISTORY
or rather such a fundamental glitch
WE ARE NOT SURE IF THE PRINCESS IS IMPRISONED OR ON
DISPLAY,
OR IF THERE IS REALLY ANY DIFFERENCE.

accept as much as you can, even a peaceable monster

to BEMONSTER, to make monstrous

"by the terrible alchemy of egotism you converted your remorse into rage."—
oscar wilde, 'de profundis'

UNSENT LETTER FROM MIAMI, 2006
you write me, bitterly, about my failure to let an event be about **YOU**, entirely.
or even more absurdly, some **time** (as if one could OWN TIME, let alone
control its content) and here I am on the eve of opening a play in which i am
both directing and acting and you FEDEX me a letter like that, excoriating me
for my bad BEHAVIOR in this highly subjective version of a night long ago,
and then behave as if i brought it up? what kind of malicious,
passive/aggressive behavior do you call this? and while we're talking about
passive/aggressive, the whole event in LA starts to look incredibly
manipulative. you consciously pushed the situation to its limits so as to reveal
me as the selfish, not-so-slightly nuts guy you had grown tired of—and want
away from. (notwithstanding your knowledge of my hypoglycemic tendencies,
the conversation you were almost having was inane and aimless). too bad
he's not going to die anymore. now you're stuck with him. it's actually quite
masterful, now that i think about it. a perfect set-up, perfectly engineered (like
the cleverest of murders in a noir film). the fact that i held out as long as i
did—and in fact did nothing but stalk away outside and tell you brusquely
where i was going, is not in your scenario. if anybody made that scene about
me, it was you. and you still do. you had your conversation—and then you
had some more after it was over. the point then, and now, is how much i
could stand, it was a test and a challenge.

    and this is knowing that past a certain point, my body chemistry takes
over and i really start to feel dizzy and almost panicked. and on that particular
night i also had poison ivy on the inside of my arms constantly irritating my
body. once again my body—and my control over it, are a major part of the
equation—causing a situation, in the moment, in which you are insisting i
ignore it—or CEASE to BE, in a very real way.

    why is *"exhibit" m*ore important than *"belonged"*? the whole premise
that this night belonged to you is bogus and beneath you and i think it comes
from something that terrifies you about your parents 'relationship—which is
that for a long time the LIFE belonged to your father. it was horrible for him to
do that, to impose it on his wife and family, but all men did it then. i do not.
and you really don't have to defend yourself from that in me. that you may

NEED to is something i can live with, that's what i mean by consort (a role i'm very comfortable with). but we MUST sort out when you are claiming dominion for YOURSELF—and when you are doing it to prove something NEGATIVE about me.

i have a right to my feelings, as do you, feelings of irritation and annoyance—and HUNGER. i have a right to reveal and express them. that is NOT rage. and i wish you would stop calling it that. yes, i was angry, and now i think you wanted me to be angry. and maybe you STILL DO.

the irony is that in a week that is <u>obviously</u> very stressful for me—all you are thinking about is your stress. (my child is in jeopardy, too. and i am working my ass off [directing and playing a leading role in sam shepard's *simpatico*]) and then you <u>choose</u> to bring all this up, two incidents from the past in which i had done a *"really bad thing"*—which was: making a time which was YOURS (a night or an entire summer) about ME. what are you doing right now? how is it different? one problem is that we are not physically together. and the other thing MIGHT be that my work is not as important as yours. after all, it's only theater. it's not a movie. (less money). it's not your career. by your criteria, this time should be mine. but i reject the entire premise. no <u>time</u> is mine. if anything it is *ours*. unless we want to be separate. and one of us does—or did. and maybe still wants to? without question one of us was out to find fault in the other—and create (unconsciously, i hope) situations which would demonstrate the worst aspects of the other. i say i hope—but i don't TRUST. i guess i can't anymore. i am fucking lost. will you ever see this, even as an <u>aspect</u> of what went down that horrid night in LA? or will you just defend and dismiss and make sure you are the victim of my mania with no responsibility on your part? do you remember how i once said i felt like you were trailing me, tracking me—waiting for me to fuck up somehow. you chortled and scoffed, more of my 'paranoia'. in fact, I scoffed. i shared it with you as an example i had observed of how <u>off</u> i was sometimes. but was i? how habitual or unconscious has your need to separate from me become to protect yourself from future pain when and if i died? how much has that become your entire basic stance with me? and how much did that feeling increase in urgency when my health became less threatened?

"*we have no reason to mistrust our world, for it is not against us. has it terrors, they are our terrors; has it abysses, they belong to us; are dangers at hand, we must try to love them. and if only we arrange our life according to that principle which counsels us that we must always hold to the difficult, then that which note still seems to us the most alien will become what we most trust and find most faithful.*"—*rilke, 'the dragon-princess'*

SHE SAYS
i called susanna just the other day
to thank her once again.
she said,
"for what?"
well
for standing by me
standing with me
sometimes in front of me
all around me
she could have folded up her tent
folded in her wings
then spread them and flown away
abandoning the nest we so carefully built
together.
it would have been completely understandable
especially to me

i had heard two men
talking on the radio
the day i made the call
about a documentary film
called *5B*
a doctor and a nurse
who had established the first hospital ward exclusively for AIDS patients
it was at san francisco general
ward 5B.
i cried so hard i had to pull over
driving down kenmore avenue
going to get my taxes done

318

clearing up a debt from the year i left her
on my way to leaving everything in tatters
go ahead
call it death.

so i called her on impulse
sitting in my ticking car
and as always
she picked up
(or she calls back right away
for which i am always so pleased,
and always a bit surprised).
when she says
"for what?"
i say
"for being so stalwart.
with such grace.."
then my throat catches, my voice falters,
and she says something about *"support"*
but i didn't quite catch it.
it haunted me for a couple of days
so i wrote and asked her;
thereby to wring out every drop of possible comfort,
if she recalled the words.
she did not remember
"i have no idea what i said,"
she says.
—2019

"all the horror of city life is personified in **pete**, *a schizzed-out scumbag of a coke freak who's been up for days suffering from totally justified paranoia. he forces* **betty** *into a confrontation that's so petrifying it's almost unbearable.* **darrell larson,** *as pete, first appears nonchalantly slithering in the background. you try to ignore him, actually subconsciously hoping he won't be in the rest of the picture, but then he insinuates his way into the lead...he's scarier than pacino in* scarface. *with* **debra winger** *as the true*

innocent and **darrell larson as the most dangerous and pathetic human on earth,** *mike's murder is an utterly original advertisement for spending the rest of your life in the country."—micharel dare, 'l.a.weekly, 'march, 1984*

"darrell larson plays a creepy but human scrounger, like a dostoevski outcast on loan to raymond chandler."—david elliott, 'usa today'

NOT HEARING X
gone thrown out of the whiskey
a gogo
suddenly whirling with nausea
passed out blam
beer in hand
facedown on the dance floor
just as X began blasting
call me wrecking ball
bumtossed onto the buzzing sidewalk
banished from the headbanging brilliance
& carried across sunset
by a plump round-faced punk
straining for severity and recklessness
with the wisp of a beard
t-shirt torn strategically
careful fraying
and his girl friend
maybe fifteen in shredded tights and safety pins
brimming with generosity
drag me all the way to my car
blocks away
below the bleary blinking strip
not sixteen himself but nevertheless
he cautions, parentally,
"be careful, man, take a nap, don't drive."
and i'm in the midst of the murder of mike
in the smeared melancholy of sunlight,
there's a fresh gash on my forehead

inexplicably
but deft make-up covers all wounds.

sometime later,
after my last shot in the picture,
brutally tossed into the trash pit
upside down at dawn
sucking the plastic bag deep into my throat,
and holding my breath
for as long as they needed me to
just to get the shot,

on my way to some forgotten home
i pulled over on highway 10, just before it turns into PCH,
and sobbed and wailed and howled *
at the final demise of doomed desperate pete
so much me
passing out of me
for then is gone.

i thought of the big rocks
tumbling
tumbling
tumbling
i thought of going down on you on your expansive bed
crumbling hillsides breaking loose
washing away beneath us,

and then
there were those
seemingly endless tracking shots
through labyrinthine hallways
following your alluring lead…

where are you now, exactly?
where's jim?
where's jack?

your indelible chortle
coming right up from your 4th chakra
goofing on the grapefruit in the market at midnight
after endearments made you recognizable
no glamour just a runny nose
and your loving jibes
and your perfect ass
and your invitations
lowering the metaphorical drawbridge for me
dimly lit but vivid
i feel you
just across the river
hard by the shining rails running into the city
huge bolts of voltage course from your heart
with the arrogance of the always frightened
i'm reminded of that looping session, when you broke all the rules kneeling
down in front of me, while they all waited for you to be ready, unbuttoned my
fly and slipped my cock in your mouth and got yourself prepared to make the
perfect sound for the scene, suddenly sexy seen from this distance.
"we're ready for you, debra…"
back on your feet
you strode to the dangling microphone and
nailed it.

together and apart
we were appreciated by the eyes of his heart lens
lens heart
some such pleasured gaze,
now we are watched over
by low flying angels
whose lanterns are the mirror moon
wrapping your beauty in blue.
—for buck, forever

WHAT I LEARNED FROM JIM
kindness is the first rule of conduct
stay with the current
keep your secrets
approve all nakedness
marry the one you love
and be together
don't
waste
time.
listen
look
with participation
turn that into art
for goodness sake never lose your teenager
make wings of your appreciation,
and pass them on.

"pete: ...betty, the good are guilty, too."—jim bridges, 'mike's murder'

PRIDE, Part 2
i felt pride when **jim bridges** and **jack larson** befriended me, adopted me, took me under their capacious wings. jim was a universally revered writer/director, whose films included *urban cowboy, the china syndrome, 9/30/55,* and *paper chase.* early in his career, he was head story editor on *alfred hitchcock presents* and did a fair amount of acting. jack was just a young actor who grew up in hollywood when he indelibly played jimmy olsen on the incredibly popular and groundbreaking *superman* tv series in the mid-1950s. his first boyfriend, monty clift, advised him to find a new line of work, pointing out that nobody would ever see him as any other character. he became an accomplished poet, playwright and librettist, including the libretto for *lord byron,* an opera by virgil thomsen. The two of them ushered me into a level of consciousness and culture that I had always hoped was out there. A real place, that if I searched and researched, I might gain entrance to. With them I found unconditional acceptance. their friendship and camaraderie with seemingly everybody on earth worth knowing, including Christopher Isherwood and don bachardy, getrude stein and alice b. toklas, Katharine

hepburn, jean renoir, and on and on, a cavalcade of greatness. and their intense interest in the whole wide world and every individual in it—an interest in human behavior, not a constant griping and chastising of perceived iniquities, but an embracing of our follies. All this they taught me and I sought to emulate. In their relationship I saw a union of equals and an uncanny ability to share that bond with others. They were a partnership forged from separate strands, together they wove themselves and those of us fortunate enough to know them, into an enormous coiled cable of inseparable connection—wound as thick, strong and enormous as the steel cables holding up the golden gate bridge.

PRIDE, Part 3

walking across the golden gate bridge with my granny and my sister, all the way across, a sunny, bounteous, stroll—my first awareness of the magnificent possibilities ahead of me, the vertiginous yet soaring feeling, the thrill of expectation—of flight, really, leap tall buildings in a single bound, somehow permitted by my granny's unconditional love (which she could never give to my mom). Holding her hand sometimes as we ambled across the span. And sometimes running ahead…awed by the cable, thicker than my eight year old body, made from hundreds of steel strands, each massive thread having a diameter bigger than my arm.

ELEGY FOR JACK LARSON

through an accident of fate, or a fateful accident, jack and I had the same last name. whatever it was, it was felicitous and just, and suited us both. We enjoyed the rhyme of history. and as far as influencing the person I strove to become—jack was by far and away more my model for what a real **man** was than my actual father ever could have been.

in a lifetime of graceful gestures, the finesse with which jack made his last exit from our company, has pride of place. those of us who witnessed this elegant maneuver, or at least the big finish, are still in awe. And also feel a deepening appreciation. His example will stand us all in good stead, sometime in our inevitable futures. In terms of the *how*, even the *when*, Jack was completely in charge.

jack's mission in life, at least one of them, was to en*courage*, and no one, at least in my experience, ever did it with more exuberance, compassion and humor. all those hundreds of times, to find him somewhere, some party, screening or private dinner, and have him say with his sideways grin, *"hello, kiddo. Hello hot stuff."* and then his ever-so-slightly salacious chuckle. with his hand lightly on your elbow, he established a special intimacy, a sly collusion, and he did this with *all* of us in his circle of friends, each in our turn.

jack practiced, indeed mastered, a kind of gossip that transcended the mundane, voyeuristic, aspects of this most human of all activities. but the way jack did it elevated the whole endeavor to the level of philosophical discourse, leavened with gales of laughter and with occasional pauses to catch one's breath, and bask in having had the great good fortune of getting to tell the tale, let alone having actually LIVED it. he was endlessly grateful— for all that had come his way, most especially his jim, and all that had been given to him to create.

i want to share with you an event from the afternoon that debra and i were fortunate enough to be chosen by jack, ever the expert casting director, to be the ones to find him, just there, sitting out in front of his door, upright in his favorite chair, his dog, charlie, sitting quietly by his right foot, which was slightly in advance of the left foot, actor-style, enabling him, if he were to so choose, to rise right on cue. he chose to stay quite still…and so did we….later in the day, once we started making calls, as loved ones gathered, we were ushered down to the bottom of the driveway by the coroner. some of us were tearful. all of us were quiet, when suddenly a STAG, a four-pointer, with the velvet still on his antlers, bounded out of the shrubbery, thirty feet or so up the slope of the road. after a moment of absolute stillness, he *approached* us, utterly unafraid, stepping up to a distance of ten or twelve feet. so that he could make eye contact with each of us, in our turn. we all gasped as one, and held our breaths.
long pause.   look.   feel.

then the magnificent creature turned calmly and strolled on up the road, disappearing around the bend. the time was right around what they call magic hour in the movies. the whole mysterious and yet so natural occurrence seemed to exemplify the wizardry and *groundedness* of this most extraordinary man. jack and jim would always say, as we parted or signed off, "we'll be together soon." i can only say, i am counting on it.
---2015

[the above elegy was delivered at jack's memorial, (another of those tributes to dear friends, i was charged with planning—as with eddie bunker, sam shepard and many other dear friends. something else i'm proud of being good at..). the event took place in the James Bridges Theater at UCLA, so named because of jack's donation to the refurbishing and upgrading of the theater. originally the room was known as melnitz 1409 and was the main screening room for the film department in which i was a freshman student in 1968. my very first class, the location of the actual beginning of my life's journey, and so much of my focus for the rest of my life and career, including film history, specifically of acting in films, was in that very room, almost fifty years earlier. on the occasion of the renaming, around 2000, they showed *mike's murder,* as representative of jim's best and most personal work. more and more and more full circles…]

"he who desires nothing, hopes for nothing, and is afraid of nothing, cannot be an artist."—anton chekhov

"as it was with Icarus
soar to the sun
soar to the sun
soar to the sun
it's only a mass of multiplied light transmuting its brilliance into the curvature of night.
like his too warm wings, the escape expands, as it contracts.
and disappears from space as impermanent as wax."
—jack larson, 'the relativity of icarus'

"if you bring forth what is within you, what you have brought forth will save you. if you do not bring forth that which is within you, what you do not bring forth will kill you."
—apocryphal gospel of st. thomas,

9. **MEDIATOR**: EVERYONE BELONGS EQUALLY IN A STATE OF UNCONDITIONAL LOVE AND UNION.

 or the world makes people unimportant and/or requires them to blend in, making comfort and belonging a substitute for love and worth.

"***coyote:*** *in the twilight of the fourth world, taiowa withdrew the spirit. i was on my own."—murray mednick, 'the coyote cycle'*

"as for me…who am neither I or not-I, i have strayed from myself and i find not remedy but despair."—nathaniel mackey, 'from 'a broken bottle traces of perfume still emanate'

"it was love that set me on the journey,
love that called me home. but it's the terror
of being just one person—one chance, one set of days—
that keeps me absolutely still tonight and makes me listen
intently to those young men above us
flying in their airplanes in the dark."
—denis johnson, from 'the monk's insomnia'

so, we have—**mnemosyne** (whose name is derived from the greek word for memory, or remembrance) who slept with zeus for nine nights in a row in order to give birth to the **NINE MUSES**: **urania** (astronomy), **polyhymnia** (sacred poetry), **erato** (love poetry), **terpsichore** (dance), **melpomene** (tragedy), **thalia** (comedy, pastoral poetry), **euterpe** (lyric poetry), **calliope** (epic poetry), **clio** (history).

in dante's *inferno,* there are **NINE CIRCLES OF HELL,** each dedicated to a
particular sin**: limbo** (general failure to live correctly, or be unbaptised in the
'one true religion, more specifically, the mormon church. at least according to
them)**, lust, gluttony, greed, wrath, heresy, violence, fraud, treachery,** in
that order of descent…

"well I've been out walking
i don't do that much talking these days
these days
these days I seem to think a lot
about the things that I forgot to do
for you
and all the times I had the chance to…"
—jackson browne, "these days"

LATE ONE SULTRY NIGHT
folks on the street legislate
then tell me why
still i meander
strike poses
rock out on shattered corners

o, that was decades ago
long gone
before she slipped through my exploded hands
and rolled on

or was that you?
find time or make time?

once i had
then i smoked my bloody eyes.

folks on the street admire my outfit
my soft leather tongue
they adjust the regulations accordingly
make me shirtless in searing sunlight
let me put it this way

so the folks on the street will yield
    [here we skip scurrilous braggadocio about going down on movie stars,
      dancing with archbishops, and so on, and confess instead...]
when i caress i gouge
my tenderness tends to splinter
and slice
but i mean
well...?
--*for saint bernadette of the library, 6:03 to 6:17, september 28, 2018*

"...okay, if you had a dot in the middle of your hand and you were going in a circle, it would have to expand and go round and round, and get larger and larger. and at some point it would have to stop, and then this same circle would have to come back around, around to the little dot in the middle of your hand."—charles mingus

ALL THE DOOMED BLONDES: Part Nine

carroll baker must be included in this pantheon, if for nothing else than her embodiment of the nymphet in *baby doll,* written by tennessee williams, directed by elia kazan. *baby doll* is a child-bride who sleeps in a crib, held prisoner by her obsessed husband, the much older karl malden, and seduced by the wily eli wallach (the only actor to survive *the misfits.* all the rest of his castmates—marilyn, gable, monty, thelma ritter—all died soon after the making of that doom-ridden film). *baby doll* was well-received especially for baker who received an academy award nomination. the protests from the legion of decency and other bastions of morality only increased the box office and the star's notoriety. she had been a highly respected member of the actor's studio, falling under lee strasberg's tutelage just like **marilyn**, **kim stanley** and **barbara loden.** but while studying at the prestigious school, she was also working as a chorus dancer in night clubs. as baker matured she was groomed to be the next marilyn monroe with a steady stream of photos explicitly designed to evoke the recently fallen goddess. then she was chosen to play *harlow* in a misbegotten biopic. the publicity campaign for the picture did her no favors, proclaiming "***harlow*** *stood for only one thing as no woman ever has—before or since.*" and in *the carpetbaggers,* a lurid potboiler, she played a drunken movie star, essentially a combination of **jean harlow** and **marilyn**. but she tired of the sex object treatment, saying it was like *"being a* *beauty contest winner instead of an actress."* baker fled hollywood and the spotlight.

by contrast, the gifted **judy holliday**, so adorably naive and yet so worldly behind her eyes, with her screechy little voice and jiggly walk, is a worthy and essential inclusion. she triumphed on broadway in *born yesterday,* a role as perfect for her as was tracy lord in *the philadelphia story* made for **katherine hepburn**. in a familiar pattern, harry cohn, who had purchased the rights to the play, refused to cast an 'unknown 'in the movie version, despite the fact that she had won a tony award in the role. the story goes that **katherine hepburn** and spencer tracy, along with the writers garson kanin and ruth gordon, conspired to convince harry cohn to give **judy** the part by casting her in *adam's rib* which charmed film audiences and convinced the all-powerful cohn to give her the role in *born yesterday* she rightly owned. she won an oscar. but after a mere ten more films, she died of breast cancer at the age of 46. george cukor said of her, *"judy holliday had in common with the great comedians ...that depth of emotion, that unexpectedly touching emotion, that thing which would unexpectedly touch your heart."*

and there you have it. although they shared many of the same sorrows— orphanhood, madness, molestation, exploitation, condescension, suicide. many of the same men: as you have no doubt noticed, the same names keep cropping up: **clark gable, william powell, elia kazan, lee strasberg, howard hawks, william wyler, george cukor, howard hughes, marlon brando, arthur miller, tennessee Williams...**each of these women brought their own unique glow to their exalted position. lombard's signature role was the ultimate madcap heiress in *my man godfrey,* very much the model for **katharine hepburn**'s performance in *bringing up baby,* and to a certain extent the slightly less flighty heiress of *the philadelphia story.* lombard's exuberance and underlying intelligence influenced the depiction of every ditzy, screwball heroine to follow. she was sexy but she wasn't overt like harlow. nevertheless, in *no man of her own* with gable, not yet her husband, they generated nearly as much heat as gable and harlow in *red dust*, which was downright pornographic at times.

in fact, **katherine hepburn** provides an interesting contrast to this tragic string of pearls. early in her career she had been repeatedly fired from production after production, for being obnoxious, strange-looking and *'just not very good'*. and yet she persevered. finally she made her broadway debut, in *the warrior's husband,* based on an old greek tale, on march 11, 1932, at the morosco theater. hepburn's first entrance called for her to leap down a narrow stairway with a stag, flank pierced with an arrow, flung over her shoulder, wearing a fetching short silver tunic. she had found the perfect role with which to proclaim to all the world her identity as the goddess artemis/diana, the huntress, independent and strict, athletic and graceful. when actaeon bursts into diana's sacred grove while she is bathing, she angrily splashes water from her spring on the hapless boy, transforming him into a stag, who is chased down and devoured by his own dogs, [see the myth of diana and actaeon. for more lurid details.] diana demands respect and obeisance but not of a sexual nature. humans are not permitted to see the goddess naked without facing punishment.. however, **katherine hepburn** may not have been a goddess of love, but she was eminently worth worshipping. she could be fantastically alluring. as in *the philadelphia story* or any film she made with spencer tracy. In *woman of the year,* the audience and tracy get a first glimpse of her at the same moment. we burst through an office door, and there she is, perched on a desk, pulling up her stockings to reveal a couple of truly gorgeous gams. in fact the shot is really of her shapely legs and then moves up the rest of her body. she takes her time straightening her skirt, as the camera pans up further. then we get to her face, and she is giving us a frank, faintly sultry look, completely unburdened with the need for approval. which, of course, makes her irresistible. it is as effective and sexy an entrance into a film as rita harworth's in *gilda.* which is really saying something. the difference is, gilda is doomed to be the victim of men's obsessions with her. she lives on it until she dies of it. there is something very fitting about the fact that in one of her last great roles, *lady from shanghai,* written and directed by her then husband orson welles, rita has gone platinum blonde.

so, who came next? after the glorious blondes herein described took their turns, who gave focus to those energies after these women flamed so brightly? as far as I can tell, no one has really taken up the mantle. In fact, it seems that the mantle is a threaadbare garment, outdated and inherently destructive. we just don't want to keep punishing the feminine principle any longer. men's atavistic terror of women terminal in fact, for all of us. we seem to be finally figuring that out.

but still, a goddess is a goddess. she is forever necessary, by definition. james hillman, a neo-jungian mythologist and writer famously declared, "*the gods have become diseases.*" but, of course, they also carry a cure. the stories evolve, the mythic narratives transform, the tales of triumph and struggle provide thereby fresh guidance and direction and insight. doesn't the celebration of the essence of love, the realm of natural lust and the pursuit of pleasure, keep us alive and vibrant, pulsating and hopeful? the stories and the gods and goddesses themselves change as we need them to. the myths we live by transform as we do, as a race. the new aphrodite, the goddess of love, one reflecting our image or the one we strive for, will inevitably arise from the seafoam, [i have one word for you: **beyonce!**] and she will show us the way to the shape of our survival—as fully formed human beings, individual inhabitants of our shared and sacred home. that's what our myths and tales, ceremonies and movies and love songs and ecstatic dances and plays and games—that's what our objects of adoration, the receptacles of our fears, and our lusts, our very **stars,** are made for—to bring us to ourselves so that we have at least a chance of saving ourselves.

"*...since the true paradises are the paradises that we have lost.*"—*marcel proust, 'remembrance of things past: the past recaptured '*

MOVING EAST/ ON THE FERRY TO THE VINEYARD/1995
drove in to new york city for the first night. me, tav and susanna. beautiful sunset on the hudson glinting off the windows of the buildings along the west side highway, the simple magnificence of this city. we make it to bill and rose's apartment on the east side. shower, relax, make phone calls, then take the subway to bleecker and have dinner at *great jones st.* (the joint we went to my very first night in new york. it was while talking to a total stranger sitting next to me at the communal tables that i first said out loud something that had been swelling up in me. i asked the guy what he did for a living and he said, "*why, do you want to marry me?*" and i said, not missing a beat, "*no, i want to marry her,*" indicating susanna who was leaning her whole body against my back, sitting next to me. she heard me she tells me later but she didn't react.) after an excellent (if noisy) meal, we stroll down to tower

records which does not impress such connoisseurs as tavish and i are. and then move on down to the anjelika for *living in oblivion*. we cab it back.

up early, leaving tav in nyc to shop. we find our way back into nyack, although not the established route. susanna and i are uneasy in our negotiations over routing. i've grown used to navigating myself. this plays out for the rest of the day. she really needs to feel that she is making the decisions. not necessarily as to content, that's not what she is concerned about. i'm concerned about her admiration for me and demonstration of same. i want everything to be an indication of how much she trusts and admires me, so every disagreement becomes proof that she doesn't. talk about tedium. but that's the tar baby i'm playing with the whole day. my sympathy goes out to peter, our architect and friend, who is patient and goodnatured. we have a nice lunch at the river house (or river cafe`...not sure what's correct. well, it's two blocks from our house, so i guess i'll get that established eventually.) and ultimately we make good decisions, together, even if yours truly is overly petulant. the best part is when we decide to use the folk sculpture of the snake, eagle and lizard as the newel post on the upstairs landing. everyone gets excited, even ken the contractor.

we take mark over to the tarrytown train station for his first trip into NYC. tav is waiting at the station and we drive on to roxbury. stop at the market. i roast a chicken. and we take a dip in the pond, even though susanna thinks it may have some toxic pollution. there is an uncharacteristic oily film on the surface. nevertheless, the water is deliciously restorative, and finally she comes in.

it's a beautiful sunset and an extremely full moon. (reason for my restive mood, but what isn't?) we settle down with ice cream and *mrs.parker and the vicious circle* which has been ominously stopped in the middle and not rewound by the previous viewer. we quickly see why. jennifer jason leigh is an absolute travesty. one feels compelled to a brutal rejection. (campbell scott is as usual very fine.) the movie is hopeless. we bail.

susanna gets up early for a swim and we hit the road—me demonstrating my road skills, especially at speeding without detection. we have time for a bite at the *leeside* in wood's hole. and now we are docking. i have personally driven from los angeles, california to vineyard haven, massachusetts. across the continent—and then some.

I CAN'T WAIT TO SEE EMMA AND LILAH!

to AGUISE: to dress; to adorn; to deck.
to AGREE: pleased; to be pleased
to AGNIZE: to acknowledge, to own, to avow.
TUMIFACIENT: eternal inflation; false vacuum.

"we are idiot, younger-sons of gods, begotten in dotages divine; and our mothers all miscarry. giants are in our germs; but we are dwarfs, staggering under heads overgrown. heaped, our measures burst. we die of too much life."—herman melville, 'mardi'

coyote: *"COYOTE CANNOT DIE!"*

TESTOSTERONE

as it turned out, longterm ingestion of the chemicals necessary to quell HIV drained patients of testosterone, an essential substance for the healthy functioning of our bodies. the drugs literally leached testosterone out of us. without it, the immune system is seriously weakened, the drugs themselves are less effective, anti-depressants simply don't work. my level, when tested, was -2; which explained why, for at least a decade, i often could not climb out of bed and out of the pit of a daily torpor until well past noon. the high octane energy i had been blessed with all of my life was more-or-less gone. my life, my marriage, my family and my work were slipping away from me—and i did not have the juice it took to turn it around. the downward spiral seemed impossible to reverse. i just couldn't muster the force. i felt like i was losing my selfhood, becoming nothing but an appendage, subsumed in the world of my in-laws; and i didn't much care, or have the will, to do anything about it. not to mention that this privileged, intelligent, elegant but natural world was the one i had yearned to belong in as a boy, dreaming and anomalous in sacramento.

and then in 2009, my doctor, paul bellman, explained that this entropy, this soggy cloak, was being carried by many in the HIV community. of course, at first it was viewed as an unwelcome side effect of what were, after all, heavy drugs. and then, suddenly, there was a solution which suggested that things did not have to be this way; and the treatment seemed to be working. with regular shots of testosterone, people were feeling much much better, stronger and vital again. after the first shot i immediately brightened. with the subsequent treatments, i felt restored to myself. i was buoyant, hopeful once more, confident in a way i had not felt in nearly a decade. my mojo was back, in spades. not only that, my body tightened up, my libido revived, markedly (not that it had really faded much…a blessing and a curse.) after years of deficiency, i was in a flush of reemergence, of restoration; of gleeful excitement, magically released from the doldrums of the last ten years. all things were once again possible. the drive to **do** was once more upon me. to buy, to consume, to fuck, to succeed, to engage, to energize, to explode, to re-explode. and best of all, suddenly i was being hit on from all sides and i was THRILLED by it. other people became energized just being around me. i took on a big project in my hometown, nyack, building a performing arts center in the middle of town called *riverspace*—and i was one of the main engines in the effort. the downside was i couldn't stop talking about it. my natural volubility, not to mention my volatility, were all amped up. my anger erupted more often. my family was becoming concerned—and occasionally frightened. i was angry that they weren't happy for me, and pleased that i was back to my old self. i especially resented my wife's resistance. i had been hanging my head, dragging myself around for years. why wasn't she delighted that i felt good about myself again? she did say, one night, that she noticed how good my body was looking. a rare bit of praise by that time. there was even a little tinge of desire in her voice. faint but thrilling.

i started taking herbal supplements to jack up even more. i got so horny, i would jerk-off while sitting in traffic on the new jersey turnpike. driving down to rutgers university where i was directing a play, a wildly sexual and violent adaptation of a greek play *big love,* by the brilliant charles mee. an adaptation of the oldest extant play, from 32 b.c., *suppliant women,* by aeschylus. i started buying flashier clothes and sex toys and books and music and thin t-shirts to show off my nipples and going to bars and sex clubs before driving home to my three-story house on the river. i felt like i could do…anything, again. and just as i had done for most of my life—i **leapt**. sometimes frantically, fleeing the hellhounds on my trail, like orestes or attis, forever on the run, their own dogs nipping at their heels. and so…in my increasing isolation, flirting with the certain plummet to come, going up in flames just to be seen…hoping against hope that i would not be rejected, that instead i would be known and accepted unconditionally, just as i am. knowing all the time that such a thing was impossible. for my soul is unacceptable, [damned, in fact, according to my dad], and my body even more so, and ' *if* *my thought dreams could be seen',* etc. often, i would sneak down to my office after everyone else was in bed and beat-off while cruising fetish websites. and then, this happened…

.

THE VERY WORST OF ALL

i had a bag of sex toys. in a black duffel. i kept it in my car.

lilah, who was seventeen and about to graduate from high school, had stopped looking at me as she passed going up the stairs. she would not speak to me. even when we were alone in the house. i didn't really know why. when i asked, she would tell me nothing. and nothing about where she was or where she was going, where she might eat or sleep. i had become a ghost to her. and all that blast of new fuel which was so exhilarating to me would stutter and flicker, frightening me further. so i bore down. i got ferocious with myself.

one night, she went out again without saying a word. i wouldn't have known she was gone but for the jangle of the bells on the back doorknob. the last couple of nights, from what i could gather, she had stayed at brooklyn's house. but she told me nothing. not if she would be back soon, or ever. i was invisible and irrelevant—and not just in the natural order or things—but willfully, deliberately, with hurt and hostility. but what was up? was she dealing with the separation that comes as high school ends, and college, and then the wide world beckons? no. this had a flavor of darkness and rage.

that night i was really horny. as i often was in those days. mostly always. but it seems now that my enforced disappearance from her world and the distancing i could feel from the other two, the mother and the sister—my beloved family was retreating from who i had become—and it was panicking me. i was more aggressive, more volatile than ever, more moody, more belligerent, more self-involved, and less willing to be shamed and demeaned and dismissed. i would push back at it when i felt it, which was a lot of the time. that demeaning attitude had become habitual, especially with susanna. so, i was demanding and cajoling. a pain in the ass—but productive and…it must be said, happy. happier than i had been in years. but feeling increasingly unseen..

so lilah left that night without a word, and i decided to have one of my extended bouts of enhanced and intense masturbation. i brought the bag inside. laid out the stuff. the dildos and nipple clamps and pumps and various inhalants and porn. i went upstairs to get a full-length mirror so i could watch myself take my body into a bliss of abuse. as i came downstairs, i saw a shadow flit out of the room, and once again the back door jangled. she had come home, she saw all the shit i had '*brought into our home*', [as she was later to say], spread there waiting on the black vinyl play sheet.

i pretended for a while that she had not seen anything. that she had not gone into the TV room, what once had been the playroom, where we had played the garden game and assembled leggo fantasies. maybe i was wrong…maybe no one had been there…maybe the worst of it all had not happened. but, yeah, i knew. even now i can hear the car racing backwards down the driveway. i knew, in my terrified heart, for sure, that nothing could or would ever repair that shock and disgust and heartbreak.

ever.

i had lost my little girl.

(there had been a night, months earlier than all of this, driving home late on 9W, long before the worst came down. after performing deviant acts in a bar in the meatpacking district, i had a sudden flash of lilah seeing me in those positions, those depraved situations. i called out her name in an agonized groan. i began to sob at this terrifying vision, this bone-chilling prophecy…somehow i knew it would happen. she would find me out…and still i went back…)

and then, i went right off the fuckin 'rails. i threw a grenade into the middle of my life. i felt like i had to escape from a trap of my own devising and that maybe i could somehow have a more authentic life, on my own……of course, inside, even before i left, i began to feel tremendous regret, shame and horror at my grotesquely reckless behavior. i could see and feel the horrible pain i was causing. and yet, i went on…

once i had moved into manhattan, all alone, the bleak reality hit me like a freight train…i had thrown it all away. *"once i had mountains/ in the palm of my hand"*….and then another T, tina, crystal meth, came to dominate my shredded life. and the sex got sicker, more frenzied…it took a few tortured years, but eventually i made my escape from new york and made it back to LA, licking my wounds in topanga. but the self-inflicted suffering persisted. i ended up in cedars-sinai in october, 2014, with my kidneys in freefall. the doctor, eyes wide as saucers, said, *"i don't know what you did, but you have two hours to live! or you'll be on dialysis for the rest of your life."* i said, i swear, *"i'll take door number 3."* i saw my children's faces, one at a time, like headshots: emma, lilah and tavish and i just refused to leave them that way. the doctor actually chuckled and we did five dialysis sessions in two days, and at the end of it, my kidneys were more or less normal. and have remained so. it's like susanna says, *"don't worry about your dad, he's like a cockroach, he'll survive the nuclear holocaust."* i consider that one the finest compliments ever paid me, actually. in the coming months on the internet, i noticed class action suits emerging about the over-prescribing of testosterone. my new doctor in LA was unable to get my medical files—after several requests. his entire practice had vanished into thin air. he had often been criticized and attacked by the AMA for not using their established protocols and other innovative treatments, even facing an attempt to take away his license. i have no idea if his liberal use of testosterone contributed to his disappearance and the dissolution of his practice. it does seem possible, if not likely, in retrospect. he retired completely in 2013, the year i left new york. but i absolutely, without a moment's hesitation, forgive my beloved doctor, paul bellman, one of the finest physicians i have ever known, because i know he was intent on keeping me alive. and i do not blame him for the devastation the use of testosterone rained down on my life. and besides, i'm still on the stuff, at a much smaller dose, of course. it is necessary to my survival...or at least that's what i need to believe now, so as to absolve..excuse..explain...those rash, erratic, out of control choices i inflicted on my loved ones. all those reckless, awful, indelible mistakes? and that overwhelming impulse to escape that has haunted me all of my life. i had to, right? after all, i did it all to stay alive...or something like that. didn't i?

"and worse I may be yet: the worst is not
so long as we can say 'this is the worst"—shake-speare, 'king lear'

"that night, i saw my first glimpse of the unreachability that would spread a wall across his face. that part of him i had once understood had begun to sink across his eyes. the part of him that could understand me was so far back, drowned already in the depths of him. i have yet to see that part again....this

was who he was: an aging hipster, clinging to his looks and coolness."—emma larson, 'in the cornucopia of your ear'

HIRAETH: (n.) a homesickness for a home to which you cannot return, a home which maybe never was; the **nostalgia**, the **yearning**, the **grief** for the lost places of your heart

BLACK SUNDAY, 2009
on that sunday,
[eleven years ago, now.]
(susanna is so good at that. remembering dates and intervals, how much time has passed…)

i called ahead knowing they were waiting, and that everything, all of it, must be said, and being frightened to my marrow. praying i could manage to represent myself in some acceptable way, so as to find forgiveness and some clear channel back into their arms and hearts—to make the fury subside.

but, i could already feel the singe. i could feel my clothes melting.
so i called ahead.
"you can't come home," she said. *"they can't be in the same room with you. if you come here they will leave."*
"but i live there. and…we were going to..talk."
"you don't live here any more. get a hotel room."
"sweetheart"
"don't call me that, i'm not your sweetheart."
"…i'm their dad, their father, why can't we sit down and talk this through?"
"because we can't—what you did to/"
"what do you think I/"
"i can't have this conversation right now."

and the line goes dead.

and the car drifts into the clouds.
and my hands go to my side and tremble.

and the sobs come.

more for the precious three i had lost, and the anguish i had caused them, than for my own sorry self.

after awhile, i call my friend andy, who i've known since the 70s in LA. he lives in nyack now, he and his wife debbie have a guest room, and i know they will not turn me away, and, in fact, they are kind and gentle and just cheerful enough.

(i met andy when he and his band, andy and the rattlesnakes, came to *cowboy mouth*, a play i directed, written by sam shepard and patti smith. andy and the snakes came for patti smith but they stayed for the beat coming off the stage, for ed harris as slim and robin ginsberg rocking cavale, an obsessed, sexy, patti avatar, and then the lobsterman, jack slater, emerging from the naugahyde lobster costume to be revealed as the rock and roll hero. [when jack died from liver disease, his memorial in seattle was held at the old town hall, more than 400 people showed up. including andy and ed and robin and so many others. he was well-loved. jack had left instructions that all attendees must affix clown noses to their faces and sing '*happy trails* ' together. one last magical moment of community added to the many provided by a true hero of rock and roll.] from then on, andy and the rattlesnakes set up every friday night after the show and played til a quarter to three. five years later, andy and the rattlesnakes headlined the party at the church when susanna and i got back from our honeymoon…still, we were more than neighbors but andy and debbie never came to our house for dinner, although i often suggested it. susanna found debbie indecipherable and a little too loud….[or at least, that's my story. and i am hopelessly subjective, as should be quite clear by now]).

as i drove through the sunset streets, past places that had become so familiar to me—such as the community center, housed in an old presbyterian church, just around the corner from our place. in the first few weeks of moving in, i had strolled up to the *nyack center*, thinking it might be a good place to begin the process of getting to know my new hometown, to find my place in it. i'd been told they gave free breakfasts to kids and drug counseling, etc.

 i figured i could make myself useful.

"you guys need to raise money for anything?"

340

"yeah, we need a new boiler?"
"how much will that cost? '
"couple of grand."
*"well, look, the holidays are coming, i can do a holiday event—readings,
music, stuff like that."*
and i did, for the next fifteen years. the holiday show became a village
tradition. still is, twenty-five years later. [i was invited back for the twentieth
anniversary. not quite to a hero's welcome, but certainly a warm embrace.

[susanna and the girls did not attend. although i did have a lovely
visit with susanna that afternoon. she gave me a tour of the garden i
had planted with so much care. the bamboo is over thirty feet high. the
peony blossoms are as big as a man's head.]

i took a left at main street, the center of town, past the starbuck's, and the
strip mall we were trying to turn into a performing arts center, a project i had
put my heart and soul into for three years, and which was now beginning to
falter, and indeed, once i was gone, entirely collapsed. the antique stores
and sushi place, the fern bars and local hangouts. i knew this would be my
last look at the hometown i had hoped would be mine forever. i saw it fade to
black. heartsick, i made it to andy and debbie's place.

*"in the complex play of human relations persons do develop dependencies,
do make emotional demands upon each other which can feed on, or even
destroy, their own lives."—henry james*

so is the past where home is? if so, then coming home, ever, is past
impossible. will it be, can it be, found in the future? when? home stays
perpetually out of reach. at least for me. a lost station on an endless train
line…and who lets you come home, anyway? there's that old saw, of course,
'home is where they can never turn you away 'or something like that…utter
bullshit, at least in my case..who gives that permission? or makes the
judgment call? turns out it comes down to this, the only home possible is right
where you are AT PRESENT. (*any place i hang my hat….*) if you can let it be.
clearly, if you have to ask—it isn't home. i guess, that's how you know where
home is.

THIS IS THE SECRET STORY

i am trying to tell
all about the trembling and the knowledge
was it the apricots?
unripe unsweet but so delicious in their firmness

how long can i hold out?
hold off?
hold in?
hold on?

for we need solace
dark energy or the end of time
in this lovely corner of the multiverse.
running into beautiful confessions
approximate nobilities
the slow lean into the first light
some damp doorway in the dark
touch of lips to lips

LEOPARDLIKE
ride willy ride
did you see the parade of plagues?
playful giant balloons shaped like
adorable smiling virus spoors
bacterium in tutus
marching mutant monkeys
running sores in gleaming sneakers
celebrity diseases lip-synching to cheerful diagnoses
funny way to start a picnic
bald, naked, and
lucky to be alive

TOPANGA COYOTES/ 2015
i went for a hike, more like a stroll, on my favorite path along the top of the
ridge dividing the canyon and the valley. the hills on the topanga side were
glowing, billowing, with tom's brilliant bush, (i must ask him the name again)
looking like snow blossoms blanketing the terrain. and the sky in which no
drones sped was doing its own big show, steamy stratocumulus, stately, like

galleons on a slowly rolling sea, over a blazing blue pacific. with dark gray rainclouds moving in over the valley. man, that pink, starting on the fringe of the clouds cloaking the disc of sun, imperceptibly turning to hot gold lace. (and of course the walk, not particularly vigorous, would have been unthinkable, inconceivable, impossible, just a few months ago which gives the whole enterprise a grandiose, celebratory air). i took a side path and got out on a promontory looking west and south. just as i approached a prime spot, a coyote ambled up over the rise, boldly out of the bush. he stopped when he saw me but he didn't bolt away. he checked me out, straight in the eyes. we had a clannish moment of recognition. he took a long look as if making a droll comment and then he took off, back down the slope. another face to face encounter with coyote, here in the canyon, the very first one, was the night i arrived. i landed at LAX rattled and shaky, hoping for the best, six thousand pounds of my goods and bads, the whole kit and calaboodle, were being trucked across the country in a semi-trailer, trailing behind me like filaments of failure, the whole shebang was unloaded into a smaller truck and then squeezed up the narrow canyon roads, all the way to my new location, deep in the twisted maze of looming rocks and trees, on a twisty paved road designated *trophy trail*. (but the stuff will take several nerve-wracking days and sleepless nights to arrive, safely and otherwise, and so began the unpacking)….now, tonight, the first night of my possibly renewed life, so dark and unknown, my son and i turn the final turn off topanga canyon boulevard heading up the road that leads to the trail, and there **he** is, as if manifesting out of the shadows, coyote himself, loping along beside the car, making the turn with us, showing us the way. kind of a rusty, reddish coat in the moonlight. gone in the blink of an eye. i ain't making this up. you can ask my boy. he saw our striding guide as well, the imaginal honor bestowed and the comfort in the animal presence.
and now, as with many nights in the last year, deep in the midnight murk, mad choruses of god's dogs howl and yip, converging on their doomed domesticated prey. their shrill cries and baleful yapping making an hypnotic song, in occasional duet with night owls, a dissonant melody of lust and praise, echoing through the canyon.

to WELTER; to roll in water or mire. to roll voluntarily, to wallow.
   *"if a man inglut himself with vanity, or **welter** in filthiness like a swine, all learning, all goodness is soon forgotten"—samuel johnson's dictionary*

"i have said that behind sorrow there is always sorrow. it were wiser still to say that behind sorrow there is always a soul. and to mock a soul in pain is a dreadful thing. in the strangely simple economy of the world people only get what they give, and to those who have not enough imagination to penetrate the mere outward shell of things, and feel pity, what pity can be given save that of scorn?"—oscar wilde, 'de profundis'

" …until you look death right in the face…until you go right up into the ass of death—right up his ass—till you find a womb of fear…then maybe, maybe…"—marlon brando as paul in 'last tango in paris'

coyote: *"COYOTE FELL INTO HIS OWN SHIT!"*

OFFAL @ CEDARS-SINAI, Fall, 2014
forced through some warp or wormhole to welter
a hopeless torpent warrior devouring my own agony
      but these bloated melonish botero boots are not my feet
          these fattened shanks are not my legs
     this balloon scrotum. this infant dick, are not my genitals
     having ingested, gulping twitching like some desperate fresh-branded
calf, this vile oily swill,
          7.2 liters of spissitude, a charmingly named concoction,
GOLIGHTLY, (poor truman would be appalled at the association)
          designed to make my gut ultracrystal clear, so as to get a
good look, camera up my ass, at just what's going on up there
meanwhile i, bloated man of sorrows, drown in my own thick but insipid
spitvenom vomit spawl, my bed a swamp of my foul excrement, beslubbered
at treacherously irregular
intervals from said anus
bespewed in rancid liquid streams
          nurses flee aghast
          a few actually yelp girlishly
          and scamper from the cesspit
          hands fluttering like startled soiled butterflies

so i am left to my own dawbed devices

344

grasping the slick bed rail, jetsam from a blasted ocean liner, still afloat
redhot from the catastrophe, engine explosion or terrorist attack, or savagely
forked lightning which impaled my guts and set me adrift in a turbulent
current
where i now cling to this noxious ladder leading most hopefully
to far less hell
alas the bed
begins to fold up on me, with a soft sinister buzz
squeezing me like a giant grinning python or anaconda (purring like that tiger
all those years ago, on the end of the bunk bed, [it may have been my
mother] while i grasped my shaking knees and stared, trembling)
the serpent from hell, dripping greenish, radioactive spit, thick golightly saliva,
bespawling it into my gurgling, chapped mouth, the better to choke me

now the tube tapping into my invaded jugular, on the right side of my neck
begins to be forced deeper into said neck, as my hospitable bed continues to
accordion,
    this same spigot will later [maybe now?] introduce an infection into my
beleaguered bloodstream, threatening once more my continued existence,
but that's a whole other campaign)
in the inescapable cauldron of my own excrescence, i scream as i have
seldom screamed and i have screamed more than a few screams.
    to my shame, of course....
and on this occasion i endeavor to be as unequivocal as i can possibly
muster, with nothing held back,,,,,,,,,,,,,,,,,,,(is this finally a prayer?)
slathered as i am with diarrhetic shit, flammable vomit, drool, spittle, snot, my
pallid face and toxic body streaming the sweat of the hanged man:

SOMEBODY GET THE **FUCK** *IN HERE* **FUCKING <u>NOW.</u> FUUUUCKKKK!**
I NEED SOME FUCKING **HELP**! *please!...FUUUCK!*

    the first saintly nurse who comes back into the fetid fray, (she has
dreadlocks long and beaded and up till now held an imperturbable, placid
expression, always moving at her own deliberate pace, hardly speaking.) now
she haughtily, imperiously declares:
    *'don't use that kind of language around me. i don't have to listen to
that, unh-uuuh'.*

then she kneels
and begins the clean-up.

SO/ WELL/ SUPPOSE
so, you ask,
how the fuck?
well, its deep
suppose its deeper than you think
or feel?
that time my father came at me like a runaway train
knocking me to the ground
or the freight i hopped, strung in my hammock, across the top of the county,
st. paul, minnesota
to portland, oregon
took two and a half days of solid banging movement
heartbeat rhythm to the dakotas,
pissing through the open boxcar door at steaming midnight in minot
i was hipped as to details by a guy who had done this ride, the burlington 99,
famous for allowing hobos to ride. [it was in the damned charter, the contract
for the railway, because burlington had been a hobo himself before being
struck by riches]. \the hippy in minnesota warned me, "*be sure you get a car
with a wiiiide open door, and keep it that way. sometimes the pounding will
creep the door closed, inch by inch, and if it closes there is no way you can
open it from the inside. you'll be in there for the duration. and don't forget to
take some newspaper or something to wrap your shit up in. no pit stops or
toilet breaks.*" the same guy suggested the hammock. not possible to sleep
on the raw wood floors, jackhammering up and down as the rails slide on
beneath you.

changing trains in spokane,
holdover long enough for a stroll
into the last real hobo jungle, established during the great depression,
inhabited ever since.
a labyrinthine warren of a least a hundred or so
squat tin and trash contrivances, once being home to hundreds of lost bodies
and ramshackle minds,
lungs breathing in the rancid smoke of the commodity culture.

and i'm shown around with great pride by a friendly tramp named willy, i'm
pretty sure that was his name,
who claimed to have built most of the slapped together shelters all by himself.
'of my own design' he declared,*'used to be a lotta guys livin'here, lotta guys.'*
looking both permanent and hopelessly deteriorated, his creations, his self,
accretions of snot, accumulated for decades and decades, stiffening his
beard.
and then, climbing back into the boxcar, exhausted by the lack of movement
falling deep asleep, in my hammock,

suddenly shaken awake
by a tramp named napoleon,
black i think,
with whom i had shared this rattler for a day
or so,
having never spoken to him,
the banging just too cacophonous even for screaming.
besides he had stayed at his end, mostly back in the shadows.
now he rasps close in my ear,
"shake it, pal. they're droppin 'us."
and sure enough the car we're in has been backed onto a sidetrack, and the
hissing train is easing out on the mainline.
so we dash, my hammock dragging and snagging behind me, backpack
thumping on my thigh,
napoleon points me to an extra engine, right behind the lead, hitching a ride,
just like us, a free ride to somewhere or other, the low step ladder makes it
easy to catch. i toss my stupid shit up to my new protector and clamber
onboard as she accelerates. napoleon gestures me up onto the huge
expansive hood of the massive spare, metal warmed by the sun, and we
stretch out our legs and lean against the windows of the conductor's cab,
finally in the open air.
(here's where he told me his name, *"napoleon"*, with a flash in his eyes,
grinning at the unlikeliness of it, the plain irony.)
and we pull into portland like emperors, triumphantly at dusk,
and then, just as we come into the yard, napoleon gives me a tap on the
shoulder, with the back of his hand, rolls easy off our perch, and right off the

train and into the brush, with a chin nod and a fist lift, as he hits the ground running, and disappears.

in portland
i hole up in a catafalque hotel where a broom leaned by the nightstand.
why?
then the grumbling from the couple in the next room,
quickly catapulting to shrieks and lamentations,
only repeated pounding on the wall
could cause surcease.
answer provided for the broom,
but still, how the fuck?
well, i'm trying
suppose it can't be explained,
forgiving is not forgetting

the day my father told me to get into the car, and my momma did not come with us.
that day he warned me about those *"bad boys"* as we drove with all of our belongings, carefully packed and lashed down in the back of the pickup, (think *beverly hillbillies*) the rest stuffed into the station wagon driven by my stepmother, betty, with my sister as surly passenger, over two mountain ranges from the central valley of california into an enormous, dry, dusty lakebed where wild mustangs still ran (and oil had recently been discovered), in the east of nevada at the crossroads of two lost highways, the settlement known as currant creek, nevada. stucco farmhouse with a big attic where me and my three cousins slept, twelve unit motel, five table cafe, single-wide trailer where my sister, father and stepmother lived, small market in a stone hut built by prospectors, catering mostly to native americans from the adjoining reservation, diesel for the steady flow of trucks, trailer park for tourists and itinerants and a small trailer behind the cafe` for kenny the fry cook. once kenny, well-groomed ex-con, invited me into his snug quarters, and put his hand on my thigh, telling me how handsome i was, i should be proud, and i fled from this peril…reluctantly.) two hundred miles from nowhere. or the nearest human outpost, a smallish city to which we drove each day to high school)… my dad told me with a serious tone tales of bad, bigger boys he once encountered in a slapped together clubhouse,

348

corrugated roof, scrap plywood, hand painted sign over the little rascals door:
'*no girlz allowed.*'
so what were they up to that rainy afternoon
when my father ducked into that shack?
…i didn't ask.

that lonely night i was home alone. father and stepmother at a card game at my uncle's. sister out on a date with her regular boyfriend. i'm watching the *bob hope christmas special,* aching with the anguish of being left out. of gropings and fondlings and openly celebrated horniness. all of us in our pegged pants and surfer haircuts, (soon to evolve to beatle cuts), and the girls in saddle shoes and pony tails, training bras and hungry eyes, would gather with our inchoate desires at the local temple to celluloid and be together there and mingle breaths. it was there where some boy threw some girl's panties up into the fluttering beam of the projector and everybody *knew.* they saw the sacramental garment. but i was not there to see it. and i yearned to worship our burgeoning bodies and more, much more.

once, at the neighborhood market i was browsing through the rotating metal rack of paperbacks. i scoped a book called *numbers* by john rechy. the fact that this book was on display at a market gives some sense of the changes in the world since 1963, that this sacred text was available for the perusal of a 12 or 13 year old boy, voracious reader, curious about all things forbidden, driven in fact to dig down into the dirt for a secret sustenance or climb to the highest branches of the tallest tree, to the far reaches of the oak or redwood, perches that could not possibly bear the weight of a human body, no matter how young, light, and indeterminate, i dangled there over this book about the adventures of a male hustler, or maybe just a sexmad man, intent on having as many lustpartners in a weekend as he could rack up. for the numbers. for the sheer exhilaration of seeing and feeling just how far he could go. (years later, cruising griffith park, i met john rechy. still muscular, tanned, elvis hair, most likely dyed, shirtless in the sun, posing in his tight tight pants and clearly defined thick dick. he was known as the american jean genet, a street genius, a bent extremity of modern literature, out there with burroughs, selby and rougher trade, like phil andros. we went back to his place, i told him the story of the young me, getting a hardon in my local grocery store, from reading his book, walking home elated in a way i could not comprehend. but i was certain, from that time forward, that i would try to find the way to the place, find the person, the thing, to shape myself, to fit the form of my wildest imaginings.) so that night, with jerry colonna and the luscious ann-margret, thanking bob for the memories. [and then, all those years later, i sat next to her in the table reads for *twice in a lifetime.* playing gene hackman's son, she picked me to sit next to. she would touch my hand every once in awhile while we read, for no particular reason i could perceive. i would stare at her skin, the impossible smoothness, and breathe in her scent. she rarely spoke, but occasionally she'd lean into my ear and whisper, *"they're all so good."]* i stripped off all my clothes and went outside, circling naked in our front yard, no trees no fence no cover for my frolic, my hand jerking at my most cherished member, my most extreme extremity. a car full of girls went by…and then they went by again, and i realized my mistake. i had left the dayworld and now i fell, crashing back into reality and i was unclothed, unprotected, unknown. my sister came home to a policeman in the driveway and one at the door. my father had to be summoned. the cops allowed as how i would not be busted for indecent exposure if my father would promise to take me to a psychiatrist, i don't think they were called therapists yet.) and he did, he took me to a gnomic little guy, with horned-rim glasses and hairy arms. he wore a short- sleeved dress shirt and a tie. he said i was perfectly normal but that my dad was afraid of me, because of how smart i was. but my protector didn't know about the nights when i climbed out my front window, prying off the screen, and sprawled out naked in the dew wet grass and came all over the moon.

still,
how the fuck?
well, let's dive on down…
suppose i'm just ashamed of my own funhouse hall of
shanghaied mirrors,
shattering all at once
when all i can do is sleep and sob,
doze-off and wake-up weeping,
dream and scream,
why keep this up?
so
dive down in the nocturinal

splayed and sprayed
with approbation and acclaim
savoring the splashing benedictions
dimly lit from all directions
sacrificed on ceramic altars
twisted mutt
altering the known commands
holy spigot midway on the bridge on the border
between dayworld and nightworld
sacred elixir gushing from meat faucets
i'm all the way open.

even in paris
there is a place
but you must dash across the bridge of smoke.
i know i am obfuscating
speaking in code
deliberately enigmatic
and that will no doubt do me in,
as the secret recording degrades.

please, don't give up on me.

well, let's face it,
shall we,
i gave up on me.
gave in,
to the smooth tapping of veins, pulsing with want,
T-shaped syringe, scorpion stinger, slender dickspike
laced with testosterone, amphetamine and tears
forming a perfect
crucifixfixfix
well, i was so lost in a pit of jagged crystal spires.
suppose i dove, soul singed,
into that chaotic tumble of lethal stilettos
sabers of oblivion driven deep
into my gaping cunt.

there i said it.
can i go now?

obviously not, because here i am. griefwracked and floating on a sturdy raft
of kindness, yes the sea is hopeless, yes the woods are dark, but once in big
sur (i remember this as if it was tomorrow), i ran and leapt, without a misstep,
out of the redwoods onto the massive boulders, tumbling all the way down to
the pacific, going against all gravities, bounding without boundary, all the
way, shape and form of peace and pain and bliss and madness and
unquenchable love.
—2015

ALOHA SUITE/ COYOTE GOES TO KAUAI, part 9
*"sometimes one would have said that the sea was becoming rough, that the
storm was making itself felt even inside the bay, and like the bay i lay
listening to the gathering roar of her breath."—marcel proust, 'remembrance
of things past: the captive'*
yes
that's it
that's the way it was
and is

storm a gathering roar
and it will hit land
with an unrelenting force
beyond our control.
you can be sure
of that.

it won't reach us here.
it can't come this far.
not inside the bay.
not inside our gate.
the trees stand sentinel.
our love stays firm
on this sacred hilltop.

and yet…her breath.
makes itself felt.
the goddess will roar
in her soul kitchen.
            the clock says it's time to close.
we stumble into neon absence.
we shamble in her blaze.
we cannot escape our shame.
no matter how much pain we inflict.
especially on ourselves.
            learn to forget…
                        …i really have to go
and this ceremony is feeble in its uselessness.
we tell ourselves a tragic tale
over and over.
and over again.

sunlight breaks through
but hope subsides
in waves of pity
we drown in too much muchness
not enough enough
a lack of lack
a fear of fear.
a general sense of sin.
even when we don't believe in it
hate strangles our hearts
even when we refuse to battle it
evil insists on its own existence.
we won't have it any other way.

so, yeah.
hurt me.
don't stop.
don't let up.
don't give up.

don't forgive.
don't come down.
and for god's sake
don't go up.
you don't belong in the temperate air.
you don't deserve it.
how many times do i have to tell you?
he and she
he and he
she and she
us and them
we walk this muddy road
hand in hand.
and then we sit on a lava rock,
lichen laced and worn by storms.
we hold each other in our weary arms.
we sing.
we kiss.
we laugh
we conjure
we relent
at last.
—*for ace and susie*
7/1/2017, kauai

NEVER TO STOP SAYING/ VALENTINE'S NOT GIVEN

samuel beckett said: "*not to want to say, not to know what you want to say, not to be able to say what you think you want to say, and never to stop saying, or hardly ever, that is the thing to keep in mind, even in the heat of composition.*"

trying to *not* die, especially in the sense of living without acknowledging that you are dying, is exactly the same as trying *to* die. except the first one is worse, because it wastes much more life.

anne carson said:

"what exactly is lost to us when words are wasted?"

why does mean mean mean?
mean meaning balanced,
golden,
mean meaning cruel
mean meaning cheap
mean meaning essence
have meaning
make sense

what does it mean that all these meanings coalesce into a particular
combination of sounds that will give you a headache if you persist in making
them for any length of time.
let's do it together
memmememememememememememeeeeeeeeeeemmmmmmeeeeeeeeean
like a drill to your forehead.

that's the kind of shit i ponder incessantly and what does *that* meeeeeeeean?
god only knows.

get over you?

how would or should or could such a thing be done?
and why would i want to…

like wayne kostenbaum said:
*"writing to speak to someone instead of the nothingness at the end of the
writing."*

cordelia could not *"heave her heart into her mouth"*.
william james said:
*"the neighbor's 'me 'falls together with all the rest of the things into one
foreign mass, against which my own 'me 'stands out in startling relief."*
which defines subjectivity itself.
or….a rhapsodic narcissism in full bore.

the size of the bullet
        the scope of the damage
                the feeling of deep ennui.
whatever the fuck that is. are you bored with your boredom yet?
and what the fuck is an undelivered valentine? isn't that an oxymoron. first of
all, just 'valentine'?, like 'frankenstein '?, the object, the creature, has usurped
the name of the creator, the deviser, the contriver…at any rate, the
progenitor, whatever….we used to append 'card' to valentine, with a
possessive 's', but now we don't need the thing, or even the little candy
hearts bearing odd sayings and abject come-ons.

the pockets have been looted
shredded paper about the dead,
mere litter,
the absence of bad luck.
letters letters letters
words words words
haunted as we are by what we failed to do.
the chimera of the undone…or the never given.
is it a valentine at all if it is not given?
it's an eternally unclosed circle.
a failure to embrace.

i realized the other night, trussed up in a sling, how much my happiness in
the moment consisted in the embracing, whole hog, and deliberately, the
condition of an infant, roughly dealt with, invaded brutally at every orifice, and
ecstatically grateful. thus my sexuality has come full circle. completing an
octave, finding the mean, having left very little out along the way.

and suddenly i am struck by, or given, a remembrance of my 6th grade class,
holding hands in a circle on valentine's day, as our teacher spins the hand-
cranked charge generator, taken from an old wooden telephone, to
demonstrate electrical current safely, and the tingling, just short of a real jolt,
passes, faintly buzzing, through each of our hands, every squealing one of
us, moving through us, connecting us, in a flash, flesh to flesh to flesh,
around the circle. some of us jump and buck, squirming, quickly leaving the
circle of trembling little bodies, culling the willing from the unwilling—those

356

who can take the charge and persist in charging up, counting out the seconds we can last…

on that day i had received two mysterious cards, from 'secret admirers'. and passed out a few store-bought ones myself. several small candies also appeared, pastel and chalky. a pink one said *'be mine.'* i had a special handmade card ready to deliver, to a secret admiree. for reasons i no longer remember i brought it back home and tossed it in the trash. or i kept it for decades, in some hidden place, and long since forgot it ever existed. or certainly who it was for…

and then i see that waitress, sometime in the 70s, with a slightly streisand face, but simpler, prettier, when i bolted back in from the parking lot, telling my friend to wait, not wanting to let this moment, this world pass by, and i saw her, standing by the swinging door into the kitchen, looking around for me…and i stayed back. i stayed back…

but to be honest…(and, really, at this point, what else is there to be?)
the ratio of **YES!**, let's do it!
to **NO!**, i am too frightened, too straight, too hung up, too ashamed, too…
all those decisions are pretty skewed to the affirmative.
there were not a lot of abstentions, actually.
probably should have been way more.
nevertheless,
i own the doing and the telling.
and i vow never to stop saying.
—*for michael kearns and queerwise, 2014*

SAY YES/ MY PROUSTIAN YEAR
"we wish to be understood, because we wish to be loved, and we wish to be loved because we are in love."—marcel proust
almost a perfect mirror
an imprecise palindrome
S-A-Y Y-E-S
blunt oblique
blind with positivity
for all intense purposes

i see the splintering sidewalks
buckling under what binds us

"the bonds that unite another person to ourselves exist only in our mind."

what connects us?
we who exist alone
we who cannot emerge from ourselves
we who know others only in ourselves.
the one who asserts to the contrary
that one is lying

"our ego is composed of the superimposition of our successive states...
endless upheavals raise to the surface of ancient deposits."

what binds us to our sorrowfullest story?
our disaster of adamantine negatives
choosing the wrong suicide
again and again
so much sadder a song than is absolutely necessary
for any of the ends we need,
endless needless needles
over and over and over and over again

please say yes instead
to the stillness in breathing each breath
affirm the aspirant clouds
tender glints of sun
glance
on her bodice
on her breasts
her glans
his glans
distal ends of their bulbous structures
tubercules
piloerections
now splashed with precipitous droplets

followed closely by spurts
spumes
spasms
whew
how'd we get here?
here in the sheer arrogance of the present
so sure so sure so sure so superior
to the fading fast past
faint futile future
and what of sleep?
what of dreams?

"we regret only what we remember"

that marcel,
he understood a thing or three
about regret
and remembrance of things past
and of our search for lost time
memories conjured from caresses
touches lingering on trembling fingertips
the taste of moistened lips
the scent of ribboned hair
the sound of morning birds

with a whispered
yeeessssssssssssssssssss
please,
say yes

but we set about building shelves
with warped wood
hungry for money
solace
grace
let the saw do the work
my dad used to say

your pain is you
you hold it close
and out of sight

a large, wide, white woman, deeply tanned, with no top teeth, sprawls in a creaking, tenuous lawn chair in the shade of a wall of concrete bricks painted a peeling ochre on the blasted street where i live. she is ensconced near the entrance to an alley strewn with detritus, reeking of piss, where distressed folks bereft of homes, gather in the fallen night, some in a welcome stupor, others up and at 'em. not begging, rather negotiating some human gesture. as i pass, the big woman smiles graciously and tosses a *"howyadoin'?"* she's seen me around. i assume the greeting is a mercantile bid but immediately do some internal chiding, for multiple negligent assumptions about a fellow person. she is reading a soiled, dogeared paperback as thick as a bible. i ask *"what are you reading?"* as i pass, and she waves the book, fluttering now as she holds it up to show me the cover announcing, not without pride, *"david balducci."* although i've never read him, i nod as if i have. *"i love it. he's such a good writer,"* she allows. making a remark exactly like someone at a posh party or on the subway, or by a crystalline pool in las vegas, perhaps a blonde in her sky blue bikini, top untied, her smooth burnished back the color of a sand dune after a rain shower. lowering her sunglasses, she closes her book, marking the page with her finger, raising up on her elbows to reveal to me the dark-rose nubbled areola of her breasts, an open place, an area, circling her erect nipples, bright pink, shadowed by her cornsilk hair…
say yes
and wonder
how'd i get here?
in this furnace sun.
some guy a few lounge chairs over says, in a midwestern twang, *"mildred, it is so hot my comb has melted in my pocket. let's get out of here."*
i pack up. i've got a movie to see.

"the truth being rather a current that flows from what people say to us, which we apprehend, invisible as it may be, rather than the actual thing that they say."

360

well, yes
may as well say yes
your story is your story
and their's to tell

they know you so well.

say
yes
yes
and again yes.

*"for there is in this world in which everything wears out, everything perishes,
one thing that crumbles into dust, that destroys itself still more completely,
leaving behind still fewer traces of itself than beauty: namely grief."—marcel
proust, 'remembrance of things past: the sweet cheat gone'*

SKYWARD
cobbled webs my legacy
federal house empty of kids
and radiant winter fireplaces.
have you ever seen
a frozen harbor,
chock full of unfaithful lovers,
suddenly melt
spreading its many treasures
skyward?

KNOWN WOLVES
"readers are repulsed by self pity."—rob sullivan
let yourself appreciate
your sense of humor
and your sky
and your highway
and your thumb out
and the grit in your eyes
and the occasional couch

and the helluva sunset
and the wreck by the side of the road
when you get here
all you have
is what you have
lost
and the girl.
i knew you when you were transparent

i am going blind
i am blinded by missing you
my eyes fill with blood and my eyelids are imbedded with tiny razors
there's no reading my way out of this
gasping at the move from blue to deeper blue
this sunset tonight disappoints
failing to save my life
or restore me to christmas
this future does not contain me
when the big one hits
you were in awe out there
a force multiplier
feelings feel really
real
and the girl.
can we forgive our shadows?

i did not mean to die
to all of you
only to make a merciful escape
false deliverance
flight path collapse
to the sorry
stuff of history
let it go
let it go
let her go.
—october, 2019

"there are no happy endings, because if things are happy they have not ended."—donald hall

"i hate endings. just detest them. beginnings are definitely the most exciting, middles are perplexing and endings are a disaster…the temptation towards resolutions, towards wrapping up the package, seems to me a terrible trap. why not be more honest with the moment? the most authentic endings are the ones which are already revolving towards another beginning…"—sam shepard

"it was all passing, for the first time as well as the last. his eyes devoured everything, yet hardly made things out. he did not know what he was thinking. it all seemed a long struggle which he could not decide if he'd won or lost. parts of it he could hardly remember. the rest was still clear. but it was all back, falling behind. there was no use trying to save anything. after a while you began to understand that. in the end you got on a train and went along the river."—james salter, 'cassada'

"we come from an unknown place and go to an unknown place. these do not concern me. but the trajectory of my life, which i share with this body, does."—jean-louis barrault

"our almost-instinct almost true/ what will survive of us is love."—phillip larkin

"as it was with Icarus, so it is with all of us."—jack larson, 'the relativity of icarus'

BENEDICTION
o to be the drastic child
        unarmed spectra
dancing into the light
        as if art tatum was
and you are the piano
wrapped in dreams
        because you am i
and i am you
in an air
we cannot capture
--12/26/2014

DRIVING HIGHWAY FIVE

a coda in three parts

NO REGRETS COYOTE/ NO DIRECTION HOME
Los Angeles to Sacramento, (Mar Vista to Marysville), and back again,
6/16-18/2016,

"coyote goes to the top of the hill/ doing the things coyotes will"—lou reed

fragments of memories
litter the fringes of the tarmacadam,
the unfurling carbon ribbon,
of highway five

golden velvet foothills,
pass away in the thrill of the grapevine,
coming down sedate,
onto highway five

right away,
the flattened corpse of a coyote with no regrets,
squashed silly on the left shoulder
of highway five

white lines drawn by the ragman's fire,
hitcher taken prisoner by the violated clouds,
the ragged, drifting, soiled, veil of smoke,
of the long white dress
of highway five

endless shades of gray roadway,
merging, from time to time,
with highway 61,
bleachers out in the sun,.
and there stands the mystery tramp,
another hitcher, thumb out, forlorn,
shooting holes in the fire on main street
on the dreadful spot,
where JD hit the strong wind area, on highway 46
just off highway five

black flags fluttering in the fields
demarcating the boundaries
of no water
on both sides
of highway five

lambs the exact color of the seared umber grass
blistered meadows where they graze
all along
highway five

hawk circling in the sudden sky,
playing with me,
far above
highway five

on the left, andersen's, where i rode the miniature railroad,
filled up on pea soup,
learned to loathe it.
now go right to rotten robbie's,
tank up with gas,
beer,
tequila,
find out i love it.
staring a hole into my scrambled eggs,
picking up her scent on my fingers.
then a quick stop at the desolation baconfest,
off highway five.

there's a sign announcing
the exit to my birthplace,
tracy, californ-i-a
dead center of the valley,
hard by the defense depot,
off highway five

passing over the steady flow of the aqueduct
question being:
'can growing food be a waste of water?'
rolling on past that tragedy,
heading off out of there,
on highway five

why don't matter
thisaway
thataway
i just get off
up aways…

    all those bleak and blasted road trips, bored out of my skull, driving with my disappointed dad, my fretful sister curled up in the backseat. me in the front, shotgun prone to car sickness, sickened by the smell of the fuel, terrified by the prospect of a future stuck in one place, this place or worse, lurching, belongings lashed to the vehicles, to yet another empty residence, just the same as the other one. relentless ballgame a scratchy mutter on the car radio, the horizon so faraway it is unapproachable as it shimmers, distorted by heat, distant dust devil glimpsed from the laboring car, hurtling ahead, going nowhere, on highway five…

    but this latest trip to visit relations was leisurely, reasonably, modestly triumphant, a reclamation through arid land, of what still holds water, dancing a jaunty two-step with my ever upbeat mom, waltzing and twirling up the polished wood runway in my younger sister's newly purchased old-time bowling alley. [within a few months my mom had danced away into the sunset. but we had that last twirl together, holding fast. we may have never really had much time together, but we made what we did have count for something.] my sister's establishment, built in the late 50s, is right there in downtown colusa and is replete, after a mere six months in she and her husband's possession, with a raft of regulars. such as, for instance, the mystery tramp named 'cowboy' who used to live in a tent down by the river until a flood flashed it away. now he goes old school and sleeps under the stars. from hat to boot he's the color of prairie, save for his lake blue eyes

368

(*oh, what did you see/ my blue-eyed son?*) or the two young chicanos, aged maybe10 and 12, brothers who can't go home for reasons unasked and unspoken, anywhere is better than there, and here, with the pins tumbling and the garlic fries, they can pitch in and have a peaceful corner over by the pro shop, all their own, airbuds in ears, wary, but starting to feel what safe might taste like.

and then there were long freewheeling talks with my older sister around her kitchen table and as we drove through the bright farmland, she being the kindest woman i've ever known, who quite simply saved my life. deeply delicate discussions about her grown-up children, her grandchildren, turbulent people all, full of the rage and hope, sadness and spunk, that churns deep in our shared DNA . after a couple of days, i head back home or its general direction, south again, somewhat sated, sometimes tearful with regret and with joy, maddened and amused by my fate as a border animal, i see the boundary but i just don't give a fuck. ('*but deep inside my heart/ i know i can't escape/ oh. mama/...*) plunging like an arrow through the brimming heart of the central valley, beatles blaring, (*i say, move over once, move over twice, o baby don't be cold as ice*), hellbent into the glare of the future, licking my wounds, soul assuaged, body knowing heart, and bone and skin and eyes and lips,

not a hit and run driver, no no,
*but a lover **for** life...*

one must,
as they say,
let it be,
released, at last,
by the fine white lines,
on the free freeway,
to drive
and thrive
on highway five.

REUNION/ ANOTHER DRIVE ON HIGHWAY 5/ OCTOBER 2018
this is a true story, as far as i can tell...

on my way
to my fiftieth everything
stop and go out of the basin
clogged going up the grapevine
and here i am,
another cruise up highway 5
getting around to everything
in the memorial interchange
even that the rain fell
and we had everything to live for.

i follow the curve of the earth
sun over my shoulder
just like death
lost
or unfound
gliding down the grapevine
and ain't it fine
one more time
into the hungry valley
all the way to mercy springs
and beyond.

there's a coyote, as always, smashed flat, fur still lush, waving in an errant
breeze, or a car passing in a whoosh,
signaling to me,
ah, here you go, again.
don't fuck it up.

hours later, memories passing like white lines,
the smells, the signs, the songs, the thrum of tire on tarmac,
as always,
i push pass the offered turnoffs, the warnings of last gas for too many miles,
i run it right up to empty

tempting fate
stretching to the edge of revenge on myself,
for all my recklesslessness and folly,
or for proof of my unquenchable promise, *(as they said of nerval, or some
other lover of george sand, "there goes a man with a promising past.")*
am i snatching defeat out of the jaws of possibility?
riding the red line of nothing?
waiting for the gasp and shudder
of no fuel.
but then…
what's that?
i spot a sign,
fate, or fortune, has tossed me a lifeline,
or maybe it's just geography.
for the next exit is my birthplace,
tracy, california,
just a mile away.
i coast to the ramp on fumes,
sweeping left, over the highway,
rolling past
low and glowering houses,
the penury of empty fields
but still no gas in sight
anywhere.
this whole glorious return
could collapse into sputters and shame,
at any moment.
i've been here before.

the way she tells it, we ran out of gas, parked down by the river…

cursing my self,
i crane around with increasing panic,
when a young couple, hip and smiling, pull up beside me, see my distress in
a glance, roll down their window,
and point
"turn right…only one block, man," and she says, *"don't worry. you made it."*

and so once again i avoid disaster,
dodging the zillionth bullet,
through the kindness of strangers,
no fault of my own.

then its back on the highway
leading to the city of my youth,
sacramento, capital of california.

when i arrive at those sacramental streets,
swooping over the river,
on a bridge i crossed so many times
it's nearly invisible to me,
all the roads are all the same as they ever were
el camino
watt avenue
auburn boulevard
fair oaks
just like always.

i take a quick shower and toke at the ramada (by wyndham)
short spin up the boulevard,
find a space, park smooth,
and amble through moonlight, under the wide sheltering branches
of an ancient oak tree,
treading purposefully on the dark lawn,
light streaming through the tall arched windows,
music welcomes,
and there they all are
inside.
i take a moment to just breathe
and stand in the shadows,
then i stride into the shindig.
the people at the table nearest to the door, as if they have positioned
themselves there to greet me, jump to their feet as i enter, arms in the air, big
beaming smiles and shouts of "*it's about time/ we were just saying/ if you
didn't show up we were gonna kill you/ you look great*" and so on. i must

admit i'm sheepish—at being late-ish (what a surprise) even though i could
not have possibly gotten there any earlier. i had driven up that day, not the
day before as i had hoped, and basically gone straight to the celebration. but
i was also taken aback at the enthusiasm, the excitement of the response.
one woman, shira, leaps to her feet and rushes to me, saying with a tug in
her throat, *"i haven't seen you, in all these years. i'm so happy.."* and there
were tears in her eyes. and it doesn't end there, other people are getting up
from other tables, coming toward me, eyes all lit up, wanting to shake my
hand, tell me how much i meant to them. how much i still meant to
them…after all these years and lifetimes.
and standing near, just one table away, is a lovely woman, slender, in a dark
grey dress, with sparkles, like night sky, smiling so broadly,
and she has the embrace i came for.
all this way.
she's the first girl i ever made love with.
cyndy
with arms spread in welcome.

> *i remember the cops rousting us, as we rubbed against each other,
> clothes askew, down by the river…*

they all repeat the same refrain as they approach: *"everyone was saying, 'is
darrell coming? is darrell coming?' some of us heard you were…but we
weren't sure."* i am…kind of overwhelmed. but then we dance. and
sometimes singly, sometimes in couples, lovely people approach and we
catch up. we all agree we all look great. and we dance. and as one of my
closer friends, jeannie b. says, later, *"you worked the room like a pro."* she
and i had gone outside to smoke a bowlful and have some time one on one,
but others followed us out and sat around the table, some of them to clear up
some serious matters. one woman, pam, confronted me on how mean i was
to her on facebook. in fact, she had blocked me she was so offended. i beg
her to restore me, completely copping to being a total asshole at times,
especially in the online context. "i just get so carried away and this shit is
really upsetting.." she forgives me and agrees to give me another chance.
anyway, jeannie and i had no time to really talk. so i messengered her on FB
a couple of days later on my return to LA and apologized for neglecting her,
since i had insisted she come, or at least encouraged her strongly. she never

had felt close to all but a few of the brightest and hippest students in our class. and we had shared an interest in theatre so we had developed a real simpatico. with no actual theater department at the school, we managed to do five productions while i was there, at norte del rio high school. one of the shows was *david and lisa*, a stage adaptation of the frank perry film, very successful in the late 60s, introducing the world to keir dullea. he played a boy who could not be touched. that was my part. shira played a girl who did not speak. jeannie and i co-directed.

she tells me they called me "magic boy", the other kids in the cast..seems they were playing with an ouija board, filling time while waiting for their scenes, and the little white teardrop-shaped device, with arcane symbols stamped on it, was sliding all over, answering questions readily, making small prophecies, connecting those who needed answers directly to the attentive dead. when i approached the group to apologize for making them wait, the device stopped dead…literally and abruptly. (she says i made some mocking remark about the game, although i don't think i did. i believed in the occult even then.) once i'd left, somebody asked the oracle, "why did you stop when darrell was here?" and the board spelled out the words "magic boy." no shit. apparently, the name stuck for the rest of the school year. although no one called me that to my face. of that i am quite certain.…now as we lay entwined she murmurs those words, "magic boy." "huh?" " that's what we all called you." and we lie there, our limbs wrapped around each other, our roots so deep, and wide, like poplars, or magic mushrooms, the largest living organism on earth, like the one that covers most of minnesota, one organism sharing the same root system. what if i hadn't made it here? in every sense. made another drive up highway 5, made it to the reunion, to this room, to this moment? what if i had decided not to stay alive at all, giving in to gravity and grief. because it is a decision, she and i prove that with every breath we take.

cyndy dances as though she is in the throes. tosses her head back and shimmies, legs spread slightly and the spangles glitter and shine.
so we dance. sometimes other women join us. very few men are on the dance floor and then only for one or two songs. this was exactly the way it was in junior high. most of the boys refused to risk humiliation performing awkward gyrations, right out there in front of everybody. most of them did not

dare to move away from the wall. i simply did not give a fuck. and i was good at it. i could do all the current steps and moves, the twist, the stomp, the mashed potatoes too, the pony, the surf, the watusi, even the jitterbug now and again. and basically, the girls loved it. so here we are dancing, exuberantly. thrilled that we can still do it. we have the moves. we have the spirit.

a slow song begins. cyndy and i become enveloped in *us*. we move right up close and murmur into each other's ears, swaying in place. occasionally making a slow whirl. there is a blue, or maybe red, or maybe both, a purple wash, over the air, and we hold each other and tell each other our stories…while we dance. we are in a kind of bubble although i am aware that we are doing this in front of our entire surviving senior class—and they are digging it. i can feel their approbation. flat-out romance is in the room. we step slightly back and look into each other's eyes. we come to rest and i kiss her shoulder, near the delicate, rhinestoned strap, and then higher on her neck. in actual fact, cyndy and i were not a couple back in school. i didn't have a girlfriend. way too complicated. so, as she and i sway in the lights, just us left on the dance floor like the bride and groom having our first dance, what the class of 1968 is witnessing in 2018 is something completely new, a fresh falling for each other. now, this celebration of relationships formed fifty years ago is somehow transforming into something much more immediate. but what, precisely is it turning into? a deepening of already existing love? a new awareness of what we all meant to each other back in our formative years? a sentimental hook-up? just old people having fun? as we dance, cyndy and i share our personal versions of our common story as best we can. comparing our memories of what had occurred all those decades ago. we have no hesitation in what we say. we are just as straightforward as we have always been with each other, even when we were sixteen. the whole length of her body is moving against mine as we gently turn turn turn…

"the cops had to take me home, they pulled right up in my driveway. the neighbors loved it, i could see them peeking out through the curtains…it proved i was the bad bad girl they said i was." "well, but, how'd i get home then. without gas?" "i guess the cops must have had some in a can." "i don't remember that part of it at all. i remember being down by the river, i remember being all over each other in the back seat. i remember being

startled as shit at the flashlight suddenly tapped on the window. so fucking loud. and for some reason i felt ashamed, found out, as if we were doing something really wrong. that we were in big trouble. i remember that you didn't seem embarrassed at all. more like irritated as you pulled down your skirt and buttoned your blouse. and a few days later we finally did it, at my apartment, when my dad and sister weren't there." the whole deed was short and sweet, performed on the narrow bed, in the room i shared with my father....

> *"i knew it was your first time, because i was trying to act all sexy, and you just wanted to **put it in...**"*

we bask and sway on the dance floor for a beat or two. "well...you knew because i told you..i told everyone during that rehearsal for *david and lisa*. you remember. i had just walked up to you in the hall and asked you to be in the play. and you immediately said yes. without even asking me what the part was..". her character was one of the participants in an ongoing group therapy, in the institution where both david and lisa had been sent, to cure them of their conditions. cyndy played what they used to call a 'nymphomaniac.' (my father had demonstrated in divorce court that my mom was in that same category. a "nympho". the term was bandied about quite frequently in those days. and the behavior was certainly grounds for giving the custody of my sister and i to our father. but not the custody of our two younger brothers. my father proved they were not his children. not by testing their DNA. no such process was available then. he brought in our next door neighbor who admitted to having sex with my mother. and that he had once come home to find her having sex with the guy who delivered the new washing machine. of course, that proved nothing. but it demonstrated emphatically that my mother was clearly unfit to raise her children. of course, this whole notion, of 'nyphomania', has been discredited now but back then women weren't supposed to *want* sex. they were supposed to resist it as long as possible. unless they were tramps like marilyn...or my mom...) cyndy was rumored to be 'loose', to 'put out', (as we so despicably labelled an unfettered sexuality in a female back then.) i guess i thought she would understand the character. but more to the point, she had a way of carrying herself, her burgeoning womanhood, that just seemed right for the part. seeing her pass in the hall would always make me turn my head, stir me to follow her with my eyes, though we rarely spoke. she seemed to understand something most of

376

the rest of us didn't get. so one day in rehearsal, while discussing sexuality and how it related to the kids in the play and their various hang-ups and symptoms, i allowed as how i was still a virgin. i don't remember the specific reason for mentioning this troubling fact. it seemed necessary to the task at hand. i think that's why i was able to be a pretty good actor, right away, as early as the sixth grade. (i played scrooge in *the christmas carol*. the teacher, mr. billings, said he chose me because i had the loudest voice. but it was more than that. i instinctively knew how to do it. you stayed open to what was under the words, the need. somehow i knew that if you want to be *seen,* you have to reveal.) after the rehearsal, cyndy came up to me, standing a little closer than usual, with that smile, she touched me lightly just below my shoulder like she was tagging me and looked me right in the eye and then she said, *"i want to be your first."*

"so on target/ so direct…"

and now, as we are dancing slow, cyndy wriggles, just a little shake, and giggles with delight. and tells me her version. *"i don't remember that, but i'm not surprised. sounds like the kind of thing i would do. i'm sure not sorry."* and she hugs me even tighter for a moment. and laughs a little more, a deep chuckle that reminds me of my mother. there's a slight pause. a breath. *"well, you know there's another chapter."* i venture, *"…i asked you why it was so easy for you. sex. why you were so comfortable about it. all the other girls—and the boys, for that matter—were so uptight, so furtive, so terrified to cross that river. but you…you told me that your uncle, no, your stepfather."* *"my father. and my brother."* *"what? another detail wrong. wow. your brother, too? this is just…did you tell me that, about your brother?"* *"probably not."* *"well, back then i felt so bad."* *"for what?"* *"for having taken advantage of your trauma. something like that. but, and this is where the whole thing just got…amazing. you saw that look on my face, of confusion and, yeah, guilt…"* *"and i said, "no i found out i liked it. it felt good. and my dad was gentle, he was tender. and when he found out my brother had also done it, too…"* *"did you tell your dad?"* *"i don't remember how he found out. but my dad went to him and said that they had been wrong and should protect me instead of hurting me. but it didn't hurt. it felt really great. they gave me pleasure. neither of them penetrated me, at all. or did it again. my father was so sorry, he said, for 'molesting me.' years later i had to look up the word. i had no idea what he meant. and when i figured it out, i just thought, that's not what he did. at all. he made me feel so good. i considered it an expression of affection." "you aren't really allowed to feel that, as far as this society is concerned." "yeah, well, that's what i felt….so, back then, sometimes i'd pick someone who turned me on and we'd get it on, make each other feel good. and….it was my choice. and, honey, i chose you." "yeah, but most people would have let the whole thing spoil their lives, poison it, but you…you just found out you liked it." "i LIKE it." there's that fetching grin again, with a glint in her gaze. i go on, "well, at the time, i must admit, i was kind of stunned at your…i don't know. your complete independence. i learned something from you, although i didn't fully realize it back then. through the years though, i realized that you taught me something fundamental about owning your own life. it's stayed with me all this time. we really can decide for ourselves what we will do with what happens to us." "yeah, i wasn't gonna let it ruin something so fantastic. absolutely not." "see, i think that's healthy, really healthy. you are..you knew how to hang on to your own joy." then the song ends. brown-eyed girl begins. "oh, shit," i say. "uh…i have to get a tequila..i'll be right back." and i hurry off the dance floor.*

brown-eyed girl is susanna's song. not just one i associate with her. it's a song she links to herself, one of her favorites. one night in anquilla, the song came on the radio and we stopped right in the middle of the road, didn't even pull over to the shoulder, clambered out and danced in the headlights. others in the car protested, until they too climbed out, cavorting along with us. just for a few measures, then we all hopped back into the car, breathless and gleeful, and went on our way. it remains, for me at least, a peak moment in our love together.

other people are coming onto the floor, drawn by the irresistible beat. vicky fong calls out to me, *"darrell, you can't leave! it's van morrison!…"* but i head for the bar…

"making love in the green grass/ behind the stadium/ with you/ my brown-eyed girl"

while i am there at the bar, really needing a quick tequila, i am gently, but firmly, accosted by another woman, who obviously has a bone to pick. *"darrell, i have something i need to say to you. do you remember me? (i did not.) we were in homeroom together. in ninth grade. and i got you to sign my yearbook. i was so excited, and proud, i got darrell larson to sign my yearbook. but then when i looked at it, you wrote something so mean."* (my heart sinks..) i say, immediately and without hesitation, *"whatever it is, i am so sorry. i can be a real asshole sometimes." "well, i mean, i have always had body image problems, i'm heavy, but you called me FATTY, you said you liked me but that i should lose weight over the summer. and then you'd like me more." "what?…what the fuck! that is just awful. please please please accept my apology…i am just appalled.." "i've never forgotten it, all these years, i've carried it around." "i would do anything to lift that burden. absolutely anything."* [and i meant all this, even though i didn't believe it had happened, at least not in quite that way, in those words. the thought flitted through my mind, 'somebody else must have written that, posing as me'. but another voice said, 'don't be fucking ridiculous. who would do that? to get revenge on me, out of envy, or some shit?' i just never thought of myself as someone who would ever be that unkind, even in ninth grade. but what difference did it make if i remembered it? or did or did not write that in her yearbook? for her it was a lifelong reality and it had caused her real pain, even anguish. i could see that in her eyes.] *"what can i do?" "well, in fact, just, well, the way you're reacting is really helping…it is. i feel a whole lot better. thank you." "can we hug it out?"* and we did. and i headed back to cyndy.

but once again i am waylaid, this time by the statuesque, beautiful as ever, mary ackerman. totally recognizable after all these years. also at the same table is another woman, joyce, who has gotten very angry at me about things i've said on facebook. she was anti-obama from the outset and i called her out on what i perceived as racism. now i don't recognize her at all but she quickly announces herself, truculent as ever. she challenges me, *"you don't know who i am, right? i'm joyce." "of course i do, you were my prom date."* (she wasn't. that was lois…i think.) mary takes my arm and moves me to another table and sits me down. *"so, tell me about your life…you left norte and …"* (once, she an i were on the the climbing structures at our elementary school, noralto. i lived right across the street. mary said something to me i never forgot. i don't remember what i said to elicit her remark, but she said to me, firmly, not harshly, *"darrell larson, stop fishing for compliments."* i'm not sure why this moment made such an impression. something about her certainty, and her kindness. now, she is full of compliments and support...) after a quick synopsis of the salient facts of my life, she says, conspiratorially, *"i brought you over here because i don't want joyce to hear me. she boards her horse at my ranch, and i never discuss politics with her. never. she's just so.." "yeah, no shit. i think she's given up on me..." "but i love your posts. i really appreciate them. i find them so informative and stimulating, and not just the political stuff. sometimes i don't understand them at all..i just go, whoop, that went right over my head.." "ah, come on.." "i enjoy them, anyway." "its hard right now, when things are so polarized. like the kavanaugh hearings were just fucking awful, for everybody." "i know..my family is so at odds. my brother is an avid trump supporter. he insisted that kavanaugh was obviously innocent and being framed, and that the #metoo movement was completely out of control. he says, why didn't she bring this up before? when it happened? why didn't she tell somebody, if it was so awful? so i told him that i had been molested by our neighbor when i was nine years old...in our backyard." "oh, mary, i'm so sorry you went through that. nine? shit. well, did that slow your brother down? or change his position at all?" "it sure shut him up. especially when i told him he was there, in the house, when it happened." "what? but you didn't say anything at the time?" "no. i didn't tell anyone."* we just sat there. she took my hand. *"you look great,"* she said. *"so do you. you were always so beautiful. i had such a crush on you." "you did not." "okay. but i really did admire you." "i felt the same about you. we all did." "how's mike?" "he's good. we divorced awhile ago."* i glance over at cyndy, still out there dancing with her friends. *"yeah,"* mary said, *"i noticed that. you better get back over there."* we stood up and hugged. and i moved on...

cyndy sees me weaving through the tables, pausing to shake someone's hand, or hug someone who says to me, *"so glad you came..."* cyndy heads for her table, and we arrive at almost the same moment. i slide into a chair, pulling her onto my lap. someone goes by and calls out, *"get a room, you two.." "i have a room,"* i say, jocularly and give cyndy a squeeze. the people around us chuckle with delight. cyndy leans down and, once again, speaks into my ear. *"i didn't tell you..but i have stage two breast cancer. right now, it's in remission. i wanted you to know, but i don't like discussing health issues on facebook." "well, for one thing it's none of their fucking business. i just talk about HIV to give other people…i don't know…to normalize it. push back on the stigma." "of course. i know. well, they did radiation, they wanted to do chemo and i just said NO. enough. i'm seeing a naturopath—and i'm just done with all that doctor shit. i told them that and everybody freaked out. i won't even do an X-ray. my body has had enough radiation, thank you very much. i'm sick of being sick." "you sure don't seem sick. you seem the very opposite of sick. what are your numbers, or whatever?" "i have no idea. fuck that." "so, see, that's exactly what i mean…you have so much fucking courage. you are such a brave, indomitable person. i'm so…impressed is too weak a word for what i feel..i'm think i'm kinda crazy about you!" "let's go dance some more."* so we do. we dance some more. some of the women form a kind of chorus line, with complicated moves and steps. i screw it up. no one seems to mind, least of all me.

as the celebration is breaking up, i get explicit. *"come back to my room, baby. let's make this even more real."* however, cyndy is a little more than tipsy and i don't want to take 'advantage' of that. suddenly i'm insecure. is what i'm feeling really happening? she came in a group and we both feel suddenly too exposed, waiting for the cars to pull around. too public. and i don't want to force the issue. it seems a bit unseemly. she moans quietly, right up close. *"i want to. sooooo much. but i came with dave, i should go home with him, the one i came with. but lets make a plan. you come and visit me—or i'll visit you." "done. what about right after thanksgiving?" "we'll figure it out. i promise."* and now we are all saying our final goodbyes. with full knowledge that we will probably never see each other again. at least many of us. this will be the last time. shira has tears in her eyes, again, and hugs me tightly. we briefly discuss death for some reason and she looks bewildered, if not distraught, at my acceptance of the inevitability of it. i tell her about finding jack, but this just seems to make her more troubled. most of us are upbeat, exhilarated, thankful. one woman shakes my hand and says, *"you lived your life on your own terms."* and i have to admit that i did just that. *"we are all so proud of you."* now, the remaining small group gets giddy. we don't want to let the last precious moments pass away…
i walk back to my car alone, feeling like i didn't have the chance to talk to everyone that i wanted to talk to.

there just wasn't enough time…!
but with cyndy i said just what needed to be said. for now.

i got where i am
as if i knew
where i was going.
my classmates stayed where they started.
at home.
or settled where they went first
and made a home for themselves there.
so now….
where am i, exactly?

on the way back to the hotel, heart full to bursting, i am startled by the sight of an ancient trailer park, haggin oaks, looking spooky, even haunted, off to the left. i recognize it as the place we moved to right after we left my mom. the last time i saw her she was sitting, crying at the kitchen table of someone else's house. we pulled out of the driveway and that was that. we did not even say goodbye. *"get in the car,"* my dad said. so i did. i can still see this image of myself, kneeling on the back seat, looking through the back window of our car, as the strange, bland, tract house grew smaller and smaller and was finally lost to sight. the pool at the haggin oaks trailer park was where i learned how to swim. my dad tossed me into the shallow end of the pool and stood there, watching me flail about. i figured out how to keep my head above water real fucking fast. after a few months living there in the park, my mother came to visit us. as i remember it, my father did not permit her to speak to me. she came to get my younger brother, jerry, and took him with her when she left. it was then that i realized that life could annihilate you, if you let it. and that it would shatter your heart, no matter what you did.

on the drive back down to LA,
i see three coyote corpses, sentinels,
two to the left, one to the right.
i consider this an omen of great good fortune to come.

2. AFTER THANKSGIVING/ HIGHWAY 5/ NOVEMBER 2018

fifty years on
we are in a room together again,
at last,
vibrating like adolescents.
and we achieve
three days and nights of forever

'did you love me forever/ just for those three days?'

in a room at the ramada (by wyndham)
a magic number
418

*how can i possibly write this story
correctly? with the nuance, the passion, the improbability?*

in the throes, that first night, i bruised her.
she came out of the bathroom, giggling, displaying her shoulders, where i
had held her too tightly, and had shaken her, pounding her body into the
mattress,
as she wrapped her legs around me,
urging me on.
now she delights in showing off the signs of how far we have gone,
proof of our abandon.
i am contrite but proud, apologizing while
touching my lips to the purple and plum thumbprints, with a splash of yellow,
tinge of green,
then i throw her down on the bed, and we go back to our assigned task,
the making of love,
over and over.
we let time stop.

*she says, wisely, but not without sorrow,
"there are no do-overs in life"…and yet, here we are seizing a second
chance.*

out on the narrow balcony, mostly naked,
with a light rain falling,

i recall the rain, that day in new york city, susanna and i pressed close, sheltered under an umbrella, waiting in line for death of a salesman, *starring dustin hoffman, the first broadway play i had ever seen. crystalline raindrops dripping around us. it feels like we are curtained off, in our own private space, and i say, hoping for the best, "will you marry me, susanna." and she says "yes", just like that. so simple and so direct.*

cyndy and i
sip maker's mark
sip herradura silver
and then tumble onto the bed some more,
i move down her body and slip my tongue into her moistened cleft,
labia, vulva, clitoris—words suggesting flowers,
then i pull myself up onto the whole length of her body, like a castoff on a white sand beach, surf pounding around us,
and slide the swollen glans, the tip of my self,
into her
slipping in so deep so slow,
as deep as i can get.
pulling out so so slow
right to the throbbing end
then back in and in and in,
and then a sudden thrust
making her groan, and call out with astonishment,
her ecstatic face
stunned at the ruckus we are making,
yeah we're loud
we bang the headboard against the wall,
the tumult
the waves
knowing at last
knowing so well now
how this is done
how the miraculous works
we've done our research, for our entire lives, with dedication, and close attention,

384

now we breathe it
we share it
because we can.

all those days, centuries, minutes ago. when i picked her up at her house,..
i pull into her driveway, in a neighborhood she calls the ghetto of sacramento,
but it's actually a lovely tract of nicely-kept houses, with a park nearby. i am
too jumpy to stay for soup which she offers, or anything else. i can't even sit
down. i cannot wait to feel her skin on mine. we kiss so fervently,in a way i
have not been kissed in so fuckin' long, i feel like i'm levitating, i hold her face
in my hands, and kiss her some more. i say, *"we gotta get out of here."* she
goes into her housemate's room to tell him, he's essentially bedridden. she
tells him she's going out and won't be back tonight. while she's out of the
room i stand, trembling, in her dark, ordinary living room, feeling disoriented.
not to mention, just plain amazed. i look at her inherited china. then we're
driving in my KIA soul, knowing exactly where we are going. we are going to
us. the talk is easy, breathy with expectation, eyes sparkling, my hand on her
thigh, squeezing.

and then we are sprawled on the bed and there is no stopping us. ever.

between these bouts, these dives, this divine absorption, we remain
entwined, and once again speak softly to each other, of our life stories, our
marriages, our children, our escapes, our regrets, our expectations, our
wants, our needs, our dreams that failed, our forgiveness deserved or
otherwise, our appreciation, our addictions, our overwhelming need to fuck
each other now and now and now. we pause. we whisper other tales,
misadventures, shameful acts that cannot be undone, triumphs celebrated—
survival and exultation. and then we plunge again…falling into cleaving. so
tight so loose so consumed.

we take a break and force ourselves to leave the room, just to catch our
breath. we go see some other classmates who gather regularly for what they
call taco tuesday. cyndy is radiant as we enter, turning the heads of
everybody at the long table. i am jubilant just to be walking next to her.
someone says to me, *"you came back!"* i point to cyndy, *"i came back for
her,"* which draws a ribald response. i take a seat next to a man that i don't

quite recognize. he tells me his name is neil and we fall into an easy catchup. we obviously share a history, as long ago as it was. we trod the same halls, dug the same girls. i notice him gazing at cyndy, totally smitten. well, who wouldn't be? i am so fuckin' proud to be with her i'm giddy. turns out neil's wife, of 47 years, died just a year or two ago, after a long illness. he seems at sea, bereft—but anxious to rejoin the world. there has been talk of a bunch of us going dancing on wednesday night. i invite neil to join us at the blues bar candy frequents, nearly every friday night, along with vicki fong and other dancing partners. as it turns out, cyndy and i pass on the dancing. its our last night—we don't want to leave room 418, no time to waste. cyndy calls vicki, and asks her to give her apologies to the gang. she calls a few others, but she forgets about neil. we find out the next day that he did show up and no one was there. we both feel terrible. I particularly feel guilty. i picture him looking around…finding nobody. especially not her…
i insist to her, "*you have to make this up to him. you gotta take him dancing..promise me.*" "*i will..i will…we'll go this friday.*" "*good. now, come over here right NOW!*"

"just a little more time/ with you with me with you…"

and then morning comes, we have our breakfast at her house. scrambled eggs and turkey bacon and something else i can't remember. strong and potent coffee, for sure. i'm already pretty jangly. she moves around, cheerfully, staying busy. she shows me the collection of found objects, feathers and stones and little crumpled drawings, sticks festooned with ribbons and threads, all of them gifted to her by her grandson. she shows me pictures of her family. every once in a while we press against each other. we just stand there, close. feeling the scent of each other. and then it is really time to hit the road. finishing my coffee, lingering over it, i notice that the amulet of st. genesius, the patron saint of actors, which jack made sure i received after his death, and which i wear around my neck and never take off, is missing. i wear it on a thin chain along with a silver coyote and a small charm that says 'mom'. [i found that on the street, glinting on the sidewalk. i'm a scavenger of shiny objects, like a crow or a blue bower bird].
i periodically rub these three talismans, reaching up and arranging them as i prefer, genesius in the middle, the small piece of turquoise on the coyote facing out—but this time the habitual, comforting, gesture comes up empty.

386

it's gone. the charm is gone. the charm is gone. i feel nauseous, and unmanned. the charm is gone. i usually remove it while having sex just to make sure it doesn't get snagged and snatched from my neck, in the thrashing about. with us, i let it go. just couldn't take the time, get calm enough to make the tiny clasp work. my hands were trembling. so fuck it, i let it go. i believed it would be protected, as it protects me. jack has been watching over me since he died and this small brass oval is the palpable connection which keeps me under his wing. yeah, i know. magical thinking. but who's to say i'm wrong? i sure as fuck don't know how the universe works. what is death, anyway? how are souls conjoined? what is love, for that matter? can it ever die, or decompose? with my girls—is it gone? or just held in abeyance. i want to know, desperately sometimes. but now, i am almost panicked at the realization that i may have lost this precious medal. out of carelessness, really. and then i look at her. i see her so clearly, the great gift of her and i say, *"well, if that's what the price was for being with you for these last three days, i'm fine with it. it was without a doubt, utterly and completely worth it."* but i kiss her, just once more, and i barrel out the door to hurtle back to the hotel, driving like steve mcqueen in *bullitt*. something in me doesn't believe it's gone. i hurry up to the 4th floor and the door to 418 is open. the maid is cleaning the room. an older woman had been the maid the day before. we didn't get up until late in the afternoon on tuesday, we kept the 'do not disturb' sign on the doorknob. when we did let her in—we could tell she was just delighted, giggling and thrilled for us. we had tried to straighten the room up a bit but she noticed the tequila and whiskey and she clearly knew exactly what was going on. this time, a younger woman is changing the sheets, making a fresh bed. she sees my distress right away and reassures me, *"i find…i find.."* she says, showing me where she had discovered the precious necklace, down in the space between the bed and the headboard. we both are completely aware of how uncanny this is, something so small being found in such a hidden place. apparently the word has gotten around, about just what was going on in room 418. i am a bit flabbergasted not to say gobsmacked, but at the same time it does seem exactly right, almost inevitable. the charm has been be restored. i dash down the hall, where the older woman with her cart is waiting for the elevator. as she sees me dashing toward her she claps her hands together a couple of times and reaches for the bin where she has tucked the lost charms. talk

about a guardian angel. when she hands the thin chain and its attachments
to me, she just shines. it seems like she is blessing our union…

the truth is we can see the past right there, before us,
all of us can,
as it recedes, across a meadow, into a line of trees, all of our friends, singing,
moving into the distance, as the sunlight softens…
we are stuck, though, in the present, motionless, almost paralyzed, but only
because there's nowhere else to go.
and the future, invisible, unknown, comes up over our shoulders,
devouring us, in a gulp, in an infinite swallow, a streaming torrent gushing
through our hearts, smoothing our souls like river stones,
a cascade a zephyr a hurricane, shoving our bonehouses along, against our
will, or with it.

> *"there's a bit of magic in everything/*
> *and some loss to even things out"*

so we make plans. we will be together at the turn of the year. we will shout
and scream and kiss at midnight. she will have the flask i gave her for
christmas, slender and silver. (actually i gave her two flasks. the first i saw in
the window of a pawn shop in the neighborhood, next to the botanica where i
get sage bundles and the figures of voodoo saints. it was propped there in
the window, looking like it was made for her to sip from. but it was only as i
wrapped this elegant, perfect gift, that i realized, wait, there is no funnel,
petite and shiny, to trickle the whiskey in through the narrow mouth. after
asking the wise women at the hardware store across the street just where i
could find such a crucial item, they advised me to go to 'things remembered'
in the westchester mall. i made the pilgrimage, and there, sure enough, they
had funnels, but they only came with flasks. so this second flask i purchased
had a dark patina like midnight sky without a moon. i wrapped them both and
off they flew to arrive by xmas eve. the best part is, when she calls to thank
me, breathless and touched, she says, *"i had a couple of funnels already"*
"whaaat?" *"but no flask to go with them."* *"no surprise at all,"* i say, *"you do
have the perfect funnel."*) i will book room 418.

i have a dream that we are dancing. we can make these gravity-defying
leaps; into the air, up and over each other, in jubilant display. but she, she,

can hover…she knows how. *"i couldn't figure out how to do it, in the dream,"* i tell her. *"i will teach you how to hover,"* she says. and i dream that she has shaved her pubic hair, not entirely smooth, trimmed to a triangle, pointing to her clit, as if i needed direction, and i dream that i hover there…**the pleasure of giving another person pleasure is the greatest pleasure of all.** the bounds we make into the sky and the solid liquid feel of cock in cunt. banging our brains out. can we say that in…whatever this is? (a written record? a report from the front lines? a remembrance of things just past?) can we be that simple? that direct?

>*"love is simple, to quote a phrase/ you knew it all along,/ i'm learning it these days.."*

and then, back in LA, i'm on fire and everybody notices it, even my landlady, who asks, with wonderment, "what has happened to you?" seems like the whole world is smiling wryly and patting me on the back, at least figuratively. and when i try to explain to my friends, or basically anyone who will listen, why i seem to be better than i've been in years, i present the facts and whoops ensue, or exclamations of amazement. how do things like this happen? through what grace or spell? right before a queerwise show at the skylight, i go to my car and call her. i'm mellow and sure, under a blanket of expecting what i want. her slogan, her mantra is: *expect what you want.* but i hear something in her voice, immediately. a reluctance, a sadness, a tenuousness, as though she's speaking from the bottom of a well. some fact has been revealed to her in the grey light of day. *"oh, baby, you're too far away,"* she says, *"you've always been too far away. even in high school, you were too far away."* and she confesses, although it's not at all necessary, that she has taken up with neil. they've already had a weekend trip to san francisco. he adores her and needs her and can give her all *she* needs. sometimes he tends to smother but she'll work that out with him. *"i can put my own shoes on!"* she insists. *yeah*, i say to myself, *and take them off with panache, as well.* about all this i could not be happier—for both of them. the man is manifestly kind and cares for her. she should have someone around who can hold her every night. someone close. i cannot give her that. i can give her three days of relative ecstasy every month or so. i can hold her in my heart. but,i cannot give her what she deserves, in the way of a constant companion. i won't be going to karaoke with her on a whim. i can't take her on cruises. i can't even let her have some space when she wants it because the vast plain between us will be perpetually present, even when i am right beside her. so be it. i will send her songs, i will tell her the truth as best i can, i will send her this attempt to catch lightning in a leyden jar, to keep the whole blessed event incandescent, to warm ourselves on the living embers when we can. and i will love her to my last breath. longer than that. 'til the last person who knows my name passes away.'til my atoms disperse, at last…

who gets a chance like this? to come full circle, to get a do-over, to do her up right? not just put it in. but to lift her up, higher and higher and then to watch her with so much gratitude and affection, skipping down the slope. dancing into the dusk, disappearing as the light fades…. and if she is to be my last, as well as my first, i'm fine with that. truly. i'm more than fine. that would be a fucking miracle.

"but sometimes at night/ right out of the blue/ i remember you…"

—*for cynthia, 2018*

Special thanks:

to Michael Ace Ontkean, for absolutely everything. and the neverending conversation.

to Joseph Alessi, the first person to make it all the way through this m(e)ss.

to Elizabeth Ruscio, actor/poet/playwright/total babe, for her early encouragement.

to Susan Hayden, intrepid Library Girl and most loyal friend, who threw me a lifeline when I washed up shipwrecked on these shores.

to Michael Kearns and the gang at Queerwise, for peace, love and understanding.

to Mitch Greenhill for putting music to so much of my life.

to Murray Mednick, for his generosity and his genius

and to the cohort of sympathetic and patient readers who have done me the great favor of reading pieces of this over the years:
Evan Burkin, John Philbrick, Ava Wynne, Julie Fulton, Karen Jensen, David Means, Kristen Andersen-Groh, David-MIchael Monasch, James Morrison, Carl Weintraub, Jordan Morgan, Jeff LeBeau & all of you I'm forgetting…i still love you just as much.

Darrell Larson is an actor/director/poet, etc. He has been in dozens of films including: *Mike's Murder, UFOria, Stepmom, Rachel Getting Married, The Manchurian Candidate, Twice in a Lifetime. Stuart Saves His Family, Frances,* On television he appeared in: *Marcus Welby, M.D.; Law and Order; Law and Order: SVU; Gunsmoke; Bonanza; The Days and Nights of Molly Dodd; Congratulations, It's a Boy,* and many more. In theater he performed as Coyote in *The Coyote Cycle,* and acted in *Action, Curse of the Starving Class, Simpatico, The Dance of Death, XA: A Viet Nam Primer, Dominus Marlowe, The America Piece, Dog Logic, Comedy of Errors, The Confessions of Doc Holliday, Mexican Day, Dreams Die Hard,*

The Gary Plays, The Hillary Game, Clearwater and so on. He directed *Are You Lookin', Cowboy Mouth, The Unseen Hand, Simpatico, Comedy of Errors, Karla, The Wizard of Oz in Concert: Dreams Come True, Psychos Never Dream, Shoppers Carried By Escalators Into the Flames, Scar,* and on and on. He taught at Columbia University in the Graduate Film Department, lectured at the Smithsonian, and hosted a classic American film festival in Kaliningrad, Russia. He lives in downtown Los Angeles.